Advances in Game-Based Learning

Series Editors
Dirk Ifenthaler
Scott Joseph Warren
Deniz Eseryel

More information about this series at http://www.springer.com/series/13094

Janna Jackson Kellinger

A Guide to Designing Curricular Games

How to "Game" the System

Springer

Janna Jackson Kellinger
University of Massachusetts, Boston
Boston, MA, USA

Advances in Game-Based Learning
ISBN 978-3-319-82569-4 ISBN 978-3-319-42393-7 (eBook)
DOI 10.1007/978-3-319-42393-7

Softcover reprint of the hardcover 1st edition 2016

Printed on acid-free paper

This Springer imprint is published by Springer Nature
The registered company is Springer International Publishing AG
The registered company address is: Gewerbestrasse 11, 6330 Cham, Switzerland

To Drew and Connor—this book is for
you and for future generations of children
in the hopes that your learning will always
be "hard fun" (McGonigal, 2011, p. 32).
With special thanks to Julia Nakhleh for her
tireless and thoughtful suggestions, ideas,
contributions, and constructive criticisms
of this book from its infancy to its fruition.
A special thanks also goes out to Beth Wilson
who reintroduced me to gaming through
MYST back in the 90s.
And I would be remiss if I did not thank
my father who instilled in me my love
of mental challenges and bought
a Commodore 64 back in the 80s
on which I played my first text adventure
games as well as video games like
Pong and Jumpman.

Preface

I'm not sure I would officially be considered a "gamer." At this point in my life, I'm more of a "gamer wannabe" or maybe a "gamer lurker" or perhaps "a dormant gamer waiting for time to free up for more gaming." The hardest part of writing this book has been resisting the temptation to play all the compelling games I have been reading about. I even created a list of the video games I want to play once this book is complete. I know others who have written in this area have been criticized for not being enough of a gamer to be considered part of the gaming community. I also know that if I took a break from writing to immerse myself in any one of those games on my list, this book would not get written. I hope that this confession gives people who do not consider themselves gamers permission to try designing curricular games. Teachers do not need to be serious gamers to apply the affordances of

There are lots of free tools teachers can use to help create their own curricular games like Tellagami, a free animation tool

video games to their classroom teaching. However, they do need to have at least some experience with games to understand how rules, players, and goals operate together as a system, but between sports and board games, I am willing to bet that almost all teachers have these kinds of experiences either as players or as spectators or both, even those who have never put their hands on a video game. This book is not for gamers; it is for teachers who seek to inspire students to engage deeply and critically with content in ways that promote problem solving, risk-taking, and fun.

Boston, MA Janna Jackson Kellinger

Contents

Chapter 1
Upping Your Game: Transforming Teaching

Students frequently walk away from homework when it is too difficult, but difficult games are another matter–kids walk away from games when they're too easy.

–Devaney 2014

Abstract This chapter begins by introducing the game behind the book, including the mission and the first quest. The overall mission serves as the vehicle for designing and developing a curricular game while the first quest prepares the reader for any resistance he or she might encounter in the process of transforming his or her curriculum into a game. The chapter supports the reader in doing so by situating curricular games within the current context of education. In order to do this, this chapter outlines how this book conceives of game-based teaching both by describing it and by contrasting it with what it is not, building on deCastell and Jenson's (J Curric Stud 35:649–665, 2003) work. The chapter delves into the needs of the twenty-first century learners (Educ Res 29:4–15, 2000) and the workforce in the twenty-first century (The world is flat: a brief history of the twenty-first century, Picador, New York, 2007; Educ Leadersh 66:20–25, 2008) and uses learning theories (How people learn. National Academy Press, Washington, DC, 2000) to demonstrate how game-based teaching can help meet these needs. Each subsequent chapter begins with the next quest in the mission, i.e., steps in designing a curricular game, and ends with a worksheet to help guide the reader in accomplishing that quest along with a rubric. Activities called challenges within chapters are designed to help the reader apply and practice the concepts. The worksheets and rubrics along

Several sections of this chapter are taken from these previous works published under my former name with permission:

Jackson, J. (2009). Game-based teaching: What educators can learn from videogames. *Teaching Education, 20*(3), 291–304.

Jackson, J. (2011). Game changer: How principles of videogames can transform teaching. In M. S. Khine (Ed.), *Learning to play: Exploring the future of education with video games* (pp. 107–128). New York: Peter Lang.

J.J. Kellinger, *A Guide to Designing Curricular Games*,
Advances in Game-Based Learning, DOI 10.1007/978-3-319-42393-7_1

with other supporting materials such as further readings allow this book to be used as a textbook by teacher education professors as well as providing supports for teachers and professors using this as a manual to guide their own self-study in game-based teaching.

Keywords Twenty-first century learning • Twenty-first century learners • Twenty-first century workforce • Educational games • Commercial Off the Shelf (COTS) Games • Gamification • Standards • Gamers • Immersion • Transfer • Constructionism • Pro-social • Zone of proximal development (ZPD) • Scaffolding

YOUR MISSION:
As you clean up your classroom, ending another exhausting but exhilarating day of teaching, you put hardcopies of the latest educational standards you are expected to adhere to in your satchel as well as the book How People Learn, *required reading by your principal, and throw your satchel over your shoulder. You hear a noise and look up. Before you, an apparition appears, stating boldly: "You are needed in the future." You look around and pinch yourself to make sure you are not dreaming. Before you know it, you are transported to what appears to be a "messy closet" (Kaling* 2011, *p. 142) masquerading as an office. You look around and notice the walls are covered with elaborate maps and a desk is littered with blueprints and schematics. You find yourself thinking, "This is not the clean, sterile space-age buildings sci-fi movies promised!" A woman behind a desk peers at you intently and starts to speak in a manner that does resemble sci-fi movies, briskly and bluntly:*

> You have been transported in time. The year is 2180. World War III has devastated the planet. Since teachers were seen as cultural gatekeepers, all sides of the war targeted them. Because there are no more teachers left to teach the next generation, we are fighting to preserve our knowledge and skills. The Expert Elders have tried to pass on their knowledge, but their complete lack of teaching ability leaves everyone frustrated.[1] Due to chemical warfare and radiation, the next generation has a range of physical and cognitive impairments. In addition, a number of survivors have offspring who struggle to learn the predominant language of English. Out of desperation, I, the Commander of the Free World, commissioned an elite group of Engineering Elders to build a time machine to bring a teacher from the past into our time and a group of Historian Elders to decide who to bring back. After poring over the remaining historical documents, the Historian Elders have chosen you based on your superior reputation as a teacher. Your **mission** is to develop a curricular tool which will engage and teach future generations and serve as a model for the Expert Elders to emulate. This involves finding the elusive Holy Grail of learning—transfer, or the ability to apply a learned skill to a new context. Do you accept this mission?

"Whoah," you think, "Me, the savior of the future?" After the initial shock of being transported to a different time, you decide to approach this as you approach teaching—breaking the abstract notion of teaching into concrete, doable actions.

[1] "Though experts know their disciplines thoroughly, this does not guarantee that they are able to teach others" (Bransford et al. 2000, p. 31).

You think about the range of teaching situations which initially felt overwhelming but ultimately became fun. With renewed confidence you say, "I do." You feel as if you have just committed yourself to a marriage—a marriage of past and future, of learning and new technologies, and of yourself to the unknown.

I used to think "I don't have time to do discovery learning, I have to cover the curriculum," but I finally learned that it does not matter if I lecture until I am blue in the face if students do not learn anything. I can "cover" all the materials I want, but what really matters is what students learn. I too often fall into the trap of thinking that students cannot learn something unless I say it or show them. The truth, however, is that students do not learn something unless they say it or do it. What led me to this epiphany was one student's description of my traditional mode of teaching: "I found the class to be very long and boring and left with very little knowledge other than the fact that if you use AIM Chat on a different computer, it changes your buddy icon." Although this hurt my feelings (no matter what people say, teaching is personal), it prompted me to reexamine my teaching methods. After vowing never to teach that class again, I relented when I realized that educators had much to learn from game designers who seem to have tapped into ways to motivate people to challenge themselves. In the fall of 2006, I converted this same course into a game-like format based on techniques derived from video games. Student learning in my classes has never been the same since.

I suspect you picked up this book because you are unsatisfied with the current educational system in the United States. If not, you should be. The current educational system in the United States is built on a factory model where masses of students are processed through a conveyer belt of education with each teacher/factory worker[2] adding knowledge to their students/products. DING. The school/factory bell rings, and students/products are passed along to the next station. While educational systems across the globe vary widely, many are founded on similar dissemination models. In a world where knowledge is at everyone's fingertips outside of school, this old-fashioned model of education is not serving students at any point along the pipeline. Too many students in the United States (22 %) are dropping out

[2]This is not meant to denigrate teachers. Teachers in the United States are working so hard in a system that is more and more being crafted to thwart their best efforts (see Ken Robinson's *Changing Educational Paradigms* video). My critique is of the system—and the role of those in federal and state governments in creating that system, not of the individuals within the system who, in many cases, are merely trying to survive. As a former high school English teacher, I know this survival mode first hand. My hope is that this book creates a means by which individual teachers can transform that system, or at least find ways to make that system work for them and for student learning, instead of against them.

of high school (Stillwell and Sable 2013, p. 4), with some cities reporting dropout rates as high as 50 % (Barab et al. 2012, p. 308). Too many students in the United States require remedial classes when getting to college (Shulock 2010). Too many businesses find their newly hired workers lacking in skills (Massachusetts Business Alliance for Education (MBAE) 2008). And too many of those students are students of color (Darling-Hammond 2010). Why are so many students so ill-prepared for the world of work? Because the achievement gap is really between how schools define achievement and how businesses do.

Business leaders have made clear the skills they need for the twenty-first century workforce: "creativity and innovation, critical thinking and problem-solving, communication and collaboration" (MBAE 2008, p. 14). These are the same skills identified by the Partnership for Twenty-first Century Skills, a group founded by business leaders in 2002 and by Friedman (2007) and Wagner (2008), both of whom interviewed a range of business leaders. Businesses are no longer vertical hierarchies like the factory model of the past, but rather have horizontal work flows with ad hoc groups from around the globe capitalizing on the various skills each bring to the table (Friedman 2007). Meanwhile, our schools are focused on standardized testing where students are passive consumers praised for regurgitating information and discouraged from risk-taking by grades which are used to reward compliance and punish mistakes. This industrial model of education does not prepare students for the world of work today.

Schools that prepared workers for the industrial age did not need to produce "big-picture" thinkers because the vast majority of workers just needed to know their part on the assembly line—whether that be in a factory or as a teacher of a subject in a high school. Now, however, workers need to be able to see connections and utilize systems thinking, i.e., see the big picture, in order to solve problems and accomplish the tasks of today's world of work:

> The world is effectively shrinking and getting more complex. For instance, we're confronted with problems of enormous complexity and global ramifications (e.g. nuclear proliferation, global warming, antibiotic-resistant microbes, terrorism, and unstable governments). When faced with such complex problems, the ability to think creatively, critically, collaboratively, and systemically and then communicate effectively is essential. Learning and succeeding in a complex and dynamic world is not easily measured by multiple-choice responses on a simple knowledge test. (Shute 2011, p. 506)

As early as 1987, Resnick pointed out the dangers of this gap between work and schooling:

> As long as school focuses mainly on individual forms of competence, on tool-free performance, and on decontextualized skills, educating people to be good learners in school settings alone may not be sufficient to help them become strong out-of-school learners. (quoted in Putnam and Borko 2000, p. 5)

As Crockett et al. (2011) point out: "It's ridiculous to continue to embrace standardized learning and standardized tests at the very same time our new economy is eliminating standardized jobs" (p. 3). Schools in the United States and a multitude of other countries have not adapted to the new realities of today.

Not only is there a mismatch between business needs and school expectations, but there is a gap between the twenty-first century learners and schools. School life is in sharp contrast to what many students experience outside of school.[3] Prensky (2001b) quotes a student who says he has to "power down" (p. 3) when he goes to school. Meanwhile, many schools are still steeped in the old pedagogy of fact-based learning. It is no wonder that "In a national study, nearly half of recent high school dropouts said that a major factor in their decision was that their classes were not interesting" (MBAE 2008, p. 12). The consequences of this gap between experiences in school and experiences out of school have large implications for teaching and learning.

As educators, what can we do about these disconnects? Fortunately, two of the three elements described here do match: students' lives outside of schools and expectations of business leaders. For example, Raines (2002) found that the twenty-first century learners expect their workplace to resemble the global advances in business Friedman describes (2007) with the following characteristics topping the list: challenging, collaborative, fun, and flexible (cited in Schrum and Levin 2009). Because students' out of school experiences include being consumers and producers in their technology-rich worlds which are experiences they often do not have in school, Project Tomorrow found that less than forty percent of US students surveyed felt their education was preparing them for their future jobs (Prabhu 2009). The experiences that best prepare the twenty-first century learners for the twenty-first century workforce seem to be taking place largely outside of school. In fact, it could be argued that by and large the outdated modes of teaching still found in schools around the world will impede students' abilities to thrive in their professional lives: "All children are getting left behind, trapped in a deficient educational model that leaves them ill-prepared for the globalized workplace of the twenty-first century" (Joseph 2008, p. 258). One teacher calls this "educational malpractice" (Holt 2013).

Matchmaking

So what exactly is it that is so engaging in students' personal worlds that is largely excluded from schools? There are lots of answers to that question: social media, opportunities to be creative and showcase that creativity for a global audience, and chances to share opinions and be a part of public debate. In this book, however, I am going to focus on one—one that defies the stereotype of youth today as having short attention spans, one that can engage people for hours on end, and one that some people, myself included, can sometimes spend years trying to finish just one of them: video games.

A Pew Research Center survey reported that 97 % of 12- to 17-year-olds play video games, with 50 % stating they played yesterday (Lenhart et al. 2008, p. 8).

[3]The video "A Vision of K-12 students today" is one of many that illustrate the contrast between students' lives, their futures, and their schooling.

Video games are not just mere entertainment, video games teach. Video games teach knowledge. Video games teach skills. Video games teach dispositions. This is why it is so important to pay attention to the video games with which youth are engaging. First-person shooter video games teach. They teach so well that the Columbine shooters used video games to practice their tragic plot, prompting one investigator to state they were "playing out their game in God mode" (Pooley 1999, p. 32). However, just as with any tool, video games have the potential to be good or bad or somewhere in between. For example, games can encourage pro-social or antisocial behaviors (Anthes 2009), although De Castell and Jenson (2003) point out that the impact of all games, including antisocial ones, must be examined within the larger culture of the players, which also may sanction violence.

Fortunately, there are more video games on the shelves than just first-person shooter games. Adventure games such as the *MYST* series require problem solving and critical thinking to complete them. Massive Multiplayer Online Role-Playing Games (MMORPGs), such as *World of Warcraft*, not only require problem solving and critical thinking but also communication and collaboration. Other construction and management simulations (CMSs) like *SimCity* and *MineCraft* require all of the previous skills plus creativity and innovation. Do these skills sound familiar? They should. These are the skills business leaders identified as necessary for the twenty-first century workforce.

PROPOSAL QUEST: After being brought into the future and meeting with the Commander, you feel the weight of your mission—the future survival of the human race. You think about your most intense learning experiences, and you realize that the times in your life when you have been most engaged in learning, engaged to the point where "time does not seem to exist" (Rieber et al. 2008*, p. 30), what you have heard some refer to as "flow" (Csikszentmihalyi* 1990*), is while playing video games. You know you are not the only one who has felt this pull: "One online game popular among college students,* EverQuest, *is jokingly known as 'EverCrack' because of the amount of time its 'addicted' players spend using it. . . . One college student recently confided to [a researcher that] he had skipped an exam because he was so close to 'beating' a video game" (Prensky* 2002*, p. 6). Despite being such powerful learning tools, you know that teachers rarely play video games themselves (Sandford et al.* 2006*), probably because they feel they don't have time, although interestingly the Greek and Latin words for school derive from "game" and teachers in Ancient Rome were called* "magister ludi *(literally,* Game Master*)" (Botturi and Loh* 2008*, p. 17). You ask yourself, "What is it about videogames that afford such deep learning experiences?" You decide to reflect on at least three different kinds*[4] *of*

[4] Just like literature, people have classified video games in lots of different ways. However, there are some generally agreed upon genres like first-person shooter, adventure, role-playing, racing games, etc. (for more, see "Video game genres" in Wikipedia). The goal of this quest is for readers to realize there are different kinds of video games, to explore some of them, and to realize that different types of games are more suited for certain types of learning. Van Eck and Gikas' Matrix of Game and Learning Taxonomies (Table 1.3) outlines their assessment of learning in video games by genre based on Gagne's five types of intellectual skills.

video games you have played in the past and play at least three new ones developed in this new era, in order to evaluate them as learning tools by analyzing their affordances, what a tool enables a user to do, and, constraints, what a tool restricts a user from doing, in terms of three ingredients of learning: content (something to learn), motivation (desire to learn), and pedagogy (way to learn). In order to do so, you start by consulting Bransford et al.*'s book* How People Learn, *particularly chapters 2 through 6, conveniently in your satchel.* **ACTION**: Play three new video games and fill out a chart listing the affordances and constraints of three new ones and three video games you have played in the past in terms of content, motivation, and pedagogy.

You decide videogames can and should be used as a learning tool. *You then* **write a proposal** *to the Commander to persuade her that videogames hold the answer to her goal—and your mission—of teaching their next generation. You include in your proposal a description of the pedagogical advantages of videogames and explanations of how to counter any constraints.* **ACTION**: Write a letter to the Commander to convince her that videogames can be used as learning tools.

OR

You decide that videogames should not be used as a learning tool. *You then, read on (particularly Table 1.1)... and either*

-return to this quest if you change your mind.

OR

-justify why video games should NOT be used to teach

Pedagogical Uses of Video Games

There are lots of examples and articles written about schools using video games to teach. However, De Castell and Jenson (2003) point out that too many educational games are structured so that the learning tasks are unrelated to the overall game structure. Some call this the "broccoli and chocolate" approach, referring to educational games that have players learn something (the broccoli), and once they have mastered it, usually assessed by a quiz, then they get to play a short video game (the chocolate).[5] As such, the learning tasks get in the way of succeeding instead of providing the basis for success. Van Eck (2007) also reiterates the need for learning tasks within games to be "endogenous," or authentic and integrated parts of the game, and Klopfer et al. (2009) warn against games that are "little more than interactive quizzes (p. 2) that test isolated facts. As Klopfer et al. (2009) aptly put it: "If your spaceship requires you to answer a math problem before you can use your blasters, chances are you'll hate the game and the math" (p. 25). Klopfer et al. (2009) advise that instead of "making a game *out of* learning" (p. 27), educational

[5] Brenda Laurel in 2001 referred to educational video games as "chocolate-covered broccoli."

Table 1.1 Pedagogical advantages of video games[a]

What are some of the best ways to foster learning?	How do video games do this?[b]
Creating a storyline (Gee 2007a; Simmons 2001; Brown 2000)	Having a back story (Turkle 1984)
Setting proximal and distal goals (Bandura 1997)	"Telescoping" (Johnson 2005), or a hierarchically organizing objectives
	Having a "win state" (van Staalduinen and de Freitas 2011) as the final goal
Inducing "flow" (Csikszentmihalyi 1990), or a state of total engagement	Through "total immersion" (Prensky 2006) leading to an "altered state" (Turkle 1984)
	"Sensory stimuli" (van Staalduinen and de Freitas 2011)
Achieving "fluency" or "automaticity" with routine matters (Bransford et al. 2000) through practice so working memory can be devoted to problem solving	"Automat[ing] knowledge" (Johnson 2005) so player can focus on higher objectives
Using "mastery learning" (Bloom 1980), or showing mastery of basic concepts and/or skills before moving on to more complex concepts/skills	"Leveling up" (Prensky 2006), or moving to a more challenging level after achieving mastery of the previous level
Having a reward system (Skinner 1953)	"Seeking" (Johnson 2005), or exploring an environment in search of further rewards
Providing instant feedback (Bransford et al. 2000)	Having "just-in-time" learning (Gee 2003), i.e., feedback that lets the player know how he/she is progressing
Using inquiry/discovery learning (Bruner 1961), a process of figuring things out often by testing hypotheses	Using "inductive discovery" (Prensky 2006)
	Involving a process where players "probe, hypothesize, reprobe, rethink" (Johnson 2005)
	Using "mistakes [as] learning opportunities" (Shaffer 2006)
Operating in the "Zone of Proximal Development" (Vygotsky 1978), i.e., challenging students without being too challenging	Using "adaptivity" (Prensky 2006), games adapting to level of player
	Operating on the "edge of regime competence" (Gee 2003), ability to play in challenge zone
Introducing knowledge when needed or relevant instead of disconnected facts (Bransford et al. 2000)	Supplying information "on demand" (Gee 2007b), i.e., when it is needed in game play
Employing "metacognition" (Bransford et al. 2000), or an awareness of one's own learning	Viewing mistakes as "opportunities for reflection and learning" (Gee 2003)
	Ability to take on multiple roles/identities (Gee 2003)
"Building on previous knowledge"/ "transfer" (Bransford et al. 2000)	Having an "action-domain link" (van Staalduinen and de Freitas 2011), i.e., applying lessons learned during game play to new situations
Fostering a "community of learners" (Lave and Wenger 1991)	Creating "affinity spaces" (Gee 2007a), or groups of people and tools on which players rely on for further learning

(continued)

Table 1.1 (continued)

What are some of the best ways to foster learning?	How do video games do this?[b]
Teaching "meaningful pattern recognition"—including recognizing disparities, identifying relevant details (and ignoring irrelevant ones), creating analogies, and understanding how elements relate to one another (Bransford et al. 2000)	"Probing" (Johnson 2005) or making meaning from one's environment
	Figuring out "rules" (van Staalduinen and de Freitas 2011) that govern how elements interact
	Solving "investigative puzzles" through pattern recognition and analogy creation (Squire 2011)
Providing "conditions of applicability" (Bransford et al. 2000), or learning when different rules apply	Employing the "principle of expertise" (Gee 2007a), once rules have been mastered, changing, or refining the rules
Employing "deliberate practice" (Bransford et al. 2000), or opportunities to tinker in ways that help the learner understand a system	Providing a "fish tank" (Gee 2007a) or "sandbox" (van Staalduinen and de Freitas 2011), simplified game spaces where players can learn the rudiments of game play through exploration
Providing "contrasting cases" (Bransford et al. 2000), or a series of cases designed to refine a concept	Constructing "well-ordered problems" (Gee 2007a), or problems that build on and refine knowledge and skills gained in previous problems
Providing "scaffolding" (Vygotsky 1978), or supports a student needs to learn something	Providing hints, tutorials, and other resources (Gee 2007a; van Staalduinen and de Freitas 2011), online communities, forums, or spaces outside and within the game space that provide supports for game play
Giving learners a "sense of control" (Csikszentmihalyi 1990)	Giving players a sense of "agency" (Squire 2011), i.e., active decision-maker
Introducing "cognitive dissonance" (Festinger 1957), i.e., when incoming information contradicts prior knowledge	Creating a "mystery" (van Staalduinen and de Freitas 2011), or encountering something puzzling
Providing a risk-reduced environment (Bransford et al. 2000)	A sense of "safety" (van Staalduinen and de Freitas 2011) that "allows for risk-taking and experimentation, thus providing players with more learning opportunities" (p. 42)
"Learning by doing" (Bransford et al. 2000)	Providing opportunities for "performance before competence" (Gee 2007a; Shaffer 2006), or doing something first in order to learn about it

[a]It should be noted that none of these elements operate in isolation, and it is the interaction of these elements that create pedagogical affordances (see Bedwell et al. 2012)
[b]It should be noted that not all video games have all of these elements

game designers should "find *the fun* in that learning" (p. 27) or "find the game in the content" (p. 31). As situated cognition suggests (Driscoll 2005), learning should be embedded in an authentic context where interrelationships and systems can be explored. De Castell and Jenson (2003) provide a framework (see Table 1.2) for the qualities that make for better educational games. These qualities will be explored more in depth throughout this book since they will serve as guideposts for your own classroom game.

Table 1.2 Guidelines for educational games adapted from de Castell and Jenson (2003) originally printed in Jackson (2011)

Games should	Games should not
Allow players to construct knowledge	"Extrinsically reward correct answers to simple factual questions"
Be interactive	Simply be "display and exposition"
Be based on a storyline	Consist of a series of random facts
Allow user to "negotiate an immersive environment"	Be a "stand-alone task completion"
Allow for "role enactment"	Limit role exploration
Enact consequences based on player's actions	Have limited feedback
Enable learning to be a "by-product" of a player's actions	Have learning be incidental to game play
Encourage exploration of an environment with multiple paths to success	Presents tasks in a "linear and lock-step fashion"
Allow for collaboration and creation of a "community of practice" (Lave and Wenger 1991)	Limit resources
Be voluntary	Be compulsory
Provide instant feedback	Provide no feedback
Have problem solving be a part of the game structure and story	Have problem solving be incidental to the narrative structure
Have built-in rewards that are intrinsic to the game	Have rewards that have nothing to do with game play
Allow the player to define and redefine his/her goals	Focus on measuring "learning outcomes" based on prescribed standards

"What's that?" you say. "My own classroom game?" This book addresses one of the main problems of using commercial off-the-shelf (COTS) video games in the classroom: they are not geared toward specific learning objectives and often lack academic content (as you may have discovered in your quest) so teachers have to bend the curriculum to fit the game instead of bending the game to fit the curriculum. Well, perhaps the curriculum needs to be bent some, or at least be a little more flexible, but a teacher's reality in today's culture of standards is "coverage, coverage, coverage." There are some video games that allow users to modify or "mod" them, in other words to change the source code to alter the game. However, few teachers have the time to learn the skills needed to do so. Instead, this book focuses on how teachers can convert their curriculum into a game. In fact, game-based pedagogy has been around for thousands of years: "Using games for learning and teaching is not new. In ancient China more than 4000 years ago, *weiqi [Go]* . . . was used to train military strategists, chief executives, high-rank officials, advisors in think tank[s], and profound intellectuals" (Jin and Low 2011, p. 396). This book is not about playing video games in the classroom and it is not about one-shot game lessons like using a *Jeopardy* format to review for a test or having problem-solving races, this book is about the "transformational possibilities" (de Freitas and Maharg 2011) of using techniques of video games to revolutionize curriculum.

Gaming, however, has largely been regarded as something students do outside of school; some even label it a "waste of time." I propose educators leverage the affordances of games by "gaming the system," in other words incorporating gaming into the current educational system. I use this phrase intentionally as it implies working within a system in ways that system did not anticipate in order to "exploit it for your own personal gain" (McGonigal 2011, p. 19). In this case, our own "personal gain" as teachers is increasing student learning and the system is that of traditional schooling whose conventions in many ways lie in direct opposition to some of the conventions of gaming. For example, using "distributed cognition" (Gee 2008, p. 32) by relying on tools and others to solve problems common in MMORPGs is a strategy traditional schooling would punish as "cheating." Intentionally making mistakes to find out what happens like gamers often do is an act that traditional schooling discourages through bad grades. Despite these contradictions between schooling and gaming, this book suggests ways teachers can use the principles of video games to transform their teaching by redesigning their curricula using game design principles and to do so within the current constraints of conventional schooling.

This book takes you through the steps to design, test, and implement a curricular game without technology (no tech), with the technology you (probably) already know (low tech), with technology you can easily learn (medium tech), and with (for most) new technologies (high tech). You do not need to learn how to program (although you can). You do not even need to learn how to turn on a computer. You can convert your curriculum into a game without any technology whatsoever. For example, the mission and accompanying quests in this book required no technology outside of the word processor I typed them on to create them. No matter what level of technology you use, your curricular games will leverage common techniques from video games in order to promote learning. For a sneak peek into ways to do this, I excerpted some "ready-to-use" teaching practices below from Mecoli (2013), practices she developed based on Gee 2005 article "Learning by design":

1. **Opportunities to Codesign**: In the game world, players are often given opportunities to help determine what will happen in the game and what direction it will take. When there are opportunities for choice in the classroom (choice of project, choice of reading, choice of day's activities), we might be able to draw upon this principle.
2. **Identity**: In the game world, players immerse themselves in certain identities. They fully take on personas. Thinking about ways we can authentically get students to see themselves as writers, as scientists, and as consumers may encourage them to more fully try on engaging identities.
3. **"Just-in-Time" Instruction**: James Gee has talked about playing video games for the first time and trying to read the game's manual *before* playing the game. He remembers how much more useful it was once he was deep into playing and could reference the sections he needed at that specific point in time. Immersing students in a task and then providing them with lessons or resources when they reach a point of need utilizes the same principle.
4. **"Fish Tanks" and "Sandboxes"**: In the gaming world, both of these phenomena are common. A "fish tank" is a simplified environment of the game where a player can gain practice. A "sandbox" is a practice world where the gamer can play around and experiment before taking on the actual level without fear of consequences. In the education world, finding ways to let our students first play around with the content of a lesson without fear of failure would accomplish the same.

5. **Skills as Strategies**: Video game players know why they need to develop certain skills. They're used in service of completing some segment of the game. Contextualizing skills in service of accomplishing authentic goals that are clear and explicit to students follows the same logic.

I do have a word of caution, however, about converting your curriculum into a game. Beware of just layering superficial aspects of video games onto your already existing curriculum, such as using badges, which can lead to the opposite of the intended outcome:

> "We're really missing out on some of the elements that make real games compelling when we just boil it down to the leaderboard and achievement levels and badges. If you don't have the fun factor in there, I'm not sure that it really qualifies as a game." [G]amification, [Gillispie] proposes, is "really just getting back to the old gold star on the chart.... You need unexpected things, you need hard, difficult choices ... telling a story that sucks people in, the continuous feedback, giving kids a challenge at just the right level, where it's tough, but not frustrating" [DiCerbo adds] ... [whereas] games-rewards structures are really "behaviorism in a disguised form" ... [which leads to students thinking], "Oh, I'm just doing this to get the reward." The result: a decrease in motivation. (Schaffhausser 2013, p. 33)

The process described in this book involves a total transformation of curriculum into a game, not piecemeal additions of badges or leaderboards that just dress up curriculum as a video game, what some call "gamification." However, some use the term "gamification" and its verb form "gamify" to simply mean converting something into a game, which is how those terms are used in this book.

Can gamifying your curriculum be done in the context of standards? It already has been. Some educational video games, like *Lure of the Labyrinth*, have been aligned with common core standards. The *Quest to Learn* schools, located in New York City and Chicago, are based on game design and tied to standards. The description of their curriculum captures the linkage between games and learning: "drop [students] into inquiry-based, complex problem spaces that are scaffolded to deliver just-in-time learning and to use data to understand how they are doing, what they need to work on, and where to go next" (Salen et al. 2011, p. xi). Although this book argues that schools should move beyond standards, standards are the reality of today's teaching. However, standards do not dictate *how* teachers have to teach those standards. Instead, standards can be used as launching pads for creativity, or, in *Quest to Learn's* case, creativity can be used to help students both meet and move beyond standards:

> Test scores, an admittedly conventional metric, show the Quest kids have outperformed peers in the New York City school system in each of the last three years, in both English Language Arts and Math, according to data provided by the school. The only exception was 2010 math scores, when the school averaged 671 compared to 675 for the city... [However] Salen [the school's founder] says how she measures performance isn't quantitative: It's the engagement she sees in students at the school—the attentive look kids have on their faces when they're playing the games; the way they're able to speak clearly about what they're learning and why it's important. (Sutter 2012)

Patrick Welsh (2013) writing about his experiences as a teacher through four decades of school reform concludes: "All of [the school reforms] failed to do what I believe to be key to teaching: to make students care about what they're studying

Table 1.3 Matrix of game and learning taxonomies by Van Eck and Gikas (2006) from Van Eck (2007, p. 274) (Copyright IGI Global, Reprinted by permission of the publisher)

Taxonomy of games	Explanation of genre	Gagne's intellectual skills
Action	Keeps the player moving and involved at all times. Primary skills are eye/hand coordination and quick reflexes. Deep thinking is generally not required	Defined concepts
		Concrete concepts
Role playing	Revolves around characters, story, and combat and takes place in large, expansive worlds. Usually collaborative, often online	Problem solving
		Rules
		Defined concepts
		Concrete concepts
Adventure	Story based on exploration and puzzle solving where the player is the protagonist. Player must determine best path through storyline and obstacles on own or with others	Problem solving
		Rules
		Defined concepts
		Concrete concepts
Strategy	Emphasize strategy and theory, often in recreations of historical or other human events	Problem solving
		Rules
		Defined concepts
		Concrete concepts
Simulations	Simulation of processes, events, or phenomenon. Emphasis is on realistic representation	Problem solving
		Rules
		Defined concepts
		Concrete concepts
Sports	Allows players to play simulated sports activity	Problem solving
		Rules
		Defined concepts
		Concrete concepts
Fighting games	Players engage in combat individually or in teams. Story is present but ancillary to fighting skills	Rules
		Defined concepts
		Concrete concepts

and understand how it's relevant to their lives." Motivation, a key ingredient in learning that is often ignored, is where game-based teaching holds the most potential as it has the potential to provide what Pink (2011) lists as essential to motivation: autonomy, mastery, and purpose.

More important than being able to meet standards, games have been found to improve student learning (see Table 1.3). Johnson (2005) tells of his 7-year-old nephew suggesting he "lower his industrial tax rates" (p. 32) to solve a problem he was having in *SimCity*, and Joli Barker (2013) describes how turning her second grade classroom into a "living video game" increased her student scores by 58 % (reading comprehension), 71 % (reading fluency), and 76 % (math). The Center for Game Science at the University of Washington found that 95 % of K-12 students who played *DragonBox* for 90 min mastered basic algebra concepts (Greenberg 2013).

But a couple of anecdotes do not prove a rule. A meta-analysis (a study of studies) of research on using academic games in the classroom found an average of a 20 percentile gain in student achievement (Marzano 2010). Other meta-analyses have found longer retention, increased cognitive gains, and better attitudes to subject matter when compared to traditional modes of teaching (Adcock et al. 2010; Clark et al. 2013; Kapp 2012; Tobias et al. 2011). The studies in these meta-analyses had participants who ranged in age from preschoolers to senior citizens and covered a wide range of subject matters. It should be noted, however, that some studies found mixed results.[6] One reason is because all video games are often lumped together, particularly in these meta-studies, including those that are the "electronic equivalent of worksheets" (Dempsey 2010, p. 85). As we will see, not all video games are equal in terms of pedagogical power.

First Things First

Before we get into the nuts and bolts of how to create a curricular game, we need to further explore what it is about video games that is so compelling that gamers will invest hours and hours of their time into solving difficult, complex, and challenging problems—with no monetary rewards and no grades attached. This is what gamers call "hard fun" (McGonigal 2011, p. 32). Most educators only dream of their students spending the amount of motivation, attention, passion, and critical thinking on their classes that some students do playing video games. Although many of the pedagogical techniques that video games employ are not new to the educational scene, teachers and teacher educators can learn from the new and innovative ways video games use these techniques. While in some cases video games are uniquely suited to leverage certain pedagogical techniques, teachers can still take advantage of lessons learned from video games. For example, just as video games can readily adjust to the levels of individual users to provide the optimal amount of challenge, what Prensky (2006) calls "adaptivity" and Gee (2003) terms the edge of "regime competence," teachers can provide students with options for different levels of achievement to emulate this in the classroom by targeting students' "zones of proximal development" (ZPD) (Vygotsky 1978), i.e., when learning is challenging but attainable. On the other hand, it would be rather labor-intensive for educators to provide a traditional curriculum as individualized as video games have the potential to be.

There are other ways video games succeed where educators struggle. Successful students learn to set and manage short-term and long-term goals; video game players do this, what Johnson (2005) calls "telescoping," without having to be told to do

[6] Aldrich explains that "part of the trap, of course, is that any new approach to education has to pass a theoretical, ideal, and rigorous standard that no traditional approach could" (quoted by Becker 2010, p. 43).

their homework. Similar to Dewey's (1938) experiential education, i.e., learning by doing, and Papert's (1980) constructionism, i.e., learning by making, Cazden (1981) argues for "performance before competence," a technique that often lies at the heart of video games. By embedding the "learning" into the "doing," learners employ discovery learning (Bruner 1961) where learners use problem solving and critical thinking to construct their own understandings of the material. As Prensky (2001a) points out, "discovery learning is what many games, and certainly all adventure games, are all about" (p. 160). In other words, video games rely on constructivism, the idea that learners build their own knowledge structures.

Hypothesis testing and discovery learning have long been used in the classroom (Mayo 2009), but video game players, who also use "inductive discovery" (Prensky 2006) or "probing" (Johnson 2005), can take risks and learn from their mistakes because they can make multiple attempts instead of a one-shot paper that is due Tuesday. When that paper is turned in, the student does not receive feedback instantaneously, and often not immediately, unlike video games, because it requires time for the teacher to grade all the papers and write individual comments. When playing a video game, though, feedback is on the spot and often "just in time," i.e., "when the learner can use it" (Gee 2007b, p. 24) and/or "on demand," i.e., "when the learner is ready" (Gee 2007b, p. 25), thus providing the assistance, or "scaffolding," necessary to help learners learn within their ZPD. When feedback is received in the classroom, students often interpret it as a "judgment" from the teacher (Gee 2007a, p. 63), whereas video games sometimes have humorous or engaging feedback, which can encourage players to make "mistakes" on purpose to find out how the game responds (Prensky 2001a, p. 159). In the classroom, mistakes result in punishment—a lower grade. When playing video games, risk-taking is encouraged due to decreased real-world consequences, or "psychosocial moratorium" (Erikson 1980), so mistakes are seen as learning opportunities (Gee (2003); Prensky 2001a; Shaffer 2006). In addition, immediate positive feedback in the form of rewards helps cement the learning: "each time the child is rewarded, his brain secretes such neurotransmitters as dopamine and acetylcholine which help consolidate the map changes he has just made. (Dopamine reinforces the reward, and acetylcholine helps the brain 'tune in' and sharpen memories)" (Doidge 2007, p. 71). Of course, as studies in behaviorism have shown us, the reward needs to be intrinsic to the task and for doing something challenging. Immediate feedback and rewards allow video game players to remain engaged in the game while still invested instead of receiving feedback after losing interest or becoming discouraged after receiving negative feedback, unfortunately what happens all too often in school.

In addition, the potential for immersion that video games offer is difficult to rival in a traditional classroom setting. This immersion contributes to what Csikszentmihalyi (1990) calls "flow," or total engagement, and what Turkle (1984) describes as an "altered state" (p. 83) that people experience while playing a video game. Csikszentmihalyi (1990) asserts that "The more a job resembles a game—with variety, appropriate and flexible challenges, clear goals, and immediate feedback—the more enjoyable it will be regardless of the worker's level of development" (p. 152). To keep players in their ZPD, video games often require a certain level of mastery before players are allowed to move to the next level, similar to what educators call mastery learning (Bloom 1980). When these elements and others are combined, video games can capitalize on human beings' natural desire to learn, or "achievement motivation" (McClelland, cited in Driscoll 2005, p. 311). A great potential lies in this intersection of best teaching practices and the capacities of video games.

Although some may argue that emulating video game players is the last thing a teacher should want his or her students to do, playing video games can foster positive qualities:

> Surveys of gamers show that they have an increased appetite for risk, a greater comfort with failure, a stronger desire for social affiliations, a preference for challenges, a capacity for independent problem solving, and a desire to be involved in meaningful work when compared with nongamers (Beck and Wade 2004). Underlying Beck and Wade's argument is a notion of changing literacies. Gamers have grown up with a medium built on assumptions unlike those in print cultures (e.g., a game engine can be tinkered with, a text is not necessarily print based or defined by book covers); game players are coauthors along with game designers, co-constructing the game-as-text through their own action (cf., Robison 2005). Gamers have grown up in simulated worlds, worlds where anything is possible, and where learning through trial and error is expected, information is a resource for action, and expertise is enacted through both independent and collaborative problem solving in self-directed tasks. (Simpson 2005) (Squire 2008, p. 658)

Gee (2003) describes video game players as being able to: take on new identities and perspectives, see themselves as active problem solvers, view mistakes as "opportunities for reflection and learning," undo a previous way of solving a problem in order to learn new ways, and take risks. In addition, gamers "regularly exhibit persistence [and] … attention to detail" (Klopfer et al. 2009, p. 1). All of these qualities Friedman (2007) argues are necessary for the changing needs in a global marketplace that relies less and less on vertical hierarchies and more and more on ad hoc horizontal groups working together to solve problems.

Pelletier and Oliver (2006) studied people playing video games in action. They found that gamers developed and revised rules and strategies for game playing based on hypothesis testing and actively worked to resolve "cognitive dissonance" (Van Eck 2007), or contradictions between their own predictions about how objects in the game might react to their actions and how the objects actually reacted. Once a video game player has mastered one skill, however, Gee (2007a) argues that good games rely on what he terms the "principle of expertise," adding a twist to something that has become routine in order to make it more challenging. It is this cycle of "pleasurable frustration and routine mastery, a cycle of storm and calm" (p. 62) that continually engages the player.

In addition, Pelletier and Oliver (2006) found some evidence of transfer of skills between games, which Gee (2007a) also found in his own self-study of learning to play *Rise of Nations*, suggesting that video games may translate into real-world applications. Certainly, the military banks on this transfer in its use of video games to train soldiers (Annetta et al. 2009). Some early research does point to such outside transfer, such as a study that found that a range of cognitive skills of senior citizens who played *Rise of Nations* increased (Anthes 2009). Shaffer (2006) reports on several independent studies that found that students not only exhibited greater content understanding after using computer simulations but were able to apply this understanding to real-world situations, even ones outside of the original domain. Studies of simulations have found that those with high fidelity do promote transfer to real-world situations, although optimal learning occurs with moderate fidelity—when limits are placed on real-world variables (Grabe and Grabe 2007)—what Gee (2007a) calls a "fishtank," or a simplified version that provides just enough for the player to see how the system fits together. The advantage of computer simulations is that as learners progress, more and more real-world variables can be introduced. In addition, simulations "make certain experiences practical and other experiences possible" (Grabe and Grabe 2007, p. 129), such as "performing potentially dangerous science activities" (Annetta and Cheng 2008, p. 5). As one of my students pointed out, "it's better to make a mistake in a chemistry game than in a chemistry lab." Even when simulations are more game like, transfer can occur, such as teaching engineers a new design software tool by having them play *The Monkey Wrench Conspiracy*—a game where they have to save the Copernicus Space Station by repairing parts (Prensky 2001a). In contrast, some studies show that traditional school learning does not promote transfer: "We have known for years now that most of the kids who can pass these tests . . . cannot actually apply their knowledge to the real world" (Gee quoted in Shaffer 2006, p. x). Because video games and simulations can provide real-world context, students make connections, see relationships, think in new ways, and see the whole instead of learning isolated or abstract facts, which increases the likelihood of skills and knowledge transferring to real-world situations.

Whether gamers are playing a real-world simulation or a fictional game, when they encounter difficulties, they seek help from their "affinity spaces," groups, and other resources that supply a "distributed intelligence" and take advantage of "cross-functional affiliation" by finding other players who have a variety of skills (Gee 2007a). This happens particularly in multiplayer games, but even in single-player games, players consult online communities and walkthroughs to scaffold their learning. In other words, gamers take advantage of teamwork, communicating across age groups and geographical boundaries based on others' skills and knowledge and thus transcending race, gender, and other demographic variables to create a "gaming culture" (de Castell and Jenson 2003) where expertise-based on mastery is recognized and honored.

Gee (2003) has written much about video game players' identities and games and asserts that taking on a new identity is a powerful learning tool. One reason is because "The ability to take on multiple roles allows players to gain multiple perspectives of a given scenario" (Annetta et al. 2006). Some games establish their game play based on attributes chosen by the player. Others allow the players to replay the game from a different character's perspective. Gee (2003) points out that taking on different roles has the potential to challenge video game players' assumptions and expand their understandings, particularly when the player is faced with choices that challenge the player's values. Annetta and Holmes (2006) (cited in Annetta 2008) found that "students who had a choice of which avatar they would like to be reported greater course satisfaction and felt closer to their classmates and instructor than students who only could choose a male or a female avatar" because it gave students a "sense of individuality" (p. 235). As one of my students noted, creating an avatar allows students to "fly their freak flag without suffering social suicide." Inhabiting a role and making choices about that identity can make learning more powerful by giving students ownership and have the potential to teach valuable lessons about multiple perspectives.

Because of these changes in thinking and behavior that technology has encouraged, Prensky (2001b) points out that "Today's students are no longer the people our educational system was designed to teach" (p. 1). To accommodate this, educators need to learn to adjust their teaching to new generations of students. Turkle (1984) describes video games as opportunities for people to "learn… how to learn." In our rapidly changing world, that should be the goal of school.

I am not the only one arguing for the use of video games and video game techniques in education, nor is it limited to those cited in this chapter. The Federation of American Scientists issued a report in 2006 "stating their belief that games offer a powerful new tool to support education" (Clark and Martinez-Garza 2012, p. 279), and the National Research Council in 2009 commissioned a committee to explore ways in which to do this (Clark and Martinez-Garza 2012). However, I do have personal experience testifying to the impact of game-based teaching from my course evaluation ratings increasing (from 2.6 out of 4 in the traditional mode to 3.9 out of 4 in my most recent game-based teaching class), to the success of my students (from 40% receiving less than a B in the traditional mode to nearly 0% in the past several years, including online courses), to student comments (traditional mode comments indicate that I was "nice" and "tried hard" but that I needed to "make class more interactive" and that students wanted "more time to explore" and to "experiment with technology" whereas game-based learning comments speak to my class "meeting students where they are" and "forcing students out of their comfort zones" while being "fun" resulting in my students "integrating technology into [their] own classroom[s], even [in] urban schools with little funding" and their students "getting really excited about using computers").

Why convert your curriculum into a game? Not to compete with outside entertainment–that has always been a challenge that teachers tend to lose whether it be to sports, television, or video games–but because games enable students to *experience* the curriculum in ways that traditional instruction does not (de Freitas and Maharg 2011). When students experience the curriculum, they do more than memorize facts or practice skills; it becomes a part of their life story and a part of their brain structure (Bransford et al. 2000, p. 116).

> *Anyone who makes a distinction between games and learning doesn't know the first thing about either.*
>
> –Marshall McLuhan, 1964

Appendix: Proposal Quest Worksheets

Video game	Genre	Pros and cons	Of supplying content	Of providing motivation	Of teaching (pedagogy)
1 (previously played)		*Affordances*			
		Constraints			
2 (previously played)		*Affordances*			
		Constraints			
3 (previously played)		*Affordances*			
		Constraints			
4 (newly played)		*Affordances*			
		Constraints			
5 (newly played)		*Affordances*			
		Constraints			
6 (newly played)		*Affordances*			
		Constraints			

	Affordances	*Constraints*
Content		
Motivation		
Pedagogy		

Suggested Proposal Quest Rubric

Criteria	"Wow! I mean, I think this might work" (3)	"Hmm, this might be acceptable" (2)	"I need more convincing" (1)	"Go back to the drawing board" (0)
Affordances	Affordances put in context of learning theories	Affordances described	Affordances listed	No affordances listed
Constraints	Constraints turned into affordances	Constraints countered	Constraints listed	No constraints listed
Student impact	Explanation includes ELLs, students with special needs, and other types of learners	Explanation includes ELLs or students with special needs	Explanation includes impact on student learning	No mention of range of students
Evidence	Research studies analyzed	Research studies cited	Evidence is all anecdotal	Little to no evidence provided
Grammar, organization, and style	Sophisticated and creative persuasive writing in context of gaming scenario; APA used correctly	Clearly written and organized; APA style used correctly	Grammar or APA style mistakes; stylistically awkward	Grammar mistakes and style makes paper difficult to follow; APA style not used
Techie (one extra point)				
Table of affordances and constraints of video games by genre included				
Tech Savvy (two extra points)				
Analysis of percentage of standards addressed				
Tech Guru (three extra points)				
Learning theory diagram that demonstrates pedagogical affordances of video games included				

ELLs English Language Learners, *APA* American Psychological Association citation style

Suggested Reading

Friedman, T. (2007). *The world is flat: A brief history of the twenty-first century*. New York: Picador.

Gee, J. P. (2003). *What videogames have to teach us about learning and literacy*. New York: Palgrave Macmillan.

Gee, J. P. (2005). Learning by design: Good video games as learning machines. *E-Learning, 2*(1), 5–16.

Gee, J. P. (2007). *Good video games + good learning*. New York: Peter Lang.

Johnson, S. (2005). *Everything bad is good for you: How today's popular culture is actually making us smarter*. New York: Penguin.

Prensky, M. (2001). *Digital game-based learning*. New York: McGraw Hill.

Prensky, M. (2001). Digital natives, digital immigrants. *On the Horizon, 9*(5).

Prensky, M. (2005). "Engage me or enrage me": What today's learners demand. *Educause, 40*(5), 60–65.

Prensky, M. (2006). *Don't bother me Mom—I'm learning!* St. Paul, MN: Paragon House.

Salen, K., Torres, R., Wolozin, L., Rufo-Tepper, R., & Shapiro, A. (2011). *Quest to Learn: Developing the school for digital kids*. Cambridge, MA: MIT Press.

Shaffer, D. W. (2006). *How computer games help children learn*. New York: Palgrave MacMillan.

Van Eck, R. (2010). *Gaming and cognition: Theories and practice from the learning sciences*. Hershey, PA: Information Science Reference.

Wagner, T. (2008). Rigor redefined: Even our "best" schools are failing to prepare students for 21st-century careers and citizenship. *Educational Leadership, 66*(2), 20–25.

References

Adcock, A., Watson, G., Morrison, G., & Belfore, L. (2010). Effective knowledge development in game-based learning environments: Considering research in cognitive processes and simulation design. In R. Van Eck (Ed.), *Gaming and cognition: Theories and practice from the learning sciences* (pp. 152–168). Hershey, PA: Information Science Reference.

Annetta, L. A. (2008). Video games in education: Why they should be used and how they are being used. *Theory into Practice, 47*(3), 229–239.

Annetta, L. A., & Cheng, M.-T. (2008). Why educational video games? In L. A. Annetta (Ed.), *Serious educational games: From theory to practice* (pp. 1–11). Rotterdam, The Netherlands: Sense.

Annetta, L. A., Minogue, J., Holms, S. Y., & Cheng, M. (2009). Investigating the impact of video games on high school students' engagement and learning about genetics. *Computers and Education, 53*(1), 74–85.

Annetta, L. A., Murray, M. R., Laird, S. G., Bohr, S. C., & Park, J. C. (2006). Serious games: Incorporating video games in the classroom. *Educause, 29*(3), 16–22.

Anthes, E. (2009, October 12). How video games are good for the brain. *Boston Globe*, p. G6.

Bandura, A. (1997). *Self-efficacy: The exercise of control*. New York: W.H. Freeman.

Barab, S., Pettyjohn, P., Gresalfi, M., & Solomou, M. (2012). Game-based curricula, personal engagement, and the Modern Prometheus design project. In C. Steinkuehler, K. Squire, & S. Barab (Eds.), *Games, learning, and society: Learning and meaning in the digital age* (pp. 306–326). New York: Cambridge University Press.

Barker, J. (2013). How I turned my classroom into a "living video game"—and saw achievement soar. *eSchoolNews*. Retrieved January 6, 2016, from http://www.eschoolnews.com/2013/03/12/how-i-turned-my-classroom-into-a-living-video-game-and-saw-achievement-soar/

Barton, K., & McKellar, P. (2011). From master to games-master: Managing disequilibrium and scaffolding in simulation-based learning. In S. de Freitas & P. Maharg (Eds.), *Digital games and learning* (pp. 226–251). London: Continuum.

Becker, K. (2010). Distinctions between games and learning: A review of current literature on games in education. In R. Van Eck (Ed.), *Gaming and cognition: Theories and practice from the learning sciences* (pp. 22–54). Hershey, PA: Information Science Reference.

Bedwell, W., Pavlas, D., Heyne, K., Lazzara, E., & Salas, E. (2012). Towards a taxonomy linking game attributes to learning: An empirical study. *Simulation and Gaming, 43*(6), 729–760.

Bloom, B. S. (1980). *All our children learning*. New York: McGraw-Hill.

Botturi, L., & Loh, S. (2008). Once upon a game: Rediscovering the roots of game in education. In C. T. Miller (Ed.), *Games: Purpose and potential in education* (pp. 1–22). New York: Springer.

Bransford, J. D., Brown, A., & Cocking, R. (2000). *How people learn*. Washington, DC: National Academy Press.

Brown, J. S. (2000, March/April). Growing up digital. *Change*, pp. 10–20.

Bruner, J. S. (1961). The act of discovery. *Harvard Educational Review, 31*(1), 21–32.

Cazden, C. (1981). Performance before competence: Assistance to child discourse in the zone of proximal development. *Quarterly Newsletter of the Laboratory of Comparative Human Cognition, 3*, 5–8.

Clark, D., & Martinez-Garza, M. (2012). Prediction and explanation as design mechanics in conceptually integrated digital games to help players articulate the tacit understandings they build through game play. In C. Steinkuehler, K. Squire, & S. Barab (Eds.), *Games, learning, and society: Learning and meaning in the digital age* (pp. 279–305). New York: Cambridge University Press.

Clark, D., Tanner-Smith, E., & Killingsworth, S. (2013). *Digital games for learning: A systematic review and meta-analysis*. Menlo Park, CA: SRI International. Retrieved from http://www.sri.com/sites/default/files/brochures/digital-games-for-learning-brief.pdf

Crockett, L., Jukes, I., & Churches, A. (2011). *Literacy is not enough: 21st century fluencies for the digital age*. Thousand Oaks, CA: Sage Publishing Company.

Csikszentmihalyi, M. (1990). *Flow: The psychology of optimal experience*. New York: Harper & Row.

Darling-Hammond, L. (2010). *The flat world and education: How America's commitment to equity will determine our future*. New York: Teachers College Press.

De Castell, S., & Jenson, J. (2003). Serious play. *Journal of Curriculum Studies, 35*(6), 649–665.

Dempsey, J. V. (2010). Elemental learning and the pyramid of fidelity. In R. Van Eck (Ed.), *Gaming and cognition: Theories and practice from the learning sciences* (pp. 82–107). Hershey, PA: Information Science Reference.

Devaney, L. (2014, July 7). 5 gaming dynamics that truly engage students. *eSchoolNews*. Retrieved November 6, 2015, from http://www.eschoolnews.com/2014/07/07/gaming-engaging-students-365/

Dewey, J. (1938). *Experience and education*. New York: Collier Books.

Dickey, M. (2011). Murder on Grimm Isle. In S. de Freitas & P. Maharg (Eds.), *Digital games and learning* (pp. 129–151). London: Continuum.

Doidge, N. (2007). *The brain that changes itself: Stories of personal triumph from the frontiers of brain science*. New York: Penguin.

Driscoll, M. (2005). *Psychology of learning for instruction*. Boston: Allyn and Bacon.

Erikson, E. (1980). *Identity and the life cycle*. New York: W.W. Norton.

Festinger, L. (1957). *A theory of cognitive dissonance*. Stanford, CA: Stanford University Press.

Friedman, T. (2007). *The world is flat: A brief history of the twenty-first century*. New York: Picador.

Gee, J. P. (2003). *What videogames have to teach us about learning and literacy*. New York: Palgrave Macmillan.

Gee, J. P. (2007a). *Good video games + good learning*. New York: Peter Lang.

Gee, J. P. (2007b). Video games, learning and "content". *Harvard Interactive Media Review, 1*(1), 24–29.

Grabe, M., & Grabe, C. (2007). *Integrating technology for meaningful learning*. New York: Houghton Mifflin.

Greenberg, J. (2013). Kids like to learn algebra, if it comes in the right app. *Wired.* Retrieved November 6, 2015, from http://www.wired.com/2013/11/zoran-popovic/

Holt, T. (April 19, 2013). The ultimate education reform: Messy learning and problem solving. *Powerful Learning Practice.* Retrieved November 6, 2015, from http://plpnetwork.com/2013/04/19/ultimate-education-reform-messy-learning-problem-solving/

Jackson, J. (2011). Game changer: How principles of videogames can transform teaching. In M. S. Khine (Ed.), *Learning to play: Exploring the future of education with video games* (pp. 107–128). New York: Peter Lang.

Jin, P., & Low, R. (2011). Implications of game use for explicit instruction. In S. Tobias & J. D. Fletcher (Eds.), *Computer games and instruction* (pp. 395–416). Charlotte, NC: Information Age.

Johnson, S. (2005). *Everything bad is good for you: How today's popular culture is actually making us smarter.* New York: Penguin.

Joseph, B. (2008). Why Johnny can't fly. In K. Salen (Ed.), *The Ecology of Games: Connecting youth, games, and learning* (pp. 253–266). Cambridge, MA: MIT Press.

Kaling, M. (2011). *Is everyone hanging out without me? (and other concerns).* New York: Crown Publishing Group.

Kapp, K. (2012). *The Gamification of learning and instruction: Game-based methods and strategies for training and education.* San Francisco, CA: Pfeiffer.

Klopfer, E., Osterweil, S., & Salen, K. (2009). *Moving learning games forward: Obstacles, opportunities, and openness.* Cambridge, MA: The Education Arcade at MIT.

Lave, J., & Wenger, E. (1991). *Situated learning: Legitimate peripheral participation.* Cambridge, MA: Cambridge University Press.

Lenhart, A., Kahne, J., Middaugh, E., Magill, A. R., Evans, C., & Vitak, J. (2008). *Teens, videogames, and civics.* Washington, DC: Pew Internet and American Life Project. Retrieved November 6, 2015, from http://www.pewinternet.org/2008/09/16/teens-video-games-and-civics/

Marzano, R. (2010). Using games to enhance student achievement. *Educational Leadership, 67*(5), 71–72.

Massachusetts Business Alliance for Education. (2008). *Educating a 21st century workforce: A call for action for high school reform.* Retrieved November 6, 2015, from http://www.mbae.org/uploads/06102008230519EducatingA21stCenturyWorkforce.pdf

Mayo, M. (2009). Video games: A route to large scale STEM education? *Science, 323*, 79–82.

McGonigal, J. (2011). *Reality is broken: Why games make us better and how they can change the world.* London: Penguin.

Mecoli, S. (2013, March). Game playing=optimized learning? *Technology in the classroom.* Newsletter for Quincy High School, p. 4.

Papert, S. (1980). *Mindstorms: Children, computers, and powerful ideas.* New York: Basic Books.

Pelletier, C., & Oliver, M. (2006). Learning to play in digital games. *Learning, Media, and Technology, 31*(4), 329–342.

Pink, D. (2011). *Drive: The surprising truth about what motivates us.* New York: Penguin.

Pooley, E. (1999, May 10). Portrait of a deadly bond. *Time*, 26–32.

Prabhu, M. (2009). Senate bill supports 21st-century skills. *eSchoolNews.* Retrieved November 6, 2015, from http://www.eschoolnews.com/news/top-news/index.cfm?i=58949

Prensky, M. (2001a). *Digital game-based learning.* New York: McGraw Hill.

Prensky, M. (2001b). Digital natives, digital immigrants. *On the Horizon, 9*(5).

Prensky, M. (2002). The motivation of game play, or the REAL 21st century learning revolution. *On the Horizon, 10*(1), 5–11.

Prensky, M. (2006). *Don't bother me Mom—I'm learning!* St. Paul, MN: Paragon House.

Putnam, R. T., & Borko, H. (2000). What do new views of knowledge and thinking have to say about research on teacher learning? *Educational Researcher, 29*(1), 4–15.

Raines, C. (2002). Managing millennials. *Generations at Work.* Retrieved November 6, 2015, from http://www.generationsatwork.com/articles/millenials.htm

Rieber, L., Barbour, M., Thomas, G., & Rauscher, D. (2008). Learning by designing homemade powerpoint games. In C. T. Miller (Ed.), *Games: Purpose and potential in education* (pp. 23–43). New York: Springer.

Salen, K., Torres, R., Wolozin, L., Rufo-Tepper, R., & Shapiro, A. (2011). *Quest to Learn: Developing the school for digital kids*. Cambridge, MA: MIT Press.

Sandford, R., Ulicsak, M., Facer, K., & Rudd, T. (2006). Teaching with games: Using commercial off-the-shelf computer games in formal education. *Futurelab*. Retrieved November 6, 2015, from https://www.nfer.ac.uk/publications/FUTL49/FUTL49.pdf

Schaffhausser, D. (2013). Can gaming improve teaching and learning? *T.H.E. Journal, 40*(8), 26–33.

Schrum, L., & Levin, B. (2009). *Leading 21st century schools: Harnessing technology for engagement and achievement*. Thousand Oaks, CA: Corwin Press.

Shaffer, D. W. (2006). *How computer games help children learn*. New York: Palgrave MacMillan.

Shulock, N. (2010). *Beyond the rhetoric: Improving college readiness through coherent state policy*. San Jose, CA: The National Center for Public Policy and Higher Education. Retrieved November 6, 2015, from http://www.highereducation.org/reports/college_readiness/CollegeReadiness.pdf

Shute, V. (2011). Stealth assessment in computer-based games to support learning. In S. Tobias & J. D. Fletcher (Eds.), *Computer games and instruction* (pp. 503–524). Charlotte, NC: IAP Information Age Publishing.

Simmons, A. (2001). *The story factor: Inspiration, influence, and persuasion through the art of storytelling*. New York: Basic Books.

Skinner, B. F. (1953). *Science and human behavior*. New York: The Free Press.

Squire, K. (2008). Video-game literacy: A literacy of expertise. In J. Coiro, D. Leu, C. Lankshear, & M. Knobel (Eds.), *Handbook of research on new literacies* (pp. 635–670). New York: Taylor & Francis.

Squire, K. (2011). *Video games and learning: Teaching and participatory culture in the digital age*. New York, NY: Teachers College Press.

Staalduinen, J. P., & de Freitas, S. (2011). A Game-based learning framework: Linking game design and learning outcomes. In M. S. Khine (Ed.), *Learning to play: Exploring the future of education with video games* (pp. 29–54). New York: Peter Lang.

Stillwell, R., & Sable, J. (2013). *Public school graduates and dropouts from the common core of data: School year 2009–10* U.S. Dept. of Education. Retrieved http://nces.ed.gov/pubs2013/2013309rev.pdf

Sutter, J. (2012). The school where learning is a game. *Gaming reality*. Atlanta, GA: CNN. Retrieved from http://www.cnn.com/interactive/2012/08/tech/gaming.series/teachers.html

Tobias, S., Fletcher, J. D., Dai, D., & Wind, A. (2011). Review of research on computer games. In S. Tobias & J. D. Fletcher (Eds.), *Computer games and instruction* (pp. 127–221). Charlotte, NC: Information Age.

Turkle, S. (1984). *The second self: Computers and the human spirit*. New York: Simon and Schuster.

Van Eck, R. (2007). Building artificially intelligent learning games. In D. Gibson, C. Aldrich, & M. Prensky (Eds.), *Games and simulations in online learning: Research and development frameworks* (pp. 271–307). Hershey, PA: Information Science Publishing.

Vygotsky, L. (1978). *Mind in society*. Cambridge, MA: Harvard University Press.

Wagner, T. (2008). Rigor redefined: Even our "best" schools are failing to prepare students for 21st-century careers and citizenship. *Educational Leadership, 66*(2), 20–25. Retrieved November 6, 2015, from http://www.ascd.org/publications/educational-leadership/oct08/vol66/num02/Rigor-Redefined.aspx

Welsh, P. (2013, Sept. 27). Four decades of failed school reform. *Washington Post*. Retrieved November 6, 2015, from http://www.washingtonpost.com/opinions/four-decades-of-failed-school-reform/2013/09/27/dc9f2f34-2561-11e3-b75d-5b7f66349852_story.html

Chapter 2
Game on! Choosing a Topic

> *In every job that must be done, there is an element of fun. You find the fun and snap, the job's a game.*
>
> –Mary Poppins

Abstract This chapter provides an overview of the process of designing curricular games while emphasizing the iterative nature of game design. In doing so, this chapter explains that this process is only a guide and encourages readers to develop their own process on the way. This chapter suggests several ways the reader can brainstorm and narrow down the topic of his or her curricular game by drawing on curricular planning techniques such as Wiggins and McTighe's (1998) Backwards Design process as well as brainstorming techniques proposed by game designers such as "growing an idea tree" (Game design workshop: designing, prototyping, and playtesting games, CMP Books, San Francisco, 2004). The chapter then helps the reader develop the topic into a theme (The art of game design: a book of lenses, Morgan Kaufmann, Burlington, 2008) in order to capture the feeling the curricular game intends to provoke.

Choose Topic — *Diagram System of Topic* — *Tell Story of System* — *Gamify Story* — *Create Quests* — *Render and Test Game* — *Teach Game* — *Reflect on Teaching*

J.J. Kellinger, *A Guide to Designing Curricular Games*,
Advances in Game-Based Learning, DOI 10.1007/978-3-319-42393-7_2

TOPIC QUEST:

After reading your proposal, the Commander arranges to meet with you. You walk into the her office eager with anticipation, head held high—after all, you are the Chosen One. When you walk in, she is in the middle of a conversation with the lead historian of the committee who chose you. You overhear her saying, "Why didn't you choose E.D. Hirsch instead of this bozo?"[1] *You clear your throat, both to announce your presence and to prevent tears from welling up in your eyes. When she finally looks up to acknowledge your presence, her face immediately tells you she read your proposal with skepticism. The ensuing conversation reveals that she lacks even a basic understanding of the learning process, making it impossible for her to understand your proposal, and her unwavering eye contact suggests an unwillingness to learn. You realize you are making the same teaching mistake you seem to be doomed to repeat—assuming prior knowledge. You lower your head and find yourself mumbling and fidgeting. After an exasperating exchange where you fear she will decide you are a fraud because you cannot even teach her, you look up in frustration. You see her ceiling has an image of the constellations that shows how they move throughout the year. You realize that she is someone who thinks in systems, a way of thinking you try to teach your students. Your confidence restored, you animatedly draw a diagram of the learning process for her.*

After glancing over it, she holds it up and says, "I just do not get why learning has to be so complicated. Why not just tell someone what they are supposed to know?"

You launch into learning theory and watch her eyes glaze over. You then say, "See? That's why. I was just telling you what I wanted you to learn, but your brain did not receive it."

She concedes your point but counters with, "I've played every decent video game out there. They are just mere entertainment!"

"Let's do a little experiment," you suggest. "I will create a game on a topic you know nothing about. If, after playing the game, you have learned something about the topic, this exemplar can be used as a model for your experts so they can design their own games to teach the next generation their knowledge and skills."

"You have ninety days," she growls. "At the end of ninety days, not only does your game need to teach me, it will have to teach a random group drawn from the next generation, after all, they are your audience. If you haven't proven yourself by then, we'll have to send you back and bring in another teacher to do this job."

She then leans over and looks you straight in the eyes and says, "And whatever you do, do NOT communicate with anyone from your time period. Bringing you here is enough of a risk. Communicating with the past could disrupt the space-time continuum and alter the course of history. Do you understand me?"

Instinctively you respond by saying, "Yes ma'am."

As you step out of the Commander's office, determined but overwhelmed, you hear her say one last thing, "Good skill!"[2] *You feel a glimmer of hope that maybe, just maybe, she thinks you can succeed.*

---

[1] E.D. Hirsch advocates for a shared "cultural literacy" and has created lists of "what every American should know" which largely reflect knowledge valued by white males in his own era, and promotes a content-based curriculum.

[2] My father who did not believe in luck would always say, "Good skill!" to me before taking a standardized test.

Where to begin? If only you could ask your video game designer friend Amy how she comes up with ideas for her video games. You think, "There must be some way to communicate with people from my time, otherwise the Commander would not have warned against it. I wonder what would happen if I tried texting her?" Do you dare?

IF YES, THEN: Knowing it is a long shot, even though you are back in your room, you bend over and covertly send a quick text in case you are being watched: "Just curious, how do you come up with ideas for your video games?" You wait eagerly for a response but of course nothing happens. Texts cannot travel through time. After staring at your phone for what feels like forever, you put it in your pocket. When you look up, you realize your door is ajar. "That's odd," you think. You could have sworn you shut the door.

ELSE: You stare at your cell phone but decide you need to figure this out on your own. It's just not worth the risk—of getting caught or messing up history, or the future, or whatever it would be. However, when you look up, you realize your door is ajar. You see a figure quickly dart away. You put your cell phone in your pocket and slam the door.

You resign yourself to relying on your own experiences. Your thoughts go back to your own attempts to plan a curriculum in your first year of teaching. You had no idea what to do so you began with day one, then planned day two, and so forth with no end goal, no "win-state," in mind. As a result, your curriculum was all over the map, map, map. Hmmm. That word seems to stick out in your mind, but you can't quite figure out why. Your thoughts return to the present mission. You then remember how important Wiggins and McTighe's (2005) *Backward Design process*[3] *was to your own teaching. Quickly, you choose a topic and brainstorm some enduring understandings*[4] *or underlying concepts you want students to learn. You choose one, but then remember you have to check to see if the Commander has any knowledge about the topic. She said she's played every video game, so you do a quick search to see if a commercial off-the-shelf (COTS) video game already exists on your chosen topic.* **ACTION**: Brainstorm topics, choose one, and list some enduring understandings.

IF a COTS does exist, THEN: you remember she said "decent" and you realize you have to determine if the video game is "decent" to see if she has played it. You play the game and ask yourself the following questions:

- Does it have language or anything explicit that might not be appropriate for students?
- Is there a possibility of nonstudent avatars' "griefing," i.e., harassing, or otherwise interfering with your students' game play? If so, is there a way to create a closed system where your students only interact with each other?

---

[3] For instructional designers, this would be comparable to ADDIE—Analyze, Design, Develop, Implement, Evaluate or to the Dick and Carey Model.

[4] "Enduring understandings" is Wiggins and McTighe's (2005) phrase for those underlying concepts that reside within a student long after the initial learning has taken place. For example, an enduring understanding might be that you do not need to speak a language perfectly in order to communicate or that there are multiple ways to solve a math problem or that no history is objective because everyone has their own biases or that today's science is tomorrow's bunk. Think about the stance you want your students to take or the mindset you want to develop.

- Does it meet your learning objectives, i.e., have a high likelihood of teaching your chosen "understanding" in a way that is "enduring"?
- Is it too expensive—both in terms of the classroom time it might take and in terms of cost for both software and hardware required to run the game? Keep in mind that students may not have the technology they need at home. If you plan on playing the game only during class time, you can purchase just one copy, display it using an LCD projector, and have the students play it as a class using either personal response devices such as clickers to make choices after a whole class discussion or by having the class vote by raising their hands. This may be difficult, though, if the environment is too exploratory, i.e., too many choices. You can purchase several and have students play in small groups or with a partner if you have access to enough computers.
- If it is a cloud-based game, i.e., available only on the Internet, is there reliable Internet access at school? Will it pass through the school's Internet filters? If your students are under thirteen, can the students access the game[5]?

IF decent, THEN: *you have to go back to the drawing board because this means the Commander has played this game and therefore knows the topic. You need to choose another enduring understanding. However, you may want to consider using that commercial game as a teaching tool yourself.*

ELSE: *you recall one of your education professors admitting that teaching is really all about "stealing" and adapting someone else's curriculum to your purposes. You remember Amy saying this is true in video game design as well: "This spirit of studying one another's games—and then 'stealing' features that work—is one reason that the games industry has grown and improved so rapidly. Commercial game designers play one another's games* all the time. *If there's a feature that works in one game, it will be adopted by others in the next production cycle. Ideas jump across games at a dizzying pace that puts academic 'knowledge dissemination' to shame" (Squire 2011, p. 8). You decide you can use the ideas from this video game and modify or "mod" them to create your own classroom game.*

If no COTS exist, THEN: *you decide to create your own game from scratch. However, you keep your list of enduring understandings just in case you run into problems and have to return to it.*

Just like you do when you plan a curriculum, you work on turning your enduring understanding into an "essential question," a question that:

- **Has multiple answers**, e.g., "What makes a poem good?"
- **Is still being debated**, e.g., "What counts as a civil war?"
- **Can be revisited**, e.g., "How does your cultural background shape your identity?"
- **Is multilayered**, i.e., students at different levels can access it, e.g., both a first-grader and a city planner could answer the question, "What makes a city?"
- **Is rich and engaging**, e.g., "What does it mean to be alive?"
- **Causes someone to rethink previous ideas or see something from a different perspective**, e.g., "How can mathematical formulas explain our world?"

[5] COPPA—The Children's Online Privacy Protection Act forbids sites that gather information to be made available to users under 13 without parental permission which is why several social media sites do not allow users under 13. Despite that, Facebook kicks 20,000 users off a day for being underage (Varlas 2011).

You realize that what you choose as your essential question can greatly alter your game. For example, if your topic is the Cold War, asking "How is the Cold War a 'war'?" leads to a very different game than asking "How could the Cold War have been prevented?" or asking "How does the Cold War affect today's foreign policy?" You realize your choice of essential question depends on the enduring understanding you want your students to experience. You run your essential question through your simple test: "Can it be answered with a yes or a no?" If the answer is no, you are ready to proceed to the next step: determining scope. **ACTION**: Write an essential question about your topic.

Because a game could last for a typical class session, for a project, for a unit, or for a whole course, such as Barnard University's Reacting to the Past *semester long role-playing games, you determine what is feasible for your purposes.* **ACTION**: Determine the scope of the game. *You remember Amy talking about a game's theme. You think that has to do with what the player experiences or feels while playing the game. You jot down some ideas.* **ACTION**: Decide on a theme. *Now that you know what your game is going to be about, you sit down to figure out the nuts and bolts, nuts and bolts, nuts and bolts. Hmmm, like a machine…*

One of my first teaching disasters happened when I incorporated gaming into my teaching. I was doing my student teaching and it nearly drove me to quit teaching right then and there. I decided to enliven my teaching by conducting a Jeopardy *review game, where groups of students would compete by answering review questions. I drew the* Jeopardy *board on the chalkboard (this was 1993), put students in groups, and had them "slap in" when they thought they knew the answer. Little did I know, while my back was turned to make changes to the* Jeopardy *board, students were wadding up paper and throwing these "snowballs" out the window. Directly beneath the classroom was the vice principal's office. He was not too pleased to look out the window to see that it was "snowing" in April in Durham, North Carolina. He came storming into the classroom to see what was going on. I vowed that if I did remain in teaching, I would never play* Jeopardy *with my students again. I later recanted and redesigned my version of* Jeopardy *with very strict rules. This version worked well and this type of one-shot classroom gaming served me for quite a while, but ultimately left me unsatisfied.*

This book is not about creating a game to be played on Tuesday. This book is about turning your curriculum into a game. Those one-shot games are fun and can be motivating (at least sufficiently motivating to get students to learn enough facts to win the game), but tend to be recall games, not games that promote deeper understanding, critical thinking, problem solving, or innovation. Do you really care if your students can name all 50 states and their associated capitals, something they could find out instantly on the Internet? Or would you rather students understand how and why state lines were drawn where they were and how capitals got chosen? Or, better yet, think about ways to redraw the states[6] and choose new capitals to better reflect today's needs, or create a new country, or even imagine a unified Earth without any continental distinctions?

After redesigning my curriculum using game design principles, my students started making statements like:

- "Having played my share of video games in my life, many of which were role-playing games, I liked being able to solve problems multiple times and how assignments and lessons would change depending on the choices we made in terms of teaching style."
- "Though I found many of the preplanning projects frustrating at first, I feel that I learned a lot from struggling through them and felt driven to submit multiple attempts in order to improve my score, something I have done while playing video games."
- "Love, love, loved the structure of this class. I never felt any pressure, as I do with other classes, so I was able to put more thought behind my submissions."

Other teachers who have turned their classrooms into curricular games have reported similar sentiments among their students (Sheldon 2011).

Before examining how to make your curriculum a game, we need to explore what we mean by "game" to begin with. The term "game" is one that people outside of the gaming industry often do not question because "you know one when you see one." However, within the gaming industry, the meaning and nature of a "game" is hotly contested. Let's start with a basic definition of a game: problem solving in a risk-reduced environment. In other words, a game is a problem space where players can try out different solutions without suffering real-world consequences. For example, raising a child or improving your health is not a game, but you can probably imagine video games about raising kids or improving one's health where the player gets to choose various actions and virtually experience the consequences of those actions or at least the results of preprogrammed algorithms hopefully based on current research. My goal is that at some point while reading this book, you gain a game designer worldview if you do not have one already. You will know you have achieved this when you start seeing games in everything.[7]

At this point, though, you may need some support, a.k.a. scaffolding, in thinking of a topic for your curricular game. To start, let's look at what the game designer Jesse Schell has to say on this subject:

---

[6]The television show *Saturday Night Live* featured a skit one time where the boundaries of the states in the United States were redrawn. The one that made me laugh out loud had the South labeled "those still fighting the Civil War" and the rest of the country, "those who got on with their lives."

[7]A warm-up activity I sometimes do when presenting about game-based teaching is to have participants partner up, name something they did the weekend before, and then the partner has to turn it into a game.

> There was one juggler who stood out from the rest. He was an old man in a powder blue jumpsuit, and his tricks were not like the others at all. He used patterns and rhythms that were unique, and his tricks, though not astonishing in their difficulty, were simply beautiful to watch.... Suddenly he looked at me, and said 'Well?... Aren't you going to try to copy me?' 'I—I don't think I would know how,' I stammered out. He laughed. 'Yeah, they never can. Know why my tricks look so different?....The secret is: don't look to other jugglers for inspiration—*look everywhere else*.' He proceeded to do a beautiful looping pattern, where his arms kind of spiraled, and he turned occasional pirouettes. 'I learned that one watching a ballet in New York.' And this one... I learned from a flock of geese I saw take off from a lake up in Maine. And this... from a paper punch machine on Long Island.... People try to copy these moves, but they can't... [because] they can't copy my inspiration.'... his advice changed my approach to creativity forever. (Schell 2008, p. 59)

This mirrors my experience with teaching. I always felt my teaching was missing something so I looked to other teachers, to books about teaching, to teacher educators, and so forth. Meanwhile, I loved playing video games. I even had the hubris to think at one point that video game designers could make their games more educational by learning techniques from educators. The turning point in my thinking occurred during a humbling moment when I realized that it is actually the other way around—educators can learn a lot from video game designers. I had to take my blinders off and look outside my own field. Now, I do not want to write myself out of a job; after all, I am a teacher educator and there is a lot to learn from other teachers and from teacher educators. But there is also a lot to learn from everywhere else, including from students. Luckily, as teachers, we not only know pedagogy, but we also know our content—that can be a good source of inspiration. It may be helpful to think about how experts in your content area derive their inspiration. How do novelists think of new books? How do scientists come up with new discoveries?[8] How do historians uncover new truths? According to Warren Robinett, designer of the first graphical adventure video game, "every verb in the dictionary suggests an idea" (quoted in Salen and Zimmerman 2004, p. 431). If you are struggling, turn to the glossary in the textbook you use for your class, and turn every verb into a game. Even if you can turn a verb into a game, there are some topics, however, you may want to avoid or at least be very sensitive about. For example, I would hope that all students would object to playing Hitler.

Schell (2008) writes that his "silent partner" is his subconscious. He advises game designers to "pretend [y]our creative subconscious is another person, what is that person like?" he goes on to describe some characteristics of his subconscious: "can't talk..., impulsive..., emotional..., playful,... irrational" (Schell 2008, p. 64). Basically, he is suggesting you tap into your 2-year-old self. He continues by saying that, like people, "If you get into the habit of ignoring [your subconscious], it is going to stop making suggestions. If you get in the habit of listening to it,... it will start to offer more and better suggestions" (Schell 2008, p. 65). He then describes

[8] Current events can be a great source of inspiration for curricular games. My father sent me an article about scientists trying to figure out why wildlife living along the river we used to live on were dying. In the article, the author stated: "the list of suspects rivals a game of *Clue*" (Pittman 2013).

an example of thinking of a surfing game when a thought pops into his mind, "'What if the surfboards were bananas?' which is crazy of course… Now you could say to yourself, 'That's stupid…' Or you could take a few minutes and seriously consider the idea: 'Ok, what if the surfboards *were* bananas?' And then another thought comes: 'With monkeys surfing on them'" (Schell 2008, p. 65). Now you have the start of a game!

The painter Salvador Dali asserted that inspiration will come if you fall asleep while holding a key between your fingers with a brass plate below so that you will wake up right after falling asleep. The chemist Kekulé supposedly figured out that benzene is a ring molecule from a daydream about a serpent biting its own tail (both examples taken from Schell 2008, pp. 64–65). However, as you know, dreams can be fleeting. One trick to listening to your subconscious is to record your ideas. My father always said, "The shortest of pencils is longer than the longest of memories." Nowadays, however, there are many more options than pencils including recording devices, such as having a digital recorder next to your bed or using your phone to record your ideas—either voice memos on your phone or calling your voicemail. You could even set up a dedicated e-mail address where you send all your ideas.[9] Fullerton et al. (2004) call your own personal database of ideas an "ideabase" (p. 142). They suggest "growing an idea tree" (p. 143) by listing several topics, a couple of subtopics per topic, and then sub-subtopics. After scanning your tree for patterns, they suggest using these patterns to apply "conditions" to your tree. For example, you might have a branch about dogs. Applying the concept of "space exploration" to that branch allows you to see that branch differently, as you might think about the dogs Russia sent into space without any means of return. This then could lead you to think of a game where the player travels back in time to convince Russia to redesign these space missions to sustain the lives of the dogs, or for the player to design the space missions him or herself, or for the player to play a dog who has to figure out how to save herself from death in space.

While everyone has their own unique approach to coming up with ideas, and every idea has its own conception to birth story, some of which are not even known by the parent of the idea, I thought it might be helpful to explore one such game idea I had and how I came up with it. I taught Homer's epic poem *The Odyssey* to ninth graders year after year when I was a high school English teacher. I wish I had thought of this Odysseus Order game back then, but it was only until I was reading material for this book that I thought of it. The game involves students speculating on what might happen if the order of events in *The Odyssey* were changed. You could even set a goal of putting episodes in the correct order in order to get Odysseus to reunite with Penelope. How did I think of this? I was thinking about how games can be replayed from different characters' perspectives to evoke different experiences. I then started toying with the idea of changing other story elements such as

[9] I got this idea from a friend who knew she did not have the time to write in a journal so instead set up an e-mail address with her son's name when he was born. Periodically, she sends an e-mail to this address with her thoughts and stories about him so he can read them when he is older.

setting, which is a common English teacher essay prompt (e.g., "write a contemporary version of *Romeo and Juliet*"). At the time, I had been reading about nonlinear narratives where the reader can experience the events of a story in random order and the reader has to do the work of putting together the clues to construct the narrative. I thought about how order *does* matter in story building, for example, if a character kisses someone before getting to know him or her, the other character might get scared off instead of falling madly in love. I then tried to think of a "string of pearls" story, a story with a series of episodes. *The Odyssey* clearly fits this bill. Conveniently, each episode has a lesson. This "core game mechanic" of exploring the impact of changing the order in a sequence can easily be applied to other subjects as well. For example, the order of scientific discoveries, the order of mixing chemicals, the genetics of a family tree, the order of operations in mathematics, and, well really, all of history. According to Gee (2011):

> Good games are nothing but well-designed problem-solving spaces with copious feedback, good mentoring from the game's design and associated fan communities, and a 'win state.' Actually (though no one should tell gamers this), having a win state and way stations—'levels'—on the way to it is just a form of 'assessment'. (p. x)

These are the nuts and bolts of creating a game. How to develop each of these nuts and bolts so they fit together like a well-oiled game machine is the thrust of this book.

As teachers, we know that a major part of teaching is matching instruction with content, i.e., some types of instruction are better for some types of content than for others. This is part of what Shulman (1986) calls "pedagogical content knowledge." Some of you might be protesting that games do not fit your content. Prensky (2011), however, argues that any subject matter can be turned into a game: "there is enough variation in what we call a 'game' that, with some imagination, a high-quality engaging and effective game that works for a large number of people can be designed and built for *any* topic" (p. 268). To demonstrate the variety of games, I have taken Callois' (2006) categories of play and placed them along continua below. Imagine these continua as a stereo equalizer, each with a slider, resulting in an infinite number of combinations leading to an endless number of games:

Agon (competition, games based on skill)-------▲--------*Alea* (gambling, games based on chance)

Mimicry (simulation, based on imitating real world)----▲-----*Llinx* (pursuit of vertigo, based on distorting the real world)

Paidia (free play with little to no rules or improvising rules on-the-spot)----▲----*Ludus* (well-regulated, rule-bound play)

Prensky (2001) provides a useful chart in his book *Digital Game-Based Learning* (p. 156) outlining which types of games better fit which types of goals. Except for learning facts, most of the goals are matched with adventure, simulation, puzzle, and/or role-playing games. Especially if you think about learning your topic like a detective piecing together clues, no matter what the topic is, it is possible to "find the game in the content" (Klopfer et al. 2009, p. 31).

CHALLENGE 2.1: I miss Amy! She would always push me to flex my creativity muscle. Back in college she would make us play that game. What was it she called it? Impromptu Game Design? She would make us create a game on-the-spot by mixing and matching game elements. I feel so rusty. Maybe I should play a round now. Let's see. The directions were to take a stack of colored index cards and assign each of the following game aspects to a color. Then, write out the different possibilities on the corresponding colors:

- *Number of players (1, 2, 5, 10, etc.)*
- *Age of players (preschoolers, grade school, high schoolers, college students, adults)*
- *Public v. private information (all information public, all private/individual, one player with private information, private information hidden to all players until they do something)*
- *Social goals ("competition, collaboration, flirtation" (taken from Salen and Zimmerman* 2004, *p. 16), backstabbing, status-mongering, challenging stereotypes, negotiating peace, provoking war, persuading someone to do something, getting someone to guess something, etc.)*
- *Site of game (classroom, school/campus, open field, woods, Starbucks, subway train, city landmark, riverbank, etc.)*
- *Amount of game play (5 min, 20 min, 60 min, 3 h, etc.)*
- *Game materials (card game, ball game, board game, computer game, dice game, etc.)*
- *Characters (hero, mentor, sidekick, etc.)*

We always played with friends, but Amy said she sometimes played by herself. We would draw cards and try to describe a game that fits those constraints in two minutes. The first round, do it with just one category. Each subsequent round, add a category. If someone cannot think of a game that fits the constraints within two minutes, they are out of the game. We would play until only one player was left, usually Amy. Then Amy would have us discuss whether or not adding more constraints made it more difficult or easier. Was there an ideal number of constraints? Were some constraints easier or harder? Now I just need to make some friends here so I can play! There was that one person who kept looking at me with curiosity during breakfast. Maybe I can recruit him to play with me. **EXERCISE**: Play the above game either by yourself, with a partner, or with a group.

As teachers, we also know that a major part of teaching involves not just matching content with pedagogy but also matching content and pedagogy with students—interests, needs, prior knowledge, and learning styles. In this case, however, an additional dimension needs to be considered since our students will also be game players. Edwards (2004) identified three different types of game players: gamists who "seek competition and challenge," narrativists who "seek story and characters," and simulationists who "like exploration and experience" (Tennyson and Jorczak 2008, p. 18). The steps in this book include ways to address all these different gaming styles.

You may have encountered educational software that does what is described above—adjusting content and complexity to fit student needs—but does so not as a game but rather as an intelligent tutoring system (ITS). In other words, there is no storyline, no role-playing, and no overarching goal, just a problem set that branches based on a student's responses. This does not promote deep learning or student motivation[10]:

> Though intelligent tutoring systems (ITS) may share similar characteristics in that the system within which a student interacts may be modified based on performance, ITS are not generally 'playful' in nature, that is, there is no element of play or competition, and the learner usually engages as a learner rather than a character or role. Therefore, ITS may often lack the motivational aspects that are inherent in many effective games. (Baker and Delacruz 2008, p. 29)

This is evident in the high dropout rates of schools that implement this type of learning (Kellinger 2012). Although ITS does add a dimension of "personalization," a new term being bandied about in education circles (basically differentiation at the individual level), when personalization simply replicates drill and skill practice with an added dimension of mastery learning, it does not foster transfer to real-world problem solving nor does it tap into students' natural curiosity, creativity, or achievement motivation.

You may worry that any of your ventures into gaming may be met by guffaws from students who are used to photorealistic 3-D graphics and real-time physics in video games. This is the "ceiling" problem—"Do commercial video games create such a high ceiling that educational games can never succeed?" (Squire 2011, p. 96), otherwise known as "compet[ing] with *Grand Theft Auto*?" (Squire 2011, p. 96). First of all, keep in mind that you are building your curriculum on gaming principles. This book shows you how to do this with no technology, technology you are probably already familiar with, technology that may pose a bit of a learning curve for you, and a lot of technology. What we will concentrate on first is building the game, and then we will worry about how to render it. You may want to start with a no technology version and then build up from there. Trust me, students will appreciate your efforts and support you in revising and refining your efforts, partially because the "floor" of "standard school curriculum [is] so low that halfway decent games will be welcomed" (Squire 2011, p. 96). This is in no way reflective of your teaching. Of course your teaching is not the floor! However, all good teachers recognize that their teaching has room for improvement. And good students (and I believe that all students have the potential to be good students) recognize and respond when teachers are trying to build bridges between the curriculum and the students' own worlds.

Squire's (2011) own experiences indicate that the "floor," not the "ceiling," is the point of comparison used by students:

---

[10] Some of my students stated that most educational games are really intelligent tutoring systems masquerading as games. As a result, they describe their students' reactions as "sighing in disdain" and using the words "boring" and "annoying" to describe using them.

> Kids compared [*Supercharged!*—the educational video game Squire helped create] to 'what they did at school' rather than 'the games they played at home'. We saw no evidence of kids rejecting *Supercharged!* because it wasn't *Grand Theft Auto*. There was not one complaint about the graphics or lack of violent content. We presented *Supercharged!* as a game, and students played it. (p. 96)

However, Squire (2011) and his team did find that:

> These kids *were* critical of bad design.... As kids grow up awash in software, their expectations evolve. Twenty years ago, when I was a kid, the computer was so interesting it really didn't matter what we did with it. We were happy just to be on the computer. Now, almost every kid has access to an iPod touch, gaming console, and personal computer. They are sophisticated consumers who expect good design. (p. 96)

This book will take you through a series of steps to help you with the design and along the way provide warning flags to help you identify and resolve design issues.

The steps outlined in this book are offered as guidance. Take the advice within as "heuristic principles rather than universal laws" (Swan 2010, p. 109) and the worksheets at the end of the chapters as ways to work out your thinking. Keep in mind that the steps are not intended to be linear, but rather recursive. With each step, you should return, revise, and refine your earlier steps and then return to the current step and think about how your revisions to your earlier steps impact the current one. If, at any point, your process of designing your game takes a different direction, please follow your own path. This is not the definitive way for teachers to turn their classroom into a game. In fact, there is not even agreement on what actually constitutes a "game":

> A well-known philosopher, Ludwig Wittgenstein, asked readers to try describing a definition for the word "game." Each time he proposed a necessary condition (a game must have competition; a game must be amusing, etc.), he would turn to a popular game that violated that condition. (Rabin 2009, p. 63)

McGonigal (2011) lists four requirements for something to be a game: goals, rules, feedback system, and voluntary participation. She uses several examples to illustrate how games must have these elements. For example, the goal of golf is to get a ball into a hole but without rules; this game would be no fun—a player would simply drop the ball into each hole (example from McGonigal 2011). Rules create challenge. The feedback system makes it possible for players to overcome the challenge and allows for mastery. All this leads to the thrill of achievement, what McGonigal (2011) calls "*fiero*" (p. 33), Italian for pride. Our mandatory school systems, however, make the "voluntary participation" part difficult. I contend that creating a game that makes learning enjoyable obviates the need for voluntary participation, but if this is a concern to you, you can always offer an alternative assignment for those who do not want to participate.

If you compare McGonigal's list—at least the first three—to the ITSs described earlier, they would fit her bill, but I would not consider them games. I would add one more element to McGonigal's list and to my earlier definition of a game, *fun*. This element is hard to pin down, especially since it can differ from person to person. For some, the fun resides in meeting a challenge; for others, in taking on an alternative identity; and for even others, immersing themselves in a storyline. However, it is this last element, fun, that I think truly distinguishes games from other endeavors.

Karl Kapp defines games as: "a system in which players engage in an abstract challenge, defined by rules, interactivity, and feedback, that results in a quantifiable outcome often eliciting an emotional reaction" (p. 7).

He then goes on to define each element of his definition:

- *System*. A set of interconnected elements which occur within the "space" of the game. A score is related to behaviors and activities that, in turn, are related to a strategy or movement of pieces. The system aspect is the idea that each part of a game impacts and is integrated with other parts of the game. Scores are linked to actions, and actions are limited by rules.
- *Players*. Games involve a person interacting with game content or with other players. This happens in first-person shooters, board games, and games like Tetris. The person playing the game is the player. Later we'll refer to the players of games as "learners." The act of playing a game often results in learning, and learners are our target audience for gamification of instruction. But, for now, in this context—defining a game—we'll stick with the concept of player.
- *Abstract*. Games typically involve an abstraction of reality and typically take place in a narrowly defined "game space." This means that a game contains elements of a realistic situation or the essence of the situation but is not an exact replica. This is true of the game *Monopoly*, which mimics some of the essence of real estate transactions and business dealings, but is not an accurate portrayal of those transactions.
- *Challenge*. Games challenge players to achieve goals and outcomes that are not simple or straightforward. For example, even a simple game like *Tic-Tac-Toe* is a challenge when you play against another person who has equal knowledge of the game. A game becomes boring when the challenge no longer exists. But even the challenge involved with the card game of *Solitaire* provides enough challenge that the player continues to try to achieve the winning state within the game.
- *Rules*. The rules of the game define the game. They are the structure that allows the artificial construct to occur. They define the sequence of play, the winning state, and what is "fair" and what is "not fair" within the confines of the game environment.
- *Interactivity*. Games involve interactions. Players interact with one another, with the game system, and with the content presented during the game. Interactivity is a large part of games.
- *Feedback*. A hallmark of games is the feedback they provide to players. Feedback within a game is typically instant, direct, and clear. Players are able to take in the feedback and attempt corrections or changes based on both the positive feedback they receive and negative feedback.
- *Quantifiable Outcome*. Games are designed so that the winning state is concrete. The result of a well-designed game is that the player clearly knows when he or she has won or lost. There is no ambiguity. There is a score, level, or

winning state (checkmate) that defines a clear outcome. This is one element that distinguishes games from a state of "play," which has no defined end state or quantifiable outcome. This is also one of the traits that make games ideal for instructional settings.

- *Emotional Reaction*. Games typically involve emotion. From the "thrill of victory" to "the agony of defeat," a wide range of emotions enter into games. The feeling of completing a game in many cases is as exhilarating as is the actual playing of the game. But at times frustration, anger, and sadness can be part of a game as well. Games, more than most human interactions, evoke strong emotions on many levels. (pp. 7–9)

Kapp (2012) concludes by tying all these elements together:

> Together these disparate elements combine to make an event that is larger than the individual elements. A **player** gets caught up in playing a game because the instant **feedback** and constant **interaction** are related to the **challenge** of the game, which is defined by the **rules**, which all work within the **system** to provoke an **emotional reaction** and, finally, result in a **quantifiable outcome** within an **abstract** version of a larger system. (p. 9)

What this text offers is a blueprint for those who want to convert their curriculum into a game but do not know where to begin, by taking the reader through developing each of these various game elements and then putting them all together to create a curricular game. The steps roughly follow Warren's (2009) nine principles for educational game design:

1. "Artificial conflict or problem-solving scenario
2. Realistic context and narrative structure
3. Rules or conditions for play
4. Learning tasks stemming from the narrative
5. Criteria for achievement
6. Instruction by pedagogical agent
7. The means for providing hard, technology-embedded scaffolds and soft, teacher-developed scaffolds
8. Means of assessment and feedback
9. Designed frustration points to engender cognitive conflict" (quoted in Travis & Young 2011 pp. 156–157)

For some, the initial steps may be all they need to be off and running. Others may want to do the steps in a different order, omit some steps, or create new steps of their own. However, for some, following this lockstep the first few times may be necessary before developing their own process. However, I do suggest you read through all the steps, even if your own process ends up taking a different path, because I include warnings about how to avoid potential pitfalls as well as other advice that may serve you on your path. I hope that for those of you who take different journeys, or even those of you who follow this one, that you write up your experiences so others can learn, in good video game style, from your mistakes as well as from your successes.

As mentioned earlier, all of these steps are recursive—they reach backward and reach forward as each step requires revisiting previous steps, revisiting previous steps requires revamping the current step, and for each step you want to keep in mind future steps. This is because all these aspects of game design, just like all the aspects of playing a game, are dependent on one another:

> Playing transformationally involves (a) taking on the role of a protagonist (b) who must employ conceptual understandings (c) to make choices (d) that have the potential to transform (e) a problem-based fictional context and ultimately (f) the player's understanding of the content as well as of (g) herself [or himself] as someone who has used academic content to address a socially significant problem. Playing transformationally integrates person, content, and context as part of a transactive system in which each type of positioning motivates and is motivated by the other types. (Barab et al. 2012, p. 309 quoting Barab, Gresalfi, and Ingram-Goble, 2010, p. 5)

There are more and more educational video games being developed, opening up possibilities for teachers to find a best fit between video game, curriculum, and student needs and questions (see Table 1.2 from Chap. 1 for a list of criteria for educational video games), but this book is written to help teachers fill the void by empowering teachers to create their own educational games. The chapters that follow begin your journey.

Step 1: Choose a *topic* (the SO WHAT?)
Step 2: Diagramming the *system* of that topic (the WHAT)
Step 3: Telling the *story* of that system (the WHY, WHERE, and WHEN) and creating the *characters* (the WHO)
Step 4: Turning that story into a *game* (the HOW)
Step 5: Embedding *puzzles and challenges* into your game (the WHAT TO DO)
Step 6: Rendering that *game*—no tech, low tech, medium tech, and high tech (how the WHO, WHAT, WHEN, WHERE, and HOW come together)
Step 7: Playtesting and making subsequent *revisions* to your game (for WHOM?)
Step 8: *Teaching* your game (by WHOM?)

Notice there is a lack of standard educational jargon like "objectives" and "assessment" in the description of the steps above. That is because these are all embedded in the game. For example, the storyline establishes the objectives or the goals of the game by answering the "Why?" question. The storyline, however, should also answer the "Why should I care?" or "So what?" question. Assessment is built in through the feedback mechanisms embedded in the game. Be aware that you may have to do some translation in order to "sell" your game to your department chair, principal, students' parents, or, in some cases, even the students themselves as they have also been mired in the same standardized testing culture as educators. One way to do this is to use the jargon du jour. For example, defending your curricular game in Common Core parlance might look like this: "The curricular game itself is a 'rich task' as it addresses multiple standards. Each level within the game has ever increasing 'text complexity' and the scaffolding within the game introduces and explains both 'general academic' and 'domain-specific' language." While you yourself may or may not embrace a particular educational trend your principal or department chair wants you to, it is better to be proactive and control how it is deployed in your classroom.

For the first step, you have chosen your topic, thought about the enduring understandings, and converted one into an essential question, but you have not yet developed your theme, an element that moves your topic from something students learn about to something students experience. Transforming your topic into a theme involves focusing it on "something that holds meaning for your players" (Schell 2008, p. 56). When Jesse Schell's team was trying to decide what a pirate's virtual experience would be based on *Pirates of the Caribbean* theme ride at *Disney World*, on his way home from work he started humming theme song "Yo ho, a pirate's life for me." He states,

> Suddenly it became clear! The *Pirates of the Caribbean* ride is not about *pirates*, it is about *being* a pirate! The whole goal of the ride is to fulfill the fantasy of what it is like to throw aside the rules of society and just start being a pirate! (Schell 2008, p. 50)

The topic is pirates, but the theme is "operating outside the law." Your topic might be the Civil War, but there are lots of different types of experiences you might want to evoke ("brother fighting brother," "grappling with secession," "fighting for your own freedom" (for the black Union soldiers), and so forth. Whichever experience you choose is the theme of your game, focusing on the *experience* can help you turn a topic into a theme.

Perhaps your topic is music, but what resonates with your intended audience is how music inspires emotion. Turning your theme into a problem statement with goals and constraints helps shape it into a game. For example, you can ask how *does* music inspire emotion? In this case, the goal or "win-state" is evoking an emotion. The constraint is through music. What a cool game that would make—the player alters musical compositions to try to make an "intelligent agent," which is an image of a person whose reactions are controlled by computer algorithms and display different target emotions. Of course, you could also do this in a no tech way by having humans be the "intelligent agents." The original title I had for this first step was "inspiring." I choose this because it is about you finding inspiration for your game but also because the theme of your game should inspire your students.

Now, run your game idea through a series of questions; "Is a game really the best solution [to explore this theme]? Why? How will I be able to tell if the problem is solved? (Schell 2008, p. 62), "Does this [theme] feel right?" "Will the [students] like this [theme] enough [to find it engaging]?" (Schell 2008, p. 77) Does this theme promise to evoke the intended experiences in the students? Does this theme help students discover answers to the essential question? Does this theme promise to create the intended enduring understanding? Can I create a game from this theme both in terms of time and technology? Does this theme meet my/the school's/the state's educational goals? Likely you will not have all these answers yet, but if the answers so far promise many yesses, then, game on…

> *I don't have a fixed design process. Quite the contrary, I believe that starting from the same beginning will frequently lead to the same end.*
>
> –Reiner Knizia, designer of the *Lord of the Rings* board game

Appendix: Topic Quest Worksheet

Content area: ________________________

Grade level(s): ________________________

Any relevant information about students: ________________________________

Topic	
Enduring understanding (underlying concept)	
Essential question (should have multiple answers)	
Scope (several lessons, project, unit, semester, year)	
Theme (experience and emotions game evokes)	
Possible game genre	
Questions:	Is a game really the best solution to explore this theme?
	Why?
	How will I be able to tell if the problem is solved?
	Does this theme feel right?
	Will students like this theme enough to find it engaging?
	Does this theme promise to evoke the intended experiences in the students?
	Does this theme help students discover answers to the essential question?
	Does this theme promise to create the intended enduring understandings?
	Can I create a game from this theme both in terms of time and technology?
	Does this theme meet my/the school's/the state's educational goals?
	Any other pertinent questions?
Initial thoughts/ideas	

Suggested Topic Quest Rubric

Quest	"Wow! I mean, I think this might work" (3)	"Hmm, this is acceptable" (2)	"I need more convincing" (1)	"Go back to the drawing board" (0)
Topic quest	Topic is developed into a theme likely for players to experience the enduring understanding and explore answers to the essential question	Topic fleshed out with an enduring understanding and one overarching essential question	Topic identified	Topic is vague, unclear, or too broad

Suggested Reading

Cameron, J. (2002). *The artist's way*. New York: Putnam.

McGonigal, J. (2011). *Reality is broken: Why games make us better and how they can change the world*. London: Penguin.

Wiggins, G., & McTighe, J. (2005). *Understanding by design*. London: Pearson.

References

Baker, E., & Delacruz, G. (2008). Framework for the assessment of learning games. In H. O'Neil & R. Perez (Eds.), *Computer games and team and individual learning* (pp. 21–37). Amsterdam, The Netherlands: Elsevier.

Barab, S., Pettyjohn, P., Gresalfi, M., & Solomou, M. (2012). Game-based curricula, personal engagement, and the *Modern Prometheus* design project. In C. Steinkuehler, K. Squire, & S. Barab (Eds.), *Games, learning, and society: Learning and meaning in the digital age* (pp. 306–326). New York: Cambridge University Press.

Caillois, R. (1959/2006). The classification of games from Man, Play, and Games. In K. Salen & E. Zimmerman, E. (Eds.), *The game designer reader: A rules of play anthology* (pp. 129–155). Cambridge, MA: MIT Press.

Edwards, R. (2004). System does matter. *The Forge: The Internet Home for Independent Role-Playing Games*. Retrieved January 7, 2016, from http://www.indie-rpgs.com/_articles/system_does_matter.html

Fullerton, T., Swain, C., & Hoffman, S. (2004). *Game design workshop: Designing, prototyping, and playtesting games*. San Francisco, CA: CMP Books.

Gee, J. P. (2011). Foreward. In K. Squire (Ed.), *Video games and learning: Teaching and participatory culture in the digital age* (pp. ix–x). New York, NY: Teachers College Press.

Kapp, K. (2012). *The gamification of learning and instruction: Game-based methods and strategies for training and education*. San Francisco, CA: Pfeiffer.

Kellinger, J. (2012). The flipside: Concerns about "new literacies" paths educators might take. *Educational Forum, 76*(4), 524–536.

Klopfer, E., Osterweil, S., & Salen, K. (2009). *Moving learning games forward: Obstacles, opportunities, and openness*. Cambridge, MA: The Education Arcade at MIT.

McGonigal, J. (2011). *Reality is broken: Why games make us better and how they can change the world*. London: Penguin.

Pittman, C. (2013, June 16). Indian River lagoon mystery ailment kills manatees, dolphins, pelicans. *Tampa Bay Times*. Retrieved January 7, 2016, from http://www.tampabay.com/news/environment/die-off-in-indian-river-lagoon-killing-dolphins-manatees/2127017

Prensky, M. (2001). *Digital game-based learning*. New York: McGraw Hill.

Prensky, M. (2011). Comments on research comparing games to other instructional methods. In S. Tobias & J. D. Fletcher (Eds.), *Computer games and instruction* (pp. 251–280). Charlotte, NC: Information Age.

Rabin, S. (2009). *Introduction to game development* (2nd ed.). Herndon, VA: Cengage Learning.

Robinett, W. (1984/2006). Adventure as a video game: Adventure for the Atari 2600 from inventing the adventure game. In K. Salen & E. Zimmerman (Eds.), *The game designer reader: A rules of play anthology* (pp. 690–713). Cambridge, MA: MIT Press.

Salen, K., & Zimmerman, E. (2004). *Rules of play: Game design fundamentals*. Cambridge, MA: MIT Press.

Schell, J. (2008). *The art of game design: A book of lenses*. Burlington, MA: Morgan Kaufmann.

Sheldon, L. (2011). *The multi-player classroom: Designing coursework as a game*. Herndon, VA: Cengage Learning.

Shulman, L. S. (1986). Those who understand: Knowledge growth in teaching. *Educational Researcher, 15*(2), 4–31.
Squire, K. (2011). *Video games and learning: Teaching and participatory culture in the digital age*. New York, NY: Teachers College Press.
Swan, R. (2010). Feedforward as an essential active principle of engagement in computer games. In R. Van Eck (Ed.), *Gaming and cognition: Theories and practice from the learning sciences* (pp. 108–136). Hershey, PA: Information Science Reference.
Tennyson, R., & Jorczak, R. (2008). A conceptual framework for the empirical study of instructional games. In H. O'Neil & R. Perez (Eds.), *Computer games and team and individual learning* (pp. 3–20). Amsterdam, The Netherlands: Elsevier.
Travis, R., & Young, M. (2011). Operation KTHMA-Reign of the Demiurge: Game worlds, greek history, and situated learning. In Myint Swe Khine (Ed.), *Learning to play: Exploring the future of education with video games* (pp. 153–166). New York: Peter Lang.
Varlas, L. (2011). Can social media and school policies be friends. *ASCD, 17*(4). Retrieved January 7, 2016, from http://www.ascd.org/publications/newsletters/policy-priorities/vol17/num04/Can-Social-Media-and-School-Policies-be-%C2%A3Friends%C2%A3%C2%A2.aspx
Wiggins, G., & McTighe, J. (2005). *Understanding by design*. London: Pearson.

Chapter 3
Behind the Game: Uncovering the Systems Underlying the Topic

If you cut a cow in half, you don't get two cows.

–old saying, quoted by Linda Booth Sweeney,
author of When a Butterfly Sneezes, 2001

Abstract This chapter draws heavily upon systems thinking (Thinking in systems: a primer. Chelsea Green Publishing, White River Junction, 2008; When a butterfly sneezes: a guide for helping kids explore interconnections in our world through favorite stories, Pegasus Communications, Waltham, 2001) in order to help the reader explore the underlying system behind his or her chosen topic. The chapter gives an overview of systems thinking while an appendix goes into further details about systems thinking. Once the reader is introduced to systems thinking and practices diagramming systems with children's books and his or her overall subject area and the system of his or her chosen topic, the reader is then instructed to both simplify and complexify the system in order to provide three different levels. These levels may eventually correspond to the different levels of the curricular game.

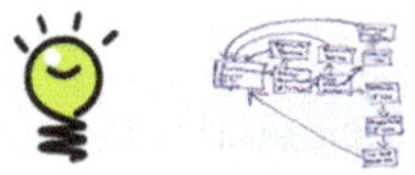

Choose Topic — ***Diagram System of Topic*** — *Tell Story of System* — *Gamify Story* — *Create Quests* — *Render and Test Game* — *Teach Game* — *Reflect on Teaching*

J.J. Kellinger, *A Guide to Designing Curricular Games*,
Advances in Game-Based Learning, DOI 10.1007/978-3-319-42393-7_3

SYSTEMS QUEST:

You run your topic by the Commander and she begrudgingly gives you the go ahead. However, you realize that 90 days to develop a video game is not a lot of time. "How can I do that as one person," you think. You know from your game designer friend Amy that video games are designed by teams of people, all with their own specialties. Plus, they have all sorts of software tools and expertise. You think, "If only I could contact her! She's helped design all sorts of video games. This would be a no-brainer for her! Deep breath. Don't hyperventilate." You realize you don't have to create a full-scale video game; you just have to use video game techniques to teach. "So," you think to yourself, "don't call it a video game. Call it a curricular game. That way I won't freak out. After all, it doesn't have to be a video game. Almost all of those affordances I discussed in my proposal like immediate feedback, learning from mistakes, and so forth don't necessarily need any technology. Even those that you would assume would require technology, like visual immersion, I could do by transforming a room into a crime scene or whatever the scenario might be. Even without technology, though, I could really use Amy's help with designing the game! What did she call it? Thinking like a designer? Design thinking? Something like that."

Now that you've cleared your head, you return back to your topic. You've played around with it in your head—converted it into an enduring understanding, an essential question, and a theme. You remember a theme is all about creating an experience. "What is an experience?" you think. "Well, an experience happens when something interacts with something else," you answer yourself. You feel something bubbling up in your head. You think back to thoughts that kept trying to enter your working memory—maps and machines, machines and maps.

"Of course! That's the answer! Machines have interacting parts and maps show how different parts relate to each other! It's been there all along! Just like drawing out the diagram of learning theory for the Commander, I need to diagram my topic!" **ACTION**: Draw a diagram of your chosen topic (not of the game, but of the topic of the game).

You remember the professional development workshop you attended on systems thinking and furiously get busy thinking through your topic as a system. But you feel like there's something missing. Playing a video game is experiencing a system, but how does a player advance *in that system. "They move through levels," you find yourself answering yourself again.*

You have a plan. You are going to draw a diagram to represent the system behind your topic. You are then going to simplify it for the first level of play. The initial diagram will be the second level of play. And then complexify it for the third level of play. **ACTION**: Draw a simplified and a more complex version of your diagram. *Yes! That's it! Busily, you get working …*

When I first taught Children's Literature, I read through textbooks on the subject and noticed each chapter was about a different genre so I used their "system" to teach it. Each week we explored a different genre—examples, characteristics, and so forth. It explored children's literature as a collection of discrete "heaps" without recognizing any relationships among genres, among authors, or among readers. This was simple but boring. I finally changed my teaching to explore children's literature as a system in different ways—by taking a historical view of children's literature, examining the impact on the audience, and exploring author's influences—but the best class of all involved having students categorize the books we had read based on that genre system, challenge the categories with some "ambiguous books," and then challenge students to create their own genres. One group created genres based on the primary emotion the book intended to evoke and thus had categories like "feel good" books, "tearjerkers," and "thrill seekers."

In chapter one, I stated that games allow students to experience the curriculum. The latest work in learning science focuses on how people abstract learning from concrete experiences:

> People store these experiences in memory... and use them to run simulations in their minds to prepare for problem solving in new situations. These simulations help them form hypotheses about how to proceed in the new situation based on past experiences. (Gee 2008b, p. 43)

The overall goal, then, is to create a game where the player/learner is:

> *transactively engaged* such that ... there exists a sense of *intentionality*, with user actions occurring in relation to a situationally meaningfully [sic] goal; *legitimacy*, with academic content becoming conceptual tools for acting on the world; and *consequentiality*, because user actions have an effect on the virtual world [by creating] *transformative play spaces*. (Barab et al. 2012, pp. 307–308)

In other words, create a game that allows players to run a simulation in order to try out a hypothesis, receive feedback, revise their hypothesis, and run another simulation.[1] Systems thinking holds the key to doing this.

If you recall, our Commander responded better to the learning diagram than to the description of arguments for video games. She is clearly a systems thinker. Her office was littered with maps and models. Systems thinkers are, quite simply, people who think in systems. However, this describes almost everyone. For example, most first-graders understand that you don't get two cows if you cut one in half. The cow is a system. All its parts work together to achieve a goal, that of survival. Once that cow dies, it no longer comprises a system because its parts are no longer working together toward a common goal: "Elements must have relationships to each other so that they can create behaviors. Until they operate together to do something as a whole, we are not looking at a system" (Rabin 2009, p. 107). However, "There are no separate systems. The world is a continuum. Where to draw a boundary around

[1] This is similar to the 7E model in science lesson planning (Eisenkraft 2003)—elicit, engage, explore, explain (generate possible explanations), elaborate (refine chosen explanation), evaluate (test explanation and refine based on response), and extend. It is also what the monsters do in the movie *Monsters, Inc.* to test their scare tactics.

a system depends on the purpose of the discussion—the questions we want to ask" (Meadows 2008, p. 97). In this case, the deceased cow does become part of a different system, or rather, its relation to the larger system it is a part of—the ecosystem—changes, either as it is eaten by another creature or as it decomposes.

There are some things, though, that are not systems in themselves, although they may be part of a system. Sweeney (2001) describes these as "heaps" and Fullerton et al. (2004) as "collections" because you can take away an element and it is still the same thing (e.g., a bowl of fruit). In contrast, in a system, you take away one thing and it makes a difference (e.g., stop eating fruit and your body won't get all the nutrients it needs). This is the whole idea behind fantasy football leagues: combinations of different elements create different effects. However, what fantasy football leagues do not take into account are (1) relationships, for example, the greatest players may not complement each other, and (2) time: the players lack the practice that creates teamwork. This is why pro bowl teams are not always so great and why fantasy football is not reality. This is always why games where you can swap the content in and out are "heaps" and those where you cannot are "systems."

We are all systems thinkers, but how we think in systems can be more or less advanced. Take the following quotes:

- "Millions of children and adults play these [violent video] games, yet the world has not been reduced to chaos and anarchy." (Kutner and Olson, cofounders of the Harvard Medical School Center for Mental Health and Media, 2008)
- "During the period in which gaming has become widespread in America, violent crime has fallen by half. If games really did make people violent, this tendency might be expected to show up in the figures, given that half of Americans play computer and video games. Perhaps, as some observers have suggested, gaming actually makes people less violent, by acting as a safety valve." (Editorial in *The Economist* 2005)
- "The opposition to gaming springs largely from the neophobia that has pitted the old against the entertainments of the young for centuries. Most gamers are under 40, and most critics are non-games-playing over-40s." (Editorial in *The Economist* 2005)

The first depicts the extremes of an either-or system with no shades of gray. The second recognizes that causes and effects are not always so obvious. The third takes a much longer view of history than the first two.

In many ways, our ultimate aim as teachers is to move our students from novice thinking toward more expert thinking. This involves increasing the complexity of our systems thinking: "Experts' knowledge cannot be reduced to sets of isolated facts or propositions but, instead, reflects contexts of applicability: that is, the knowledge is "conditionalized" on a set of circumstances" (Bransford et al. 2000, p. 31). My US history teacher in high school explained to students how natural geography impacted artificial boundaries, much in the same way Bransford et al. (2000) use geography to depict moving from novice to more expert thinking:

> Geography can be used to illustrate the manner in which expertise is organized around principles that support understanding. A student can learn to fill in a map by memorizing states, cities, countries, etc., and can complete the task with a high level of accuracy. But if the boundaries are removed, the problem becomes much more difficult. There are no concepts supporting the student's information. An expert who understands that borders often developed because natural phenomena (like mountains or water bodies) separated people,

> and that large cities often arose in locations that allowed for trade (along rivers, large lakes, and at coastal ports) will easily outperform the novice. The more developed the conceptual understanding of the needs of cities and the resource base that drew people to them, the more meaningful the map becomes. Students can become more expert if the geographical information they are taught is placed in the appropriate conceptual framework. (p. 17)

Although I am too young to remember, seeing the first photograph of Earth from space changed people's perspective of the world as separate countries to a planet within a larger system.[2] As teachers, we want students to be able to see the bigger picture while also understanding how the elements interact within it.

Sometimes we do not use systems thinking, for example, by seeing items as unrelated to each other. The story of several blind people feeling and describing different parts of an elephant, each seemingly unrelated, is an example of this. Sometimes we infer systems where none exist, for example, assuming correlation equals causation. Sometimes we think in simple linear systems, i.e., direct cause and effect relationships. Meadows (2008) uses the example of believing that using twice the amount of fertilizer will yield twice the crop as linear thinking. However, this linear thinking could be flawed. It could be that there is a threshold where too much fertilizer causes the crop to decrease. This adds complexity to the system. My example of linear thinking from my own life is thinking that raising twins is twice as hard as raising a singleton. However, what is probably closer to the truth is that raising twins makes some things twice as hard (such as carrying two babies instead of one), other things easier (such as the two of them entertaining each other so I don't have to be the entertainer), other things impossible (such as being unable to have one parent take both sledding when they are not old enough to sled on their own), other things about the same (feeding them bottles at same time), and most things somewhere in between (buying enough food to please two but if one doesn't like something, the other one might).

One way to add even more complexity to our system is by seeing one system as embedded in other systems. For example, Bronfenbrenner's (1979) ecology systems theory depicts relationships among smaller systems and larger systems through the use of concentric circles. Below is my own depiction of levels of systems thinking:

Nonsystem: unrelated isolated bits; *some people are just smart*
Belief system does not represent reality: *larger head size → more intelligence*
Simple system (e.g., causal chain): *genetics → intelligence*
Complex system (e.g., feedback loops): *reading → learning more → more curiosity → reading → learning more → more curiosity…*
Complex system plus knowledge of how to leverage leverage points: *creating cognitive dissonance challenges people to think critically*
Complex system + understanding that understanding is always partial: open to new or more complex understandings; anticipates unintended consequences, *future understandings of the world will challenge our current understanding of the world*

[2] Frank White (1987) describes this paradigm shift in his book *The Overview Effect*.

Invent a new system: *creating a paradigm shift such as moving from believing that our brains are hardwired from birth to recognizing the lifelong plasticity of our brains*

What does all of this have to do with video games? Not only are video games systems or, as Rabin (2009) puts it, "systems running on systems" (p. 64), they help uncover systems:

- "Videogames are particularly useful tools for visualizing the logics that make up a worldview." (Bogost 2007, p. 74)
- Because time is compressed in a game, it is easier for players to see cause and effect. For example, it may take years for an increase in property taxes to cause people to move out of a neighborhood in reality, but only a few 'moves' in a game for that to happen. (Kapp 2012)
- "[Video games] situate meaning in a multimodal space through embodied experiences to solve problems and reflect on the intricacies of the design of imagined worlds and the design of both real and imagined social relationships and identities in the modern world." (Gee 2003, p. 48)
- "James Paul Gee (2005) argues that what gamers learn is embodied empathy for a complex system. Video game players develop a feel or intuition of how systems work. This systemic thinking is valuable because it helps people solve problems holistically, rather than focusing on single-cause solutions. Video game players learn that if you change one variable, for instance, the type of ships available, it affects the entire system (e.g., the placement of cities). Systemic thinking isn't valued much inside schools today (particularly because it isn't captured well by standardized tests), but this type of thinking is important everywhere outside school, from ecology to engineering to politics. If video games can support systemic thinking in these areas, they could be powerful educational tools indeed." (Squire 2011, p. 5)
- "Videogames are an expressive medium. They represent how real and imagined systems work. They invite players to interact with those systems and form judgments about them." (Bogost 2007, p vii)
- "Books typically tell stories or make arguments. Films typically tell a story from the point(s) of view of a character or characters. Games, in contrast set up *relationships among rules* that players *design* within" (Squire 2011, p. 158)
- "games are at their essence systems for producing meaning through active experience." (Macklin and Sharp 2012, p. 385)
- "Games are systems made up of interconnected parts that work together: a combination of rules, goals, narrative content, signs and symbols, interactive design, and the platform through which they are delivered, whether they be a deck of playing cards or a next-generation game console." (Macklin and Sharp 2012, p. 383)

Our second task to curricular game-building, then, is to depict our *topic* as a system. Before we do so, however, let's learn a little bit about how systems work and ways to depict systems.

What is a system? A system contains interconnected elements (some systems thinkers use the word "objects") that produce patterns of behavior. So our first step is to list the elements in our system. Go back to the *topic* you chose in the previous chapter, and list all the elements encompassed by that topic. For example, if your topic was pirates, your list might look like this: ship, flag with skull and crossbones, eye patch, peg leg, bandana, parrot, sword, and booty. Do not worry yet about the game, we are not looking for game elements. Right now we are just exploring the topic to set ourselves up for designing the game later. Think of this chapter as "prewriting" in the game composition process. As such, do not worry about making an exact list; right now we are just brainstorming. Notice, all the items on my pirate list are concrete. However, elements can also be abstract, for example, confidence. Meadows (2008) reminds us to "pay attention to what is important, not just what is quantifiable" (p. 175). For example, I would argue that creativity and innovation are important, but because they are not easily quantifiable, standardized tests tend not to measure them, resulting in creativity and innovation sometimes being left out of the education system.

You might be tempted to list "adventure" for our pirate example. Keep in mind the difference between the goal of the overall system, the feeling or experience that the system aims to create, and elements of that system. What is the goal of your system? Survival is the most basic goal of most systems: "An important function of almost every system is to ensure its own perpetuation" (Meadows 2008, p. 15). As you can see, with our pirate example, basic survival would be a primary goal. You might even want to make a version of Maslow's Hierarchy of Needs[3] for your theme. A pirate's version might look like this: survival, gold/booty, bragging rights, comradery, and adventure.

Keep in mind that elements have properties or qualities that can be static or dynamic. In checkers, the color of a piece is static, but location and type dynamic: "Checkers have only three properties: color, location, and type. While the location of checkers changes, their color never does. The type of checker can change from 'normal' to 'king' if it reaches the other side of the board" (Fullerton et al. 2004, p. 108). Elements also can perform certain behaviors: "potential actions that an object might perform in a given state" (Fullerton et al. 2004, p. 109). For example, checkers can either move or jump. In games, these behaviors are defined by a set of rules. Normal checkers can move to an adjacent square or jump an opponent's checker as long as the movement is forward, i.e., toward the other side of the board. A king checker has the same behaviors but can move in either direction. Most importantly for our system diagram, elements are in relationship with other elements (black and red checkers are in opposition to each other such that jumping one of the opposite color will result in its removal from game play).

Think about the relationships among the elements you listed. Is there a hierarchy? Are elements clustered based on proximity? On need? On values? Do certain elements attract or repel others? Is there an inverse relationship between certain elements? How does cause and effect work among elements? Are there multiple causes? Interacting causes? Or are they just correlations? Although we will do this in a more systematic way later on in this chapter, go ahead and try your hand at depicting these relationships in a diagram. We'll call this your "working model."

[3] Maslow described a hierarchy of human needs, one needs to be met before a human can satisfy the next, in this order: physiological, safety, love/belonging, esteem, and self-actualization.

Let's practice by using children's literature. There are lots of examples in children's literature of simple causal chains: "This is the farmer sowing his corn, That kept the cock that crowed in the morn, That waked the priest all shaven and shorn …." The farmer kept a cock, the cock crowed, the crowing woke the priest, and a whole other series of events happened. These forms of children's literature serve to teach the enduring understanding that one action leads to another (cause and effect). There are also examples of causal loops in children's literature. The story *If You Give a Mouse a Cookie* by Numeroff (1985) leads the reader through a causal chain, or endless loop, started by giving a mouse a cookie that ends up back at the beginning, giving a mouse another cookie. There are even examples of endless loops such as "There's a Hole in My Bucket" which begins with a hole in a bucket and suggestions to fix the hole that lead to a need for water which cannot be attained or contained because "there's a hole in my bucket."

CHALLENGE 3.1: You think back to that professional development on systems thinking your principal made everyone attend. Drawn from the book When a Butterfly Sneezes *by Sweeney, every teacher had to choose one of five content areas closest to what they taught and had to* **diagram the plot** *of an assigned children's book:*

- *Social Studies—*Butter Battle Book *by Dr. Seuss*
- *Math—*Anno's Magic Seeds *by Anno*
- *English—*Black and White *by Macauley*
- *Science—*The Lorax *by Dr. Seuss*
- *Foreign Language—*The Sneetches *by Dr. Seuss*

Then, each content area group had to **diagram the system of their content area**. *You remember the teachers were challenged to see how many different types of content area systems they could think of. You do that now to practice your systems thinking.* **EXERCISE**: Diagram the plot of the book associated with your content area. Then, diagram your content area. Challenge yourself by trying to think of at least two other ways you could diagram your content area.

To help you visualize how you might depict a system, Sweeney (2001) suggests "thinking like a bathtub" (p. 35). The amount of water, or the *stock*, is determined by the *flow*, the amount of water flowing in and out of the bathtub. You can see how this analogy might work with lots of different types of systems:

> we need to understand the difference between the national deficit (a flow—the rate at which we borrow) and the national debt (a stock—the accumulated debt). Reducing the deficit … will not reduce the level of debt. It will slow down the rate at which the debt accumulates—but the debt itself will still keep accumulating. (Sweeney 2001, p. 36)

Stocks are a stored amount of something, i.e., anything that can be measured (water, money, lives in a video game, health, amount of self-esteem); flows are changes in the amounts of your stock, i.e., rates of change. Inflows increase your stock; outflows decrease your stock. Dynamic equilibrium occurs when the inflow and outflow occur at same rate.

In keeping with the bathtub analogy, some systems thinkers distinguish between inflows and outflows by calling them "faucets" (inflows) and "drains" (outflows). You can use arrows to depict the direction of the flow. The handles on the faucets and the drains indicate leverage points where the "flows," or rates of change, are controlled. In our pirate example, gold, or "booty," would be our main stock. The inflow would be determined by our ability to take over other ships and the outflow determined by how many other pirates we encounter who are able to take over our ship. Stocks play an important role in the relationship between inflows and outflows as "stocks allow inflows and outflows to be decoupled and to be independent and temporarily out of balance with each other" (Meadows 2008, p. 24). Imagine if you had no pantry, refrigerator, grocery store, or restaurants and had to grow and harvest food at the same rate at which you eat it. In these ways, stocks absorb the ebbs and flows of a system.

We have described a simple system. However, systems are rarely simple. So far we have described closed systems, systems that function within itself (e.g., a terrarium). An open system has an exchange with its environment (e.g., semipermeable cells). It may be more useful to think of systems as being more open or less open since systems exist within other systems and interact with other systems (nested systems, subsystems, hierarchies, etc.). For example, another professor was telling me about a time when she realized her class was lost so she scrapped her plans and had them do a concept mapping exercise instead. As a result of this exercise, one of her students wrote in his response paper that this exercise allowed him to move from seeing works of literature as discrete books to be read and analyzed (i.e., each work of literature its own closed system) to seeing literature as "a global subject that encompasses language, literature, culture, history, and politics" (i.e., works of literature as elements within an open system). We see this in education as well. People tend to think of schools as closed systems and get frustrated when school reforms do not work. As Diane Ravitch (2013) keeps trying to tell us, schools are not closed systems and we need to take into account how other systems, such as the cycle of poverty, impact learning. We have some powerful examples from history that speak to the impact switching from a closed system to an open system, such as China opening its doors to trade. In our pirate example, outside systems such as weather and trade routes would impact our system. When the weather becomes unstable, so does our pirate trade.

Keep in mind, too, that drains also serve as faucets into another stock. When a pirate does not achieve his or her primary goal of survival, we have the outflow not only of his or her stock of gold into most likely another pirate's stock (or maybe a stock of hidden treasure to be found by someone later) but also of the stock of his or her life. Because drains are also faucets, we have cemeteries. As you can see, our simple pirate system quickly becomes more and more complex. One system's outflow becomes another system's inflow.

It is important for us to recognize the complexity of systems, but we also must be able to comprehend the system. To acknowledge the complexity of systems within systems without gumming up our simple system, systems thinkers use clouds to depict what happens before and after the segment of the system they are studying. Since "all system diagrams and descriptions are simplified versions of the real world" (Meadows 2008, p. 18), systems thinkers use clouds at either end of stock and flow charts to signify the boundaries of their system diagram.

What we have not taken into account so far is the element of time. Systems function over time resulting in the emergence of patterns of behavior. In some cases, results lead to consequences that produce greater results. This is called a *reinforcing feedback loop.*[4] For example, greater births lead to more potential parents which can lead to greater births; pirating software leads to increase cost of software which leads to more piracy of software. Compound interest is another example of a reinforcing feedback loop. The more interest you earn, the greater your stock of money, the more interest you earn on it. In other words, the rich get richer, or "whenever the winners of a competition receive, as part of the reward, the means to compete even more effectively in the future" (Meadows 2008, p. 127). You can see this in the accumulation of privilege in the United States. Between the 1930s and 1950s, the federal government instituted a program to help people buy houses. Less than two percent of the recipients of this program were nonwhite because of a practice known as "redlining" or deeming houses in minority neighborhoods as non-desirable.[5] The wealth from home ownership then gets passed on to the mainly white children due to miscegenation laws (de jure discrimination) as well as social taboos against interracial marriage (de facto discrimination). In this case, some white people are given an advantage over people of color which accumulates into larger and larger advantages over time. The corollary of this, of course, is that the poor get poorer, i.e., the cycle of poverty.[6] Part of this is because those in power built highways and designed cities in ways that the poor and minorities were isolated from resources, including from jobs (Seitles 1996). Looking at the rich and poor in this country without taking into account the historical forces that led to those disparities in the first place can lead to very different conclusions about the income gap. This is why snapshots in time do not reveal the full picture.

Other systems involve *balancing feedback loops* where the results lead to consequences that mediate future results. For example, our bodies' temperature control system keeps our temperature within a certain range. When it is too hot, perspiration cools us off; when it is too cold we shiver (see Sweeney 2001, p. 28). The thermostats in our houses work much the same way, although they use different mechanisms to do so: "Any balancing feedback loop needs a goal (the thermostat setting), a monitoring and signaling device to detect deviation from the goal (the thermostat), and a response mechanism (the furnace)" (Meadows 2008, p. 153). Basketball and football both have balancing feedback loops. When one team scores, the other team gets the ball and thus the opportunity to score. We can also see this in terms of educational goals and assessments designed to give feedback on attainment of those

[4] Systems thinkers describe feedback loops as vicious "amplifying to make something greater" or virtuous "making something less" (Sweeney 2001, p. 27); however, I think those terms can be misleading because they are laden with value judgment so I prefer escalating and de-escalating.

[5] There is evidence that "redlining," unfortunately, still happens today.

[6] Meadows (2008) points out that "Because the poor can afford to buy only small quantities (of food, fuel, seed, fertilizer), they pay the highest prices. Because they are often unorganized and inarticulate, a disproportionately small part of government expenditure is allocated to their needs. Ideas and technologies come to them last. Disease and pollution come to them first. They are the people who have no choice but to take dangerous, low-paying jobs, whose children are not vaccinated, who live in crowded, crime-prone, disaster-prone areas" (p. 129).

goals. Too often, however, education fails to provide a response mechanism so we just end up knowing that we are failing. It is also important to keep in mind that:

> The strength of a balancing feedback loop is important relative to the impact it is designed to correct….A thermostat system may work fine on a cold winter day-but open all the windows and its corrective power is no match for the temperature change imposed on the system. (Meadows 2008, p. 154)

In terms of education, this means that education cannot be the sole panacea for the world's problems. Another problem that can occur with balancing feedback loops is when the feedback is ignored. The feedback has to be strong enough to be listened to:

> Suppose any town or company that puts a water intake pipe in a river had to put it immediately downstream from its own wastewater outflow pipe… Suppose (this is an old one) the politicians who declare war were required to spend that war in the front lines. (Meadows 2008, p. 157)

In order for a balancing feedback loop to work, the feedback must register and there must be a response mechanism in place.

Often systems involve both reinforcing and balancing feedback loops. In these situations, one type of loop can dominate or they can help balance each other out. For example, inheritance tax serves as a way to offset the accumulation of privilege, i.e., "a way of starting the game over with each new generation" (Meadows 2008, p. 130). In ecology, imagine two species in the same environment competing for the same resources. If one species reproduces faster, it will use more resources (assuming each member consumes approximately the same amount of resources) and deplete those resources for the other species (you can replace "species" with "companies" for economics). However, the "winning" species also depletes the resources for itself, and then its own population will diminish: "exponential growth cannot go on forever" (Meadows 2008, p. 126). In terms of games, a game is no fun when the rich keep getting richer and the poor keep getting poorer, even for the rich. The rich may have fun at first, but when winning comes too easy, the game loses its challenge and therefore its fun. In the reality game show *The Amazing Race*, those who win one leg get to start the next leg ahead of the others (reinforcing feedback loop), but often the game is manipulated to "level the playing field," what game designers call "rubberbanding,"[7] by making everyone wait, for a ferry, plane, train, some place to open, etc. so everyone catches up to each other, thus inserting a balancing feedback loop. This makes the race more exciting because it keeps it close. Games are not exciting when one team is almost guaranteed to win. A prime example of this is the Olympics. Sports where one country dominates (like the United States in basketball) have low viewership. Even when it seems there is no end to a reinforcing feedback loop, sometimes "losers, if they are unable to get out of the game of success to the successful, and if they have no hope of winning, could get frustrated

[7] A video game example of rubberbanding (courtesy of Julia Nakhleh) occurs in *Mario Kart* where the further behind in the race a player is, the more powerful "power up" items he or she gets. Players in dead last are more likely to get a booster rocket that can really speed him or her up, whereas first-place players are more likely to get bananas, which can slow down your opponents if they drive over the bananas, but not by a lot.

enough to destroy the playing field" (Meadows 2008, p. 130).[8] This might explain various instances of social unrest.

Good systems thinkers develop an ability to take the long view in order to take into account *emergent properties*, traits that develop in a system over time (e.g., team spirit, kids getting antsy on a long trip, etc.) (examples from Sweeney 2001, p. 25), as well as potential unintended consequences. According to Sweeney (2001), "before the Nashua Indians made any decision, they weighed its potential impact on seven generations to follow" (p. 34). In a study I conducted with queer teachers, one of my participants described viewing homophobic incidents he had experienced as mere "blips" on his radar screen. Clearly, this teacher took the long view and saw the larger impact he had on his students as more important than the homophobia directed toward him. Meadows (2008) points out that:

> One reason why systems of all kinds surprise us [is because] we are too fascinated by the events they generate. We pay too little attention to their history. And we are insufficiently skilled at seeing in their history clues to the structures from which behavior and events flow. (p. 91)

Instead of reacting to events, search for patterns of behavior, examine the structures that contribute to these patterns, and then look to the mental models that contribute to these structures in order to develop a long view. Sweeney (2001) calls this "lowering the water line" (p. 31) in reference to only ten percent of icebergs being above the surface of the water.

This short introduction to systems thinking is less than the tip of the iceberg. For more about systems thinking, see the suggested readings at the end of this chapter and the appendix at the end of the book.

You know you are a systems thinker when:

- "Someone tells you that population growth causes poverty [and] you[] ask yourself how poverty may cause population growth" (Meadows 2008, p. 34)
- You are cleaning caterpillar droppings off your patio table and you think, "A drain is also a faucet"
- You think, "trees [are] the opposite of animals [because] trees take in carbon dioxide and produce oxygen; animals take in oxygen and produce carbon dioxide" (example from Meadows 2008, p. 16)
- You find yourself telling your three-year-old who is describing how cat food goes into the top of the container and comes out the bottom, that it then goes into the cat's mouth and later comes out of the cat's bottom

Modeling a System

We used the bathtub analogy to describe systems which also provided us with a useful way to depict systems—as a stock and flow chart (Fig. 3.1):

[8] *Spoiler alert*: For example, in the novel *Catching Fire*, Katniss literally destroys the playing field when she fires her arrow into the force field surrounding the playing field.

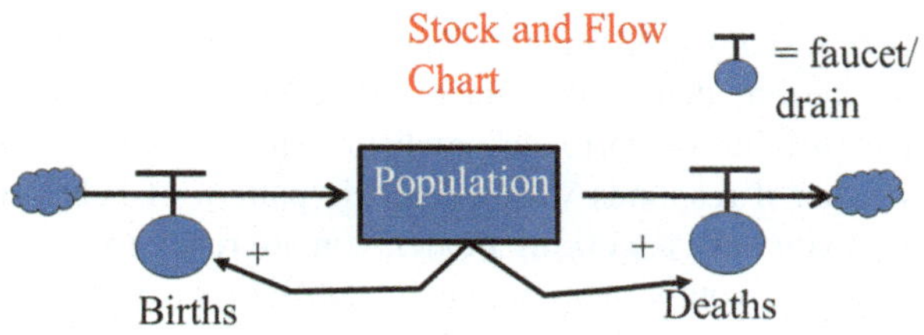

Fig. 3.1 Population stock and flow chart

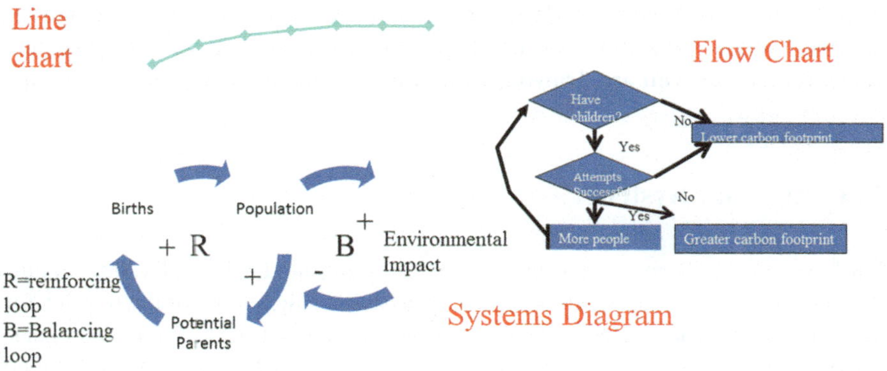

Fig. 3.2 Other ways to depict population

However, there are many other ways to depict the same system. Below are three such ways to depict the same system (Fig. 3.2).

With all of these models, you can see the potential for running simulations to see what might happen if certain variables are increased or decreased. Keep in mind, however, that "Dynamic systems studies usually are not designed to *predict* what will happen. Rather, they're designed to explore *what would happen*, if a number of driving factors unfold in a range of different ways" (Meadows 2008, p. 46). I would actually change the word "would" to "might" due to unpredictable factors. Systems are embedded in other systems and have their own systems embedded in them. Systems themselves and therefore models of systems are always simplified versions of reality. They are designed to help us make sense of reality, but they do not depict or predict reality. For example, none of the models above take into account a number of other factors that may work to increase or decrease number of births: improved birth control, impact of abortion legislation, influence (or lack of) of sex education, and so forth.

One of the reasons a system is greater than the sum of its parts is because rearranging the elements results in a different system. To test your working model, first see if swapping elements in and out make a difference. If it does not, you have a heap/collection and not a system. Then see if moving the elements around makes a difference. If not, you need to define relationships among elements better. Finally run some mental simulation by changing the value of some of the elements and thinking through how that would impact other elements. To see if your model works for depicting your system, determine if the results are likely: "Model utility depends not on whether its driving scenarios are realistic (since no one can know that for sure), but on whether it responds with a realistic pattern of behavior" (Meadows 2008, p. 48). Once you have a working model, you are ready to level[9] it.

When you do "level" your system, it may be useful to use different types of models to represent the system at different levels. For example, one of my students used a stock and flow chart for the simple version of her system, a line chart for the middle, and a flow chart for the more complex version of her system. Think about which model both fits your system and the level of complexity you are trying to depict. Don't forget, you can always create your own model as well. Although the hope is that this "prewriting" work will help lay the foundation for your curricular game, **remember, you are drawing a diagram of your topic, not of your game.**

Leveling Your System

It is impossible to become an instantaneous expert in a field. Gladwell (2008) claims it takes 10,000 h of practice to develop expertise in an area. One of the reasons for this is because learners need to be able to learn the elements of a system and understand how they relate to each other at a very simple level before they can understand a more complex model:

> Anderson (2000) presents three stages of skill acquisition leading to the development of a domain expert. In the cognitive (novice) stage, learners begin to understand the processes or concepts related to the domain through the acquisition of declarative or foundational knowledge. Learners at this stage require a high level of detailed information about the domain area and any necessary supports for understanding or visualizing. In the associative (experienced) stage, connections are made linking individual knowledge units together into procedural knowledge. At this point, the level of detail is reduced, as the learner is able to create larger chunks of information. Learners can begin working autonomously as long as proper scaffolding is provided. In the final level of knowledge development, the autonomous (expert) stage, connections among essential domain knowledge are internalized and learners can make automatic associations. Supports can be gradually faded as learners are able to perform tasks without the support of an expert model. It is in this stage that learners are able to think conditionally, divergently and transfer knowledge from one problem set to an isomorphic problem. (Adcock et al. 2010, p. 154)

In other words, a novice needs declarative knowledge (the "whats" or elements of a system) that is discrete with a lot of detail about the context. To learn this, the novice needs high amounts of support. An experienced thinker uses associative (how the "whats" are related) and procedural (and how) knowledge and needs less context and medium support. Experts have developed conditional knowledge ("what happens when") and need little detail and little to no support in order

[9] By "level," I don't mean reduce it to rubble; I mean create different levels of your system. Isn't that interesting? We have a word that also means nearly its opposite (level to destroy; level to create). There are several other words like this in the English language. Some names for these include autoantonyms, contranyms, and antagonyms.

to understand what happens in different contexts. This movement goes from understanding the elements, to how they interact, to being able to run hypothetical simulations for various scenarios.

This is a simple model of how people learn. However, I find that complexifying a system is more complex. It can involve adding more elements, including breaking some elements into different parts, adding more systems both macro and micro, understanding change over time, developing more nuanced relationships among elements, and so forth. For example, a simple model might depict the skin absorbing vitamin D through sun exposure. A more complex model might include that it is the UVB rays only that create vitamin D, that the amount of melanin in the skin allows more or less UVB rays to enter, and that too much UVB results in a sunburn. Even more complex might have that UVA rays deplete vitamin D, that glass windows block UVB rays while allowing UVA rays through, that the sun is only high enough in the sky for humans to receive UVB rays between 10 and 4 (also prime time for sunburns), that geography plus the time of year impacts angle of sun and thus the amount of vitamin D, and that vitamin D remains dormant/stored in the body until it is needed by the immune system when it gets "supercharged." Putting all of this in a modern-day context where people tend to work in offices all day, particularly during 10 and 4, where the only natural light, if any, is filtered through windows leads to vitamin D deficiency and thus weakened the immune system resulting in an increase in various diseases which impacts the population in various ways and, of course, is in combination with the types of foods we eat, amount of exercise, how we sleep, and so forth. We can also view this in terms of skin color and geography, with those who have darker skin originating from more tropical areas to those with lighter skin originating from areas that get less sunlight and then ponder the ramifications of migration (and discrimination). Our simple "sun exposure produces vitamin D that our bodies need" system can quickly become increasingly complex but we need to understand the most basic model in order to be able to comprehend the more complex ones.

Research on learning from simulations bears this out. The more a simulation resembles the real world (fidelity), the more difficult it is for novice learners to learn the system. Part of the reason for this is that the cognitive load is too high.[10] However, the less fidelity a simulation has, the less likely the learner is to transfer their learning to the real world. Optimal learning tends to take place in the moderate fidelity zone (Grabe and Grabe 2007, p. 129). However, we know learning takes place over time. Novices need a simple system. When they become intermediate learners, they need a system with moderate fidelity and expert learners one with high fidelity. As learners move from novice to expert, they need to apply their learning in various contexts in order to generalize their learning across contexts to then be able to apply

[10] According to the information processing theory, humans can only hold ±7 chunks of information in their working memory. Novices see all items as discrete and lack the ability to chunk or categorize items and have difficulty to pick out relevant items from irrelevant ones. The greater the ability to chunk, the more information someone can work with, i.e., greater cognitive load. This is why "chunking" items such as the alphabet (a lot of young children believe "lmno" is one letter), our phone numbers, use acronyms, etc. allows us to remember and do more. I get anxious when I have too much on my mental to-do list, even when each individual item is minor, because I feel like I am losing track of everything. Writing things down and categorizing items lessens my anxiety.

it to new contexts, i.e., transfer. James Paul Gee (2008a) explains how games can enable learners to do this:

> Context here then means *goal-driven problem space*. As players move through different contexts—each containing similar but varied problems—this movement helps them to interpret and, eventually, generalize their experiences. They learn to generalize—but always with appropriate customization for specific different contexts—their skills, procedures, principles, choices, and uses of information. This essentially solves the dilemma that learning in context can leave learners with knowledge that is too context-specific, but that learning out of context leaves learners with knowledge they cannot apply. Players come to see specific in-game solutions as part of more general types of approaches. (p. 26)

In order for us as teachers to facilitate movement from novice thinking toward expert thinking, then, we need to level our system, i.e., create a simple version, a moderate version, and a complex version. Movement between versions involves applying learning to different contexts.

This replicates how our brain works. Our brains create mental models that simplify reality. Schell (2008) uses a concrete example to describe how this works:

> Charlie Brown seems like a person even though he doesn't look like anyone we know because he matches some of our internal models. We accept his giant head because our minds store much more information about heads and faces than the rest of the body, since so much information about a person's feelings come from their face. If instead, he had a small head, and giant feet, he would immediately look ridiculous, because he wouldn't match our internal models at all. And what about his lines? It is a challenging problem for the brain to look at a scene and pick out which objects are separate from each other. When it does, below our conscious level, our internal visual processing system draws lines around each separate object. Our conscious mind never sees these lines, but it does get a feeling about which things in a scene are separate objects. When we are presented with a picture already drawn with lines, it has been 'pre-digested' in a sense, matching our internal modeling mechanisms perfectly, and saving them a lot of work. This is part of why people find cartoons and comics so soothing to look at—our brain needs to do less work to understand them. (p. 117)

In describing ways that the video game *Civilization* (*Civ*) is a simplified version of the world,[11] Squire points out that:

> If the model gets too complex, you can't observe the consequences, and then it is not entertaining or educational. Many educators make this mistake (let's include everything so that it's realistic), which makes a model less useful for learning. We don't want a 1:1 map of the world; we want a model to illustrate ideas. This is why many science researchers use simplified models. (Squire 2011, p. 23)

You want your system to be simple enough to see the impact of one's actions so that learners can "manipulate variables [and] observe the impact on the overall system [thus] learn to recognize meaningful patterns" (Kirkley et al. 2011, p. 389). In other words, KISS your system: "Keep It Simple, Stupid." Take the diagram you have drawn of your system and simplify it.

One way to simplify your system is to strip it down to its most essential elements and depict them as a linear causal chain (A causes B, B causes C, C causes D, etc.).

---

[11] Originally *Civ* leaves out slavery and religion but in later versions adds them in, thus complexifying the system.

Another way is to hold one (or more) variable(s) constant. For example, I had a student who created an assignment where her students had to be an organism within a specified ecosystem. Students had to create a "Facebook" page for their organism with a picture of it, likes, dislikes, and status updates. Students "friended" other organisms and posted comments on each other's pages. If "prey" friended a "predator," they would then be eaten. This immediate feedback helped them learn how the elements in this system interacted. However, the environment initially was unchanging. By holding the environment constant, she was able to introduce students to a simplified version of an ecosystem.

Rabin (2009) describes this as the difference between simulation and emulation—a simulation models elements working together in a system; emulation assigns a behavior to an object. For example, in a flight simulator, all the elements have to interact with each other as they would in reality in order for the plane to fly (simulation), whereas in an airstrike game, the planes fly on their own (emulation) and the player just presses the button to release bombs. By automating certain behaviors, you can reduce the level of complexity. The "perpetual running" games do this by having the avatar in constant motion. By offloading moving the avatar forward, the player just has to react to environmental cues by jumping, ducking, moving side to side, and turning left or right. What is important to simulate and what can be emulated all depend on what you want students to learn. Emulate as much as possible in order for players to focus on the simulation/learning part. Later levels can have students simulate what was emulated in lower levels.

For the next level of medium complexity, you want to add in more elements as well as feedback loops. Games are an ideal medium for learners to start to conceptualize a system with feedback loops:

> Lectures, readings, and videos all have the weakness of being linear, and a linear medium is a very difficult way to convey a complex system of relationships. The only way to understand a complex system of relationships is to *play* with it, and to get a holistic sense of how everything is connected. (Schell 2008, p. 446)

Bogost (2008) describes how this occurred for his son:

> My [five year old] son soon realized the dilemma facing him [in the game *Animal Crossing*]: the more material possessions he took on, the more space he needed, and the more debt he had to assume to provide that space. And the additional space just fueled more material acquisitions, continuing the loop. This link between debt and acquisition gives form to a routine that many mortgage holders fail to recognize: buying more living space not only creates more debt, it also drives the impulse to acquire more goods. More goods demand even more space, creating a vicious cycle. (p. 117)

As Simmons (2001) points out, "Reality in the information age is nonlinear. Actually, reality has always been nonlinear but things moved slowly enough that we could pretend like we lived in a linear and predictable world. Not anymore" (pp. 36–37). To increase the level of complexity of your system, turn the causal chains into causal loops and depict how they interact.

To complexify your system even more, play with the boundaries, add new elements, reverse elements, ask questions, and seek alternative explanations: "Even though simulations are premised on the notion of fidelity to their referent, the very fact that they are dynamic systems means they allow for the exploration of alternative permutations" (Salen and Zimmerman 2004, p. 455). For example, as I stated earlier, my work in this area began with me wondering why video game designers did not seek out educators to make their video games more pedagogically powerful. It was not until I reversed my thinking that I realized that video game designers are the ones who have the keys to learning.

The highest level of systems thinking is creating a new system by questioning the old. If germs are the reasons humans get diseases, why is it that there are some people who always get the office cold and others who never do? Asking this question allowed Dr. Francis (2002) to propose a new system of understanding disease where there is only one disease, that of malfunctioning cells, and only two causes of cellular malfunction: nutritional deficiency and toxicity. Will Wright, creator of the *SIMS*, observes that "the games that tend to be more creative, have a much larger solution space, so you can potentially solve this problem in a way no one else has" (Fullerton, et al 2004, p. 133 quoting Celia Pearce's interview with Will Wright). The highest level of complexity allows players to invent their own systems. Similar to how I changed the way I taught children's literature, if you were teaching genre, you might create a game where the players are librarians having to classify and shelve children's books by genre. In the first level, the player would have to shelve books where the genre is very clear. The next level might involve the librarian classifying books that cross genres, for example, a book that could be classified as fantasy or as science fiction, and the players have to justify the decisions they made. The final level might involve the players inventing their own system of genres. Think about how you can create a simple system, have some examples that challenge that system, and then give students the opportunity to create their own system.

Leveling Up

Now that we have at least three levels of complexity to our system, in order to teach, we need to think about ways to move students from one level to the next. Asking your essential question ("what makes a city?," "what are the criteria for historical significance?," "what makes a good poem?") may be a good entry point for novice learners. That way, you can introduce the basic elements (or have the learner introduce them or select them) for the most simple level.

Once a learner has mastered the basics, getting the learner to question those basics can move a learner from a simple mental model to one with a moderate level of complexity. This creates *cognitive dissonance*[12] in the learner. In other words, it creates a discrepancy between the learner's mental model and the outside world (or,

[12] Leon Festinger wrote a book in 1956 titled *When Prophecy Fails* to explore this idea of cognitive dissonance—when reality contradicts someone's inner world. Jean Piaget developed the ideas of *assimilation*, fitting the outside world into one's internal schema (e.g., "if all you have is a hammer, then everything looks like a nail"), and *accommodation*, changing one's internal schema to match outside reality.

Fig. 3.3 My worldview

Fig. 3.4 World logo

in our case, the game world). Some call this a "discrepant event" where the outcome is nonintuitive. For example, when I was young, I thought that the world looked like this (Fig. 3.3).

At the time, an international organization used a graphic that had children holding hands and circling the globe similar to this (Fig. 3.4).

This directly contradicted my own mental image. I was faced with three choices: live with this contradiction (something humans are averse to doing), assimilate this contradiction by somehow incorporating the external information into my own mental model, or accommodate this contradiction by changing my mental model. As I slowly realized that everyone else viewed the world this way, I changed my mental model.[13] Challenging learner's misconceptions, which sometimes are just oversimplified models, by presenting them with contradictory data motivates learners to resolve those contradictions by modifying their mental models.

[13] This then introduced a new contradiction as I did not understand why those children did not fall off the earth. I had to live with that cognitive dissonance until I developed a more accurate understanding of gravity.

I know a science teacher who begins her biology unit by bringing in a burning candle and asking her middle school students if the flame is alive. Her students know it is not, but cannot explain why as she points out that it needs oxygen to live, it moves, it reproduces (by lighting a match off the candle), and so forth. This works as a great hook for teaching her students the elements of life. By getting students to question their own criteria for life, students are much more prone to remember them than they would be if she just said these are the elements. Introducing questions like "why are there mammals in the sea?" or "are songs poems?" can inject cognitive dissonance. So can creating an "event," i.e., something that disrupts the system (Bogost 2007, p. 74). For example, my student who created the Facebook ecosystem simulated the effects of a natural disaster, thus disrupting the simple mental model students had created. Initially, she had held the environment as a constant. By turning it into a variable, she then forced her students to complexify their own mental models of an ecosystem. Removing a predator would seemingly increase the population of its prey, but having the prey's population diminish over time would counter students' intuitions and force them to revise their mental model to take into account the depletion of resources caused by overpopulation. Making eye contact with a stranger by US custom would invite friendliness, but do so in another culture might provoke hostility. There are a number of misconceptions in every field that can be used. As teachers, however, we often forget our own misconceptions we encountered along the way. There may be some, perhaps, we did not encounter at all, particularly if our ways of thinking match those honored in the field. Examine student work; observe students' behaviors; listen to students' conversations; try to uncover the misconceptions your students have.

To move students from moderate to a higher level of complexity, you can also have students experience the system from a different perspective. Gee (2003) describes how the game *Sonic the Hedgehog* challenges players' perspective, what he calls "cultural model" by allowing the player to play as Sonic or as Shadow, Sonic's nemesis. In the Facebook ecosystem, students who were prey could then be predators and vice versa and so experience the system from a different perspective. Squire (2011) points out that this perspective-taking ability can be an affordance of video games: "global leaders shouldn't make policy decisions based on playing *Civ. However, Civ* does enable players to see history and geopolitics from different perspectives" (p. 23). Allowing players to play from a different point of view gives them a wider and deeper understanding of the system. Another option might be allowing them to play in "god" mode, in other words, being able to manipulate all or almost all of the elements within a system.

Labeling Your Levels

As teachers, we have been "labeling our levels" ever since rubrics became popular. At first, I labeled the levels of my rubrics with different gradations without giving much thought to the messages these labels sent. It is important, however, to realize that student work and the labels we put on it are personal. Although we know we are not labeling students when we grade work, sometimes it feels that way to the student and, unfortunately, sometimes teachers do label students in our heads when we do this.[14] It was not until I read about effort-based learning that I changed the lowest level of my rubrics to "not yet" instead of "unsatisfactory."

Jesse Schell (2008) advises "us[ing] every means possible to reinforce [your] theme" (p. 49). Now is your chance. Instead of labeling your levels "Beginner, Intermediate, Expert," reinforce your theme by selecting names from that topic. For example, the video game *RollerCoaster Tycoon* uses the levels of "Apprentice, Entrepreneur, and Tycoon," which fit a game about economics. For a game about lifespan development, you could use "Caterpillar, Chrysalis, Butterfly." Sports have their own levels: "Rookie, Experienced, Veteran." These do not have to be formalized labels, but rather how people talk about differing levels of experience. I changed my rubrics so that the levels of extra-credit that revolve around technology are labeled: "Techie, Tech Savvy, Tech Guru." Think about what labels for levels might work for your topic.

Conclusion

Dale's Learning Cone depicts the more active the learning, the greater the understanding. The top tier has "simulating the real experience, doing the real thing, teaching it to another person" (Crockett et al. 2011, p. 92). This chapter discussed how to "simulate the real experience," but the next chapter argues that making the experience part of a larger story with a larger goal adds an even deeper learning level to Dale's Learning Cone. As we will explore in the next chapter, stories speak to us at deep levels, can change our core values, and can inspire us in unbelievable ways.

Games are the most elevated form of investigation.

–Albert Einstein

Appendix: Systems Quest Worksheet

Theme: ______________________

Deeper enduring understanding: ________________________________

Revised essential question: ___________________________________

[14] This is true of both positive and negative labeling and can blind us to what is happening in the classroom. For example, when I was a high school teacher, I had a strong student who had been plagiarizing all year long, but I did not discover it until the final research paper because I did not question her writing until it became so blatant I realized the paper was too good for even her to write it.

Elements of chosen **topic** (add more rows as needed)	Element	Properties	Static or dynamic	Behaviors
Primary goal of the system				
Hierarchy of goals				
Working model: initial diagram of how elements are related to each other				

Suggested Rubric for Systems Quest

Quest	"Wow! I mean, I think this might work" (3)	"Hmm, this is acceptable" (2)	"I need more convincing" (1)	"Go back to the drawing board" (0)
Systems quest	System at three levels of complexity	System with feedback loops	Causal chain or causal loop	System is unclear

Suggested Reading: Nonfiction

Meadows, D. (2008). *Thinking in systems: A primer*. White River Junction, VT: Chelsea Green.

Sweeney, L. B. (2001). *When a butterfly sneezes: A guide for helping kids explore interconnections in our world through favorite stories*. Waltham, MA: Pegasus Communications.

References

Chasing the dream. (2005, August 4). *The Economist*. Retrieved November 1, 2016, from http://videogames.procon.org/view.source.php?sourceID=009370

Adcock, A., Watson, G., Morrison, G., & Belfore, L. (2010). Effective knowledge development in game-based learning environments: Considering research in cognitive processes and simulation design. In R. Van Eck (Ed.), *Gaming and cognition: Theories and practice from the learning sciences* (pp. 152–168). Hershey, PA: Information Science Reference.

Barab, S., Pettyjohn, P., Gresalfi, M., & Solomou, M. (2012). Game-based curricula, personal engagement, and the *Modern Prometheus* design project. In C. Steinkuehler, K. Squire, & S. Barab (Eds.), *Games, learning, and society: Learning and meaning in the digital age* (pp. 306–326). New York: Cambridge University Press.

Bogost, I. (2007). *Persuasive games: The expressive power of videogames*. Cambridge, MA: MIT Press.

Bransford, J., Brown, A., & Cocking, R. (2000). *How people learn: Brain, mind, experience, and school*. Washington, DC: National Academy Press.

Bronfenbrenner, U. (1979). *The ecology of human development: Experiments by nature and design*. Cambridge, MA: Harvard University Press.

Crockett, L., Jukes, I., & Churches, A. (2011). *Literacy is not enough: 21st century fluencies for the digital age*. Thousand Oaks, CA: Sage.

Eisenkraft, A. (2003). Expanding the 5E model: A proposed 7E model emphasizes "transfer of learning" and the importance of eliciting prior understanding. *The Science Teacher, 70*, 56–59.

Francis, R. (2002). *Never be sick again: Health is a choice, learn how to choose it*. Deerfield Beach, FL: Health Communications.

Fullerton, T., Swain, C., & Hoffman, S. (2004). *Game design workshop: Designing, prototyping, and playtesting games*. San Francisco, CA: CMP Books.

Gee, J. P. (2003). *What videogames have to teach us about learning and literacy*. New York: Palgrave Macmillan.

Gee, J. P. (2005). Learning by design: Good video games as learning machines. *E-Learning, 2*(1), 5–16.

Gee, J. P. (Ed.). (2008a). Learning and games. In K. Salen (Ed.), *The ecology of games: Connecting youth, games, and learning* (pp. 21–40). Cambridge, MA: MIT Press.

Gee, J. P. (2008b). Video games, learning, and 'content'. In C. T. Miller (Ed.), *Games: Purpose and potential in education* (pp. 43–53). New York: Springer.

Gladwell, M. (2008). *Outliers: The story of success*. Boston: Little, Brown, and Company.

Grabe, M., & Grabe, C. (2007). *Integrating technology for meaningful learning*. New York: Houghton Mifflin.

Kapp, K. (2012). *The gamification of learning and instruction: Game-based methods and strategies for training and education*. San Francisco, CA: Pfeiffer.

Kirkley, J. R., Duffy, T., Kirkley, S., & Kremer, D. (2011). Implications of constructivism for the design and use of serious games. In S. Tobias & J. D. Fletcher (Eds.), *Computer games and instruction* (pp. 371–394). Charlotte, NC: Information Age.

Kutner, L., & Olson, C. K. (2008). *Grand theft childhood: The surprising truth about violent video games*. New York: Simon and Schuster.

LeBlanc, M. (2004/2006). Tools for creating dramatic game dynamics. In K. Salen & E. Zimmerman (Eds.). *The game designer reader: A rules of play anthology*. (pp. 438–459) Cambridge, MA: MIT Press.

Macklin, C., & Sharp, J. (2012). "Freakin' hard": Game design and issue literacy. In C. Steinkuehler, K. Squire, & S. Barab (Eds.), *Games, learning, and society: Learning and meaning in the digital age* (pp. 381–402). New York: Cambridge University Press.

Meadows, D. (2008). *Thinking in systems: A primer*. White River Junction, VT: Chelsea Green.

Numeroff, L. (1985). *If you give a mouse a cookie*. New York: HarperCollins.

Rabin, S. (2009). *Introduction to game development* (2nd ed.). Herndon, VA: Cengage Learning.

Ravitch, D. (2013). *Reign of error: The hoax of the privatization movement and the danger to America's public schools*. New York: Knopf Doubleday.

Schell, J. (2008). *The art of game design: A book of lenses*. Burlington, MA: Morgan Kaufmann.

Seitles, M. (1996). The perpetuation of residential racial segregation in America: Historical discrimination, modern forms of exclusion, and inclusionary remedies. Journal of Land Use and Environmental Law. Retrieved from http://archive.law.fsu.edu/journals/landuse/Vol141/seit.htm?referer=www.clickfind.com.au

Simmons, A. (2001). *The story factor: Inspiration, influence, and persuasion through the art of storytelling*. New York: Basic Books.

Squire, K. (2011). *Video games and learning: Teaching and participatory culture in the digital age*. New York, NY: Teachers College Press.

Sweeney, L. B. (2001). *When a butterfly sneezes: A guide for helping kids explore interconnections in our world through favorite stories*. Waltham, MA: Pegasus Communications.

White, F. (1987). *The overview effect: Space exploration and human evolution*. Reston, VA: AIAA.

Fiction

The following give the reader a chance to view a system as an insider and an outsider.

Any book from the Magic School Bus series.

Atwood, M. (1998). *The Handmaid's tale*. New York: Knopf Doubleday.

Lowry, L. (2002). *The Giver*. New York: Random House.

Chapter 4
Game Face: Telling the Story

> *Truth, naked and cold, had been turned away from every door in the village. Her nakedness frightened the people. When Parable found her she was huddled in a corner, shivering and hungry. Taking pity on her, Parable gathered her up and took her home. There, she dressed Truth in story, warmed her and sent her out again. Clothed in story, Truth knocked again at the villagers' doors and was readily welcomed into the people's houses. They invited her to eat at their table and warm herself by their fire.*
>
> –*Jewish Teaching Story*

Abstract This chapter delves into the pedagogical power of storytelling (The story factor: inspiration, influence, and persuasion through the art of storytelling. Basic Books, New York, 2001). It encourages the reader to tell the story of the system by choosing an element or elements within the system to serve as a protagonist(s). The chapter discusses both conventional and unconventional plot and character development by exploring ways video games have exploded narrative possibilities. By finding leverage points within the system, the reader then branches the narrative by exploring alternative paths the protagonist(s) can take. Building on Turkle's (The second self: Computers and the human spirit. Simon and Schuster, New York) groundbreaking work about how people relate to technology, this chapter also explores how to create a game story and characters that foster empathy, motivation, and immersion.

Keywords Empathy • Presence • Transitional objects • Avatar • Identities • Race • Gender • Hero • Non-playing characters (NPCs) • Plot • Counterfactual analysis • Cut scenes • Boss level • Rubber-banding • Golden path • Branching

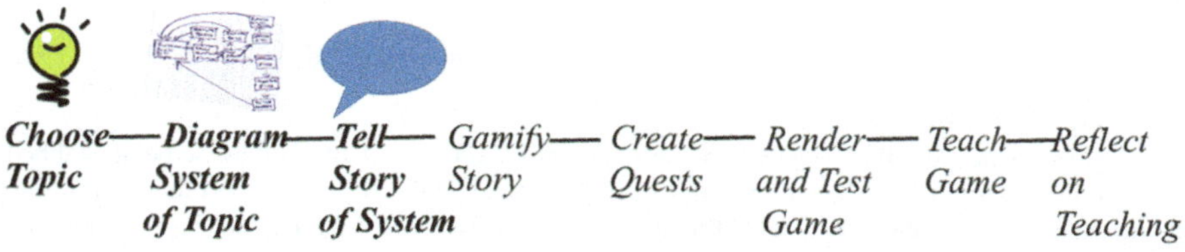

J.J. Kellinger, *A Guide to Designing Curricular Games*,
Advances in Game-Based Learning, DOI 10.1007/978-3-319-42393-7_4

STORY QUEST:

You get the nod of approval from the Commander after showing her your diagrams. As a matter of fact, you think you detect a look of satisfaction.

"Ahh," you think to yourself, "I'm almost there."

When you look over the diagrams you've drawn, though, you realize they are just that. Diagrams. They in no way resemble a game. As you contemplate the next step, you realize you have an abstract representation of your topic; you need to turn it into a concrete way for students to experience your theme. You remember the experiment your cognitive psychology professor did where she told you the rule: "A card with an even number on one side must have a vowel on the other side." She then showed you four cards, A, 7, D, *and* 8, *and asked how many and which cards need to be turned over to see if any of them violated the rule. After much deliberation, the class figured out that you need to turn over the* 8 *to see if it has a vowel on the other side and the* D *to see if it has an even number on the other side. Since the rule says nothing about odd numbers, it doesn't matter what's on the other side of the seven, and since a vowel could be on the other side of either an even number or an odd number, it doesn't matter what's on the other side of the A. She then gave you a new rule, "Anyone under 21 is not allowed to drink alcohol," and showed you four new cards:* beer, coke, 18, *and* 25. *When the same task went from abstract to concrete, it quickly became clear that you only need to turn over* beer *and* 18.

"How do I make the abstract concrete?" Thinking back on your best teachers, you realize they made the abstract concrete by telling stories. For example, you remember the bystander effect because of the impact the Kitty Genovese[1] *story had on you. Then you think back to all the story-rich games you have played, adventure series like* MYST, *and even casual games like* Angry Birds *have some sort of plot, and you remember your surprise at discovering the game story written inside the* Candyland *box. You ask yourself, "What story does my system tell?"*

IF you are a visual learner, THEN you draw: Immediately you start seeing the boxes in your diagrams and their connectors as comic strips. You start storyboarding, *drawing a comic book version of your story where each box represents an action in the story and breaks between boxes represent transitions in action. You rethink it and start drawing arrows to indicate where you think the different boxes would fit better. After creating a complete mess, you start over with sticky notes for each comic strip box, placing them on the paper, drawing arrows to indicate the flow of the story, and labeling the arrows to describe the transitions. But still, you struggle with creating a coherent story…*

ELSE you write: You start to dive into writing the backstory but can't figure out where to begin. You realize you have a lot more thinking to do before you can put words on paper.

[1]According to the *New York Times*, 37 witnesses heard and/or saw Kitty Genovese being stabbed to death in Queens in 1964, yet not a single one of them called the police to report the crime while it was happening. Psychologists label this the bystander effect: the more bystanders there are, the less likely one of them will take action because each one feels the responsibility is spread among all bystanders and therefore feels less compelled to take action.

You realize, you cannot tell a story without characters in that story. You sit back and start the laborious process of birthing characters. At breakfast, you find yourself tapping your pencil, yes pencil. You also quickly realize that the eraser at the end of your pencil has become your new best friend. How sad. Your best friend is an object. You've been so caught up in your mission, you haven't even befriended anyone here. Well, there is that one guy you have had weird smile exchanges with. You look up and notice him glancing at you furtively. "What is he up to?" you think. He looks like he is doing what your parents used to call "the pee-pee dance." "Weird. Maybe he's just weird. Or maybe he's trying to tell me something!" You look around, put your pencil down, and head to the bathroom.

After spending a really long time delaying, especially since you didn't have to go to the bathroom in the first place, you decide he is just weird and get ready to exit when he walks in. Without looking at you, he immediately checks all the stalls to make sure no one is around. You realize that the bathrooms, despite being unisex which you find odd, are the one place where there are no security cameras in order to respect people's privacy. "Ahhh, no wonder he wanted to meet me here. I wonder what he has to tell me?" Instead of talking to you, he rushes by you and whispers "only use this at night." Having no idea what he's talking about, you go back to your breakfast completely perplexed. You decide that maybe he is experiencing some of the psychological aftereffects of being in a war. You shake your head to help you focus and get back to what you were thinking.

"I don't even have the skeleton of a story. Hmmm. Maybe I first have to put flesh and blood on a skeleton. Who should my characters be? Which perspective best tells my story? Or can it be told from multiple perspectives?"

You think back to the system you designed. Now you have to embody that system. You try to identify which elements are "actors" in your system—their behaviors impact the whole system—and which elements are "reactors" in your system.

"Perhaps," you think, "the actors should be the players and the reactors the nonplaying characters or NPCs. But it's not that simple, is it, since actors are also reactors."

You decide to start from step one: identifying, describing, and defining the main character. You go back to your topic and look at the overarching goals. "Whose goals are these in the system?" you ask yourself. Answering that question starts you on the path of giving your story life or, rather, lives. Hmm, just like some video games have "lives."

You finish your breakfast, place the items in the corresponding recycling bins, and shove both your hands in your pockets—what your ex calls your "thinking pose." When you do, you discover something in your pocket. Your new "friend" is the opposite of a pickpocket. Perhaps he does have a purpose after all. You start to pull it out to study it, but then you remember you are constantly being watched. It takes all your willpower to wait until you return to your room where you can examine it in the safety of your own bathroom.

ACTION: Brainstorm ideas for your story and create character sketches of potential characters.

Part I: Birthing Characters

When one enters the magic circle [of a game], the game token is no longer a piece of plastic, the game token becomes "you."

–Richard Swan 2010

I have created multiple classes that are structured as curricular games. The first few used the story as a narrative vehicle designed to deliver the content which was leveled and could only be unlocked as students earned a certain number of points. Then, I started using more game-like elements such as content-based problems embedded as mini-games that derived from the story but also drove the story. In the latest game-based class I created, the narrative is the content instead of the frame for the content. This allowed me to create nonplaying characters (NPCs) that represent different points of view. As the narrative progresses, the characters' relationships among each other are revealed to be more and more complicated, allowing for a more complex system to emerge and the students as the protagonist to explore their own positionalities within this system.

In the last chapter, we diagrammed a system of our topic. Now, we need to populate that system. This section offers guidance in doing so. The first step is to choose the perspective from which to act on the system:

> Role-play should be seen as a fundamental skill used across multiple academic domains. Whether it be children on a playground acting out and deciphering the complex universe of Pokémon, Orville Wright pretending to be a buzzard gliding over sand dunes, or Albert Einstein imagining himself to be a photon speeding over the earth, role-playing enables us to envision and collaboratively theorize about manipulating entirely new worlds. (Jenkins 2009, p. 52)

Role-playing allows people to empathize with the actors within a system, what Gee (2008) calls "embodied empathy for a complex system" (p. 32). Gee goes on to describe what this might look like:

> Scientists often talk and think *as if* they were inside not only the simulations they build, but even the graphs they draw and the models they build. They do this to gain a deeper feel for how variables are interacting in the system. For example, consider the following remark from a physicist talking to other physicists while looking and pointing to a graph (an abstract model) on a blackboard. (Points to the right side of the diagram) "When (moves finger to left) I come down (moves finger to right) I'm in (moves finger to left) the domain state."… This is much like gamers who say "I died" in *Doom* or "my army was crushed" in *Rise of Nations*. (Gee 2008, p. 31)

Just as scientists use this technique to better understand a system, some teachers use this technique to aid students in doing the same: "In science education… research shows that students often find it helpful to identify with individual elements in a model, and then view phenomena from the perspective of that element" (Gee 2008, p. 31). Indeed, one of the teachers I interviewed for a previous study describes using this very technique:

> If you were standing on the nucleus of an atom and you were to look down, what would you see?... If you're carbon, and you're in this environment with all these other atoms, how are you going to feel? What are your needs going to be so to speak? (Patrick in Jackson 2007, p. 143)

This same teacher goes on to argue for the necessity of teaching empathy as a skill: "empathy I think is I would say the most powerful human tool. We don't spend enough time either talking about it or working on it and if we all had more empathy, I think we would all not step on each others' toes and hurt each other as much" (Patrick in Jackson 2007, p. 144). Empathy begets empathy and can change the culture of a classroom or even a school: "A 2001 University of British Columbia study found that 88 % of children who had completed the Roots of Empathy program showed a decrease in aggressive behaviors such as bullying. 'When empathy goes up, bullying goes down,' Gordon said" (Blanchard 2007). Extrapolate this to a global scale and you can hypothesize how empathy can change the course of history. Hmmm, sounds like a potential video game.

Empathy coupled with a feeling of helplessness, however, can lead to despair. Sweeney (2001) proposes designing instruction in such a way that students also feel they have agency within systems:

> Ideally, we want [our children] to be able to see the systems they are embedded in, to understand why troubling things happen, and to figure out what they can do about them. ... we want them to adopt a mindset that they are part of a larger system, *and* that they can make a difference even as one person in that world. (p. 14)

This sense of "presence," of feeling that one is in the game, forms from a combination of immersion and role-play. Presence plus interactivity leads to the sense of agency or "satisfying power to take meaningful action and see the results of our decisions and choices" (Murray 1997, p. 126). Because the player is the hero, i.e., the one making the decisions, games have an advantage over literature or film because they can engender this sense of agency:

> In a video game, players make things happen; they don't just consume what the 'author' (game designer) has placed before them. In good games, players feel that their actions and decisions—and not just the designers' actions and decisions—co-create the world they are in and shape the experiences they are having. Their choices matter. What they do matters. I would argue that all deep learning involves learners feeling a strong sense of ownership and agency, as well as the ability to produce and not just passively consume. (Gee 2008, p. 35)

By having players act upon a world and have their actions create consequences within the game world, i.e., be meaningful, players play an active role in constructing their own understandings of the material.

Combining these ideas—that of role-playing as a means of developing empathy, of understanding systems dynamics, and of creating a sense of agency—we have an argument for Gee's (2008) "embodied empathy for a complex system" as a means for enabling students to learn, to see through the eyes of others, and to use these new understandings to act upon the world in a way that promotes social justice. Gee (2008) argues that video games can be a useful platform to do so:

> Video games, under the right circumstances, may well be able to encourage (and actually help players to enact) an "attitude" or "stance" similar to the one taken by scientists studying complex systems. This stance involves a sort of "embodied empathy for a complex system" wherein a person seeks to enter imaginatively into a system, all the while seeing and thinking of it as a system, rather than as a group of local or random events. This does, indeed, seem similar to the stance players take when [video gamers] play… and seek to figure out the rule system that underlies the virtual world… We can go on to ask whether video games could create such empathy for the sorts of complex systems relevant to academic and other domains outside of entertainment… Shafer's "epistemic games"—games which model sorts of professional practices—already give us a good indication that even young learners, through video games embedded inside a well-organized curriculum, can be inducted into professional practices as a form of value-laden deep learning that transfers to school-based skills and conceptual understandings. (p. 32)

This explanation describes how video games can become "transitional objects." Papert (1980) uses the term "transitional object" to describe what he calls "objects to think with." As he continues to describe these transitional objects, it becomes clear they are also "objects to feel with": "You can be the gear, you can understand how it turns by projecting yourself into its place and turning with it" (p. viii). The term "transitional objects" is also used to describe items, often blankets, that children substitute for a parent when a parent is not around, deriving comfort and love from such transitional objects. Papert argues that the cognitive dimension of transitional objects derives from this affective dimension. For Papert, gears were such transitional objects. He even describes falling in love with gears. For Papert, gears symbolized the complicated ways cause and effect occurred in the world.[2] Turkle (1984) uses the term "fusion" to describe this complicated relationship of identifying with an object and Papert (1980) the phrase "syntonic learning" to describe learning that derives from "fusion" with an object. Over the years, some cultures have adopted various "transitional objects" as a means for viewing the world: the mechanics of clocks as a metaphor for the universe, bodies as machines, and the mind as a computer. Video games serve as "transitional objects" for me as the constructs behind video games shape how I view the world. According to Turkle (1984), this is true for others as well.

This connection between the self and the game can promote learning: "Moreno and Mayer (2000, 2004, 2005) found that personalizing games [addressing the player as 'you', 'I', or as a nickname] increases learning and transfer" (Tobias et al. 2011, p. 200). Part of this may be due to increased emotion correlating with increased memory and retention, as the limbic system in the brain labels something emotional as important and tells the brain to pay attention to it. However, too much emotion can actually inhibit performance, for example, the pressure of high-stakes tests, where the brain gets overwhelmed and shuts down. This means there is a window,

[2] "I found particular pleasure in such systems as the differential gear, which does not follow a simple linear chain of causality since the motion in the transmission shaft can be distributed in many different ways to the two wheels depending on what resistance they encounter. I remember quite vividly my excitement at discovering that a system could be lawful and completely comprehensible without being rigidly deterministic" (Papert 1980, p. vi).

or optimal range, of emotions for learning. The size and range of this window differ for every person. Even though playing a video game can simulate feelings of something being "high stakes" through identification with the goals of the avatar, the lack of real-world consequences actually makes video games "low stakes." This combination of a high-stakes feeling with the knowing that it is actually low stakes regulates the amount of emotion a player experiences so emotional valence tends to stay in the learning zone.

Who Is the "You"?

When playing Wii at the early age of two, my twins would point to one of the Mii's on the screen and say, "That's me" or "That's my brother," even when the Mii looked nothing like either one of them. Similarly, many gamers have described identifying with an avatar (Turkle 1984). However, Salen and Zimmerman (2004) argue that it is not that simple. Instead they describe a game player as "a character in a simulated world, a player in a game, and a person in a larger social setting" (Salen and Zimmerman 2004, p. 454). Fine (1983) describes an instance of a researcher observing two avatars meeting for the first time in a role-playing game: "Jerry seems surprised and asks: 'Don't the two of you know each other?' Barry comments, 'Not in this game'" (Fine 1983/2006, p. 597). Will Wright, creator of *The Sims*, describes how these multiple personas can play out while playing a video game:

> It's actually very interesting in The Sims how the pronouns change all the time. I'm sitting there playing the game and I'm talking about, 'Oh, first I'm going to get a job, then I'm going to do this, then I'm going to do that.' And then you know when the character starts disobeying me, all of a sudden I shift and say 'Oh, why won't he do that?' or 'What's he doing now?'.... I think that's something we use a lot in our imaginations when we're modeling things. We'll put ourselves in somebody else's point of view very specifically for a very short period of time. 'Well let's see, if I were that person, I would probably do x, y, and z.' And then I kind of jump out of their head and then I'm me, talking to them, relating to them. (Fullterton et al. 2004, pp. 137–138 quoting Will Wright, creator of *The Sims*, in an interview by Celia Pearce)

As Salen and Zimmerman (2004) explain it, "a game avatar is simultaneously both subject and object: on one hand a mask to be worn, and on the other a tool to view and manipulate" (p. 526), or as Brown (2008) puts it: "[My avatar] conceals and reveals my personality" (p. xii). Gee (2007) explains that as players, we take on the goals of the character we inhabit, but we also "project" ourselves onto that character as we determine how those goals are achieved.

This triple identity stance—that of avatar, of player, and of person—can play out in complicated ways. An avatar matching a player's racial or ethnic identity can interfere with game play because the player might focus on how that avatar represents, or misrepresents, his or her race/ethnicity (Tobias et al. 2011 citing research by Moreno and Flowerday 2006).

A possible exception is a white player playing a white character since many white people do not recognize white culture (McIntyre 1997). But if all the avatars, nonplaying characters (NPCs), and animated agents are white, then the game signals only white people can be scientists, doctors, heroes, etc., and/or can take action on the world. Same goes for game characters all being male. Whoopi Goldberg describes how the first African American science fiction character impacted her: “When I was a little girl, it was like, ‘Oh, we are in the future.’ Uhura did that for me” (Nemetz 2014). Having authentic representations of those who are underrepresented can affect people in very personal ways.

You may think, well, let players choose the characteristics of their avatars, and indeed, there are strong arguments for doing so:

> Yee (2005, 2006) found that players noted that they enjoyed the creative aspects of modifying their avatar’s initial appearance and subsequent customizations, with some players even going as far as inventing fictitious background stories for their avatars. Players also reported being invested emotionally and psychologically in what happened to their avatars. Thus, successes and failures as realized through the avatar can have a psychological impact on players.[3] (Anderson 2010, p. 67)

When given a choice, people tend to make their avatars the same race as themselves (Tobias et al. 2011 citing research by Moreno and Flowerday 2006). By doing so, gamers may play their own identity to see how it is represented. Anything they find objectionable, though, can break the “magic circle” (Huizinga 1955), or internal world of the game.

Since we are talking about using video games in a pedagogical context, these multiple identities can serve as teachable moments. For example, if all the role-playing choices are female and males resist playing a female, this might generate a discussion on what messages students have received that may have led to that resistance,[4] that is, if that is part of the point of the game/class. However, these “teachable moments” might distract from learning goals or even be barriers. For example, one of my white male students objected to role-playing a black female high school student because he knew that he could not realistically do so without coming across as perpetuating stereotypes. Possible solutions include using animals, aliens, humans with nonhuman colors, gender-neutral humans,[5] or a third gender as avatars and NPCs. You may even design a game from a first-person perspective so players literally see through the eyes of their avatar, thus rendering choosing characteristics unnecessary.

McGonigal (2011) argues that when an avatar is designed to look like a “mini-me,” people are more likely to be inspired by its feedback. She cites a study on “vicarious reinforcement” (p. 162) where look-alike avatars who lost or gained

---

[3] Jesse Schell (2008) even predicts that the avatars we create may “be passed on to children and grandchildren, giving our future descendants a strange connection to their ancestors” (p. 370) much like a family crest.

[4] As a teacher I have found that putting the spotlight on the messages students receive by asking, “Why do you think that?” instead of the student himself or herself generates a much more productive discussion.

[5] This can pose difficulties with the English language (and with other languages). It can also challenge our own internalized gender distinctions. I remember having difficulty following a short story that used gender-neutral pronouns because I couldn’t visualize the characters. To counter society’s primacy on gender, my wife and I left gender intentionally vague resulting in our children using gendered pronouns interchangeably until they were four.

weight based on person's exercise level proved more inspiring than random avatars. She describes this desire to exercise more as doing so "in order to make the Mini happy" (p. 162). However, avatars can also serve as a "macro-me," possessing powers beyond the real-world person: "Avatars are not an escape from our 'self,' they are, rather, a longed-for chance of expressing ourselves beyond our physical limitations" (Filiciak quoted by Brown 2008, p. 140). This includes not just actions but looks as well, as sometimes people create their avatars to look like their "idealized" self. When playtesting an early version of a class I gamified, my sister asked, "Why is Rachel in your game?" referring to Rachel from the television show *Friends*. I had subconsciously chosen an avatar who looks like Jennifer Aniston, the actress who played Rachel on the TV show *Friends* and someone I would not mind looking like.

CHALLENGE 4.1: After waiting for what feels like the longest day in the world, it is finally nightfall. You were too afraid to fiddle with your newfound object during the daylight, even just to look at it, after the whispered warning. You casually stroll into your bathroom, or at least try to, in case the security cameras are watching. Excitedly, you take it out of your pocket, but your close inspection only reveals that it is a black box. Turning it slowly over and over again in your hands reveals nothing. It doesn't seem to do anything! Exasperated, you give up. "Just a weirdo," you think. You return to your bedroom to contemplate what characters you would have in your game. As you do so, you reflect on past avatars you have created. You smile at yourself as you realize your avatars in some ways trace the development of your own "ideal self." "Well, I can't communicate with Amy, but I can guess at this point she would have me describe what or who my 'ideal self' avatar would look like."

EXERCISE: Describe what your "ideal self" avatar would look like.

Castronova (2002/2006) explains how virtual worlds can provide fertile ground for being "bigger than life": "Unlike Earth, in [Virtual Worlds (VWs)] there is real equality of opportunity, as everybody is born penniless and with the same minimal effectiveness. In a VW, people choose their own abilities, gender, and skin tone instead of having them imposed by accidents of birth. Those who cannot run on Earth can run in a VW. On Earth, reputation sticks to a person; in VWs, an avatar with a bad reputation can be replaced by one who is clean" (p. 824). It is this transcendence where "the player is more powerful in the game world than they are in the real world" plus simplicity where "the game world is simpler than the real world" (Schell 2008, pp. 271–272) that creates a sense of agency in a player. However, a game cannot be too simple or too transcendent; otherwise, challenge is removed from the game.

Because heroes have motivating goals like saving the world, being the "hero" engenders this sense of agency (Prensky 2011). Keep in mind, however, there are many ways a player can be a hero—sometimes being a hero can even involve helping the supposed hero of a story. Knowing your students can help you create a game where you "hook the audience by creating empathetic and archetypal game characters with similar hopes, dreams and fears of the target audience" (Hirumi and Stapleton 2008, pp. 135–136). Athletes and others use positive visualization by playing a movie in their head where they perform flawlessly before competing to enhance their performance. When you see yourself doing something on the screen, you can imagine yourself doing it in real life.

A player writes her own story into the hero of the video game so sometimes it is better to leave out details and characteristics to allow this to happen:

> By limiting information about the player character's motivation, personality, and background, game designers create blank slates, characterless characters, more easily adaptable to the player's own identity— such as Darth Revan at the outset of Knights of the Old Republic, a character purged of memory and personality. What makes a memorable character in fiction and film, in fact, stands at odds with what makes an effective player character. (Brown 2008, p. 18)

Schell (2008) describes how controlling detail is used in comics to create both familiarity and unfamiliarity:

> In… *Understanding Comics*, McCloud makes the interesting point that the less detail that goes into a character, the more opportunity the reader has to project themselves into that character. McCloud further points out that in comics, it is often the case that characters or environments that are meant to seem alien, foreign, or scary are given a lot of detail, because more detail makes them more "other." (Schell 2008, p. 313)

Schell (2008) goes on to describe how this can be done in a way that the player feels empowered through his or her avatar:

> The idealized form and the blank slate are often mixed. Consider Spider Man, for example. He is an ideal form: a powerful and brave superhero, but the mask that covers his face makes him almost completely iconic—a blank slate that could be almost anyone. (p. 314)

In the game story for this book, I was very careful to make sure the "you" was not associated with a particular content area so I would not alienate any of my readers. Allowing players to fill in as many details as possible helps players identify with the protagonist.

One plausible way to do this is to have the protagonist experience amnesia. The goal of the game could be for the protagonist to recover memories of his or her life story. A complication could be that NPCs present conflicting stories and the protagonist has to choose who to believe and which memories to stitch together as his or her own. In this way, the player creates his or her own backstory, allowing the player to immerse him or herself into the game:

> characters are the agents through which dramatic stories are told, and they can function this way in games as well, providing a way for us to empathize with the situation and live vicariously through their efforts. But characters in games can also be vessels for our own participation, entry points for us to experience situations and conflicts through the guise of a mask we create and direct. (Fullterton et al. 2004, p. 34)

Because of this, "we have seen comparatively jaded adolescents become animated as they take on the personas embedded in game characters" (Coulter et al. 2012, p. 332). It is the role-playing aspect that serves as an entry into immersion.

Keep in mind that the main character does not have to be human (or alien) but can be an actor in your system such as a virus or a charged particle. Jesse Schell (2008) points out that we embody nonliving things all the time in real life:

> We have the ability to project ourselves into just about anything we control. When we drive a car, we project our identity into the car, as if it is an extension of ourselves. Examining a parking space, we will often say "I don't think I can fit in there." And if another car collides with our car, we don't say "He hit my car!" Instead we say "He hit *me*!" (Schell 2008, p. 312)

When choosing an element to be the main character, think of something that navigates your system and therefore will experience the whole system, not just one aspect of the system. By being an element in the system, the player gets to view how that element "makes decisions" in that system. For example, I had one student whose protagonist in his curricular game was a water droplet making decisions as it traveled through the water cycle. Having students play elements within a system allows students to experience the system:

> Empathic projection is a useful method of problem solving. If I can imagine myself in the place of another, I can make better decisions about what that [item] can do to solve a particular problem. Also, in games, you don't just project your feelings into a character, you project your entire decision-making capacity into that character, and can become them in a way that isn't possible in non-interactive media. (Schell 2008, p. 124)

Schell (2008) says "let players express themselves" (p. 362), but I would say, "let players express the character or element they are playing" because there is something freeing about being someone or something else, particularly for teenagers who often feel like they cannot break out of their stereotype yet are in the identity exploration phase of their lives. This can be done easily by having students dress up as characters. While students, particularly teenagers, may feel inhibited about this, you can have a costume/prop closet where students can choose from and wear or hold a prop during your class. A single prop can represent a lot, for example, someone carrying a sword signals something much different than someone carrying a candle. A single eye patch can conjure up the whole world of piracy.

Having students "be" the subject matter infuses learning with a deeper connection: "the subject-object distinction that exists… between students and much of what they learn in school, disappears" (Bricken (1991) quoted in Richter and Livingstone 2011, p. 109). Gee (2008) explains how this works:

> Microcontrol has well-known cognitive effects. Humans feel their bodies extend only so far as the space over which they have small-scale control, which for most of us is a space quite close to the body.… Video games… offer humans… microcontrol over objects in virtual space. This gives us the feeling that our bodies and minds have extended into this virtual space and that the spaces of the real and the virtual are joined. (p. 31)

This ability to "lose oneself" in the game by embodying something else is one of the more powerful effects of gaming and of learning.

You can also create a game where the player is the ultimate decision-maker, i.e., a "god game," where the player views the whole system and can control variables within it.[6] You could also create a game where the final level is a "god" level so that after playing as an element in the system, the player gets to control all the elements. To make this plausible, you could set up the scenario so that if the element chosen as the main character makes the right decisions, i.e., follows what game designers call the golden path, the element then gains control over the whole system.

---

[6]When I say being a "god," I do not necessarily mean playing "God." I simply mean putting the player in a position to control all the various aspects of your system. For example, we are "gods" to our bodies and control what we eat and when, how we exercise and when, what toxins we are exposed to, etc., but clearly we are not "God."

Character traits should match character functions. For example, if you create a character who is a control freak, then that character should have extremely neat appearance. If not, the sloppy exterior contradicts the controlling interior. Gredler (1992) explains that, as the game designer, you should:

> establish bona fide roles for the participants in which they are to carry out important tasks that are functional in the particular social microcosm…., provide sufficient documentation on an issue or a problem (such as memos, newspaper articles and maps) so that the participants can behave in a professional manner…, and design the simulation so that behavioural contingencies support the conscientious execution of the assigned role by the participants. (p. 15)

In other words, behaving like the role should be supported and rewarded by game mechanics and game play, what Jones (1984) calls "reality of function" (quoted in Gredler 1992). Make sure what the character cares about is also true to life:

> For instance, Richard Berg's Campaigns for North Africa claims to be an extraordinary realistic simulation of the Axis campaign in Africa. Yet you, as a player, spend a great deal of time worrying about the locations of individual pilots and how much water is available to individual battalions. Rommel's staff might worry about such things, but Rommel assuredly did not. Who are you supposed to be? The accuracy of the simulation is, in a sense, undermined, not supported, by the level of detail. (Costikyan 1994/2006, p. 206)

Characters' thoughts and actions need to be plausible in order to be believable.

In developing characters for your story, keep in mind that "The author develops characters that the audience can identify with to invite them into the action, and once empathic to the characters' plight, the audience goes wherever they are lead" (Hirumi and Stapleton 2008, p. 148). To do so, ask yourself: "Is my avatar an ideal form likely to appeal to my players? Does my avatar have iconic qualities that let a player project themselves into the character?" (Schell 2008, p. 314). You also need to keep in mind the overall goal of your game. If the goal of your game is personal transformation such as losing weight, you probably want to have your students choose or define their own avatar so they can be inspired by a "mini-me." However, if your goal is to learn concepts or skills, you might want to choose the avatar for them or create a "blank slate" avatar. If the goal is for students to experience a different perspective or different perspectives, the character they embody should have different experiences than they have had.

Your characters should not remain the same over the course of the story; otherwise, you have a pretty boring game. In many stories, the protagonist has to change in order to overcome the obstacle or else there would be no challenge involved. Dynamic characters are characters that change throughout a story or, in our case, as a result of game play. This adds not only dramatic engagement, but it can also be a source of leveling up and/or complexifying the story/system. Think about how the characters/elements in your system change based on events and interactions with other characters/elements. Think about how you can convey those changes in your character's actions and/or appearance: "Being able to select which components of your subject to ignore and which to retain and abstract is an absolutely critical game design skill" (Salen and Zimmerman 2004, p. 439). To determine this, ask yourself "what is meaningful in the context of a particular situation?" (Salen and

Zimmerman 2004, p. 440). While I am not a fan of badges and find that sometimes teachers think that using "badges" is a curricular game when actually they are just using a reward system by substituting badges for grades (old wine in new bottles), think about how "badges" can signify changes in your main character. In this case, I do not mean a badge in the traditional sense, although if the main character is a military general or a girl scout, it may be very appropriate to use traditional badges, but rather what I mean is what types of props, appearance, actions, words, changes in costume, changes in behavior, and so forth could signify the changes occurring in the character.

As the protagonist transforms, so does the student/player behind the protagonist:

> These types of games have the potential to be very transformative in terms of the players' identities. The players can view the world as a scientist, using scientific tools, seeing how and why it's interesting, and using science to have a direct impact on the world. (Clark and Martinez-Garza 2012, p. 280)

Yee and Bailenson (2007) call this the Proteus[7] effect (cited in Richter and Livingstone 2011, p. 110); in other words, the behavior and characteristics of an avatar in a virtual world are reflected in the player's persona. For example, when someone has a tall avatar, they display confident behavior. In this way, "[game]play offer[s] the player the opportunity not simply to play the game but also to 'play out self.' Elsewhere we have documented how game play tends to bind itself into students' personal lifeworlds (Dodge et al. 2008)" (Barab 2012, p. 321). Because of this "projective identity" (Gee 2007), role-playing allows tweens and teens to take on different identity roles in a "safe" way as consequences in games occur virtually, not in real life, thus allowing for the identity exploration needed, according to Erik Erikson, to successfully resolve the identity formation stage of development.

So far we have been talking about creating a game with one protagonist. However, you can have students, or groups of students, role-play different elements within a system. For example, players can play the roles of stakeholders with competing agendas. Squire (2011) provides an example of the goal of a game being determining the future of a lake and the students role-play environmentalists, developers, local residents, and so forth with goal of finding consensus among the various needs and desire. In describing students playing the game *Revolution* where students role-play characters in Colonial Williamsburg from different social classes, Brown (2008) explains how having multiple protagonists adds another dimension to role-playing games:

> [The game] positioned students in a particular role and encouraged them to experience the unfolding drama as an insider, empathizing with the distinctive concerns of their virtual persona as they attempted to achieve various personal goals. … At times, the multiplicity of perspectives stimulated a rich discussion as multiple students articulated their unique experience of a particular social theme and challenged each other's interpretation of events. (p. 125)

[7] In Greek mythology, Proteus is a sea-god who can change shape.

McGonigal (2011) used the personality strengths developed by Seligman and Peterson (2004) to build characters for *Lost Ring*, her global collaborative game for the 2008 summer Olympics:

> *Sofia*: I bring wisdom, creativity, and cleverness to our mission. I am one of the knowledge seekers.
> *Thumos*: I bring courage, energy, and determination to our mission. I am one of the adventurers.
> *Chariton*: I bring heart, humanity, and charm to our mission. I am one of the connectors.
> *Dikaiosune*: I bring leadership, direction, and focus to our mission. I am one of the pilots.
> *Sophrosune*: I bring balance, self-control, and an open mind to our mission. I am one of the advisors.
> *Mythopoeia*: I bring optimism, vision, and artistry to our mission. I am one of the truth finders. (p. 289)

Notice all of these character descriptions involve complementary and complimentary positive traits, making them ideal for students. One thing you want to avoid is having one student be "the bad guy." [8] While some students may relish this role, this is certainly something you do not want to foster and could lead to parental backlash. Think about the repercussions of having a student play Hitler. While you could have students choose a role for themselves or switch roles for each mission, students love taking *Cosmo*[9]-type quizzes about themselves so you could have students take a Values in Action inventory or any other personality quiz and assign roles that way. McGonigal (2011) went on to assigned specific tasks for each role:

> *Sofia*: You are the best engineers. Study the labyrinth plans—and arrive early to design and build the labyrinth. *Thumos*: You make the fastest runners. Get blindfolded and go for it! *Chariton*: You are the best coaches. Cheer on your team and trash-talk others. *Dikaiosune*: You make the best captains. Keep our team strong and focused on getting faster. Keep your wall coordinated and working together! *Sophrosune*: You make the best referees. Make sure everyone follows the rules. Keep time of the best scores. *Mythopoeia*: You tell the best stories. Take film and video of the game! And spread news of the best times from other cities-help your local team keep up-to-date on how the rest of the world is training. (p. 291)

As teachers, we are taught to assign specific roles to students for small group work to ensure everyone contributes. This takes it to a new, much more motivating level than just simply assigning someone to be the scribe and someone else to be the presenter.

When designing a game with multiple protagonists, you need to think about who would interact with whom. In the Colonial Williamsburg example, interaction patterns would largely be determined by social class, but other contexts might not be so clear. The "interpersonal circumplex," a graph with dominant versus submissive

[8] I learned this the hard way when giving my students some backstory for the high school students they would role-play. I was deriving these backstories from high school students I taught. I listed on one of the index cards "this student has killed someone else." My wife delicately pointed out that I probably should not have someone play the role of a murderer.

[9] *Cosmopolitan*, or *Cosmo*, is a magazine in the United States that is known for having personality tests and other self-quizzes.

on one axis and friendly versus hostile on the other, might help you to think through who would interact with whom as characters often interact more with characters closer to them on the graph.

Having multiple protagonists with specific character traits and roles allows a sense of community to evolve within the game world:

> Without community, you simply have a bunch of independent players running around the same environment. Players won't be drawn in, and there won't be anything there to bind them. The key to creating community, therefore, is interdependence. In *EverQuest*, we forced interdependence in several ways, and although we've been criticized for it, I think it's one of a couple of reasons behind our success. … By creating a class-based system, players NEED each other. By creating an environment often too challenging for a solo player, people are compelled to group and even form large guilds and alliances. All this builds community. (Brown 2008, p. 153 quoting McQuaid, one of creators of *EverQuest*)

After playing the game, students could debrief and share their perspectives or even switch roles and play the game again from a new perspective. Both the teamwork aspect and the perspective-taking ability are twenty-first-century skills identified by business leaders as needed in the twenty-first-century workforce (see Chap. 1).

Who Are the Others?

Unlike having a "blank slate" protagonist that allows players to write their own story into the character, key nonplaying characters (NPCs) should have a detailed backstory to make them believable. That is, unless, of course, you want the backstory of an NPC to be a mystery where part of the game play involves figuring out the backstory of an NPC:

> In order for a game world to be convincing and immersive, the characters that exist within that world need to be compelling and three dimensional [Sheldon04]. Because the characters are three dimensional, they need to be built upon a frame to provide support, otherwise they are no more interesting than a pile of goo. A large part of this frame is composed of the character's backstory. This includes all the major details that brought them to this point in their lives and explains why they are in their current emotional state. The audience need not know all the details of the history, but by providing one for the character, it deepens the character and makes the other elements of his character make sense [Krawczyk06]. The character needs roots, and these roots should show in what the character says and how the character acts. The other part of this frame is the character's attributes, such as his motivations, goals, aspirations, attitudes, character flaws, and temperament. Ask yourself, "Why is this person here, and what do they want?" The more layers and depth built into the character, the more alive and human they will seem and the more they will strengthen the player's feeling of immersion. Again, the audience may never overtly see these attributes. However, by the writer knowing these attributes and taking them into consideration when writing a character, the character and their dialogue become that much more believable. A trick for adding believability and defining and strengthening characters is to deliberately design flaws into the characters. For example, a companion NPC might be scared of dogs, or have a really short attention span, which might get him into a bit of trouble. Adding character flaws can add humor, interest, and realism to the story and further enrich the game world. Character flaws can also be beneficial to add to the hero. A hero that is just a wee bit too arrogant could

> cause fun things to occur in the storyline as his mouth gets him in trouble. As long as he is a likeable hero, his flaws will not only be tolerated, but will also make him seem more authentic and human. Additionally, watching NPCs perform and have a life outside of the interaction with the character also makes them more believable. (Rabin 2009, p. 160)

In order to flesh out NPCs, identify the character's goals and norms "(composed of rules or principles or guidelines) by which to act and evaluate one's actions" (Gee 2008, pp. 24–25). These rules do not have to be complex. A few simple interacting rules can lead to complex character behavior:

> Nonplayer characters [in *Halo*] have three simple impulses that drive them: (1) perception of the world around them (aural, visual, and tactile), (2) state of the world (memories of enemy sightings and weapon locations) and (3) emotion (growing scared when under attack, etc.). These three sets of rules interact—each consulting the other—as a decision-making system in a character. The result is semirealistic behavior within the game. The non-characters do not follow a script written by a designer but rather make their own decisions based on the situation they're in. (Fullterton et al. 2004, p. 126)

Now, you may be thinking, "How am I going to program a software tool to do this?" Keep in mind there are multiple ways to render your game. This could be done as easily as giving a student an index card with a rule on it (e.g., "Whenever someone asks you a question, you answer the opposite of the truth."). For right now, worry about creating the game. We will work out the details of rendering it later.

There are some archetypal roles that NPCs can play:

- *Hero*: typically the player
- *Mentor*: someone who advises the hero just in time with hints and warnings; may appear at certain times or be able to be called upon at any time
- *Threshold Guardian:* the gatekeeper who allows player to pass to next level once hero has proved his/her worth by successfully completing a challenge (think of the Sphinx riddle)
- *Herald*: bearer of news; sometimes makes predictions (like the witches in *Macbeth*)
- *Shapeshifter*: a character who can morph into different beings
- *Shadow*: someone who is the opposite of hero. This can be the dark side of the hero like Voldemort in the *Harry Potter* series; someone who places obstacles for the hero or causes the initial, major problem to solve
- *Trickster:* someone who is not who he/she seems like Snape in the Harry Potter series or someone who plays jokes or tricks like Brer Rabbit in the Uncle Remus tales. (taken from Volger's (1998) character types cited in Dickey 2011, p. 136)

Of course, as game designer, you can combine archetypes, for example, the hero could also be a trickster or the herald a shapeshifter and so forth. You can also split an archetype into its different characteristics. For example, Baylor (2003) found it was better to separate out cheerleader and mentor into separate agents (in Anderson 2010, p. 68). These are just some ideas of character types. There is a whole world of literature, movies, people in your life, and your own imagination to draw from.

Just like we talked about multiple protagonists interacting with each other, keep in mind that even if you have a singular protagonist, he, she, or it will be interacting with NPCs:

> The relationship between the hero and the supporting characters should evolve over time and change upon increasing interaction. If a hero repeatedly visits an NPC, the attitude toward him should change and become increasingly friendly, or wary, depending on the relationship. (Rabin 2009, p. 161)

Again, you can use rules to program this so that the third interaction elicits a different reaction from the NPC than the first or even the seventh. You could have a curve where the NPC gets more friendly but then more irritated as the main character initiates more interaction.

The Helpers

Often in stories and in games, there are characters who help the main character achieve his, her, or its goal. For example, in the *Harry Potter* series, Harry Potter has Hermione Granger and Ron Weasley. In real life, when faced with a problem, we often consult others, sometimes even doing so until we get the answer we secretly want to hear:

> The nature of problem solving is often a collaborative effort involving our seeking help and advice from many sources, both to gather the information needed as well as to help with the problem-solving strategies. Sometimes the people we interact with have the knowledge we need; sometimes they have strategies for getting that knowledge.... we should seek assistance from multiple characters and they should seek assistance from us; sometimes we will have information that is needed, and sometimes they will have it. (Van Eck 2007, p. 297)

Think about who the helpers might be in your story. Remember that they do not have to be characters; they could be creatures or "an object that moves around on its own, initiating actions" (Robinett 1984/2006, p. 699), elements, sources of information, signs strategically placed in the background, and so forth.

The Hinderers

In addition to helpers, stories and games often have hinderers, people, creatures, objects, etc., that make achieving the goal more difficult. This chart outlines different types of hinderers.

Role of actor	Motive of play	Role of counteractor
To overtake	Race	To stay ahead
To catch, tackle, tag	Chase	To outdistance, dodge, or elude
To overcome a barrier, enter a guarded area, overpower a defense; to injure psychologically or otherwise	Attack	To defend an area or a person, to ward off, to be on guard
To take person, symbol	Capture	To avoid being taken
To tease, taunt, lure; to mistake or unsuccessfully attack	Harassment	To see through, to move suddenly and punish an attacker, to bide time
To find by chance or clue (object, person)	Search	To hide, to cover or mislead, to feign
To spring prisoner; to be savior	Rescue	To be jailer, to guard against escape
To tempt a forbidden action	Seduction	To resist, to have self-control

–From Salen and Zimmerman 2004, p. 464 based on Brian Sutton-Smith's work

Keep in mind, though, the opponent can be the teacher or even the player (e.g., beating your own best time in a race or your high score). The game itself can also act in a manner similar to a character: "the closer a game approximated an active adaptive agent, the more intense the gameplay experience" (Swan 2010 p. 124). For example, the game can act as a human opponent. In the *Hunger Games*, the players are not only playing each other, but they are also playing the dynamic environment being manipulated by the game makers, an environment that sometimes feels as though it has a personality of its own.

Helpers as Hinderers and Vice Versa

There can be instances where it is unclear whether someone is a helper or a hinderer, such as Snape's character in the *Harry Potter* series,[10] or when someone switches back and forth or even acts as a helper and a hinderer in the same breath. You can have an unreliable narrator or character so it is set up so the player is not sure who to trust. For example, in the *Myst* series, you do not know which brother to trust. In different disciplines, you can take two opposing camps or even one prevailing thought that was trumped by another and anthropomorphize these ideas. A good guy/bad guy switcheroo can create drama by having an NPC alternate between being a good guy and a bad guy, but you must make this plausible. Blurring the line between good guys and bad guys could even be an enduring understanding of your game.

The Helped

In order to have a helper, you need someone to be helped. So far, we have talked about this in terms of someone helping the main character achieve his, her, or its goal. However, the helper could be the main character in which case you need an NPC to be the helped: "In care-taking games, such as *Viva Piñata* where players have to support an ecosystem of 'living,' wild-roaming piñata animals, we develop empathy for them and become invested in their well-being" (quoting Donath, an MIT researcher studying the emotional attachment people have to virtual creatures). Just like being the hero can give the real-life player a sense of agency, helping can engender empathy[11] and foster caretaking skills: "Naturally, then, the happier our

[10] The fact that Snape could kill Dumbledore to make you think "ok, he really was a bad guy after all" and then have it turn out he was a good guy all along I think was literary genius!

[11] "Wolves (dog ancestors) don't have nearly the range of facial expression of domesticated dogs. Dogs appear to have evolved this ability as a survival skill. Dogs that could make the right faces could capture our empathy, and we, suddenly feeling their feelings, became more likely to take care of them" (Schell 2008, p. 123).

virtual creatures appear to be as a direct result of our actions, the more satisfied we are as effective caretakers" (McGonigal 2011, p. 163). There have been interesting studies done with teachable agents where a student tutors a computer agent[12] whose progress is determined by how the computer agent does on quizzes (Blair et al. 2007). According to Dempsey (2010), "tutoring is the most effective tool we know about to increase achievement and retention" (p. 97). Certainly, as teachers, we come to know our subjects at a much deeper level when we teach it.

Considerations

Although I have used literature and film as examples throughout this chapter, there are some distinct differences between telling those stories and telling a story in a game:

> The perception of many developers is that story is primarily dialogue. Not only is that not true, but a lot of dialogue is usually not ideal in a game, and will try most players' patience. Instead, think of the story as a series of conflicts and obstacles that build upon each other. Place these conflicts within a classic story structure, and a story is created. (Rabin 2009, p. 143)

Rabin (2009) goes on to provide concrete advice for in-game dialogue when it is needed:

> Furthermore, a video game is not a place for lengthy expositions, no matter how well written. Dialogue should be fairly brief and to the point, while still keeping it conversational and in character. A short delivery also makes it more likely that the player will absorb what was said. If the dialogue is too long, much of what was said is often quickly forgotten by the player. By keeping it brief, it maintains the pace of the game and keeps the focus on the necessary facts. However, players do not usually take kindly to orders without being provided with some sort of motivation to follow them. When giving players directions, it is important to make sure they not only know what it is they have to do, but why it is they have to do it. They need to know, and care, why it is so important to the NPC that they go and find the NPC's lost amulet. It would also be important in this situation to provide a reason for the NPC to want this amulet. Why is it so important to him and how does getting this amulet help him or her achieve their larger goals? By fleshing out the motivations behind an NPC's actions, it creates a more human-like character. It makes the game feel more compelling and authentic. (Rabin 2009, p. 162)

Keep in mind that dialogue does not have to be verbal. A lot can be conveyed through body language. Schell (2008) describes how body language can be used to negotiate status:

> Typical low status behaviors include: fidgeting, avoiding eye contact, touching one's own face, and generally being tense. Typical high stats behaviors include: being relaxed and in control, making strong eye contact, and, weirdly, not moving your head while you speak. (p. 322)

There are lots of other ways to convey story as well, including setting, background, journals, and so forth. Part of the game play, too, can be the players filling in the story themselves.

---

[12] An avatar is a computer character controlled by a real-life person. An agent is a computer character who is programmed to respond in various ways.

One thing you need to decide about your game is if you, as the teacher, will play a role in the game itself:

> Because we took on the roles of the fictional characters within the simulation, it was obvious exactly when the students encountered problems or could not understand substantive or procedural issues—more so than in traditional classroom settings. We could then respond to them in character in a way that helped them overcome their problem or correct their mistake, while maintaining the flow of the simulation. (Barton and McKellar 2011, p. 241)

Helper, though, is not the only role teachers can play. Earlier I cautioned against making a student the "bad guy." If there is a bad guy in your story, you can always play the bad guy. In a class that I recently gamified, I play the high school principal who has hired the students as private investigators. As the semester plays out, students figure out that I am not only the principal but also the vice principal, as I have become a tyrannical control freak and taken over the school.

Plot Section of Story Quest

Now that you have fleshed out some characters, you realize you need to have them do something or rather several things!

> *IF you decided to draw out your story like a comic strip, THEN you start to storyboard. You aren't the tech guru and find it much easier to sketch out your storyboard on paper instead of a computer.*
>
> *ELSE you start to write out your story.*

ACTION: Either draw or write a rough draft of your game story.

As you work, you find yourself erasing and scratching out your ideas until you are back at the beginning. You find yourself stuck.

"Writer's block. More like writer's lock. Amy was always the key to unlocking my creativity with her different exercises." You hate to admit it, but you end up thinking, "Amy, I need you!"

You head to breakfast. Slowly chewing the gruel they call oatmeal, you feel like something is missing. You realize your friend is no longer in his usual spot sussing you out. You look around, finally spotting him among a gaggle of people, laughing and joking. However, you get the sense he is doing so in order to appear "normal" out of fear of getting caught. "Getting caught for what?" you think. "For giving me a useless black box? Whatever." You continue with your breakfast, but then something catches your eye. He and his friends are all wearing Google glasses. You realize he is one of the Engineering Elders. Maybe there is more to that black box than you realize.

You remember the first time you found an Easter egg in a video game. You were so excited to find this hidden surprise, you scoured every inch of the rest of the game, moving your cursor systematically from left to right trying to cover the screen, waiting in anticipation for your arrow to turn into a hand. The next time you saw Amy, you told her about your discovery and subsequent search for more. She laughed and said, "You went on a pixel hunt![13] *Easter eggs are a lazy designer trick—easy to create, hard to find." You remember you got mad at her for diminishing your fun. "Who cares if they are lazy," you thought, "they are still fun to find." You come back to the present and realize maybe that's what you need to do now, go on a pixel hunt.*

That night in your bathroom, you move your index finger applying light pressure across the black box as if you are reading Braille. You get to a spot that feels different, although you can't name how. Suddenly, a mini USB port pops out. Your eyes open wide as you realize this will fit into your cell phone. Maybe you can text the past after all!

Excitedly, you attach the device to your cell phone. Do you dare use it to try to communicate with Amy? Will doing so disrupt the space-time continuum?

> *IF you decide to text Amy, THEN you decide to test it out in an innocuous way. Surely, just contacting Amy couldn't be so bad, you decide. After all, that shouldn't give away that you are in the future. Tentatively you type, "What's up?" and press send. Almost immediately you get a response: "Nothing. Where u been?" Yikes! You put the phone down like it's a hot potato. You didn't even think about time passing in your present. Breaking out in a sweat, you decide it's better to continue channeling Amy instead of communicating with her.*
>
> *ELSE: You decide it's better to continue channeling Amy instead of communicating with her.*

Part II: Creating the Storyline(s)

Storytelling is the most ancient form of education.

–Joan Halifax

What we have created so far is a simulation[14] with characters. However, our ultimate goal is to create a game. Much has been written, and argued, about the difference between games and simulations. I find that with most definitions of either, you can interchange the word "game" for "simulation" and vice versa. One distinction we can make between simulations and games is that simulations are simplified versions of our reality, whereas games are simplified versions of *a* reality, whether that reality be our reality or an alternative one.[15] These simplified, or perhaps amplified might be a better term, realities comprise the game world or "magic circle"

[13] From Sheldon (2004, p. 189).

[14] I do not want to diminish the importance of simulations. Boston medical personnel simulating medical emergencies before the marathon bombing took place meant the amount of time taken for decision-making was greatly reduced as it had been predetermined which types of injuries would go to which hospitals, ways to transport patients had been worked out, and so forth. These prior simulations led to lives being saved.

[15] I would argue, though, that any alternative reality derives from our reality. Can humans create something truly original, i.e., not derivative from anything else? There is a scene in the movie *Star Wars* where the characters are in this liminal space, a bar on the edge of the universe where the patrons are bizarre and rough-looking creatures. However, a closer examination of these aliens reveals that they are all just mash-ups of various animals: an elephant trunk here, armadillo face there, and so forth.

(Huizinga 1955). As Kafai (1995) points out, "If France is one of the better places to learn to speak French, then a math land, or a mathematics culture, in which one can learn 'to speak mathematics' would be a better place to learn mathematics" (Kafai 1995, p. 3).

Transforming our system simulations to games involves creating a world in which our learners experience our theme. How do we create this new world? Bruner (1990) explains that "once understood in the context of the narratives that give it meaning, law becomes not merely a system of rules to be observed, but a world in which to live" (quoted by Barab 2012, p. 306). Just like Truth in the parable at the beginning of this chapter, dressing up the diagrams we created in the previous chapter in story can operate as an interface for learners by making the topic meaningful and providing motivation to play with the system:

> The story or fantasy element… is the "backstory" which transforms an arbitrary learning task into something of personal importance and relevance to the learner… Paradoxically, it is the fantasy element of the game that can make the link to the real world. (Macleod 2008, p. 22)

Stories do so because they "meaningfully position the person with intentionality, content with legitimacy, and context with consequentiality" (Barab 2012, p. 274). Story not only gives learners a reason to experiment within a system, it also allows them to experience that system in a way that does not feel overwhelming.

Storifying your curricular game is the most crucial step to ensure that your curricular game is not just your curriculum dressed up in game garb. I cannot stress this enough. Just because a teacher has students choose their own avatar, calls groups "guilds," and uses the term "experience points" instead of grades, that does not constitute what I mean by curricular game. I have even read accounts of teachers who use the phrase "fighting monsters" to refer to students doing their homework. Think about the message that sends about homework. There are also teachers who turned not the classroom content but classroom management into a "game" where students get "experience points" for listening and doing what they were told. A story does not guarantee that your curricular game will not fall into these traps, but a curricular game without a story definitely will.

Remember that our ultimate goal is to enable our students to *experience* the curriculum. Simulations allow students to *experiment*, but we can take further steps to immerse our students in our curriculum to allow them to *experience* it. LoPiccolo et al. (2012) states that *Guitar Hero* and *Rock Band* aimed to "capture the feeling" of the experience of being a rockstar (p. 110). Because "Stor[ies]…simulate experience" (Simmons 2001, p. 79), they promote feelings that experience engenders and might explain why "the brain, it seems, does not make much of a distinction between reading about an experience and encountering it in real life; in each case, the same neurological regions are stimulated" (Paul 2012, p. SR6). An experience in my life speaks to the power that stories have. When my father was in the hospital after having a stroke, I read him the second book in the Harry Potter series. Nine months later when we watched the movie, he insisted he had seen the movie before. When I told him he had not, he said he had to have seen the movie before because he knew the plot. I explained that was because I had read him the story. He had no recollection of actual reality—me reading the story to him—yet he remembered the alternative reality, the story itself!

The experiential effect of stories also helps explain why "classroom activities that are anchored in narrative structure have been shown to be quite powerful for learning" (Travis and Young 2011, p. 158). For example, in the last chapter, I presented the example of asking students if a candle is alive as a means of introducing cognitive dissonance. Imagine the difference between a teacher asking if the candle is alive versus pretending the candle is alive and even giving the candle, or the flame, a name. Although both challenge students' thinking, the second creates a new world that challenges students' realities, thus they become much more motivated to resolve this cognitive dissonance. Unfortunately schooling, at least traditional schooling, tends to operate on the transmission model where

> domain concepts, practices, methods, and principles are stripped of the legitimate situational frames in which they have meaning and value [and therefore] run the likely risk of becoming facts to be memorized rather than useful tools for operating in the world. (Brown, Collins, and Duguid, 1989) (cited in Barab 2012, p. 323)

Simmons (2001) points out that stripping facts of context runs a greater risk of facts being ignored, misinterpreted, or manipulated to fit someone's previous story:

> A good story helps you influence the interpretation people give to facts. Facts aren't influential until they *mean* something to someone. A story delivers a context so that your facts slide into new slots in your listener's brains. If you don't give them a new story, they will simply slide new facts into old slots. (Simmons 2001, p. 51)

A powerful example of how stories can create these new slots, i.e., a paradigm shift, occurred in my home state of Massachusetts. When the state legislature first voted on same-sex marriage in 2004, barely 25 % of the state legislators supported same-sex marriage. Three years later when the final vote was taken that secured same-sex marriage in Massachusetts, over 75 % of the state legislators supported same-sex marriage. In an era when flip-flopping was seen as a fatal political move, the reason cited over and over again by legislators who changed their vote was the impact of constituents' stories (Wangsness and Estes 2007).

The ultimate goal of education is that of transfer, i.e., being able to apply prior knowledge to new situations, which becomes even more imperative in an age where it feels like technology is changing the future at a rapid fire pace. To promote transfer, we created diagrams with differing levels of complexity including applying knowledge to new situations. Simmons (2001) argues that story is one way to introduce complexity:

> Our tendency to try to create teaching that is *clear* creates an unintended consequence of oversimplification.... Clarity is overrated in teaching. Story allows you to reintroduce complexity over tidy 'skill-set modules' so that the skills you teach also teach people to think about why and how they might use a new skill. (p. 19)

As a result, learners create conditional knowledge, not just declarative knowledge. Brown (2000) describes a study on Xerox technician workers that found they learned not through memorizing a list of instructions for fixes but rather through listening to the stories of other Xerox technicians. As a result of this study, the company gave Xerox technicians walkie-talkies and then a website where they could share their stories, which "increased the learning curve of tech reps by 300 %"

(Brown 2000, p. 17). This speaks once again to experiential learning—learning from one's own experiences as well as those of others.

In traditional stories, "narrative comprehension is an active process by which viewers assemble and make hypothesis about likely narrative developments on the basis of information drawn from textual cues and clues... test[ing] and reformulate[ing] their mental maps of the narrative action and story space" (Jenkins, 2004/2006, p. 681), just like we discussed in designing systems. However, Jenkins adds that, "In games, players are forced to act upon those mental maps, to literally test them against the game world itself" (p. 681). In this way, video games have the potential to take stories to another level by allowing players to co-construct the narrative as the player's "actions... determine the direction of the unfolding story" (Barab 2012, pp. 321). Game designer Trent Polack explains that in games "Story sets the stage for meaning. It frames the player's actions. We, as designers, are not telling, we're not showing, we're informing the doing—the actions that players engage in and the feats they undergo" (McGonigal 2011, p. 101). In doing so, games allow people to become someone else and try new things without real-world consequences. It is in trying new things that players learn by "plac[ing] the learner in situations in which enlisting academic content becomes necessary for advancing the storyline" (Barab 2012, pp. 322). This contrasts the traditional transmission model of learning: "In such game spaces, information is sustenance, and players actively and aggressively *pull* it from various resources as it's needed and actively employ it to progress. This is in stark contrast to the traditional classroom model, where information is selected by the system and *pushed* upon the students. In the game space, users *play* in order to learn the *game*—as opposed to learning first and playing later." (Rabone 2013, p. 2) Stories provide context and give people a reason to learn knowledge. Video games take this a step further by providing opportunities to apply this knowledge to direct the story itself.

Now I hear you protesting and saying but not all video games have stories! You are correct. There are some games and video games that do not. These are often casual games—games people play as time-fillers. Because of this, players do not want to get wrapped up in a story because they want to be able to put down the game at any point, for example, when the subway train arrives or the doctor calls them into her office.

CHALLENGE 4.2: *"Creating a story is hard! What would Amy do? Hmmm. She would tell me to 'flex my creativity muscle.' No, she would actually make me flex my creativity muscle. I know! She would have me take an abstract game like Tic-Tac-Toe, 20 Questions, Checkers, or Tetris and give it a storyline and then ask: Does the storyline make the game more compelling?"*[16] *Since I decided to channel Amy, I need to answer my own question. If only she were here to guide me!*

[16] "I played Liar's Dice with some school-age kids recently, which is a completely abstract dice game. They liked the game, but after a few rounds, one of them said, 'Let's pretend we are pirates playing for our souls!' which was greeted with enthusiasm all around the table" (Schell 2008, p. 263). In a similar vein, my children are playing a game that begins with a cut scene of aliens landing on earth. In the first level, they have to get one of the aliens through a series of mazes by giving it instructions using arrows. When they were three, my twins determined on their own that the point of getting "Blue Fuzz" through the mazes was so he could find his friends even though nowhere in the game does it say this. I just hope this is how it turns out, otherwise, my children will be very disappointed and sad for Blue Fuzz.

EXERCISE: Think of a game story for a game that does not have one. Now think of two more stories that would work for that game.

In responding to the challenge above, perhaps you came up with a fantastical storyline. Fantasy is great as long as it operates within the world of plausibility. We started off this section discussing creating a new reality, a new world. In order for people to suspend their disbelief, therefore believing in this new world, it must have internal logic:

> Writers are often taught to distinguish plausibility from possibility. When something is considered possible, it is capable of happening in the real world: planes may fly, but muscular men in a cape and tights alone cannot. However, in creative writing, you are free to suggest any kind of truth as long as it is plausible within the rules of the universe you've described in your fiction; there must be an explanation that makes sense in the particular context of the environment. As it relates to a player's map of the premise, we can view plausibility as the domain (area) of the player's map. When an object or situation is implausible, it is beyond the border of what the player can (or is willing to) map acceptably." (Rabin 2009, p. 122)

In other words, "A story does not have to be realistic, but it must be plausible" (Dickey 2011 p. 140). Let's compare these two premises by fourth graders in Kafai's 1995 *Game Design Project*, both intended to teach fractions:

> "You are a monkey. You are going to Island Snow. There are blue birds at a lake and a mountain. First go to the lake, then to the mountain. And last to the GOLDEN MOUNTAIN. You have to get the Golden Snow from the GOLDEN MOUNTAIN to cure the king monkey, Contrae, because he is sick. At the island, you will meet the monkey you just saw turned into a goon by the evil wizard. Use the arrow keys to move. He will ask you a fraction problem. If you get it wrong, you will become mentally deformed. Good Luck!!!"
>
> VERSUS
>
> "You want to go to the home of Zeus but the map was ripped up by the Greek God Hades. All of the Gods and Goddesses have a fraction of the map. You are to go to the Gods and goddesses one at a time and they will ask you a fraction problem. If you get it right, you will get a fraction of the map. When you get the whole map you will be at the gate of Zeus' home. The bull at the gate will ask you three hard fraction problems. If you get them right you will go inside Zeus' home and get to become the God or Goddess of Fractions and meet Zeus!" (from Kafai 1995, pp. xiv–xv)

Both are technically plausible, but if you can swap content in and out (e.g., in the Golden Mountain scenario, any type of content question could be asked and it would not change the nature of the game), the story pushes the edge of plausibility. There is no reason within the world described that questions would be asked about fractions. Remember that the content must be integral to game. To increase plausibility, you could have the protagonist figure out how to mix fractions of different chemicals to produce the medicine to cure Contrae. The wrong ratios could lead to Contrae getting sicker, have no effect on her illness, cause an explosion, and so forth. In the second story, the map being ripped into pieces does provide a stronger context for exploring fractions as the fractions of the map need to be reassembled into a whole; however, it still has the same "content swapping" aspect of the first one as the Gods and Goddesses could ask any content question. To make the content integral, focus the fraction problems on reassembling the map. It can be tempting to use story to dress up quizzes, such as having a "vocabulary battle" among teams of students. Instead, create tasks where students have to pull the information in order to accomplish something. For example, one of my students created a game about the Underground Railroad where the escaped slave has to decide whether or not to go to a Contraband Camp. Students may not know what a Contraband Camp is and would have to look that up (which could be a hint in the game or you could have them look it up externally) in order to make their decision. Having to know what a vocabulary word means to understand the directions creates an authentic reason for students to pull the information, making it much more likely students will remember it because it has context. Tasks where you push information onto students by having them memorize and regurgitate information do not.

Although the fraction game scenarios described above lacked content-game play coherence, the students were able to employ several aspects of narrative game spaces. Their premises constructed "microworlds" where the player is the protagonist with short- and long-term goals. However, you also want to consider the messages their stories told. In both, they also reflected students' attitudes toward fractions—that fractions are obstacles to overcome. As you develop your storylines, think about the messages they send. In this case, you would want a storyline where fractions are tools to help the protagonist think and achieve a goal, not obstacles to obtaining a goal.

There are various ways to use story to make your abstract diagrams concrete. One is to think about the contexts in which the story can be told. For example, *Cuckoo Time!* is a game which uses gears, pulleys, levers, and pendulums to teach elementary physics within the setting of a cuckoo clock. Schell (2008) described the theme of *Toontown* as "work v. play" so "the story of Toontown Online became a story of robot executives (the Cogs) trying to turn colorful Toontown into a dingy office park. The Toons team up to fight off the Cogs with gags and practical jokes, and the Cogs fight back with office supplies" (p. 55). If you want to create a game about waitressing, the theme might be balancing (e.g., balancing dishes, balancing customers, balancing bills), or maybe, you want to do a game about balance, so your story is about waitressing. Schell (2008) claims that "to truly communicate with someone, you must speak the language of their childhood" (p. 102). You might want to study the media of your students' childhood: What games did they play? Television shows/movies did they watch? Books did they read? You can always find this out with an interest survey. Whenever I pull out children's books to make an academic point, my students always perk up—no matter what age.

Another way to come up with a storyline is to do some "What if…?" exploration or have that be the core game mechanic itself. For example, what if the North had not intervened when the South seceded? What if Al Gore had become president instead of George Bush, Jr.? What if gravity acted as a centrifugal force instead of a centripetal one? What if we had wheels instead of feet? What if Romeo and/or Juliet had lived? What if the Earth lacked a magnetic field? What if dinosaurs never became extinct? This type of "counterfactual analysis" allows students to understand a system by changing its variables. While you may be concerned it teaches wrong history, science, etc., making it clear that this is hypothetical allows students to better understand the systems in their own reality. You can always use debriefing as a time to compare the game world to the real world.

Playing around with hypotheticals is a common English teacher trick used to highlight the impact of setting, plot sequence, pacing, character development, allusions, audience, etc., by having students explore what would happen if one of these aspects were changed. It would be interesting to create a game where students vary major story elements like the dials on an equalizer and, better yet, to have students create their own game where they do this. They could do this with a work of literature or even to create their own story. This would take my *Odysseus Order* game to a new level! Allowing students to experience something differently each time not only creates "play" but also gives insight into how the overall system operates.

Another way of using story is to come up with a concrete analogy for your system:

> metaphors play a crucial role in defining our shared understanding, and in turn, our concepts... Clever design benefits from metaphors in which the source domain (the one in which the metaphorical reasoning takes place) provides a utilitarian vehicle to reach the target domain (the subject matter). (Dempsey 2010, p. 99)

Using metaphors avoids the problem of players expecting a complete one-to-one match between the system in the game and reality:

> In fact, for many simulations, it might be best to avoid the notion of 'total fidelity.' It turns out that striving to reproduce complete reality has drawbacks. More notably, the more realistic the environment, the more likely the player will focus on the imperfections in the simulation rather than the substance of the game. (Hirumi and Hall 2011, p. 64)

This statement about simulating reality leading to a search for imperfections presumes the learner understands reality enough to make a comparison. When a learner does not, analogy allows the learner to connect new learning to prior understandings: "people learn through analogy by mapping relational structure from a concrete or relatively familiar domain to an abstract or relatively unfamiliar domain" (Reese 2010, p. 234). For example, I know how delivery trucks, packages, and garbage trucks work but I am struggling to understand how cholesterol works in my body. An explanation that begins with using my prior knowledge that oil and water do not mix to explain why cholesterol (oil) needs LDL apolipoprotein (delivery truck) to deliver its cargo (cholesterol) through blood/water to its destination (organs) and then HDL apolipoprotein (garbage truck) to pick up the excess cholesterol waste (garbage) and deliver it to the dump (LDL receptors in the liver) makes understanding how cholesterol works more accessible. As Noah Falstein, design columnist for *Game Developer* magazine, claims, "Most good ideas ... involve combining dissimilar things in novel ways" (quoted in Fullterton et al. 2004, p. 146). A participant in one of my studies described how using an analogy with a parking garage allowed his students to understand how electron clouds in atoms worked. Analogies make material accessible by creating bridges between the new content and students' prior knowledge.

Personifying the elements in your system is another way to use story to make the abstract concrete:

> Suppose that in a game world, we personify elements as people having characteristics analogous to their namesake elements. So we would have the muscle men Chromium, Manganese, and Iron, the attractive Chlorine, Fluorine, and Iodine, the Casanovas Lithium, Sodium and Potassium, the super rich Platinum, Gold, Silver, and Copper. A goal in this game might be to rescue Silver, who is being held hostage by the seductive Chlorine (the compound silver chloride, used in photographic paper)… the player could use a magic powder (free electrons) to sprinkle over Silver to reduce his attraction to Chlorine, so that he can be set free. …along the way the player would have to avoid the dangerous Arsenic and Plutonium, distracting Arsenic with Gallium, or using Lead as a shield from Plutonium's rays. (Levin and Kareev 1980, pp. 40–41 quoted in Greenfield 2010, p. 18)

One way to do this is to turn one of the elements of your system into a superhero. Following McGonigal's recipe for recovery after suffering from a concussion can help you develop a superhero story, as I have excerpted here:

> "**Mission #1**: Create your SuperBetter secret identity. You're the hero of this adventure. And you can be anyone you want, from any story you love….You're about to borrow their superpowers and play the leading role yourself. I chose Buffy the Vampire Slayer as my story line. That made me Jane the Concussion Slayer, and that made my symptoms the vampires, demons, and other forces of darkness I was destined by fate to battle against. The point of this mission is to start seeing yourself as powerful, not powerless.
>
> **Mission #2:** Recruit your allies. Every superhero has an inner circle of friends who help save the day. … it gives people who want to help, but don't know how, something specific and actionable to do… [and] achievements feel more meaningful when someone else gives them to you.
>
> **Mission #3**: Find the bad guys. To win this battle, you need to know what you're up against
>
> **Mission #4**: Identify your power-ups [items that enhance your abilities such as power pellets in *Pac Man*]
>
> **Mission #5:** Create your superhero to-do list. Not every mission is possible, but it doesn't hurt to dream big. Make a list of goals for yourself, ranging from things you're 100 % positive you can do right now to things you might not have been able to do even in your wildest dreams before you got sick or hurt. Everything on your list should be something that would make you feel awesome and show off your strengths." (McGonigal 2011, pp. 135–139)

For the mission in this book, I used "the chosen one" archetype. However, I just as easily could have used a "competition" storyline where teachers are competing to be chosen to go into the future. While I eschew games where content can be swapped, that is different from employing an archetype to structure your story. There are lots of archetypes you can tap into to help you create your story. Having students interview for a job, for example, as a NASA scientist as one of my students did for her game, easily allows you as game developer to test students' prior knowledge through the interview process, provides a natural gateway or chokepoint—that of being hired—gives you a reason to impart new knowledge through orientation, and then allows you to create a first task on the job where students have to apply that new knowledge. Common storylines like having students be private investigators, figure out how to survive after an apocalypse, fight off aliens, escape after being captured, time travel, recover memories after having amnesia, and so forth might provide a way to design content-based tasks. Movies can also be a good source for storylines. Since we are not creating commercial games to sell, teachers are covered by the "Fair Use" policy and thus can adopt and adapt freely. For example, Lee Sheldon (2011) points out that following curricular game story is very similar to "best-selling books and blockbuster movies":

> A game story could be built challenging students to uncover two secret societies intent on protecting, on the one hand, science, and on the other, art throughout the centuries. Arcane clues could be discovered in poems; strange connections between rhyming couplets and mathematical theories could emerge. And the ultimate realization for the class might be that a combination of the two could be the key to saving our civilization. (p. 248)

You should still give credit to your inspiration. This way students do not feel like you are unjustly ripping off an idea and you are modeling good citation habits. Feel free to steal ideas from games as well. For example, one of my students created a physics-based *Can you Escape?* game where each room required solving a physics problem to escape out of the room. A storyline surrounding this kind of game could involve an eccentric millionaire who set up these tests to see which of her heirs is worthy of her fortune or a devious criminal who takes pleasure in designing elaborate traps.

No matter which angle you take on developing your story, a large part in creating your story is to develop a goal, or a mission, much like the first step of determining your intended outcome in Backward Design:

> All games have a premise that ties together the environment and action, relying on a set of rules that the fictional universe will be bound to. The premise can be formed with just a few words. A fine example comes from the middle of the 1980s, when a player could sink a quarter into *Robotron: 2084* and, with five words, be transported into an understandable future place: "Save the last human family." It is impossible for a game to completely lack a setting, though it may be radically abstract with nothing for the mind to grasp—completely indescribable as a real place, but our minds are not so quick to fail us as is our language. Within the first few moments, a premise is forming in our minds whether the game is providing it for us, or we have to invent it on our own. We need context to guide our experiences and the mapping of our actions. The premise is the source of the game's individual context. (Rabin 2009, p. 121)

Because learning involves making sense of our environment by attending to and interacting with elements within that environment in order to achieve a goal (such as resolving cognitive dissonance) and testing new understandings by interpreting feedback, goals drive what we do and how we learn within an environment. For example, after hearing that *Green Eggs and Ham* by Dr. Seuss was actually about the Cold War, I read the same book very differently than before in order to resolve the cognitive dissonance between viewing *Green Eggs and Ham* as a silly children's book and this new information that it is a serious historical commentary. Because I had a specific goal, in this case answering my own question about how *Green Eggs and Ham* is an analogy for the Cold War, I attended to different details, such as the indecipherable text on a newspaper that resembles the Russian alphabet, and interpreted aspects symbolically such as the color green as representing American money/capitalism. Therefore, the goals you set in your storyline shape what players attend to and learn from the game. Oftentimes a story or a game's premise involves "an event that upsets the status quo" (Fullterton et al. 2004, p. 91), in which case the goal is to reestablish the status quo. Keep in mind too, each player could have a different set of goals such as a predator and prey within an ecological system.

Many games (as opposed to simulations) declare the first person to reach a goal the "winner" and the rest of the players as "losers." However, the New Games Movement of the late sixties and early seventies challenged this notion. The goal of the New Games Movement was to create games that were noncompetitive. If you have ever held the edge of a parachute and, along with the other players, used the parachute to bounce a ball, you have the New Games Movement to thank. For our purposes, all students who reach the goal should be considered winners, no matter how much scaffolding or time they require.[17]

The conflict is what prevents the protagonist from easily obtaining the goal: "there should always be some element that works against player success" (Salen and Zimmerman 2004, p. 387). Remember from English class, conflict is not just person v. person, it can also be person v. nature/environment, mind v. body, person v. government, person v. self, and so forth. Person v. self can entail someone's own lack of knowledge, a conflict within someone's value system, someone's lack of skill, etc. One way to make an internal conflict explicit is to create cognitive dissonance. For example, if someone has a stereotype that gay people are promiscuous, stories about long-standing gay relationships create cognitive dissonance (although I have found that, in order to keep stereotypes intact, people often label this contradictory evidence "an exception to the rule"). It is the conflict that drives the storyline: "When game conflict provides a narrative context for action, your players will help you tell your game's story, infusing their own actions with narrative meaning" (Salen and Zimmerman 2004, p. 388). Schell (2008) describes how this is employed in the movie industry:

> It is an old maxim of Hollywood screenwriting that the main ingredients for a story are (1) A character with a goal and (2) obstacles that keep him from reaching his goal. As the character tries to overcome the obstacles, interesting conflicts tend to arise, particularly when another character has a conflicting goal. This simple pattern leads to very interesting stories because it means the character has to engage in problem-solving (which we find very interesting), because conflicts lead to unpredictable results, in other words, surprises (which we find very interesting,), and because the bigger the obstacle, the bigger the potential for dramatic change (which we find very interesting). (Schell 2008, pp. 270–271)

Every system has a reason to run, i.e., a goal. Think about what might happen within or outside your system that can make that goal harder to achieve, i.e., the obstacles. That is your conflict.

Although the lines between simulations and games may be blurred, having specific challenges along the way to achieving a goal can gamify a simulation. For example, I designed my English methods class as a simulation—students role-played

[17] This challenges the old notion that grades should reward students who achieve something the fastest or the easiest or within a certain time period and instead introduces a performance-based model where the assumption is that every student will eventually be able to achieve a skill and should be rewarded for doing so, regardless of how long it takes.

both a teacher and a student. Students had much success and some fun along the way, and this version garnered my highest course evaluation rating in my history of teaching that course. Still, I was not satisfied. Although it had game elements, I felt it was not quite a game. Although I feared that I might take something good and mess it up by trying to make it better, I felt compelled to add challenges with very concrete goals in order to gamify this class. Now students still role-play a teacher and a student, but they do so in order to complete challenges with very specific goals, such as getting another student to pass a quiz after tutoring him or her in a new language. Just as in video games, students get the opportunity to try and try again until they succeed. They cannot move on to the next challenge until the previous one is accomplished. This type of storyline is called "rivers and lakes" or "string of pearls"[18] since players have to go down a linear path (i.e., achieve a specific goal) in order to access the next lake/pearl or exploratory environment.

I have been using the terms "goal" and "challenge" pretty interchangeably; however, "According to Crawford (2003), 'the point is the challenge, not the goal' (p. 38). Going to the grocery stor[e] is a goal, but it is not normally a challenge" (Swan 2010, p. 112). What makes something a challenge is when there are constraints. If you are not worried about your wealth or health, it is a goal. However, limiting resources and/or setting conditions, in this grocery store scenario operating within a tight budget or shopping for your child's newly diagnosed diabetes, makes something like going to the grocery store a challenge. A common constraint is limiting resources:

> The limitation of resources presents a possible barrier to the player's progress in the game. It introduces another element of risk or uncertainty in the game. For example, players may wonder whether to use the resource now, whether they will need the resource later, or whether they will find more of the resource when they need it. Thus, the judicious design of resources is another way to shape challenge and conflict. (Swan 2010, p. 114)

Remember that resources do not have to be objects; they can include health, experience, safety, and so forth. There are also teacher-controlled resources. For example, some teachers use "homework passes" as incentives that students can use judiciously or wantonly. Think, though, about the messages these "rewards" can send. In this case, a homework pass signals that homework is not essential and that doing homework is an unwanted chore. Choose your rewards/resources wisely.

Keep in mind our rule about relating everything to your theme: "A meaningful challenge is defined as an attainable goal of endogenous value [i.e., that has meaning within the system of the game] that entails conflict constrained by operational rules and limited resources" (Swan 2010, pp. 112–113). Your story creates this endogenous value, i.e., gives the challenge meaning, by setting an attainable goal, engendering conflict, setting conditions/rules, and limiting resources. Some of these aspects of the storyline you may want to make explicit (e.g., having a short video or

---

[18] Some gamers may pejoratively call this "railroading," i.e., forcing players to go down a certain path. Although this can be a way teachers can ensure all students learn the required material, it is good to keep in mind balancing free play and directed play.

animation (i.e., a cut scene) where a nonplaying character (NPC) directly states the goal), some discoverable (e.g., players might figure out a rule by testing something), and some attainable (e.g., players might unlock additional resources by solving a puzzle). Of course, you decide which is which. You might even make the goal discoverable (e.g., in the video game *Portal*, the protagonist is dropped "in media res" (in the middle of the action) and has to figure out what the goal is) or the rules attainable (e.g., after achieving a level, an NPC states a hidden rule). The trick is figuring out which should be which and balancing them. If the whole story is explicit, then it is a story and not a game. If every aspect of the story is only discoverable, players may quickly reach a frustration level that turns them off of the game or may not discover the story at all.[19]

All of this talk of "missions" and "challenges" or "quests" might remind you of hero stories. Joseph Campbell's *Hero with a Thousand Faces* explores the hero archetype in depth. Christopher Vogler, a writer and producer in Hollywood, summed up Campbell's hero archetype in his book *The Writer's Journey*, which Schell (2008) sums up in his book *The Art of Game Design*:

1. **The Ordinary World**—Establishing scenes that show our hero is a regular person leading an ordinary life.
2. **The Call to Adventure**—The hero is presented with a challenge that disrupts their ordinary life.
3. **Refusal of the Call**—The hero makes excuses about why he can't go on the adventure.
4. **Meeting with the Mentor**—Some wise figure gives advice, training, or aid.
5. **Crossing the Threshold**—The hero leaves the ordinary world (often under pressure) and enters the adventure world.
6. **Tests, Allies, Enemies**—The hero faces minor challenges, makes allies, confronts enemies, and learns the workings of the adventure world.
7. **Approaching the Cave**—The hero encounters setbacks and needs to try something new.
8. **The Ordeal**—The hero faces a peak life or death crisis.
9. **The Reward**—The hero survives, overcomes their fear, and gets the reward.
10. **The Road Back**—The hero returns to the ordinary world, but the problems still aren't all solved.
11. **Resurrection**—The hero faces a still greater crisis, and has to use everything he has learned.
12. **Returning with the Elixir**—The journey is now well and truly complete, and the hero's success has improved the lives of everyone in the ordinary world. (pp. 273–274)

In Joseph Campbell's interview with Bill Moyers, he shows how *Star Wars* fits this archetype, but I will use a more contemporary example to point out aspects of the hero archetype: *Finding Nemo*, a movie about a clown fish, Marlin, who is trying

[19] Lee Sheldon (2004) provides an example of game players complaining about the lack of story in *EverQuest*, while the game designers countered that the players just hadn't discovered it yet.

to find his son, Nemo. In a typical hero story, the hero starts in ordinary world (e.g., Marlin taking Nemo to school) but gets a "call to adventure" where the hero has to go into an unfamiliar world (both Nemo in challenging his dad and venturing into the open sea and Marlin in finding his son); the hero experiences several tests/challenges/trials (both Nemo (using pebble to block the filter in the fish tank) and Marlin (facing sharks, riding the current, going through the jellyfish tentacles, etc.)) on the way and may or may not have assistance (Nemo has his fellow fish tank mates and Marlin has a fish he encounters on his journey named Dory); the hero faces the ultimate challenge (getting Nemo out of the fish tank in the dentist office) in order to get the final reward (father and son being reunited); and the hero returns a changed person or, in this case, fish (Marlin and Nemo both gain self-confidence and Marlin learns to trust his son).

CHALLENGE 4.3: "Ok, I flexed my creativity muscle, but I'm still no closer to coming up with a story," you think. "WWAD? Well, I already know WWAS (What Would Amy Say?): 'game designing is stealing'—taking others' ideas and adapting them. I would always respond 'just like teaching'. Now that I think of it, really, all of literature is stealing too! What was that quote about all texts really just being remixes?" (Erstad 2008). Anyway, I'm sure Amy would have me make a chart and identify the elements of the hero archetype in at least two different stories (e.g., The Hobbit, Odysseus, *and* The Matrix[20]). *She encourages creativity but she also recognizes the importance of structure. However, I don't think she would want structure to get in the way of creativity. One of my students once used the phrase 'loose fitting tool.'* That seems appropriate here as there might not be a perfect fit for every single aspect. Once done, you look at your charts and say to yourself, "WWAT? What Would Amy Think?

EXERCISE: Identify different elements of the hero archetype in at least two different stories.

Placing a learner in the position of being a hero can change his or her mindset: "If you can convince them they are on a hero's journey, they can begin to see obstacles as challenges, and choose behaviors more befitting a hero than a victim. Change their story and you change their behavior" (Simmons 2001, pp. 38–39). Think about the impact this might have on students. Instead of seeing themselves as victims subject to a curriculum (and standardized tests) that are done *to* them, students can start to see themselves as having agency to learn and to change their world. Some people tend to have an internal locus of control, a feeling that their efforts make a difference in their lives and the lives of others, while others have an external locus of control, a feeling that no matter what they do, they cannot control their fate. There are several self-quizzes online you can take to ascertain your locus of control, although I would caution that it probably changes depending on the context. People with an internal locus of control, i.e., sense of agency, tend to be more successful in school and in life (Driscoll, 2005, p. 312). Studies on effort-based teaching have

[20]According to Schell (2008) the writers of *The Matrix*, are said to have used Vogler's book as a guide.

demonstrated the positive impact of agency on learning (Resnick and Hall 2005). When students' actions make a difference in the game world, they start to develop a sense of agency in their own world and view learning as a result of effort, what Carol Dweck (2007) calls a "growth mindset."

You might worry that following this hero archetype might make your story seem cliché. However, clichés, stereotypes, schemas, allusions, symbols, archetypes, and so forth can help you easily introduce backstory without spending a lot of time telling, what Mateas and Stern (2006) call "evoked narratives" (p. 673). When you have an NPC with an eye patch and parrot on his shoulder, you don't have to explain that this NPC operates outside the law because most people will conjure up all their pirate associations. Furthermore, as Schell (2008) points out:

> clichés have the tremendous advantage of being familiar to the player, and what is familiar is understandable and comprehensible. It has been said that every successful videogame finds a way to combine something familiar with something novel. Some designers would never make a game about ninjas, because ninjas have been done to death. But what if you made a story about a lonely ninja, or an incompetent ninja, a ninja dog, a robotic ninja, or a third grade girl who leads a secret life as a ninja? All of these storylines have the potential to be something new and different, while having a hook into a world the player already understands. (pp. 279–280)

Remember that all stories are really just mash-ups of other stories: "the author is simply a collaborator with other writers, citing them and reworking their ideas" (Diakopoulos 2005, quoted in Erstad 2008, p. 189). Do not be afraid to tap into these cultural gold mines.

Once you've written out your backstory, rip it to shreds. Ok, not literally, but we are going to parse it out. One thing traditional schooling has gotten wrong is the impulse to tell the backstory first:

> The backstory, which consists of all relevant parts of the story that occurred prior to the story opening, is often an important part of whom a character is and why he is where he is and why he has to do what he has to do. However, uncovering a backstory can be tricky. It is often instinctive for a writer to want to present the audience with the backstory all at once in the beginning. Doesn't the player need to know these details to understand the story? Usually not. Oftentimes, giving it all to them at the beginning backfires, and the audience winds up feeling dumped upon and wonders why they are given all this information about a person they have yet to care about. It is equivalent to hearing your Aunt Myrtle drone on and on about a childhood friend. The audience is left thinking "so what," and this is not a good way to grab attention. It also has the effect of ruining the suspense. Part of the mystery is discovering what led the player to be in his current predicament. It is okay for the audience not to know, and, in fact, it is intriguing to them. It causes them to ask questions and then want to know answers, further engaging them. Another problem with presenting the backstory at the beginning is that the player doesn't know what details are important to focus on, or what details are important from the backstory. This means that key information presented here isn't always absorbed and is often quickly forgotten. Instead, it is preferable to drop a player in the middle of the action, engaging him immediately, and then have the backstory unfold through plot and narrative elements. This is especially true in games, where the impatient player wants to get right to the action. Though many games in the past have used cinematic cut scenes at the beginning of a game, this is not always the best place for them, as they often go ignored. Some players do enjoy this, so it is okay to include them, but just allow the player the option of skipping the cut scene and make sure that any essential information in the cut scene is given to the player in another form elsewhere. Don't

> forget that in games, unlike written stories, the story is there to serve the game and that the goal is active engagement and interactivity, not passive absorption. So, if there are details from the past that the player needs to know to understand the storyline, allow those details to be uncovered through active gameplay. For example, if you need the player to know that he is an orphan, have him meet someone who describes how his parents die. If he is in a destroyed city that was brought down 20 years ago in an alien attack, have clues in the environment, such as signs, posters, radio broadcasts, city alerts, and anything that is natural within the environment. *BioShock* does a good job of this in uncovering the details of what happened in the city, Rapture, prior to the start of the game. You can also add NPCs that say things like "Yes, ever since our city was destroyed by aliens 20 years ago, fresh water has been hard to find." This way, the player learns about the backstory actively and while engaged, instead of passively absorbing it. (Rabin 2009, p. 150)

My original mission text read: "*The year is 2180. World War III has devastated the planet. Those left are fighting to preserve their culture, knowledge, and skills. Despite having experts, because all sides of the war targeted teachers since they were seen as cultural gatekeepers, there are no teachers left to teach the next generation, and the experts are rapidly dying off. The content matter experts have tried, but their complete lack of teaching ability leaves everyone frustrated: 'Though experts know their disciplines thoroughly, this does not guarantee that they are able to teach others' (Bransford et al. 2000, p. 31). Out of desperation, the Commander of the free world commissioned an elite group of scientists to build a time machine to bring a teacher back to the future. She appointed a group of historians to decide who to bring back. After poring over the remaining historical documents, the historians have chosen you based on your superior reputation as a teacher. Your mission is to develop a curricular tool which will engage and teach future generations and serve as a model for the content matter experts to emulate. This involves finding the elusive Holy Grail of education*—transfer—*or applying learning to new situations. The text that follows along with the embedded quests will help you achieve your mission.*"

Notice this first version involves "telling" ("gamers hate telling" (Prensky 2002, p. 10)). My second version does a better job of showing:

As you clean up your classroom, ending another exhausting but exhilarating day of teaching, you put hard copies of the latest educational standards you are expected to adhere to in your satchel as well as the book How People Learn *that your principal expects all teachers to read and throw your satchel over your shoulder. You hear a noise and look up. Before you, an apparition appears, stating boldly: "You are needed in the future." You look around and pinch yourself to make sure you are not dreaming. Before you know it, you are transported to what appears to be a "messy closet" masquerading as an office. You look around and notice the walls are covered with elaborate maps and a desk is littered with blueprints and schematics. You find yourself thinking, "This is not the clean, sterile space-age buildings sci-fi movies promised!" A woman behind a desk peers at you intently and starts to speak in a manner that does resemble sci-fi movies, briskly and bluntly:*

> *The year is 2180. World War III has devastated the planet. Those of us who are left are fighting to preserve our culture, knowledge, and skills. Since teachers were seen as cultural gatekeepers, all sides of the war targeted them, thus there are no teachers left to teach the next generation. The Expert Elders have tried to pass their knowledge on, but their complete*

> *lack of teaching ability leaves everyone frustrated. Out of desperation, I, the Commander of the Free World, commissioned an elite group of Engineering Elders to build a time machine to bring a teacher back to the future and a group of Historian Elders to decide who to bring back. After poring over the remaining historical documents, the Historian Elders have chosen you based on your superior reputation as a teacher. Your* **mission** *is to develop a curricular tool which will engage and teach future generations and serve as a model for the Expert Elders to emulate. This involves finding the elusive Holy Grail of education*—expertise and transfer. *Good skill.*

"Whoah," you think, "Me, the savior of the future?" You decide to approach this as you approach teaching—breaking the abstract notion of teaching into concrete, doable actions.

You may have picked up on some of the initial text appearing in the second version. However, I employed the trick of having an NPC say this, instead of an omniscient, abstract narrator, in order to embed some telling inside the showing.

Remember you do not want to "show" everything; "game narrative is by definition incomplete: 'It must be in order to leave room for the player to bring it to fruition' (Pearce 2004, p. 146)" (Van Eck 2007, pp. 296–297). Starting "mis-en-scene" (in the middle of the scene or plot) is a good way to create suspense by making the initial goal figuring out the goal. For example, my children play a game that starts off with the main character/player running away from flying monkeys. This incites the player to ask several questions: Why is he running away from the flying monkeys? What did he do to provoke them/why are they attacking him? Is his goal simply survival or is there a larger goal? Where is he? Who is he? You do want to make sure, however, that the meaning/objective becomes clear at some point or at least provide a clue early on (e.g., finding a hidden note) that points to an objective; otherwise, "the players roam around but have no idea where they're supposed to go or what they're supposed to do" (Fullerton et al. 2004, pp. 287–288).

One way to avoid the roaming player syndrome (something I have definitely experienced as a game player!) is to begin not just "mis-en-scene," but "in media res" (in the middle of the action) with what Rabin (2009) terms an "inciting incident" (p. 144), an event that calls the hero/protagonist to action: "For many gamers, if they are not drawn in within the first 10 min, they are lost and may not choose to ever attempt to play the game again. This means beginning the game with immediate action and conflict. It can be brief and minor, but ideally, there should be an immediate obstacle for the player to overcome right from the outset" (Rabin 2009, p. 144). This is similar to having a "hook" when teaching a lesson, except that the consequences for not figuring out the game "hook" can be dire or at least the player needs to feel that is the case. Keep in mind that, just like every lesson needs its own hook, each game level needs its own "inciting incident."

There are several ways to reveal the story as the game progresses. After a challenge is completed, you can reward players by revealing more of the storyline. Parsing out the story motivates players to continue playing:

> The story also provides the player with the motivation to continue playing and a reason to press forward through game obstacles. The player is continually rewarded with uncovering new parts of the story as he plays the game. This maintains his sense of immersion and creates a more fulfilling game experience. (Rabin 2009, p. 140)

"Cut scenes," or in-game mini videos, are one way to do this. I have played video games with computer monitors strewn throughout with messages left from the past (or sometimes the future), often from the people who were there and now are missing and the player has to figure out why. You can also have NPCs tell more of the story. Or you can have the protagonist find a journal (another common video game feature) or some other clue (e.g., a newspaper article which, of course, can be strategically torn to create more "missing information"). You can also employ the "Fog of War" where players can only see their immediate surroundings, thus creating a sense of uncertainty and forcing them to remember previously visited terrain. In terms of your curricular game, there are lots of non-tech or low-tech ways to do this which we will discuss in much more detail later. For now, just think about how you can slowly reveal information to create suspense.

Of course, you need to hint that information is concealed to motivate your learners, just like authors do to create suspense. For example, saying "squirrels are *usually* timid…" (Simmons 2001, p. 98) makes a reader wonder what this brazen squirrel did. Delaying information ("I heard something yesterday that made me want to give Martin a big old bear hug (pause) …") (Simmons 2001, p. 102), saying something incongruous or not explained "I would speak up but I don't want to get labeled with the 'A-word'" (Simmons 2001, p. 78), or anything that leaves a reader wondering what will happen next creates "cliffhangers" and the desire to continue in order to find out the outcome.

One game designer describes this as "engineer[ing] 'memorable moments'" (Squire 2011, p. 89). Sometimes we as teachers "engineer teachable moments," but all too often they take us by surprise, and we have to make the snap decision of whether or not we have time to discuss the "AIDS is a punishment by God" comment by one of our students (a comment one of my students made when I taught high school) or move on with what we had planned. There will probably be surprising "teachable moments" in your game-based curriculum; however, planning "memorable moments" can help cement learning. For example, one of my students "LOVED" the "trick" in one of my courses where both choices led to the same outcome with an attendant explanation. I have also had students express surprise and excitement at discovering the various "Easter eggs," or hidden information, I dispersed throughout my curricular game. One student told me she was so pleased with herself, she could not help but brag to her boyfriend. I still remember when I was so frustrated in a video game because I could not figure out what to do next. I had opened the doors to a building, walked in, clicked on every object in the room, and explored every nook and cranny. After hours of frustration, I did the one thing I had not done—close the doors to the building I was in—from the inside. When I did, I saw that there were secret tunnels hidden behind the doors, tunnels that were concealed when the front doors were open. This was a memorable moment—one that actually transferred to real life when I went to stay at a friend's condo and realized that what I was seeing inside did not fit the footprint of the building when I walked around the outside. After investigating, I discovered that behind the open front door which could only open so far due to the proximity of the refrigerator was an entryway to a bedroom. Discovery is the essence of all mystery stories and really all stories. For example, in the children's story *Detective Blue*, the fact that Goldilocks and Miss Muffet are the same person (Miss Goldilocks Muffet) is not revealed until nearly the end of the story, causing the babysitter of my children to issue an audible "ahhhh" when she got to this point.

This element of surprise capitalizes on the optimal behavioral maintenance system[21] by providing information at random (or after achieving something which can feel random because you do not know when the next time might be) to get rush of dopamine. It is the "not knowing" when you might get another one that compels players/learners forward. For example, in the popular television show *Jeopardy*, players do not know which square contains the "Daily Doubles" where contestants have the opportunity to double the amount of their points, creating this element of surprise.

Gee (2007) refers to parsing out information like this as providing it "just in time," i.e., "when the learner can use it" (p. 24). However, sometimes you want to provide some information "just before time." For example, I moved noticing the blueprints, maps, etc., on the Commander's wall to when you first enter the office instead of during the second exchange. During the second exchange would be "just in time," but, by putting it before, the reader may think of the fact that she is a visual learner before the character does. If not, when the character does, the reader thinks, "Of course! I should have noticed the clues," giving the sense that learners can be more active players instead of passively ingesting a story. There are other instances where you might want to put information "just after time" to give the learner a chance to figure it out on his or her own.

Learners, however, should have enough of the backstory (what English teachers call "exposition") in the first stage of a game before moving on to the "rising action." The rising action usually consists of several related and increasingly difficult tasks. Rabin (2009) warns, though, that you don't want to "send the character out on meaningless, empty quests to fill time" (Rabin 2009, p. 144), i.e., "busy work." Fullerton et al. (2004) describe how the video game *Donkey Kong* creates rising action:

> In *Donkey Kong*, Mario is the protagonist. Mario's girlfriend, Pauline, has been kidnapped by the giant ape, Donkey Kong, and taken to the top of a building under construction. Mario's goal is to save Pauline before time runs out. To do so, he must climb the levels of the building, traversing girders, elevators, and conveyer belts, while avoiding flames, barrels, and bouncing rivets thrown at him by Donkey Kong. Each time Mario reaches Pauline, Donkey Kong grabs her and carries her off to the next higher level. Each level builds in difficulty, creating rising tension for the player. (p. 101)

As you can see, in this case every time the player thinks he or she has reached the goal, the goal line is moved. Although this creates frustration, Gee (2007) explains that it is "pleasant frustration" (p. 36) as the player is continually challenged within their zone of proximal development (Vygotsky 1978), i.e., challenge zone, creating what Czikszentmihalyi (1990) calls "flow."

[21] B.F. Skinner found in his studies on operant conditioning, or influencing behavior through a system of rewards and punishments, that after associating a reward with a behavior, offering that reward after a random number of times was the most optimal way to maintain that behavior.

All this leads up to the climax or "boss level," where the player has to prove him or herself: "Finally, in the climax of the game, Mario must not only avoid Donkey Kong's attacks, but also fight him directly by [figuring out that] removing all the rivets on every floor of the level [will topple him]. After the rivets are removed, Donkey Kong falls head first onto a stack of girders and is knocked out, allowing Mario to rescue Pauline and resolve both the formal and dramatic tension." (Fullerton et al. 2004, p. 101). The "boss" consists of a foe, real or metaphorical, that contains all the skills of the previous foes in one "boss." This is often a win or lose all situation, or at least game designers want to make it feel this way: "Players expect this portion of the narrative to be intense and worth the investment they have given up to this point. This means the stakes should be high and the drama intense. The players need to feel like they have won. It is up to the writer to make sure that the clues and story elements that lead to this moment make sense and that it connects to the rest of the story" (Rabin 2009, p. 145). For example, the television show *Jeopardy* employs the possibility of a "dramatic reversals of fortune" (LeBlanc 2004/2006, p. 451) in the climax of the game, Final Jeopardy, where players can bet any value from zero to the amount earned on the final clue.

"Rubber banding" is an algorithm from racing games where if a player gets too far ahead, the speed of the computer-controlled cars increases to catch up so the player does not lose excitement or the player gets special tools to use like in *Mario Kart*. Rubber banding is one way to build up the rising action. The reality television show *Amazing Race* used to have time stamps, but did away with that in favor of which place teams were in. By doing so, producers could use the editing process to create the illusion of teams battling it out. This is also called "handicapping" or "negative feedback system" where the game is designed to try to keep the distance among players (or between the player and the game system) as close to zero as possible in order to create dramatic tension through dramatic uncertainty. In this way, the outcome feels close, like a tossup, and it "assures that the climax occurs late in the game, at a moment when one player's lead is large enough—and the time left in the game is short enough—that the feedback system cannot bring the players together before the end of the game" so creates the "dramatic arc" and can use a positive feedback system to bring on the climax if the game stagnates (Le Blanc, 2004/2006, pp. 448–449).

After the climax is the resolution. It is at this point that everything should come together and make sense. Sometimes authors employ "deus ex machina" ("god from a machine"),[22] where someone or something enters at the end of a story to resolve the conflict. This final explanation in good books, and good games, should make the reader/player want to go back and reread/replay the game with this new enlightenment. In your case, it can be revealing all the inner workings of your system.

You may be concerned that your game story sounds "cheesy" or "lame." Remember, though, that your students are not comparing your curricular game to commercial off-the-shelf (COTS) games or even to the latest blockbuster movie.

[22] From a practice in Greek tragedies where a god or goddess would enter the stage by a machine (a crane or a trapdoor) in order to resolve the conflict at the end of a play

They are comparing it to the teaching they have already experienced which, most likely, was not "storified." I asked my students directly if they thought the game story in this book was cheesy. They said that it made the material more interesting and that they looked forward to the next installment because it broke up the "textbook" portion of the text. Trust me that students will appreciate your efforts and may even contribute details to your game story or even write one of their own!

The quest for this section of the chapter directs you to create a storyboard for your game story complete with boxes for each scene of the action and dialogue bubbles to represent the main point of the scene. In other words, create a comic strip of your story. While it may be fun to use fancy software to storyboard your story and you are of course welcome to do so, keep in mind the recursive nature of this process. You will be making changes to your game story as you design quests, figuring out how everything fits together, and revising it to make it doable in your classroom context. The number one advice my students had for future students was to not spend time creating a fancy storyboard with comic strip software, particularly if you have to learn the software. Instead, they suggested either writing out your game story or drawing it out by hand and scanning it into the computer or taking a picture of it. While some of my students created really elaborate digital storyboards and had fun doing so, they realized in retrospect that the technology got in the way because the time they spent figuring out the technology could have been spent on the game story itself. They also got frustrated because they ended up making so many changes to their game story that changing their digital storyboard to reflect those changes would have been extremely time-consuming. Unless you are already facile at using comic strip or storyboarding software or plan to use this for your curricular game, I suggest saving the technological learning curve for rendering the game itself.

Branching Section of Story Quest

You stand back and look at what you have done so far. You smile with satisfaction but then your smile begins to fade. You realize you've created a great movie, but it is a linear causal chain. You ask yourself, "where is the game in this?" Reflecting on what you've read about video games, you realize the crucial element is that the player is in the story, directing the action, or at least the player's actions are affecting the direction of the story. You think back to the Choose Your Own Adventure[23] *series you read as a kid where you would read until faced with a decision and then jump to the page the text directed you to based on your decision. You smile fondly as you recall marking each page as you read through to make sure you followed every possible path and the one time you thought you had but noticed there was a page without a tick mark! Your need to exhaust all possibilities kicked in as you traced back to figure out the path you missed. You then recall another children's book series,* Encyclopedia Brown, *where the reader is challenged to solve mysteries*

[23] Jenkins (2004/2006) calls *Choose Your Own Adventure* books "lifeless [with] mechanical exposition" (p. 671). Perhaps this is true in comparison with today's video games, but they certainly offer the reader opportunities to direct the narrative in ways other books do not.

faced by Encyclopedia Brown. You even remember some of them, like the one where a character claims to have just returned from somewhere, yet Encyclopedia Brown observes a baby playing on the hood of the car. You have to turn the page to read the conclusion—that the character must be lying because otherwise the hood of the car would be too hot for a baby to be playing on it if the car had just been driven. So Choose Your Own Adventure *meets* Encyclopedia Brown. *Now you have a place to begin. But how to depict this?*

> *IF you decided to storyboard your story, THEN you think, "Let's see. I'm really creating a decision tree. Hmm, like a flowchart! I can use boxes to represent events, diamonds to represent decisions, and lines with labels indicating the decision path." You start converting your storyboard into a flowchart, much like your systems diagram, but this time shrouded in story.*
>
> *ELSE: You take your narrative and write out the choices as IF-THEN, ELSE statements.*

ACTION: Either draw a flowchart or use IF-THEN, ELSE statements to branch your story.

Part III: Branching Your Story

A good game is a series of interesting choices.

–Sid Meier, creator of *Civilization*

To reconstruct your storyboard or your written narrative, go back to your diagrams and find the leverage points. Think about "what if…" scenarios and alternative paths, competing goals, and so forth. For example, one of my students took a work of fiction, identified different decisions that the protagonist made throughout, and thought through what might have happened if the protagonist had made different decisions. In doing so, she provided historical evidence for the consequences of taking alternative paths. What she did was to create a branching narrative.[24]

You should be thinking, "Whoah, branching can get exponentially complex pretty quickly!" Yes, if you imagine a branching tree where limbs never intersect. BUT, you can have forced intersections where two or more storylines converge. You can do this through false choices, by introducing a nonfactor variable (something that players may think is a factor but is not OR something that typically would be, but mediating circumstances make it a nonfactor), by creating an intervention that leads players back to another path, etc. You can also have dead ends. You may even build in an option to "start over" or, as my twins would often say when they were two, "try again," a saying from their first video game (what the crabs say when the player fails to launch them into their shells in *Ima the Iguana*). You can also have players die but return as ghosts or in dreams or the players can continue playing as ghosts or zombies and so forth. You can have students who have completed a task serve as advisors or even judges on

[24] According to Barab (2012): "Simply providing critical decisions... within a story... seems to foster commitment to the activities in ways that narratively immutable curriculum does not... [as] students' responses . . . involved audible gasps when they witnessed the consequences of their choices" (pp. 317–323).

that task until all students complete it, thus "rubberbanding" game play to resolve the problem of some students proceeding much faster than others. You can also have players "save" a game state so he/she can return to it later. In this way, you are developing a "game [that] evolve[s] in response to our choices" (Squire 2011, p. 22):

> The difference from a linear story is that the audience has agency as the player and the experience arc is "specified by rules and not events" (Crawford, 2003). Instead of a linear plot, it becomes a dynamic "metaplot" where the player participates in the unfolding sequence of problems and obstacles that develop characters and forwards [the] story. Instead of linear plot points placed by the author, the influence of the audience gains meaning through interactions with the game to compel and not disrupt the story or game flow. … the challenge lies with the author to create a journey that reaches the same emotional waypoints as a linear plot, but the audience is allowed to reach them in their own way. (Stapleton and Hughes 2003 quoted in Hirumi and Stapleton 2008, pp. 148–149)

The "emotional waypoints" can be the movements from one level to the next. Rich Hilleman, from *Electronic Arts*, says that an average game playing session is about an hour, which is a common amount of time in a class period in the United States. Hilleman explains that "designers plan 'mini-arcs' of about one hour into the overall game progress. … At the end of each mini-arc, the designers try to make sure the player encounters a 'memorable moment' of gameplay" (quoted in Fullerton et al. 2004, p. 285). One way to think about your game is to think of each level as a subplot in the overall plot of your game.

To create this effect, you can design your game so that the decisions (or at least the ones that do not end in "game over") all lead to the same challenge that all players have to complete in order to move to the next level. Rabin (2009) describes how some game designers accomplish this:

> The spine of the game consists of all of the narrative elements that are absolutely necessary for the player to experience in order to complete the game. The game can have many side plots and subquests; however, in the spine are only the plot points that the player must pass through to progress in the game. Along with the spine is the golden path. The golden path is the optimum path a player would take through the game in order to experience the game as intended and to experience the maximum rewards. It is the duty of the writer to encourage the player to stay on the golden path and force him to return to the spine, without making it feel unnatural. The player needs to know the reason to move to the next area and perform the next task. It doesn't work to merely tell the player, "now move onto the library," or "now kill the emperor," without giving him a reason to do so. The writer must provide appropriate motivation for the player to execute the next task. (Rabin 2009, p. 152)

In this way mastery (game play) is rewarded by meaning (narrative). Beware, though, if the funneling back to one path becomes too obvious or too forced, players might feel "railroaded," a term some gamers use to describe feeling like they are forced to take a certain action. One way to avoid this is to allow players to explore future environments but lack the skills or resources to do anything. After wandering/wondering around, they then can return to a previous area where they can take action. You could also have two (or more) protagonists played by teams of students. In order to find the golden path, both teams need to make the correct decision. This introduces some uncertainty since failure could mean both teams were wrong or just one team, but you do not know which one. Another pitfall that teachers can fall into is to turn following the golden path into getting the correct answer on a multiple choice-type questions. While you may have some recall tasks built into the game, you want as many performance tasks as possible. In your branched narrative you will probably have some dead ends, and you may have an optimal path, but you do want your players to have some leeway so building alternative paths that still lead to the same gateways to the next level is ideal.

Not every game, however, has a golden path or even a spine. You can design a game where there are multiple successful paths or even where the order of the episodes does not matter ("modular storytelling" (Rabin 2009)):

> Imagine, for example, a 10-day vacation. Each day of the vacation, something new and interesting happens. It really doesn't matter in which order the days happen. Each day is a story in and of itself, and they add up to one large experience, or story, called a vacation. (Rabin 2009, p. 148)

Foreign language teachers could design a game where students choose where to go on vacation or, more interestingly, pretend to go on vacation while hiding from your family that you are actually on a secret mission. Each location poses a different challenge where students have to use the target language accurately enough to pass the challenge, and doing so could reveal a new clue.

You can make the goal of the game creating the narrative ("chaotic story" (McGonigal 2011) or "fragmented fiction" (McGonigal 2008)): "Instead of telling a story, we would present the evidence of that story, and let the players tell it to themselves" (Sean Stewart, lead writer of *I Love Bees* quoted by McGonigal 2008, p. 202). An English teacher might create a game where the game randomly generates different aspects of a story (setting, protagonist, conflict, etc.), and the players have to create a story from these building blocks. The "boss" level could involve students (or groups of students) figuring out how their different stories can merge into one larger story. A social studies teacher could have a protagonist with amnesia who finds clues about his or her past that they then have to reconstruct or a time traveler who has to figure out which time period she has been transported to. A geometry teacher could have students create Facebook pages where each student is a different shape. Each shape then posts and comments on others' status updates to create a story. For example, the square could tell the rhombus to "straighten up." There are numerous possibilities of story creation within game design.

You can even design a game that is one big exploratory environment. Terms for these kinds of games include "sandbox games" (Schell 2008), "emergent narratives" (Salen and Zimmerman 2004), and "narrative pregnant game spaces" (Mateas and Stern 2006):

> where the game elements are not as formally scripted. Instead, the player is given an environment and a set of tools to manipulate that environment. Content is implicit and is made up of stories, goals, and objectives that players create for themselves, and these can be completed in any order the players choose. The story comes from what the player thinks and feels while playing the game. This is most often seen in simulation games, such as *The Sims* series. (Rabin 2009, p. 148)

A game about genetics could be an emergent game where a player creates and breeds creatures which are subject to the rules of genetics. Some of these sandbox games even have the ability for players to take snapshots of their game play and create scrapbooks to document their experiences and create their own narrative arc.

Remember that it is the experience that matters, so think about how you want your learners to experience the curriculum, linearly, modularly, chaotically, emergently, and so forth. You may even want your learners to experience the game from different perspectives. To do so, have your game replayable as different characters so players experience the same events but from different characters' points of view. In English, this can be used to teach point of view,[25] social studies to experience a historical event from different perspectives and teach about bias, science to see how different elements in a system experience that system differently (ecosystem, human body, etc.), math to show how a mathematician can try to solve the same problem using different methods, in foreign language, how people across cultures experience the same holiday event (Day of the Dead, different independence days, etc.), and so forth.

Now that you have written the story of your game, keep in mind that this is still a work in progress:

> Following that story too slavishly, at the expense of the other [game] elements, is a common mistake—and an especially silly one, since story is, in some ways, the most pliable of all the elements! Story elements can often be changed with just a few words. (Schell 2008, p. 275)

Schell (2008) tells the story of game developers who thought they would have to scrap their game because they couldn't keep drawing distant terrain so they were going to create a foggy world, but they could only create green fog. The game developers then realized they could "change the story to solve the problem" (quote from the children's television show *SuperWhy*) so that "the evil aliens who had taken over the planet had done so by shrouding it with toxic gas" (Schell 2008, p. 275). One of my students designed a post-apocalyptic game where the players find a scientist on the side of the road. Initially, there was no explanation for why the players had to figure out the solution when the scientist would know how to do it all along. Adding language about the scientist being found gasping for air on the side of the road creates the explanation that a lack of oxygen has killed some of his brain cells but not others. This also allows the scientist to provide plausible scaffolding as he remembers some, but not all, of the science he once knew. In these ways, the game developers changed the story in a way that maintained, or rather created, internal consistency within the game world.

If the world, a character, or an object contradicts itself, "the integrity of the entire fantasy world" is compromised—"the compromised characters and setting will seem phony from the point of contradiction onward, and it will be difficult for the guest to sustain projection" (Schell 2008, p. 256). Some call this "Nuking the Fridge" from the fourth *Indiana Jones* movie when Indiana Jones survives a nuclear blast by getting into a lead-lined refrigerator. The lack of credibility of this feat shook audience members out of their suspension of disbelief, causing them to then question the rest of the plot. I found out the dangers of this the hard way when I forgot that the backstory of one of the "students" that was being role-played in my class had lost her mother and I, as puppet master, introduced an "event" by storming in and pretending to be this "student's" angry mother. By doing this, I burst the "magic circle" (Huizinga 1955) of our role-playing game and threw the whole class off, not to mention being extremely embarrassed.

[25] Several novels have been written so that the reader reads about the same event from different perspectives (*Instance of the Fingerpost* by Pears and *As I Lay Dying* by Faulkner are two examples).

As a game designer, though, sometimes you need to ditch reality to get a point across when reality distracts from that point (remember that you can point out differences between reality and your game world as you teach it or after you teach it during debriefing). For example, when Jesse Schell designed a *Pirates of the Caribbean* game, his design team had the flags at the tops of ships flying the same direction as the sail because wind is what drove the boats but found that their audience was used to flags on cars' antennas, which go the opposite direction of the car. They got so tired of playtesters pointing out that the "flags went the wrong way"—at least in the playtesters' minds—that they changed the direction of the flags and "people stopped asking about them, because now they looked 'normal'" (Schell 2008, p. 278). In this case, the direction of the flag was not integral to the story, so changing it eliminated a distraction without changing the intended experience.

If you do have something "weird" in your story, introducing it early can make it seem less weird and more consistent. For example, Schell (2008) describes a hamster game that involved "hamster cannons." Before the cannons were deployed in the game, the game designers showed the outside of the pet shop with signs that read "Special! Hamster Cannons on Sale!" (p. 279) so players didn't question it when hamster cannons were used to shoot one hamster into another's cage. You may think you have your story written now, but you will be making ongoing changes not only to create a sense of internal consistency within your game world but also to accommodate the quests you will design later.

CHALLENGE 4.4: "Earlier I added a story to a game, but now I'm trying to make a game out of my story. Just like good video games, I should practice before taking on this challenge." You take a popular story like the Hunger Games *and think about how you might make it into a game. Once done, you do the mental gymnastics of imagining how Amy would evaluate your work. "Enough channeling of Amy!" you think. "Maybe I should take the risk of contacting her."*

EXERCISE: Mentally convert a movie into a game.

As we have explored in this chapter, the basic formula of the standard story arc of exposition, rising action, climax, and denouement can be complicated in many different ways. How players experience this in video games, according to Davidson and Lemarchand (2012), is in three stages:

1. Involvement (introduction to the game)
2. Immersion (flow state)
3. Investment (commitment to finishing the game)[26]

When people lose immersion is when they quit. According to game designers Davidson and Lemarchand (2012), immersion is maintained through a balance of "meaning and mastery" (Davidson and Lemarchand 2012, p. 100), i.e., narrative and game play. If a player gets stuck in game play, for example, being unable to unlock a treasure chest or endlessly fighting orcs, the player loses interest out of frustration. While random events can add an element of surprise and of playfulness, too many random events shift a player's internal locus of control to an external one, causing a

[26] This parallels the process Ito describes in her observations of how youth engage with digital media—they start "hanging out" or observing how others behave in a space; then they start "messing around" or trying things out; then they "geek out" or specialize in something (Squire 2011, p. 47).

loss of meaning and agency and ultimately of immersion. If the story gets too long-winded, the player loses interest out of lack of interactivity. One of the first video games that I played, *Jumpman*, made this cycle extremely explicit as the game rewarded completing a level which involved jumping on moving boards, climbing ropes, etc., with a *cutscene*, in this case the next animated segment of a storyline about a robot going into space. Because I enjoyed the game play of *Jumpman* and I wanted to see how the story unfolded, I entered Davidson and Lemarchand's (2012) "investment" stage. Sadly, I never did complete *Jumpman* (although I came very close) which leaves me with a sense of being unfulfilled twenty years later when I think about it (apparently it is still available—maybe I will play it when I retire). In your curricular game, you will need to provide enough scaffolding for students to complete the game without losing interest. Because students will approach your game with differing levels of abilities, you will need to design the game so students can access differing amounts of scaffolding. Branching your game story is one way to do this. Future chapters will explore other ways to support students all the way through the end.

Conclusion

Role-playing can be one of the most insightful pedagogical tools. When I was a high school teacher, I had my students do "impromptu skits" as a pre-reading activity for *Othello*. One of the scenarios was for the students to act out a white father discovering his white daughter had eloped with a black man. Seeing my black students act out their stereotypes of white people was eye-opening. I knew these stereotypes about white people existed; I even had a student who periodically would make blanket statements about white people like "white people can't dance" forgetting that I was white (or pretending to forget) and then would apologize to me later. But to see these stereotypes in action in a safe way really brought them to life and allowed me to get a small glimpse of how some of the black youth in my class characterized white people. Talk about a teachable moment for the teacher! It was also the hardest I have ever laughed as a teacher or I think my students have ever laughed in my class.

Creating a story in which students role-play provides context for the game and motivation for the players. Story is the means by which your students *experience* the theme of your game. However, games are more than stories. They are dynamic enterprises where players can experience multiple story paths and even influence the direction of the story itself. Games allow people to *be* the protagonist, not in the way that stories or film do, but in an even more immersive way because games give the audience authorship. In this way, students direct their own learning as they navigate the game world as their character. Making decisions and experiencing the consequences of those decisions as an element within a system not only provide a venue for hypothesis testing, feedback, and revision but also impact a students' identity as decisions made might result in his or her game character dying from the plague, saving the world, or altering the course of history.

Education is a matter of "learning to become" rather than "learning about."

–Hamish Macleod 2008

Appendix: Story Quest Worksheet*

Topic: ___________________________

Possible Protagonist				
Story of system through Protagonist's eyes				
Possible Goal of Protagonist				
Possible Conflict/Obstacles/Constraints				
Potential Backstory—either text or storyboarded, highlight just the parts absolutely necessary for the player to know at the beginning of the game, if any				
Branching—redo story using sticky notes and drawing lines to depict branched narrative as a flowchart				
NPCs	Name	Function		Description

Suggested Story Quest Rubric

Quest	"Wow! I mean, I think this might work." (3)	"Hmm, this is acceptable." (2)	"I need more convincing." (1)	"Go back to the drawing board." (0)
Story Quest	Compelling storyline and characters likely to help students achieve game goals	Clear how plot ties to learning objectives	Basic plot described but unclear how it relates to learning objectives	Story is unclear

Suggested Reading: Nonfiction

Jenkins, H. (2004). Game design as narrative architecture. In N. Wardrip-Fruin & P. Harrigan (Eds.), *First person: New media as story, performance and game* (pp. 118–130). Cambridge, MA: MIT Press.

Papert, S. (1991). *Mindstorms: Children, computers, and powerful ideas*. New York: Basic Books.

Shaffer, D. W. (2006). *How computer games help children learn*. New York: Palgrave MacMillan.

Sheldon, L. (2004). *Character development and storytelling for games*. Boston: Cengage Learning.

Simmons, A. (2001). *The story factor*. New York: Basic Books.

References

Anderson, B. (2010). MMORPGs in support of learning: current trends and future uses. In R. Van Eck (Ed.), *Gaming and cognition: Theories and practice from the learning sciences* (pp. 55–80). Hershey, PA: Information Science Reference.

Barab, S. (2012). Introduction to Section III. In C. Steinkuehler, K. Squire, & S. Barab (Eds.), *Games, learning, and society: Learning and meaning in the digital age* (pp. 271–278). New York: Cambridge University Press.

Barton, K., & McKellar, P. (2011). From Master to Games-master: Managing disequilibrium and scaffolding in simulation-based learning. In S. de Freitas & P. Maharg (Eds.), *Digital games and learning* (pp. 226–251). London: Continuum.

Blair, K. P., Schwartz, D. L., Biswas, G., & Leelawong, K. (2007). Pedagogical agents for learning by teaching: Teachable agents. *Educational Technology, 47*(1), 56–61.

Blanchard, J. (2007, December 29). Anti-bullying program aims to teach students empathy. *Seattle Post- Intelligencer.*

Bransford, J., Brown, A., & Cocking, R. (2000). *How people learn: Brain, mind, experience, and school*. Washington, DC: National Academies Press.

Brown, H. (2008). *Videogames and education*. Armonk, NY: M.E. Sharpe.

Castronova, E. (2002/2006). Virtual worlds: A first-hand account of market and society on the Cyberian Frontier. In K. Salen & E. Zimmerman (Eds.), *The game designer reader: A rules of play anthology* (pp. 814–863). Cambridge, MA: MIT Press.

Clark, D., & Martinez-Garza, M. (2012). Prediction and explanation as design mechanics in conceptually integrated digital games to help players articulate the tacit understandings they build through game play. In C. Steinkuehler, K. Squire, & S. Barab (Eds.), *Games, learning, and society: Learning and meaning in the digital age* (pp. 279–305). New York: Cambridge University Press.

Costikyan, G. (1994/2006). I have no words and I must design. In K. Salen & E. Zimmerman (Eds.), *The game designer reader: A rules of play anthology* (pp. 192–211). Cambridge, MA: MIT Press.

Coulter, B., Klopfer, E., Sheldon, J., & Perry, J. (2012). Discovering familiar places: Learning through mobile place-based games. In C. Steinkuehler, K. Squire, & S. Barab (Eds.), *Games, learning, and society: Learning and meaning in the digital age* (pp. 327–354). New York: Cambridge University Press.

Czikszentmihalyi, M. (1990). *Flow: The psychology of optimal experience*. New York: Harper & Row.

Davidson, D., & Lemarchand, R. (2012). *Uncharted 2: Among Thieves*—How to become a hero. In C. Steinkuehler, K. Squire, & S. Barab (Eds.), *Games, learning, and society: Learning and meaning in the digital age* (pp. 75–107). New York: Cambridge University Press.

Dempsey, J. V. (2010). Elemental learning and the pyramid of fidelity. In R. Van Eck (Ed.), *Gaming and cognition: Theories and practice from the learning sciences* (pp. 82–107). Hershey, PA: Information Science Reference.

Dickey, M. (2011). Murder on Grimm Isle. In S. de Freitas & P. Maharg (Eds.), *Digital games and learning* (pp. 129–151). London: Continuum.

Driscoll, M. (2005). *Psychology of learning for instruction. Boston*: Allyn and Bacon.

Dweck, C. (2007). Mindset: *The new psychology of success*. New York: Ballantine Books.

Fine, G. (1983/2006). Frames and games. From shared fantasy: Role-playing games as social worlds. In K. Salen & E. Zimmerman (Eds.), The game designer reader: A rules of play anthology (pp. 578–601). Cambridge, MA: MIT Press.

Fullerton, T., Swain, C., & Hoffman, S. (2004). *Game design workshop: Designing, prototyping, and playtesting games*. San Francisco, CA: CMP Books.

Gee, J. P. (2007). *Good videogames + good learning: Collected essays on videogames, learning, and literacy*. New York: Peter Lang.

Gee, J. P. (Ed.). (2008). Learning and games. In K. Salen (Ed.), *The ecology of games: Connecting youth, games, and learning* (pp. 21–40). Cambridge, MA: MIT Press.

Gredler, M. E. (1992). *Designing and evaluating games and simulations*. London: Kogan Page.

Greenfield, P. (2010). Video games revisited. In R. Van Eck (Ed.), *Gaming and cognition: Theories and practice from the learning sciences* (pp. 1–21). Hershey, PA: Information Science Reference.

Hirumi, A., & Hall, R. (2011). Presenting content information and facilitating instruction: Design techniques for advancing game flow. In M. S. Khine (Ed.), *Learning to play: Exploring the future of education with video games* (pp. 55–78). New York: Peter Lang.

Huizinga, J. (1955/2006). Nature and significance of play as a cultural phenomenon from Homo Ludens: A study of the play element in culture. In K. Salen, & E. Zimmerman (Eds.), *The game designer reader: A rules of play anthology* (pp. 96–120) Cambridge, MA: MIT Press.

Jackson, J. (2007). *Unmasking identities: An exploration of the lives of gay and lesbian teachers*. Lanham, MD: Lexington Books.

Jenkins, H. (2004/2006). Game design as narrative architecture from Jenkins, H. In K. Salen & E. Zimmerman (Eds.), *The game designer reader: A rules of play anthology* (pp. 670–689). Cambridge, MA: MIT Press.

Jenkins, H. (2009). *Confronting the challenges of a participatory culture: Media education for the 21st century*. Cambridge, MA: MIT Press.

Kafai, Y. (1995). *Minds in play: Computer game design as a context for children's learning*. Hillsdale, NJ: Lawrence Erlbaum Associates.

LeBlanc, M. (2004/2006). Tools for creating dramatic game dynamics. In K. Salen & E. Zimmerman (Eds.), *The game designer reader: A rules of play anthology* (pp. 438–459). Cambridge, MA: MIT Press.

LoPiccolo, G., Squire, K., & Chu, S. (2012). Interview with Harmonix. In C. Steinkuehler, K. Squire, & S. Barab (Eds.), *Games, learning, and society: Learning and meaning in the digital age* (pp. 108–120). New York: Cambridge University Press.

Macleod, H. (Ed.). 2008. Games in learning. In M. Pivec & M. Moretti (Eds.), *Game-based learning: Discover the pleasure of learning* (pp. 17–23). Lengerich, Germany: Pabst Science Publishers.

Mateas, M., & Stern, A. (2005/2006). Interaction and narrative from *Expressive AI*. In K. Salen & E. Zimmerman (Eds.), *The game designer reader: A rules of play anthology* (pp. 642–669). Cambridge, MA: MIT Press.

McGonigal, J. (2008). Why *I Love Bees*. In K. Salen (Ed.), *The ecology of games: Connecting youth, games, and learning* (pp. 199–227). Cambridge, MA: MIT Press.

McGonigal, J. (2011). *Reality is broken: Why games make us better and how they can change the world*. London: Penguin.

McIntyre, A. (1997). *Making meaning of whiteness: Exploring the racial identity of white teachers*. Albany: State University of New York Press.

Murray, J. (1997). *Hamlet on the holodeck: The future of narrative in cyberspace*. Cambridge, MA: MIT Press.

Nemetz, D. (2014, June 24). Whoopi Goldberg explains why she wanted to be on Star Trek. *Yahoo TV*. Retrieved from https://tv.yahoo.com/blogs/tv-news/exclusive-video-whoopi-goldberg-star-trek-213710247.html

Papert, S. (1980). *Mindstorms: Children, computers, and powerful ideas*. New York: Basic Books.

Paul, A. M. (2012, March 17). Your brain on fiction. *New York Times*, p. SR6.

Prensky, M. (2002). The motivation of game play, or the REAL 21st century learning revolution. *On the Horizon, 10*(1), 5–11.

Prensky, M. (2011). Comments on research comparing games to other instructional methods. In S. Tobias & J. D. Fletcher (Eds.), *Computer games and instruction* (pp. 251–280). Charlotte, NC: Information Age.

Rabin, S. (2009). *Introduction to game development* (2nd ed.). Herndon, VA: Cengage Learning.

Rabone, D. (2013). How 'game mechanics" can revitalize education. *eSchoolNews*. Retrieved from http://www.eschoolnews.com/2013/02/12/how-game-mechanics-can-revitalize-education/3/

Reese, D. (2010). Introducing Flowometer: A CyGaMEs assessment suite tool. In R. Van Eck (Ed.), *Gaming and cognition: Theories and practice from the learning sciences* (pp. 227–254). Hershey, PA: Information Science Reference.

Resnick, L., & Hall, M. (2005). *Principles of learning for effort-based education*. Pittsburgh: University of Pittsburgh, Institute for Learning, Learning Research and Development Center.

Richter, J., & Livingstone, D. (2011). Multi-user games and learning. In S. Tobias & J. D. Fletcher (Eds.), *Computer games and instruction* (pp. 101–124). Charlotte, NC: Information Age.

Robinett, W. (1984/2006). Adventure as a video game: Adventure for the Atari 2600 from inventing the adventure game. In K. Salen & E. Zimmerman (Eds.), *The game designer reader: A rules of play anthology* (pp. 690–713). Cambridge, MA: MIT Press.
Salen, K., & Zimmerman, E. (2004). *Rules of play: Game design fundamentals*. Cambridge, MA: MIT Press.
Schell, J. (2008). *The art of game design: A book of lenses*. Burlington, MA: Morgan Kaufmann.
Sheldon, L. (2004). *Character development and storytelling for games*. Boston: Cengage Learning.
Sheldon, L. (2011). *The multi-player classroom: Designing coursework as a game*. Herndon, VA: Cengage Learning.
Simmons, A. (2001). *The story factor*. New York: Basic Books.
Squire, K. (2011). *Video games and learning: Teaching and participatory culture in the digital age*. New York: Teachers College Press.
Swan, R. (2010). Feedforward as an essential active principle of engagement in computer games. In R. Van Eck (Ed.), *Gaming and cognition: Theories and practice from the learning sciences* (pp. 108–136). Hershey, PA: Information Science Reference.
Sweeney, L. B. (2001). *When a butterfly sneezes: A guide for helping kids explore interconnections in our world through favorite stories*. Waltham, MA: Pegasus Communications.
Tobias, S., Fletcher, J. D., Dai, D., & Wind, A. (2011). Review of research on computer games. In S. Tobias & J. D. Fletcher (Eds.), *Computer games and instruction* (pp. 127–221). Charlotte, NC: Information Age.
Travis, R., & Young, M. (2011). Operation KTHMA-reign of the demiurge: Game worlds, greek history, and situated learning. In M. S. Khine (Ed.), *Learning to play: Exploring the future of education with video games* (pp. 153–166). New York: Peter Lang.
Turkle, S. (1984). *The second self: Computers and the human spirit*. New York: Simon and Schuster.
Van Eck, R. (2007). Building artificially intelligent learning games. In D. Gibson, C. Aldrich, & M. Prensky (Eds.), *Games and simulations in online learning: Research and development frameworks* (pp. 271–307). Hershey, PA: Information Science.
Vygotsky, L. (1978). *Mind in society*. Cambridge, MA: Harvard University Press.
Wangsness, L., & Estes, A. (2007, June 15). Personal stories changed minds. *Boston Globe*. Retrieved from http://www.boston.com/news/local/massachusetts/articles/2007/06/15/personal_stories_changed_minds/?page=full

Fiction

Any of Edward Packard's *Choose your own adventure* series (these books have branched narratives).
Faulkner, W. (1930/2013). *As I lay dying*. Toronto, ON: HarperCollins. (This novel has the same events described by different characters)
Gaarder, J. (1991). *Sophie's world: A novel about the history of philosophy.* New York: Farrar, Straus and Giroux. (This novel teaches the history of philosophy through story)
Pears, I. (1998). *Instance of the fingerpost*. New York: The Berkley Publishing Group. (This novel has the same events described by different characters)

Chapter 5
The Game Plan: Converting the Story into a Game

> *The designer creates an experience.... The game enables the experience, but it is not the experience.*
>
> *–Jesse Schell, 2008, CEO of Schell Games and creative director of the first massively multiplayer game for kids, Toontown Online, as well as several rides at Disney World*

Abstract This chapter assists the reader in assembling all of the various game elements developed so far into a curricular game using a design document as a tool to do so. In the process, this chapter helps readers determine the genre, specify the core game mechanic, think through player configuration, design the game space, establish the scoring mechanism(s), and propose rules. As the reader engages in this process, he or she is encouraged to think about how each element impacts another and how together they contribute to the gaming experience.

Keywords Resources • Objects • Core game mechanics • Design document • Scoring • Win-state • Rules • Timing

J.J. Kellinger, *A Guide to Designing Curricular Games*,
Advances in Game-Based Learning, DOI 10.1007/978-3-319-42393-7_5

DESIGN QUEST:

IF you chose to write out the story, THEN you need to go back to the drawing board. Literally. The Commander merely glances at what you wrote before she declares "too many words" and waves you off with a dismissive hand. You remember your friend Amy mentioning that game designers storyboard their game as part of the design process. Thinking back to the maps and schematics in the Commander's office, her need for a learning theory diagram before you could win her over, and her secret pleasure at your diagrams of your topic's system, you realize visual is the way to go if you want her approval. You get out your sticky notes and start arranging your story.

ELSE, you can proceed with the Commander's approval.

You stare at your board of sticky notes, each one with a different aspect of the branching storylines: "I have all these ideas scattered around but, just like a mousetrap is not a mousetrap until the board, spring, and cheese are all assembled in the proper way, what I have is not a game, just a bunch of pieces. How do I go about turning these 'heaps' into a game? I feel like I've just been shuffling parts around for days! My time is running out. I really need some scaffolding. Damn the space-time continuum! I'm going to contact Amy."

IF you decide NOT to text Amy, THEN you get stuck, not knowing what to do next.

ELSE: You run to the bathroom and hurriedly text her, knowing that if you hesitate, you might not have the courage again: "Been busy. Hey, just curious, how do you put your video games together?"

You stare at your cell phone in anticipation. As you do, you notice the time. In your hurry, you forgot to make sure it was nighttime! You realize it's dusk. Dusk, does that count as night time? Maybe it will be ok if Amy doesn't text back until night time. But what if she doesn't text back until tomorrow? Who knows what the time difference between the future and the past is? Does it make a difference if I'm in the same time zone? You leap back as your phone buzzes.

"Just like you put together your lessons, dummy. You are so busy complaining all the time about lesson plans, you never pay attention to my struggles with assembling a design document that pleases everyone!"

Amy always has been a bit blunt, but always helpful.

"A design document. Ok, let me think about how a lesson plan might translate into a design document." You try to recall the different aspects of a design document Amy has talked about. Quickly you scribble out your initial ideas.

Lesson plan	Design document
Unit goals	*Game goal or mission*
Objectives	*Core game mechanic*
Background of students	*Target audience*
Materials	*Game objects*
Procedures	*Game events (branching story, quests, etc.)*
Assessment	*Chokepoints, scoring mechanisms*
Accommodations	*In-game scaffolding*

ACTION: Write out a design document for your curricular game.

"Now I feel like I know what I'm doing!" You realize that you should have figured this out on your own; after all, this is using Carol Lee's (2001) Cultural Modeling, i.e., making connections between prior knowledge and new knowledge, on yourself! Silently you thank Amy, not daring to do it by text, and get to work.

When I designed my first game-based course, I had students earn points over the course of the semester with only one deadline: the end of the course. This meant that students could wait until the very end and then frantically try to rack up points—putting a time crunch on them and on me. I quickly learned that students needed multiple deadlines so I gave reaching each level its own deadline. Because students needed to earn a certain number of points to reach a new level, I had to institute a "revise and resubmit" rule, which, by far, is the most favored rule by my students. The consequences for me, however, are that not only do I have a lot more grading, but because students need to earn points to move ahead in the course, I have to grade assignments almost immediately, otherwise I get very disgruntled students. I did have one disgruntled student express extreme displeasure at having to wait for me to grade something until I pointed out that he could have used the syllabus to work ahead. Now I make this 'course cheat' explicit to give me a little leeway in grading assignments.

It is important to remember that creating a game is a second-order design problem—we are not creating the gaming experiences, we are creating the conditions for the gaming experiences to emerge (Salen and Zimmerman 2004). Just like with teaching, we cannot create or force learning (as much as we try!); instead we create conditions in which learning is likely to occur.

To create these conditions, Marc LeBlanc (2004/2006) describes a game design process that starts at the end:

> When we play a game, our experience can be described as a kind of causal flow that starts with its mechanics ("all the necessary pieces that we need to play the game"), passes through dynamics ("the actual events and phenomena that occur as the game is played"), and ends with aesthetics (the "emotional responses we have when we play")... As game designers, ... we begin our work with a set of aesthetic objectives—emotional responses we *hope* to evoke in the players. Our task is to work backward, determining what dynamics will accomplish our aesthetic objectives, and from there design game mechanics that will create those dynamics. (pp. 440–441).

Wiggins and McTighe (1998) suggest starting with the goals of the unit in their backward design process, we should start with the goal of the game and think about how to structure the game to help players achieve that goal. In doing so, our students should be constantly revising their mental model to come closer and closer to resembling the expert model. However, we want to make sure that the ultimate feeling we want our students to experience is fun, that is, hard fun.

Jesse Schell (2008) advises game designers to begin designing a game experience in this way: "Step 1: Figure out what your theme is. Step 2: Use every means possible to reinforce that theme" (p. 49). Go all the way back to chapter two when you distilled your enduring understandings into a theme. It is important to recognize that a game's theme is what you want players to experience. This is closely linked to what a game teaches, as that is determined by the game play, i.e., what the players do in the game. As Johnson (2012)) points out, "*Super Mario Bros.* … is a game about timing, certainly not about plumbing" (p. 34). Johnson (2012) warns, though, that, "when a game's theme and mechanics are sharply divorced, players can react negatively to the dissonance. Such a dissonance can leave players feeling lost, perhaps even cheated. Thus designers should strive to keep the two in harmony" (p. 36). I disagree.

A really advanced designer could develop a game where what the game is about is really just a vehicle for the game's mechanics which is then used to teach the academic material. Through reflection and perhaps through scaffolding provided by the teacher or the game, users can make the connection between the game world and the academic content. That would be a cool design trick. For example, as Johnson (2012) himself points out, the game *World of Warcraft's* mechanics teaches about natural selection, although few would identify that as the content. The "game" in this book ostensibly involves creating a curricular game; however, the quests about developing a proposal to satisfy the "Commander" also help prepare teachers to argue the value of educational games with their Commander/principal if they encounter resistance—something that may or may not be immediately obvious from the Quests. This is what Chatham (2011) describes as a "Trojan horse approach" (p. 78) and MacCullum-Stewart (2011) terms as "stealth learning" (p. 111). Using a metaphor to teach the content can help students connect their prior knowledge to new knowledge. However, sometimes you can embed "stealth learning" into your curricular game without an elaborate metaphor. For example, the curricular game in this book embeds common programming language such as IF, THEN, ELSE statements and WHILE loops.

In the storytelling chapter, you were prompted to create your game world. The distance between the game world, or content of the game, and the theme, or academic content, can vary. In some instances, it might make sense to have them mirror each other; in others, a metaphor for your topic might make sense. Because my students are studying to be teachers, most of my curricular games involve students becoming new teachers. However, one of my curricular games has my students be a private investigator. Throughout the curricular game, connections are made between how a private investigator looks for clues and patterns to make inferences and how teachers look for clues and patterns to better understand their students. Educators talk about students' knowledge, skills, and dispositions, but too often focus almost exclusively on the knowledge perhaps because that can be easiest to measure. I have found, though, in curricular games focusing on the skills and dispositions can create a learning situation where students end up pulling the knowledge for their use instead of having knowledge pushed on them. In your curricular game, you want to make sure what your students are doing in the game are the skills and involve the dispositions that you want students to learn whether or not you use a metaphor as a vehicle to do so or not.

Matching theme and mechanics means "finding the game in the content" (Squire 2011, p. 90), what Rieber (1996) describes as endogenous games. If your game is no more than a worksheet in game format, it is not the type of game this book, or scholars in this area, endorse: "Games, like teachers, come in a wide variety of 'goodness.' Unfortunately, most games are not good. In fact, most are bad, often drills in disguise" (Prensky quoted by Korbey 2013). Games that are "drills in disguise" often borrow from established games. For example, the game *Math Invaders* is essentially *Space Invaders* except that the player has to shoot numbers to equal the target number. Clearly, this is not an endogenous game. If the user had to use math to calculate the trajectory and/or speed, however, then the math would be endogenous to the game. Bogost (2007) uses the phrase "procedural rhetoric" to refer to the messages that a game's mechanics send and describe what happens when there is a mismatch between theme and mechanics:

> One common pitfall [of] borrowing a procedural form from existing game or game genre and skinning it with new graphics… *Congo Jones* adopts no procedural representation—and therefore no procedural rhetoric—of its own. Instead, it borrows the notion of progress through abstract obstacles as an object lesson for deforestation's struggle against the World Bank (who had supported logging in the Congolese rainforests). The game makes no claims about possible reasons to oppose the World Bank, nor how to do so, although it does succeed in positing the World Bank as an archetypal opponent, the 'boss monster' of the game. The game might or might not be effective in building 'awareness' about the issue, but it certainly does not mount a procedural argument about the topic. Or more precisely, it does not mount its *own* procedural rhetoric; it adopts processes of obstacle avoidance and goal pursuit from platform games and reinscribes them onto deforestation… Another common technique is to borrow gameplay and apply a textual skin—a verbal rhetoric—atop it. An example of such a game is *P.o.N.G.* … the result is a direct copy of *Pong* in which the ball is replaced by words that might arise in discussions of globalization … The player must bat these back and forth with the paddle, as one might 'exchange words' in a conversation on the topic. (p. 50)

This does not mean we as teachers and now as curricular game designers should not look to other games for inspiration. As a matter of fact, good teachers know that teaching is all about stealing—borrowing others' ideas and adapting them to our own classroom needs. Game designers do the same. However, to do so uncritically can result in disaster.[1] In order to critically examine your own curricular game, you need to practice critically examining the games of others.

How can you tell if a game is embedded in the content? If you can change the content without changing the game play, you should rethink your game. For example, if players pretended to race to different countries to complete math tasks and the first to get to the end wins, the game is simply a shell to deliver the content because you could switch out the math tasks and swap in science tasks and the game would be the same. To move it toward being more endogenous, you could have math tasks specific to a country's culture, for example, a math game traditionally played by a culture or math used in a common job in a country, but even that feels a little contrived. Even if your game has English tasks based on a piece of literature from that country, it still feels arbitrary because there is no reason for players to be racing to different countries. But, say, if you teach Spanish and each task is rooted in the culture of a Spanish-speaking country, then racing around the world feels more related to the content area. You could even have all the tasks related to the ways different cultures celebrate a common holiday like Day of the Dead, Christmas, or

[1] One teacher described to me what it was like to work in a cutthroat school where the competition to teach upper level senior classes was fierce. She said that veteran teachers would leave bad tests lying around the copy room so unsuspecting novice teachers would think the veteran teacher accidentally left it behind and use it for themselves, resulting in poor reviews.

their Independence Day to highlight what makes each culture's celebration unique. However, if you had an ultimate goal in racing to the different countries and each task a step toward reaching that goal, for example, tracking down a stolen painting,[2] then you have an endogenous game!

In order to "find the game in the content," you need to go back to your enduring understanding and describe what it looks like, or better yet, what it feels like. This may involve deepening your enduring understanding. For example, if your enduring understanding is: "Students will understand that the struggle between Communism and democracy sparked the Cold War tensions," think about why there was a struggle to begin with. Why couldn't the two types of government coexist? Why did one see the other as a threat? Were they fighting over scarce resources? Or did they each believe they had a "manifest destiny" to spread their form of government? What is at the heart of historical struggles among or even within countries? Deepening your enduring understanding requires going beneath the surface of the specific content to find the underlying concepts. For example, instead of "Students will understand how Dunbar uses masks as a symbol in 'We Wear the Mask'," a better enduring understanding would be about how authors use symbolism. Deepening your enduring understanding is not about divorcing it from the specific content, but exploring the deeper concepts that underlie multiple contexts. This will help you discover what you want students to experience in your game, i.e., the theme. If you want to emphasize that the Cold War was about fighting for scarce resources, then design a game where students fight over scarce resources. However, if you want to emphasize that the Cold War was about the drive to spread what world leaders believed to be the best way to live and altruistically, or selfishly, wanted everyone to live that way, then that would lead to a very different game.

Genre

In Chap. 1, we analyzed the pedagogical affordances and constraints of video games. In doing so, we aggregated our data by genre. Before you read on, look back to see if there is one genre that rose above the others in terms of pedagogical affordances. See if your answer matches Richard Van Eck's (2007): "Adventure games have … the greatest potential for addressing all levels of the learning taxonomy" (p. 276). He goes on to explain how he came to that conclusion:

> Adventure computer games are narrative-based problem-solving activities in which the storyline drives the actions of the player and the movement through the game through a continuous cycle of hypothesis formation, action, and feedback …[They] are situated in environments that are generally immersive, allows (and even require) exploration, are driven by narrative and story, and often require hypothesis formulation, testing, revision,

[2]Two of my students independently came up with the stolen painting idea and ended up working together to create a curricular game for beginning Spanish students where students had to use their Spanish to catch trains, get information from an informant in a café, and so forth. While their technology version worked well, the no tech version involved transforming the classroom into a train station one day, a Spanish café the next, and so forth, creating quite a sense of immersion—and fun!

and re-testing. These kinds of strategies are conducive both to adventure game play and to problem solving. Adventure games thus address all levels of the learning taxonomy, and in particular focus on the highest levels. Problem solving skills (also sometimes referred to by educators and parents as critical thinking skills) are among the most highly desired goals in education, but they are typically among the most difficult to address in any instructional medium. Adventure games are well aligned with exiting pedagogical theories such as situated cognition and learning (e.g., Brown, Collins & Duguid, 1989; Lave & Wegner, 1991), anchored instruction (e.g., Bransford, Sherwood, Hasselbring, Kinzere, & Willams, 1990; CGTV, 1990, 1993, 1996) and discovery-based learning (e.g., Bruner, 1960), all of which have been shown to promote problem-solving skills. (p. 276)

If you did not play an adventure game for one of your three in the first chapter when you did the preparation work for the proposal quest, take a moment (or hours) to explore one now. I highly recommend the *MYST* series, but there are lots of others out there. Your curricular game does not have to be of the adventure genre, but I do recommend that you at least consider what your curricular game might look like if you did use this genre to structure it.

Goal

Go back to your enduring understanding and theme on your Topic Quest Worksheet. Your theme should describe the feelings you hope to evoke that will underscore your enduring understanding. For example, if your enduring understanding is that humans should be respected in clinical research, your theme should be about empathy. If your enduring understanding is that you do not need to be a perfect speaker of a new language in order to communicate, your theme should capture that feeling of connecting with someone who speaks a different language. If your enduring understanding is about the benefits of democracy, your theme should be about the feeling of being able to make a difference in this world through the political system. Start with the feeling you want to evoke in order to develop the goal of your game.

Now think about how your game can convey the goal. According to Schell (2008), "The more easily players understand the goal, the more easily they can visualize achieving it, and the more likely they are going to want to play your game" (p. 148). As teachers, we are told we need to put the objectives on the board. Certainly, I contend there is a need to put learning in context, make explicit how a lesson relates to the overall unit goals, and explain why we are doing what we are doing in the classroom; otherwise, learning feels arbitrary and disconnected. However, instead of putting the goals/objectives up front, having students discover the goal as part of the game play can incite curiosity:

Players begin each game by tackling the obstacle of *not knowing what to do* and *not knowing how to play*. This kind of ambiguous play is markedly different from historical, predigital games. Traditionally, we have needed instructions in order to play a game. But now we're often invited to learn as we go. We explore the game space and the computer code effectively constrains and guides us. We learn how to play by carefully observing what the game allows us to do and how it responds to our input. As a result, most gamers never read game manuals. In fact, it's a truism in the game industry that a well-designed game should be playable immediately, with no instruction whatsoever. (McGonigal 2011, p. 26)

Imagine what might happen if your students entered the classroom and there was no teacher. Instead, students have to explore the classroom to discover a note that states that their teacher has been kidnapped. That would certainly get everyone's attention (although it could also get you fired). The point is introducing an element of mystery can motivate students much more than objectives listed on the board.

Below is a list of common game goals from Fullerton et al. (2004, pp. 54–60) for you to use for inspiration:

1. Capture/chase = Capture the other side while avoiding being captured
2. Race = First to complete something
3. Alignment = "Arrange your game pieces in a certain spatial configuration or create conceptual alignment between categories of pieces" (p. 55) such as *Tic-Tac-Toe*, *Connect Four*, and *Tetris*
4. Rescue/escape = Either you escape or help someone else escape
5. Forbidden act = Trying "to get the competition to 'break the rules' by … doing something they shouldn't" (p. 57) like *Taboo* and *Twister*
6. Construction = "To build, maintain, or manage objects" (p. 58) such as *Sims*
7. Exploration = Explore new worlds (often in combination with other game objectives)
8. Solution = Solve puzzles like in *Myst*
9. Outwit = "Gain and use knowledge in a way that defeats the other players" (p. 60) like *Trivial Pursuit* or *Clue*

Keep in mind these can be combined and are not the only types of game goals. Each player can even have his or her own goal, or an individual goals and a collective group goal.

Core Game Mechanic

The core game mechanic is how players achieve the goal. For example, the goal of a racing game is to complete something first, but this could be done by doing many different things: answering trivia questions, driving a car, running a footrace, and so forth. The core game mechanic is the skill that the player performs and perfects over the course of the game:

> The core game mechanism can be defined as the one action a player repeats most often while trying to achieve the game's overall goal. Games are repetitive by nature. While the meaning and consequences of what a player does may change over the course of game, the core action tends to remain the same from beginning to end. For instance, in chess, the core action is moving your pieces on a grid in an attempt to capture your opponent's pieces. That single action defines the entire game. (Fullerton et al. 2004, pp. 172–173)

For the Odysseus order game that I described earlier where students have to place Odysseus' adventures in an order that makes sense, sequencing is the core game mechanic. The players sequence and re-sequence the order of events to figure out the optimal order for Odysseus to learn what he needs to learn and apply to the next challenge. You could have a game where the core game mechanic is determining criteria, for example, what are the criteria for historical significance to decide what to include in a textbook or a museum. In my English Methods course game I described earlier where students role-play students and teachers, teaching English is the core game mechanic. Initially, students learn and practice individual aspects of teaching and practice them on a small scale (tutoring), a medium scale (small group discussion), and a large scale (whole class teaching). During whole class teaching, students initially can pause the action to reflect, but for the boss level, students must put it all these aspects of teaching together without a pause option and complete their lesson within the allotted time. We defined our ultimate goal in chapter one as getting students to *experience* the curriculum: "Core mechanics create patterns of behavior, which manifest as experience for players" (Salen and Zimmerman 2004, p. 317). If there is no repetition, then the actions feel arbitrary and not meaningful. The development of skills occurs by advancement through repetition. However, this repetition must build on itself by increasing the challenge level after the player has demonstrated mastery. By proceeding through "well-ordered problems" (Gee 2007, p. 35), games create meaning. You will know you have achieved this when you receive student feedback like this: "You took us on a great journey, and each step felt logical and sequential."

Your core game mechanic should be skill–based and not left to chance. For example, the core game mechanic in soccer of kicking the ball accurately is skill–based. Flipping cards over in the game of *War* is chance. To determine if your core game mechanic is skill–based, ask yourself the following questions: "Can experts generally be sure they will defeat novices?" (Schell 2008, p. 186). Could the player at the end of the game beat him or herself from beginning of game? Is it likely that the students will be different by the end of game and if so, how? Chance games are relaxing, casual games because the outcome is up to fate. Skill-based games are intense learning games. However, you can alternate between relaxation and tension by combining chance and skill. Schell (2008) points out that "dealing out a hand of cards is pure chance—deciding how to play them is pure skill" (p. 182). For example, to teach about epigenetics, you could create a game where the genes each player has are chance since you do not choose your parents, but what a player does with his/her set of genes is skill. In defining your core game mechanic, make sure it is skill–based, but do not be afraid to insert an element of chance.

Player Configuration

When you open up a new board game, one of the first items in the directions is how many players the game is designed for. Most likely you are designing a game for a whole class, but you can always "chunk" your class into a smaller number of players. For example, if your game is about World War II, you might want to "chunk" your class into the number of countries involved in World War II by grouping your students and having each group play a different country. You can even design a single-player curricular game by having the whole class play as one player. The class, then, would be making decisions together either unanimously, representatively, by majority vote, or by any other mechanism you determine. If you are teaching in a school with little technology, perhaps the only technology is your own personal technology, you can project your laptop or tablet onto the screen[3] and have the class vote on each decision. This can be an ideal way to foster critical thinking as students are forced to make their thinking visible, or rather audible, and take into account the perspectives of others. This way decisions are not made willy-nilly just to get through the game. If you are concerned about students using trial-and-error instead of critical thinking skills, put them into groups. Even just having partners can force students to articulate their thinking. Partners can also solve the problem of not having enough computers. Partners can take turns being the designated "driver," the one controlling the computer, and the other the "navigator," telling the driver what to do. If you really want to foster persuasion, require that all decisions be unanimous. Another interesting way to do this would be to have each student take a turn at being the ultimate "decider," and the class has to persuade him or her on which decision to make. Of course if you do it this way, you would have to make sure there are enough decisions to go around.

If your first goal is figuring out the game goal, you might want to have students do this as a class so learners do not feel lost on their own, incompetent, and/or isolated, particularly if they are the last one to figure it out. On the other hand, if students are learning an individual skill, particularly if the game is real time and not turn based, you might want the first step to be one where they can practice in isolation (and get feedback) before performing their skill in front of others. This might be an ideal situation for learning a foreign language since students often progress at different rates. Particularly if students are playing as individuals, you want to think about "which is more important: that my game is a reliable measure of who has the most skill, or that it provide an interesting challenge to all players? If I want players of different skill levels to play together, what means will I use to make the game interesting and challenging for everyone?" (Schell 2008, p. 176). In one of my classes, students have a choice of "teaching" at one of three schools: Traditional High School, Hybrid High School, or New Literacies High School. No matter which school they choose, they have to complete the same set of tasks. However, how they complete them is dependent upon the school they chose. By having my students choose the school, I can accommodate various degrees of technological expertise while having students learn the same set of pedagogical skills.

One of the biggest considerations not just in designing a curricular game but in education, and even in life itself, is competition versus cooperation. Competition can motivate people to do things that they do not typically like to do. McGonigal (2011) describes how the game *Chore Wars*, an alternate reality game where players rack up points by doing actual chores successfully (e.g., dusting without knocking anything off the shelves), had her and her husband sneaking around trying to beat each other at scrubbing the toilet in order to get experience points in the game. Conflict creates drama and competition fosters conflict. However, with competition

[3] LCD projectors have really come down in price, so if your school does not have an LCD projector and you can afford one, it might be a good investment. If you do, don't forget to take it off on your taxes. There are also lots of mini-grants available to teachers if you can't afford one yourself.

among individuals, there are winners and losers, and the last thing you want to do is to make your students feel like losers.

In a lot of games, there are losers, and you could contend that the potential for losing is part of the unspoken contract when someone agrees to play a game. However, the game of school is not voluntary. Some argue that schooling is about separating out those who "can" from those who "cannot," and some teachers control for this through bell curve grading that dooms a percentage of students to failing, even if they did fairly well. I would like to think all of my students can get an A. Schell (2008) asks, "'What percentage of players do I want to be able to complete this game?' and then design for that" (p. 178). I try to design for 100% completion. To do so, I provide a lot of support, clearly lay out how to get an A by having students earn points, and have a revise and resubmit policy. As a result, my students do almost all get As with very few exceptions and still report being challenged no matter what level of expertise they entered with:

- I came into this course with little knowledge of technology and how it could be useful in the classroom. The course helped me to find ways to integrate technology into my classroom, even though it is an urban school with little funding. Excellent class!
- This course was unbelievably helpful to me. Before taking the class I would say that I was afraid of technology. [The professor] helped me realize my own potential with computers and technology, and I have since begun to incorporate technology into my teaching practices. I have already been able to share a lot of the skills that I have learned with my students who are now getting really excited about using the computers in my classroom. Though I spent a lot of time doing the work for this class, I think that I have learned more than in any other course I have taken in [this] program.
- Even though I have a strong background in technology this course helped me put it to a more practical use.
- Janna truly meets her students where they are and allows them to grow from there. This is so important in this class because everyone seemed to have different backgrounds with technology.
- Thanks so much… I learned a ton in your class! I'm clearly not a computer guru, but I feel much more comfortable than I ever have, and that's what it's all about, right? You really forced me to get out of my comfort zone. Thanks again!
- Thank you for helping me face my technological fears.
- As hard as I have struggled through certain parts of your class, I feel that I have learned more from you than I have in many other classes and appreciate why [another professor] recommended you to me both for my own lack of technological experience and for the quality of techniques that you incorporate in your own classes. I have learned as much about teaching as I have about technology in your class, and I plan to incorporate and utilize as many aspects of your teaching as I can in the upcoming year. I guess that is what teaching is all about. (quotes originally published in Jackson 2009, pp. 300–301)

There are ways that games can foster competition without having an individual loser. One way is the "last-person standing" game where essentially everyone loses except for the winner, the "last-person standing." This might be good for a game that lasts less than a class period, but for an ongoing curricular game, you would need to figure out what to do with the ever-increasing group of "losers." Some possibilities include having students return as ghosts, turn into advisors or guides on the side, return in dreams, and so forth. Another way is to have individuals compete against themselves. I used to volunteer with a friend of mine who was a basketball coach. Our volunteer job was to assemble brown-bag meals for people with AIDS. She would see how many she could put together in a certain amount of time and then try to beat that. There was no actual competition, but she created her own internal competition. My niece knows she can never beat her father in the game of *Qwirkle*, so her goal is to beat her previous score. Individual competition allows players to operate in their own ZPD. Another way to foster competition without having individual losers is to have the whole class play together to try to beat the game: "[people] seem to be happiest when we are putting our signature strengths to good use in a group setting" (McGonigal 2011, p. 292). Even though the class might be playing as one "player," you could have individual roles assigned to students or groups of students such as reporter, researcher, scribe, and so forth. In this way, you can ensure that each individual contributes to the whole class decision-making process.

Perhaps the best way to foster both cooperation and competition is by having students play as members of a team. This can blunt the edge of being a loser by losing as a group and therefore dispersing the feelings of loss. It can also foster collaboration: "Collaboration is a special way of working together. It requires three distinct kinds of concerted effort: *cooperating* (acting purposefully toward a common goal), *coordinating* (synchronizing efforts and sharing resources), and *cocreating* (producing a novel outcome together)" (McGonigal 2011, p. 268). Using the jigsaw approach,[4] where groups of students become experts on a different topic or skill and it is only when each topic or skill is brought together that a whole is formed, can promote collaboration within a small group and among groups. Gee (2008) calls these "cross-functional teams":

> Each member must have deep expertise in a specific area, that is, specialized knowledge (their 'function'). At the same time, each team member must have a good knowledge of each other team member's special skills, both so that he or she can integrate with that person smoothly in practice and so that he or she can carry out some of the team member's functions even if one or another team member is missing (crossing functions). That is, each team member must have extensive knowledge in addition to intensive knowledge. (p. 33)

This allows for players to "have their knowledge valued and used by others" (Stevens et al. 2008, p. 58), thus enhancing their sense of ownership, agency, and contribution to game play.

One version of a lesson plan template I used in my teaching has students clearly identify both the students' roles and the teacher's role in the procedures. When students wrote procedures that were teacher centered, such as lecturing, they would not think about what students could be doing, such as filling out a graphic organizer. When students wrote procedures that were student centered, they often did not give any thought as to what the teacher should do, that is, until they taught the lesson and they found themselves awkwardly gazing at students while students were free-writing. Think about what role you, as the teacher, should play in your curricular game.

Some video games have the option of a "Co-op mode" where "gamers work together to defeat an [Artificial Intelligence (AI)] opponent" (McGonigal 2011,

[4]A common version of the jigsaw approach has groups of students become experts on something and then each expert goes back to their home group to teach the other members of their home group.

p. 272). Instead of literally designing an AI opponent, you, as the teacher, can be that opponent. As game master/teacher, you can manipulate the game so you end up being the loser. Students, particularly younger students, love beating adults because it gives them a temporary sense of power over those who rule their world. However, it does set up a competitive dynamic between the teacher and the students and prevents the teacher from being the "guide on the side" helping students defeat opponents, beat the clock, figure out puzzles, overcome obstacles, or solve dilemmas. Earlier I mentioned the driver/navigator pairing. You could have the teacher be the driver and the students be the navigators telling the teacher what to do. You could even have the first level, be teacher as navigator and students as drivers, and then switch roles for a higher level. As teacher, you could also be a nonplaying character (NPC) playing a mentor or even personifying an object being acted upon. For example, in a game about the digestive system, the teacher could be the food that the students act upon. The goal of the game then would be for the food to successfully move through digestive system to provide nutrients to the body and for the waste to be eliminated. For some students, causing the teacher to have to "be" human waste would be the ultimate reward. In the curricular game that guides this text, the teacher could be the Commander giving blunt and harsh feedback, but could also be Amy giving advice on the side.

While the directions contain the number of players, the age of the players is often right on the outside of the box so consumers can choose an age-appropriate game before having to shell out money. Of course we want to design our games to be age appropriate, but we also want them to be gamer appropriate. Earlier we discussed some different types of players. Fullerton et al. (2004) provide a much longer list:

- Competitor: "plays to best other players, regardless of the game."
- Explorer: "curious about the world, loves to go adventuring. Explorers seek outside boundaries—physical or mental"
- Collector: "acquires items, trophies, or knowledge, the collector likes to create sets, organize history, etc."
- Achiever: "plays for varying levels of achievement. Ladders and levels incentivize the achiever"
- Joker: "doesn't take the game seriously—plays for the fun of playing. There's a potential for jokers to annoy serious players. On the other hand, jokers can make the game more social than competitive"
- Artist: "driven by creativity, creation, design"
- Director: "loves to be in charge, direct the play"
- Storyteller: "loves to create or live in worlds of fantasy and imagination"
- Performer: "loves to put on a show for others"
- Craftsman: "wants to build, craft, engineer, or puzzle things out" (p. 90)

One glaring omission from the list above is the socializer: "Adding [a social] element to your game creates an unpredictable, emergent layer that is often enough for many players to stay hooked on a game" (Fullerton et al. 2004, p. 267). It may help to reduce this long list into general groups: those who act on the world (achievers), those who interact with the world (explorers), those who interact with other players (socializers), and those who act on players (imposers) (from Bartle, cited in Schell 2008, p. 110). While we know it is impossible to please all our students all the time, we can try to design a game for most of these types of players by appealing to players' desires to "live out fantasies," for "social interaction," for "exploration and discovery," for "self-expression and performance," for "construction and destruction," for "stimulation," for "collection," and for "story".

Game Space

One of the first things players do with a board game is to take out and study the board because the board should convey what the game play will be like. A *Monopoly* board signals that players will be rotating around the board continuously, whereas *Sorry!* has launching pads and home bases indicating a once around the board. *Chutes and Ladders* has a path that goes from one end to the other. The game board circumscribes the game space—the boundaries within which the game is played. Think about what would happen if there were no boundaries in sports. Keep in mind too that time is a boundary as well. If there were no time boundary in basketball, games would go on forever, that is, unless you imposed a point boundary (first team to reach a certain number of points wins). Game space is not just the physical features; it also includes the nonphysical boundaries that delineate the game as well.

The game space is the most prominent physical feature of a game that helps create the "magic circle" surrounding a game: "The play theorist Johan Huizinga calls the abstract space that the boundaries of games create the 'magic circle,' a temporary world where the rules of the game apply, rather than the rules of the ordinary world" (Fullerton et al. 2004, p. 78). You see this need to draw boundaries between the game world and the real world in children's play as they designate where a cave, fort, nest, and other play spaces reside. Items within these play spaces take on game-based meanings: "although the sequence of letters H-O-N-K-I-E has meaning as a racial slur *outside* of the context of a game of Scrabble, *within* it the sequence has meaning as a six-letter play worth a number of points on the board" (Salen and Zimmerman 2004, p. 43). If someone came up to you, balled up their fist, and moved it in a circle, you would be perplexed. But if they did so in the context of a game of *Charades*, you would know they were about to act out the title of a movie. The magic circle works because the players within the magic circle agree to those shared meanings, although sometimes negotiating meanings is part of the game play itself.

Think about the space that your system occupies and objects within that space. Is it bounded or continuous? Are the boundaries impervious or permeable or perhaps there are openings in the boundaries? Are there spaces within that space (and even spaces within those spaces)? What are those boundaries like? How do objects traverse within the space? (e.g., think of how different objects move through the human body, a restaurant, an ecosystem, a country, etc.). Do the attributes (or the state of an attribute) of objects change depending on their location within that space? Are there other triggers? How does the player know that or should a player know that? How can you represent that space? This may seem overwhelming, but simple signals can conjure up whole worlds. For example, you can use tape on the floor of your classroom to designate the walls of a room, a game board, graph paper, or the outline of a body. A black flag with a skull and crossbones "communicates a time in history, a general location, manners of dress and speech and other social roles and rules from the world of piracy quickly and wordlessly" (Swan 2010, p. 115). In other words, symbols that say a lot without saying anything can help you quickly establish your game world.

Perspective can also say a lot without words. If you study the *Mousetrap* game board, you realize you are looking down on the room from the ceiling. How do you want players to view your game space? Do you want a "bird's eye" view like the *Mousetrap* board? Or a side view like being on the sidelines of a sporting event? Or an "isometric" view looking down from an upper corner? Or a first-person view such as looking through the eyes of a mouse navigating a maze? Or an "over-the-shoulder" view? Or do you want players to be able to toggle among types of views? Perhaps you want a first-person view until a level is completed and part of the reward is a bird's eye view, such as of the maze the player just successfully navigated. Schell (2008) calls this "the binocular effect," showing detail at the beginning through a close-up view and then viewing at a distance with little detail. This is similar to what people do when watching a play because "once someone has seen [the characters] close-up, they can map that image onto the tiny figures they see on the stage in their visual imagination" (Schell 2008, p. 302). Or you could do the opposite, like the beginning of many movies, where the overview of the setting is shown and then the camera zooms in for a close-up of what the director wants viewers to focus on at the beginning. Zooming back out can then allow players to view the game world with new eyes after experiencing it from within.

The game space is what gives players the feel of the game. According to Rabin (2009), third-person point of view allows players to relate to the protagonist: "It becomes easier for players to identify, empathize, and understand the character because they can see it" (p. 105). However, Schell (2008) argues that fewer features of the protagonist allow the player to map himself or herself onto the protagonist, and first-person point of view would have no features at all. The features of the landscape (landmarks, signs (directional and identification), thresholds, boundaries, paths, intersections, and so forth) help orient the player and convey expected player action. For example, an intersection signals a decision point; a boundary conveys the rule "you cannot go beyond this point." Schell (2008) describes how J.R.R. Tolkein names remote features in his story world to create the sense that there are no boundaries:

> J.R.R. Tolkien's worlds are famous for being deep and rich—one way he achieves this is through a trick he referred to as 'distant mountains.' Throughout his books, he gives names to distant places, people, and events that are never actually encountered in the book. The names and brief descriptions make it seem like the world is larger and richer than it is. When fans would ask him why he didn't add more detail about these things, he would reply that he could tell them all about the distant mountains, but if he did that he'd need to create more distant mountains for those distant mountains. (p. 351)

Not only can the game space give players a feel for the game; game space can also indirectly control players' actions within a game. The game *Connect Four* is configured with seven columns, forcing players to have a piece in the center for horizontal or diagonal connect fours; thus "the battle for control of [the center column] draws players into conflict with each other quickly and makes the overall experience more exciting" (Fullerton et al. 2004, p. 236). If *Connect Four* had eight columns, this conflict might not occur. Schell (2008) describes how a real-life game space uses a prominent landmark to direct park goers' actions:

> Walt Disney knew that there was some risk of guests entering the park and milling about the entrance, unsure of where to go. The castle is placed such that the guests' eyes are immediately drawn to it upon entering the park, and their feet are quick to follow. Soon the guests are at the Disneyland hub, with several visual landmarks beckoning them in different directions. Indirectly, Walt was able to control guests to do just what he wanted them to do: Move quickly to the center of Disneyland, and then branch out randomly to other parts of the park. Of course, the guests are seldom aware of this manipulation. After all, no one told them where to go. All the guests know is that without much thinking, and with total freedom, they ended up somewhere interesting and had a fun entertainment experience. (p. 289)

Think about how you can use your game space to influence player's actions while making them feel like they have free will. If you want to show gradual transition, use gradients, curves, and pastels; if you want to indicate contrast, use primary colors and sharp boundaries. Design your game space to convey and shape players' experiences.

While "the primary purpose of architecture is to control a person's experience" (Schell 2008, p. 330), music and color can also be used to influence actions. For example, owners of fast-food restaurants paint their interiors and exteriors red, orange, and yellow colors because those colors make us hungry; grocery stores play slow music to make us linger and shop longer. Schell (2008) challenges his readers to think of what audio effects and/or music might make players do the following: "Look around for something hidden; destroy everything possible without slowing down; realize they are heading the wrong way; move slowly and carefully; worry about accidentally hurting innocent bystanders; go as far and as fast as possible without looking back" (pp. 292–293). Just like in movies, music in video games can be used to make players feel certain emotions and is becoming popular even outside of game play. In 2011, "Baba Yetu," a song written for *Civilization IV*, became the first video game song to win a Grammy (Kuchera 2011). Game space not only influences the physical experience of the game, it stimulates emotions as well.

Game Objects

Objects within your game space should also operate to reinforce your theme. For example, if your game takes place in a library, likely objects would be books, book shelves, tables, and those green-hooded lamps that seem to be in every library. Schell (2008) describes how he and his team designed *Pirates of the Caribbean: Battle for the Buccaneer Gold*, a virtual reality experience at *Disney World*, so that functional items also served as thematic items: fishing nets as the place to hold bags, air conditioning vents aimed so the air blows on players' faces to feel like the ocean breeze, and so forth.

Objects should convey their functionality: "Picturing 'knights' as horses helps us remember that they can jump around the board in ways the others cannot. By giving details that help our imaginations better grasp their functionality [makes] the game become much more accessible to us" (Schell 2008, p. 200). In doing so, features should be borrowed from the real world, otherwise making players memorize what features signal what can unnecessarily increase cognitive load:

> Has Dr. Seuss over influenced sim design? ...Feeding a planet of snicklewhacks (or whatever) puts a level of contrivance that simply doesn't resonate with enough people. Any game element, almost by definition, appeals to some while turning off others... Let's say that I need body language to suggest my creature is sick. I would rather the designer research the real-world body language than make up new ones. ("The juntiopians turn blue and spotted when sick.... ")... I believe a good short-term goal for visual fidelity in the whole "big skills" area (project management, stewardship, relationship management, and so on) is about the level of a *New Yorker* cartoon. Real, but abstracted, including exaggerations and holes. The nice thing about that is that it provides an accurate representation of most systems as well. (Aldrich 2009, pp. 463–464)

One way objects convey meaning is by being similar to, or different from, other objects: "if two objects behave the same way, they should look the same. If they behave differently, they should look different" (Schell 2008, p. 136). If one is a smaller version of another, having the same features can convey this: "the boss monster [having] something in common with his minions" (Schell 2008, p. 337). Think about how your objects relate to each other and how you can design the features of your objects to show these relationships.

Game players tend to be averse to excessive dialogue, so game objects, for example, a creature turning blue to indicate it is sick, can help convey the story without words:

> Another way to convey the storyline to the player is through artifacts. Artifacts are items like posters, radio broadcasts, journals, letters, photos, CDs, laptops, and other items that contain information that advance the narrative. Leaving information on artifacts to be discovered by the player leaves the player feeling in control. They can choose when and for how long to view the item, and they decide what significance it has to the plot. The trick here is to keep the player's interaction with the item brief and the amount of information small on each item to prevent the player from being overwhelmed by information. (Rabin 2009, p. 156)

Game objects can serve many functions including reinforcing the theme, showing relationships, and advancing the plot.

Game objects can also indirectly control player's actions. One way to do this is by using objects, or a lack of, to limit players' choices: "When we built our virtual pirates attraction with a wooden ship's wheel and ... cannons, no guest ever asked whether they could sword fight as part of the game—that option never entered their minds" (Schell 2008, p. 287). Objects can also help players set goals. Schell (2008) provides the example of a fake fly on urinals in Amsterdam's Schipol Airport to give users a place to aim, and therefore less mess (p. 286). Objects, though, can also distract players from what game designers want them to do. Jesse Schell tells the story of a video game scene where the designers wanted the players to go to the throne in the middle, but the playtesters flew around the room on their magic carpets instead. To solve the problem, they drew a bright red line on the floor leading to the throne. When playtesters were asked why they followed the red line, they said, "What red line?". Schell (2008) realized, "it was seeing the columns, and the chandeliers that put the idea of flying around into their minds. The red line was so visually dominant in the scene, that it stopped them from noticing the other things, and so the idea to do these other things didn't even occur to them" (p. 291). Objects can convey goals, whether we intend for them to or not.

One problem with objects, though, is that most of them cannot move on their own. You can enable players to pick them up and carry them to other locations. You can also have NPCs transport them. Another solution can be to use creatures to do this work as well:

> The bat … flaps from room to room carrying along an object, periodically the bat tires of its current trinket, and discards it in favor of a new object to carry off. Without the bat, non-creature objects would never move from the spots where the player dropped them. The effect of the bat is to move objects around, to disturb the predictability of the game. The bat is the game's confusion factor. (Robinett 1984/2006, p. 702)

Objects can be static or dynamic. If dynamic, you will need to think about the rules that govern their behavior. You can use case-based design, where the designer designs paths for every possibility, or rule-based design, where the designer devises rules that govern object behaviors. For example, if a lever requires a certain weight to open a door, the designer could define objects as heavy, medium heavy, or light and code for each instance. Or, the designer could give each object a numerical weight and program the lever only to operate when a certain weight is achieved and even so that it doesn't operate if objects on it are too heavy (example from Salen and Zimmerman 2004, p. 445). This "programming" can be done by having a player roll a die and the teacher moving the lever or having a card telling the player how to determine if the lever moves. Objects should not just be eye candy in games. They should be active contributors to game play.

Resources

Resources are objects that have some value in the game. Schell (2008) compares and contrasts two games to show the difference converting objects into resources can make. The game *Bubsy* involved a cat moving up levels by defeating enemies and, while doing so, collecting yarn balls but the number of yarn balls ended up having no value. *Sonic the Hedgehog 2*, on the other hand.

> was a similar platform game, but did not suffer from this problem In *Sonic 2*, you collect rings instead of yarn balls, and the number of rings collected is very important to players—the rings have a lot of endogenous value. Why? Because carrying rings helps protect you from enemies, and every time you collect 100 rings, you receive an extra life, which increases the chances you will be able to complete all the levels. In the end, Sonic 2 was a much more compelling game than *Bubsy*. (p. 33)

However, you want to make sure that you do not imbue objects with too much value: "'Super units' as they're sometimes called, ruin the gameplay by becoming so valuable that none of the other units matter … Every unit can be balanced by giving it a special advantage ["killer moves"] and a corresponding drawback ["an Achilles heel"]" (Fullerton et al. 2004, p. 238). Rotational symmetry like in *Rochambeau*, a.k.a. rock, paper, scissors, where X beats y which beats z which beats x, can balance out the value of resources.

Resources, of course, should be in keeping with the theme of the game and do not necessarily have to be tangible objects from the real world. For example, health, knowledge, questions (as in the game *Twenty Questions*), available actions, and time can all be resources. What makes all of these valuable is scarcity: "Resources are, by definition, items made valuable by their scarcity and utility. In the real world, and in game worlds, resources can be used to further our aims; they can be combined to make new products or items; and they can be bought and sold in various types of markets" (Fullerton et al. 2004, p. 27). Scarcity does not necessarily mean that there is a limit to how much of that resource is available; it can also mean that resource is hard to get. Love is limitless, but love can sometimes be hard to find.

Resources really represent economic systems, even if they are not necessarily currency, so economic questions can help us determine how resources can be used in our game: "Are the resources fixed or can they grow and/or decline as the game progresses? How are prices set—fixed or controlled by market forces? Is the trade of resources mediated by a currency? Is trade mediated by agents (like shopkeepers and/or bankers?)? What are the rules about trading resources among participants?" (Fullerton et al. 2004, pp. 126–127). If you do use a currency in your game, consider "How can my players earn money? Should there be other ways? What can my players buy? Why? Is money too easy to get? Too hard? How can I change this? Are choices about earning and spending meaningful ones?" (Schell 2008, p. 204). Resources are objects with value, but they should also convey meaning.

The starting point in a game is also a resource. Symmetrical games are games where all players have the same starting position, although you still have to balance who goes first in turn-based games. This is often done either by randomness, by spinning a spinner or throwing dice, or by some aspect of a player that is irrelevant to game play such as youngest player goes first. In order to avoid chance playing a major role, make sure the first move is relatively insignificant in terms of overall play. However, an asymmetrical game where players start with different resources that can be changed through game play such as *Poker* mimics real life more closely. Just like real life, players need places to keep their resources. Consider what can be stored, where items can be stored, how they can be stored, how they can be retrieved, how they can be organized, and how players can see what is in their inventories.

In all games, and in life, information is a resource. Think about how much information players need about the underlying system of the game at any given point and how information about the underlying system is revealed throughout and through game play. Some information is only known to the game; some private to individual players; some private to groups of players; and some public: "a great way to create drama in a game is to make an important piece of private information suddenly become public" (Schell 2008, p. 140). The game of *Clue* is all about information as a resource. An in-game journal allows players to store the information they have earned.

Scoring Mechanism

Players need feedback on where they are in the game—for motivation, to get a sense of the relationship to the whole, and to revise their hypotheses. In order to measure progress, you need a way to keep score. A score should measure how well the student model of the system matches the expert model of the system. To do this, you would need to design a scoring model with a "measurement scale, the scoring criteria, performance descriptions of each criterion at each point on the scale, and sample responses that represent various levels of performance" (Baker and Delacruz 2008, p. 28), in other words, a rubric. In schooling, typically the points earned represent the student model and 100 points the expert model. The discrepancy between the student model and expert model is measured in terms of the percentage of the student model that matches the expert model.

Once you have a scoring model, you can design a cybernetic system. A cybernetic system uses a sensor (scoring function) to take in information from the environment (current game state). A comparator (controller) then evaluates that information based on an established range. If the score is outside of the established range, an activator (game mechanics) takes action on the environment (game state) to change the environment (game state) to reflect this discrepancy and/or if it falls within the range to change the environment (game state) to reflect this success (Marc LeBlanc cited in Salen and Zimmerman 2004, p. 218). If we think about this in terms of a typical classroom, the sensor is the teacher who "reads" the assignment and is the comparator who evaluates that information by comparing it to the scoring model (rubric) and the activator who takes action by grading the assignment. In both the classroom and a game, failure could mean stasis and success change (e.g., ability to move to the next level); failure could mean change (e.g., the bomb blows up or you flunk out) and success stasis; or both could mean changes in different ways (e.g., success you advance, failure you flunk out). You then need to decide how the system will respond when performance falls outside of that given range and how it should respond when it falls within the range. This then gives the student feedback about how much their model matches the expert model. Keep in mind, though, that a failure state does not have to be one and done: "It is significant that it takes two collisions with the dragon, not one, for the cursor to be swallowed. Merely colliding with the dragon is not fatal. Thus the interesting chase-bite cycle is made possible. Most video games define simple one-time collision with enemies as fatal and irrevocable, and thereby miss a chance to create a more interesting interaction" (Robinett 1984/2006, p. 702). Failure can also be partial, allowing the player to recover without having to restart the game, such as losing health points when hit in a battle.

One way to create rising action is through "escalation," or having point values increase as the game progresses. For example, in the popular television show *Jeopardy*, the second round doubles the points. In Final Jeopardy, players can bet any value between zero and the amount earned making the amount earned important, but also giving other players that chance to catch up (i.e., rubberbanding). It also creates a meaningful choice as the player has to decide how much he or she should bet based on confidence in their ability to answer a question in that subject area and the difference between their score and their opponents' scores.

Allowing players to choose between doing a lot of little tasks for a few points or one big task for a lot of points is another way to create meaningful choices. However, you need to make sure that the scoring system reinforces the core game mechanism: "My concern was that it encouraged quantity over quality. Students quickly learned that three C's were better than one A in terms of course points, so they churned out work to get points rather than focusing primarily on the quality of the work" (Hodgson 2013, p. 55). One problem with grades, and some scoring systems, is that they put a cap on high performance. Students can earn an A+, but they cannot earn anything above an A+ so students quickly learn that going above and beyond an A+ does not get measured and therefore is not valued. Goodhart's law states that "When a measure becomes a target, it ceases to be a good measure." The scoring system should not be the goal of the game, but rather be a way of providing students feedback about their game play.

You may even opt to have your scoring system be progress in the game instead of numerical points. For my English Methods class, students have a series of challenges with specific performance targets (e.g., leading a small group discussion with an exchange of at least three students in a row without teacher intervention). They cannot move on to the next challenge until they meet their current challenge. Students who complete all the challenges earn an A, all but one challenge a B, and so forth. What I am concerned about in teaching this class is that students possess the skills necessary to student teach, whether or not they can write an "A" lesson plan. Your scoring system should not only reinforce the theme of your game but also reflect the values you want to engender.

Game Events

The events in your game should flow from your story. Do not forget, though, that you can manipulate your story to create certain game events. Perhaps, however, I should not talk in terms of the game story, but rather the game stories: "Games with only one path to victory can become predictable" (Fullerton et al. 2004, p. 290). Not only are they predictable, but they are not replayable. Multiple paths to victory also solves the problem of students giving away a crucial piece of game information to other students, either in another class period or students who might have you the following year. You can also have players choose different objectives for different game play. However, one advantage you have in designing a curricular game versus a commercial video game is that your students are likely to only play your game once. It may make sense with your particular game to have a "golden path." If that is the case, you need to stress to students that the same rules around cheating on a test apply to playing the game and make it clear when it is acceptable to collaborate with others in their class and/or share information with those outside of class and when it is not.

Schrier (2007) found that "some participants, however, desired a more linear game. They felt that because the game was open-ended, it did not feel as goal-oriented. They were unsure of their status in the game as they navigated it because there was little feedback on whether they were gathering enough evidence or finding enough historic figures. Some felt that there were too many choices at once and they wanted more of a progression of events" (p. 264). Schrier (2007) redesigned the game to satisfy both the achievers and the explorers:

> In the redesign, I established new mini-objectives as role-specific secret missions. These objectives functioned as checkpoints that helped direct the participants' navigation of the content. Interestingly, the Redesign trial participants especially did not seem overwhelmed or frustrated, but thrived in the nonlinear environment because they liked to 'figure something out for [themselves].' These participants enjoyed having agency or control over how they navigated the game world… For example, one participant liked that in this game, the results were not pre-established and she needed to create the 'game ending' herself. … A nonlinear world with well-placed boundaries and sufficient direction seemed to support the pedagogical objectives of encouraging alternative views of history, and also engaged participants by enabling them to have enough control over their game experience to encourage them to use their critical thinking skills as well as their imagination. (p. 264)

Optional "secret missions" or side quests can allow achievers to move through the game directly by bypassing them, while satisfying explorer's need for more open-endedness. Secret missions can also be used as rewards: "not only do they not have to complete it, they actually have to *earn the right* to complete it, by discovering its secret location" (McGonigal 2011, p. 129). Optional secret missions are also a great way to differentiate learning by providing enough challenge for high-achieving students without frustrating other students.

In the story chapter, we discussed the typical narrative story arc: exposition, rising action, climax, and resolution. However, we can also look to learning theories to help shape our game's narrative arc:

> **Initial Hook reveals objective**: The beginning needs to grab the students' attention. This can be done by having the game start 'in media res' (in the middle of the action) by introducing a mystery, setting students on a mission, or creating cognitive dissonance. The goal might be conveyed directly, such as an NPC telling the player the mission. Many adventure games do this by beginning with a short video called a cut scene. Sometimes the initial objective might be to figure out the goal, creating an air of mystery when you find yourself somewhere and you don't know where or why or what you are supposed to do. In the play *Romeo and Juliet*, it's the opposite. The whole story is told in the prologue and purpose of reading is to find out the details to figure out how that all happened. Most games fall somewhere in between where the player is only given partial knowledge or perhaps the overall goal but the details and back story are learned through playing the game. *Corresponding learning theories*: Gagné's (1985) reception/expectancy stage; Hunter's (1982) anticipatory set; Merrill's (2002) Problem; Eisenkraft's (2003) Engage; Keller's (1984) attention stage.

> **Secondary Hook activates prior knowledge**: This is where a mini-success or partial success reveals more information. The game starts to establish the backstory and build background knowledge but in doing so, the game should activate prior knowledge. This can be done by requiring the student to use prior knowledge to solve the first problem or use analogies to make connections between the students' prior knowledge and the subject matter. *Corresponding learning theories:* Gagné's (1985) retrieval stage; Hunter's (1982) objectives; Merrill's (2002) activation; Eisenkraft's (2003) Elicit; Keller's (1984) relevance.

Character interactions model behaviors and norms: The inner workings of the system are revealed as the player has to discover the rules that govern the system through the responses generated by playing the game. Gee (2008) provides an example of this from *SWAT 4* where shooting without announcing that you are police results in an "unauthorized use of force penalty" (pp. 24–25). *Corresponding learning theories*: Gagné's (1985) selective perception; Hunter's (1982) teaching stage; Merrill's (2002) demonstration; Eisenkraft's (2003) Explain; Keller's (1984) relevance.

Puzzles, quests, and challenges allow players to develop subskills within the whole context: Players learn, practice, and master subskills that are part of a larger skill through scaffolding and feedback. *Corresponding learning theories:* Gagné's (1985) semantic encoding; Hunter's (1982) guided practice; Merrill's (2002) application; Eisenkraft's (2003) Elaborate; Keller's (1984) confidence.

Boss challenge provides an opportunity for players to put all subskills together: The game requires players to use all subskills at once. This could also involve applying skills in new contexts. *Corresponding learning theories*: Gagné's (1985) responding stage; Hunter's (1982) independent practice; Merrill's (2002) integration; Eisenkraft's (2003) Evaluate; Keller' (1984) satisfaction.

After Action Review gives players the chance to reflect on their game play: Debriefing after the game or level allows players to think about alternatives, the values embedded in the game, and the messages of the game. *Corresponding learning theories*: Gagné's (1985) reinforcement and generalization; Hunter's (1982) closure; Merrill's (2002) integration; Eisenkraft's (2003) Extend; Keller's (1984) satisfaction.

REPEAT with each level increasing in complexity and expanding the player's options.

The narrative arc and the story events within it shape how our students experience the game: "What is the player actually doing from moment to moment in the game? How are these moments connected in a larger trajectory of experience? How does the experience of play become meaningful? What, above all, is the play of the game?" (Salen and Zimmerman 2004, p. 326). We can make these game moments memorable by tapping into common human pleasures:

"**Anticipation**. When you know a pleasure is coming, just waiting for it is a kind of pleasure.

"**Delight in Another's Misfortune**. Typically, we feel this when some unjust person suddenly gets their comeuppance. It is an important aspect of competitive games. The Germans call it *schadenfreude* (pronounced shodden froyd).

"**Gift Giving**. There is a unique pleasure when you make someone else happy through the surprise of a gift. We wrap our presents to heighten and intensify the surprise. The pleasure is not just that the person is happy, but that *you* made them happy.

"**Humor**. Two unconnected things are suddenly united by a paradigm shift. It is hard to describe, but we all know when it happens. Weirdly, it causes us to make a barking noise.

"**Possibility**. This is the pleasure of having many choices and knowing you could pick any one of them. This is often experienced when shopping or at a buffet table.

"**Pride in Accomplishment**. This is a pleasure all its own that can persist long after the accomplishment was made. The Yiddish word *naches* (pronounced 'nock-hess') is about this kind of pleased satisfaction, usually when referring to pride in children or grandchildren.

> "**Purification**. It feels good to make something clean. Many games take advantage of the pleasure of purification—any game where you have to 'eat all the dots,' 'destroy all the bad guys,' or otherwise 'clear the level' is taking advantage of this pleasure.
>
> "**Surprise**. … The brain likes surprises.
>
> "**Thrill**. There is a saying among roller coaster designers that 'fear minus death equals fun.' Thrill is that kind of fun—you experience terror, but feel secure in your safety.
>
> "**Triumph over Adversity**. This is that pleasure that you have accomplished something that you knew was a long shot. Typically this pleasure is accompanied by shouts of personal triumph. The Italians have a word for this pleasure: *fiero* (pronounced fee-air-o).
>
> "**Wonder**. An overwhelming feeling of awe and amazement." (Schell 2008, pp. 111–112)

Marc LeBlanc describes how games tap into human pleasure: "Sensation: game as sense-pleasure; fantasy: game as make-believe; narrative: game as drama; challenge: game as obstacle course; fellowship: game as social framework; discovery: game as uncharted territory; expression: game as self-discovery; submission: … submission to a rule-based system" (Salen and Zimmerman 2004, p. 334). While it might be impossible to design a game that satisfies every human pleasure, incorporating game moments that make it likely for your students to experience pleasure, including "pleasant frustration" (Gee 2007, p. 36), creates memories and makes it more likely that the understandings that are fostered become enduring ones.

However, it is not just pleasure that games evoke. J.C. Herz argues that playing games tap into our basic survival instinct (Salen and Zimmerman 2004, p. 336). Games can also meet Csikszentmihalyi's (1990) eight components of "flow": chance of completion and of non-completion, conditions for concentration, clear goals, immediate feedback, actions remove self from everydayness of life, sense of control, trade concern for self for enhanced sense of self, and alters sense of time. The first four are conditions of the game and the last four effects of playing the game. Czikszentmihalyi (1990), however, points out certain paradoxes of flow. Put in gaming context, gamers need both the chance of completion and non-completion; focused concentration (on game world) while losing concentration (on real world); clear goals without clear ways to achieve them; a sense of control within lack of control; trading concern for self for enhanced sense of self; and altered sense of time creating sensation of both "hours pass by like minutes, and minutes can stretch out to seem like hours" (Czikszentmihalyi 1990, p. 49). One repeated theme you will see throughout this book is that game design, like teaching, is all about balance.

Another paradox of a flow state is the importance of lulls in order to give players a chance to reflect: "Pauses give your listener time to participate, to think, and to process your story. Good timing encourages your listener to dance with you … People will participate in your stories if you let them, and they participate even more when you let them have some of the good parts" (Simmons 2001, p. 100). I am currently watching a television show that is a nonstop drama which makes it not only exhausting to watch, but there is no time for any one drama to be satisfactorily resolved. Instead, games should tap into the "rhythmic pleasure" (Salen and Zimmerman 2004, p. 341) of action and reflection.

As mentioned earlier, games are all about making choices. Michael Mateas points out that "If Choices>Desires, then the player is overwhelmed. If Choices<Desires, the player is frustrated. If Choices=Desires, the player has a feeling of freedom and fulfillment" (Schell 2008, p. 180). The nonvoluntary nature of classroom games has players start off feeling like they have no choice. Giving players an initial expressive choice (role-play role, overall goal, avatar traits, etc.) can make the game feel voluntary. However, you do not want to overwhelm your players with too many choices once they start playing the game. Remember, "just learning to play a game at all is a challenge" (Schell 2008, p. 178) so make the first level easy. Keep the choices and the challenges focused on the learning objectives. You may have played a video game where the player had to learn a new language and you thought that was really cool (what Mayer and Moreno (2002) call "seductive details" (quoted in Barrett and Johnson 2010, p. 289)), but inventing a new language just for the sake of fun that is unrelated to your learning goals will at the very least distract your learners and at the most overburden them and prevent them from learning the material. For example, I initially used the word denouement when listing the typical plot sequence. This is a domain-specific word that mostly only English majors will know. Since this is not a book designed to teach literature, I changed it to "resolution," a much more common word. However, I would encourage you to incorporate the language of the field (what are called Tier 3 words) that your game targets. For example, in a game about electricity, you could have a billboard that says (Ω=Ǿ or "ohm=naught," i.e., resistance is futile). Not only does it teach, but it makes players feel like they are learning a secret language and thus becoming part of that content area's discourse community.

Players make choices dependent upon their prediction of the consequences. Using the variable ratio schedule can increase the excitement of making these choices: "Sometimes the player will be attacked when he opens a door or rounds a corner, but usually he is not. The experiential result of this design strategy is that in *Half-Life*, deadly threats seem to lurk in every dark shadow and beyond every closed doorway" (Salen and Zimmerman 2004, p. 348). However, be careful about adding too much surprise:

> When you are working on your game, if you discover that things are too predictable, resist the immediate temptation of quick fixes like 'adding randomness.' Before adding chaos, look to player performance and strategy first. Hiding a little information (for example a fog of war) is often all that you will need to get the excitement back. A deterministic system can still have plenty of mystery and uncertainty. Just remember that it is seldom fun for the player if randomness plays a key role in a player's success. Random fates tend to frustrate players. If you do decide to introduce randomness, look for parts of your game systems where the unsystematic behavior won't be too obvious or out of place. For example, you might hide this a bit by using a random outcome in a supporting role; somewhere in your system that will subtly and quietly affect the overall result. (Rabin 2009, p. 96)

Look to the system to determine how much randomness and chance to introduce. You do not want your game to become "man versus random number generator" (Bartle 1996/2006, p. 765). If you decide you want something to sometimes happen, look to how often it typically happens in real life and use that to determine how often it happens in game play. For example, if you created a game about raising a child, you might use the real-life probability of having an autistic child. On the other hand, you might want to increase the odds of something happening. You want your airplane pilot to have practiced emergency situations repeatedly in a flight simulator, not just on the rare occasions that they might occur.

However, perhaps you want to generate something that is not an either/or event, but rather a scale. For example, perhaps your game calls for a hurricane, or maybe is even about hurricanes, but hurricanes vary in intensity from a scale of 1–5. By adding a zero to represent a tropical storm instead of a hurricane, you could have players roll a six-sided die to determine intensity. The probability of having a category five hurricane would then be the same as having a tropical storm. However, in real life there are more tropical storms than category five hurricanes (thank goodness!) so you might want a system where the chances of getting a tropical storm are much greater than a category five hurricane.

There are other scales of probability that are not exponential but rather follow a bell curve. There is a nice bell curve distribution of different probabilities of adding up two die: "in the game *Dungeons and Dragons*, players generate (virtual) skill attributes with values ranging from 3 to 18 by rolling three six-sided dice. As a result, you see a lot of attribute values around 10 or 11, but very few at 3 or 18, and this is exactly what the designers wanted. How would the game be different if players simply rolled a single 20-sided die to get their attributes?" (Schell 2008, p. 161). Of course, you also have to consider the weight of the consequences. For example, if you know another child at your child's school has a disease which is highly contagious, if you just followed the laws of probability, you would keep your child home and you would lose a sick day. But, if you take into account that the consequences of this disease are only a short-lived rash, you might send your child to school. However, if the consequence of the disease is losing an arm, you would keep your child home. You would probably even do so if the probability of your child contracting that disease was very low.

Often, however, players are unaware of the probability of certain events happening. As Schell (2008) points out, "Estimating chance is a skill" (p. 167). If you don't tell players the probabilities, "you must be aware of the 'perceived possibilities' that players have arrived at, because it will determine how they play" (Schell 2008, p. 165). Many people have probability fallacies such as "overvaluing the long shot," "the tendency to think of successive chance events as additive," "the Monte Carlo syndrome" (string of bad luck has to be followed by good luck), "overemphasis on good outcomes," "lightning striking twice," and "luck" (Salen and Zimmerman 2004, p. 186). Despite having the tendency to overestimate the chances of negative consequences, teenagers tend to be drawn to unknown risks, presumably to encourage independence from parents or, in the case of animals, to draw them toward exploring new environments so one geographic area does not become overcrowded (Szalavitz 2012). Because of this, "allowing teens opportunities to safely experiment—for example, a simulator that shows sober teens what drunk driving is like—could also help, by making an unknown risk seem more real and known. Allowing teens the opportunity to take risks in a safe context could also help them develop expertise that underlies gist-based thinking" (Szalavitz 2012), making simulation games the perfect venue for teaching teenagers decision-making skills.

However, you do not want to make too much known in your game: "Imagine how incomplete you would feel if, before the game, you were already declared the winner. Imagine how purposeless the game would feel" (Bernard DeKoven quoted in Salen and Zimmerman 2004, p. 174). This is because "if the outcome of the game is completely predetermined—then any choices a player makes are meaningless, because they do not impact the way that the game plays out" (Salen and Zimmerman 2004, p. 174). Most games do have predetermined outcomes, as the goal of the game is to achieve a certain win state. What is uncertain is which player will reach it first. This is a tricky one for us as teachers, however, because we want all of our students to be winners. Salen and Zimmerman (2004) follow this up by saying "Uncertainty is a central feature of every game … [it] is a necessary ingredient in giving a game a feeling of purpose … of meaningful play" (p. 174). Uncertainty, however, does not need to lie in who will be the winner, but rather in the outcome of the game. Perhaps your game does have a set "win state" in order to convey that the goal has been achieved. In that case, the uncertainty can reside in how the game will play out like in *Romeo and Juliet* where the chorus creates suspense by telling the outcome, but the reader/viewer wonders how the outcome happened. This is why we do not want to know the outcome of a sports game before we watch it. There is little point in watching it if we know the outcome, unless we are a player reviewing it to improve our game. However, we might want to watch specific plays or events, for example, fast-forwarding just to see how the touchdowns occurred. Some game events, such as when Joe Theismann broke his leg during a football game, are so interesting in itself that the particular event has risen in importance above the game. Only diehard sports fans remember who actually won that game where Joe Theismann broke his leg so dramatically. Many video games have the ability to capture game play through a recording device such as a camera, video camera, or journal. You may want to consider doing the same with your game by using actual cameras, video cameras, or journals.

Cut scenes and scripted events occur when the player does not have control over the action and instead is viewing the actions of others. Cut scenes are like little movies that show action away from present location. Scripted events are actions that take place at the location but the player has no control over how the action is played out. For example, this could be an NPC doing something in background or the player entering a room and the camera swinging around to show something important. Cut scenes and scripted events can be a great way to advance the plot by introducing new information or adding a new conflict. For example, I introduced my own "scripted event" in my English Methods class when I subtly left the room and stormed back in with a sign that said "irate parent" and berated the poor student who was currently teaching for failing my child. The student then had to decide how to react. However, Rabin (2009) cautions that because cut scenes/scripted events "take control of the action away from the player," [they] "should be used with caution" (p. 154). Rabin (2009) also warns against forcing the player to watch a cut scene or scripted event over again if the player replays that section. Instead, the game should have the option of skipping over them.

On the other hand, "a *triggered event* is one that is preplanned into the script and is prompted to occur once the player has activated a certain mechanism in the game" (Rabin 2009, p. 157). Triggered events can create the illusion of control by allowing the player to make choices that do not impact game play—that way you do not have to program in what happens for each choice (e.g., whether to wear a green or a blue hat) but can have choices that trigger events unrelated to the spine of the story such as causing two NPC cars to crash in *Grand Theft Auto* and watching the drivers jump out and fight each other (example from Rabin 2009, p. 158). Triggered events can also be in response to failing or succeeding in a task and therefore providing the player feedback on the consequences of his or her actions and thus prompt further action.

Another way to create the illusion of agency is to have players choose the order in which they encounter the material. To do this, write all game events down on note cards. Then, determine which events have to occur in a particular sequence and which do not. Color code or use some other marker to differentiate between the two. Place the events (note cards) that have to take place in a certain order in that order. Then, take the remaining events (note cards) and put them with ordered events in a way that makes sense. This is called "gating":

> This way, while each plot point is not encountered in a linear manner, each group is. One way of keeping a player within a group is not giving the character a type of skill or enough hit points until he has completed all of the challenges within a grouping. He can go to later groupings, but will be unsuccessful in his attempts to defeat the later challenges. A writer can go further and allow different choices to effect what challenges the player will encounter within the grouping; however, inevitably, all characters will wind up experiencing the same number of groupings. (Rabin 2009, p. 158)

Depending on the scale of your game, you can think of these groupings either as lessons within a unit or units within a course. Keep in mind, though, that "players should never spend so much time in a sub-game that they forget what they were doing in the main game" (quoting Sid Meier, Schell 2008, p. 147). Also, if a player encounters a grouping he or she is not yet prepared for, the game should in some way make it clear that the player needs to do something else first. While you want your game events to be memorable, you want to do so in a way that helps achieve your overall unit or course goals, not create frustration in your players.

Teaching through simulations and case-based teaching has the problem of overly contextualizing the material as students end up knowing how to do something only in those specific instances. I heard a story about someone who, because she lived at Boston University (BU) her first 4 years in Boston, learned how to get around Boston only in relation to BU. After she left BU and lived elsewhere in Boston, she could only get places by first going to BU and then going to her destination instead of going directly to her destination. Gaming levels can solve the problem of over-contextualization by having students perform a task in multiple contexts: "With multiple contexts, students are more likely to abstract the relevant features of concepts and develop a more flexible representation of knowledge" (Bransford et al. 2000, p. 78). To create these different contexts, ask "what if" different parts of the problem were changed. To succeed, players have to develop general rules that would apply to all (or most) situations, and conditional rules that apply to specific situations. Giving players the opportunity to experience the core game mechanic from as many different perspectives or different situations as possible can help student thinking move from concrete to abstract and help them distinguish between general rules and conditional rules.

The final outcome of your game, or the win state, should tie back to the beginning to provide a sense of closure. Like the Hero's Return in the hero archetype where the hero returns home much wiser, revisiting the beginning allows students to reflect on how the game has changed them. However, "you never want to drag out the ending. Think of your game as a movie. Once you've passed the climax, wrap it up fast" (Fullerton et al. 2004, p. 237). The final outcome of your game also must be rewarding, especially since most likely you will not have a single winner (being the sole winner can be enough excitement in and of itself). This is why graduations have such "pomp and circumstance." One way to make the ending rewarding is to have a surprise ending, tie up some mystery, or bring seemingly disparate pieces together in a way that makes the whole system make sense and may make players want to play game again with new knowledge. For example, in the movie *Murder on the Orient Express* (spoiler alert), you find out at the end that all the suspects teamed up to commit the murder. If you want to do this, think of something important you can withhold until the end. You can even have the class play the game again with this new knowledge, or at least speculate on what it would be like to play the game again during the debriefing.

Rules

Reading a book or watching a movie involves a "suspension of disbelief" (Samuel Taylor Coleridge 1817), so does agreeing to operate within the rules of a game world, or entering the "magic circle" (Huizinga 1955). The goal of *Charades* is to get your teammates to say the title of a book or movie. You could just tell them the title and ask them to repeat it back. However, it is much more fun to try to get your teammates to guess the correct title by acting it out. The players of *Charades* have a tacit agreement that each person will not say the title but will attempt to pantomime it. It is the rules that constrain actions that create the game: "Easy games do not do well in the marketplace because gamers want tough challenges" (Charsky 2010, p. 204). Establishing a goal and instituting rules create these unnecessary obstacles that make achieving that goal a challenge as players attempt to figure out the best way to do so. Oftentimes discussions that sometimes verge on arguments over the nuances of the rules became a part of the game play itself. Almost every game of *Charades* involves discussion over what behaviors are allowed; *Scrabble* has its own official dictionary of words players can use; and spectators of sports feel a part of the game as they assert their own interpretations of how the rules apply to players' actions.

Play is "the experience of rules set in motion" (Salen and Zimmerman 2004, p. 326). Without rules, a game becomes a task:

> To design a game is to construct a set of rules. But the point of game design is not to have players experience rules—it is to have players experience play. Game design is therefore a second-order design problem, in which designers craft play, but only indirectly, through the systems of rules that game designers create. Play arises out of the rules as they are inhabited and enacted by players, creating emergent patterns of behavior, sensation, social exchange,

> and meaning. This shows the necessity of the iterative design process. The delicate interaction of rule and play is something too subtle and too complex to script out in advance, requiring the improvisational balancing that only testing and prototyping can provide. (Zimmerman quoted in Fullerton et al. 2004, pp. 204–205)

As Zimmerman states, creating a game is really about creating balance, including balance between freedom and constraints. This is what Bogost (2007) calls the "simulation gap" or "the gap between rule-based representation and player subjectivity" (p. 43). As we saw, ironically, rules are required for fun. In games like *Taboo* or the *$64,000 Pyramid,* the contestants try to get their partner to guess a word without saying that word. If there were no rules, the contestant could just tell his or her partner what to say. It is the constraint of not being allowed to say it that makes it fun. However, we all know that too many rules ruin the fun: If the contestant was given a script for what to say in order to get the partner to guess, that would "suck the fun out" of the game. Both too much and too little freedom also limit learning. So, you need to consider what balance between affordances (what your game allows students to do) and constraints (what students are not allowed to do) promotes both learning and fun.

CHALLENGE 5.1: Too afraid to contact Amy again, you reflect back on some of those games Amy made you play in college. You recall one where in a small group of people, she had you begin with one person listing two rules, covering the first rule, but the next person can see the second rule. The next person creates two new rules and covers all but one and so forth. The last person would write out the winning condition. At the end, the rules would be uncovered and together we would have to design a game (from Salen and Zimmerman 2004*, p. 16). Except for your secret friend who has made it clear he wants to remain secret, you don't even have one friend to play this with. Perhaps you can play another game to help you think about how rules govern game play. You think of a game you have played, what type of player that game appealed to, and challenge yourself to change a rule in a way that makes that game attractive to another type of game player.* **EXERCISE:** Change a rule in a game to try to make that game more appealing to a different type of game player. Then play the game to see if you achieved the anticipated results.

Rules are the grammar of a system. They define how everything interacts. Often rules change when the game is in different modes or the player is at different levels. It is amazing how many words can be created out of the rules that govern the interaction among the 26 letters of the alphabet. Change the rules by changing the language, and you get a whole new set of possibilities. Instead of imposing limitations, rules create potential: "When the rules of an emergent system are set into motion, the internal relationships between the objects begin to transform the attributes of the elements. These transformations then affect change in the objects' internal relationships, further altering their attributes, resulting in loops and patterns of behavior" (Salen and Zimmerman 2004, p. 160). This leads to unpredictability, i.e., every game is different; thus, a player's experience is different every time: "'Simulation authors,' says Gonzalo Frasca, 'do not represent a particular event, but a set of potential events. Because of this, they have to think about their objects as systems and consider which are the laws that rule their behaviors. In a similar way, people who interpret simulations create mental model of it by inferring the rules that govern it'" (Bogost 2007, p. 64). This is quite a contrast to factory-based schooling.

Earlier I cited my example of redesigning *Jeopardy* for the classroom. I changed the rules because the goal in the classroom was for all students to learn, not for one person to emerge the winner. The real *Jeopardy* has a positive reinforcing feedback loop so that when someone gets something right, they get another turn by having "control of the board," i.e., getting to choose the category and amount of points. I changed this in my classroom version to a balancing feedback loop so that one team does not dominate. Even when a group got something right, the next team got a turn; and when a group got something wrong, the other teams got a chance to answer in rotating order, thus making it in their best interest to pay attention to other teams' turns. If no team got it right, the original team got another turn. In real *Jeopardy*, contestants experienced a negative reinforcing feedback loop—if they got something wrong, they lose points. In my classroom version, groups only lost points during final jeopardy so that way they were encouraged to take more risks.

Marc LeBlanc devised a set of guidelines about how balancing and reinforcing feedback loops impact game play. Reinforcing feedback loops destabilize game play, thus creating challenge. However, you do not want your game too imbalanced or players lose motivation. For example, if you only had ladders and no chutes in *Chutes and Ladders*, one lucky player could quickly get far ahead. Balancing feedback loops stabilize game play. However, you do not want a game too stable; then there is no progress and no drama. Salen and Zimmerman (2004) supply an example to demonstrate this: if all players return to the beginning once a player gets ahead in *Chutes and Ladders*, you have a balancing feedback loop but no movement. Reinforcing feedback loops can speed a game's end by rewarding the winner. Balancing feedback loops can prolong a game by forgiving the loser. For example, in *Chutes and Ladders*, and many other games, players have to get an exact number to enter home. Balancing feedback loops magnify late successes; reinforcing feedback loops magnify early successes (Rabin 2009, p. 113). Keep in mind that sometimes unplanned feedback loops occur. Think about how rules can create balancing and reinforcing feedback loops for different effects: "Every rule adjustment results in a change to the play of the game, and you will never be able to test out every possible rule variation, or even a tiny fraction of them. That is why anticipating how changes to the formal structure of a game affect its play is one of the core skills that game designers must develop" (Salen and Zimmerman 2004, p. 168). An often ignored rule in the game of *Monopoly* states "If you do not wish to buy the property, the Banker sells it at auction to the highest bidder" which "adds a strategic layer to a game that most people believe is based primarily on the luck of the die" (Morris 2013). Keep in mind a rule might not be an explicitly written rule. For example, you can change the number of players and the size of the game space, play with cards instead of on the computer, make public information private or vice versa, put a card back in the deck instead of a discard pile or vice versa, change the win state such as making basketball winnable by reaching a certain number of points instead of a certain time, and so forth. Think about how you might modify the rules to make tic-tac-toe playable by three players.[5]

[5]Example from Fullerton et al. (2004, p. 50).

Game designers distinguish between *operational rules* (how the player can interact with other players and NPCs or "rules of engagement," e.g., football players are punished for grabbing another player by the facemask) and *constitutive rules* (how players can interact with the game world or the world's "natural laws," e.g., football players cannot make a play outside the boundaries of the field) (Swan 2010, p. 115). However, game designers recognize that there are other rules that emerge from game play. Bluffing in poker is an emergent behavior that derives from the rules and is so common, it has become an implicit rule ("players may act like they have a better hand than they do") in and of itself (example from Salen and Zimmerman 2004). Some would argue, though, that implicit rules are not really rules, but rather strategies. For example in the game of *Jotto*, where one player thinks of a word, the other players guess words, and the initial player says how many letters in the guessed word are in the target word until the target word is guessed; some rules include only five letter words can be used and there can be no letter repeats. Some strategies include using the process of elimination, guessing words with letters of high frequency, identifying vowels in the target word, and thinking of letter combinations (e.g., if no U, then likely no Q). However, you could say that the player who knows the target word being honest about the number of shared letters would constitute an implicit rule, not a strategy. Whether or not the other players are allowed to collaborate or work individually is often an unwritten rule that needs to be agreed upon by those playing the game.

Below is a descriptive list of different types of rules that shape game play:

- "*Operational Rules*. These are the rules that describe how the game is played. When you want to play a game and someone explains that you can't open the door until you collect the right key, he is describing an operational rule. Or he tells you that collecting 2000 tokens allows you to buy a cooler snowboard, which is also an operational rule. Once you gain a basic understanding of operational rules, you can play the game.
- *Constitutive Rules or Foundational Rules*. These are the underlying formal structures dictating game functionality. An example is the mathematical formulas used to calculate how many times the number 6 will appear on a die. These tend to be abstract and need only be understood by the designer of the game. However, occasionally a player can determine these underlying rules and use them to his or her advantage. In the 1990s a group of math students from MIT used a method of counting cards in the card game Black Jack to win millions of dollars at casinos in Las Vegas. They achieved this feat by moving beyond the operational rules governing the game such as 'the cards from 2 through 9 are valued at their face value' and 'the 10 card, Jack, Queen, and King are all valued at 10' to the foundational rules such as 'We are playing with three decks, which means there are 156 cards and that means there are a total of forty-eight high cards and four of them have been played already, so the probability that the next card is a high card is .28.'
- *Implicit Rules or Behavior Rules*. These are the rules that govern the social contract between two or more players, in other words, the rules related to being a good sport about the game—game etiquette. These are implied rules and are usually not written. Yet, they have a powerful influence over the game. If they are violated, it is usually a penalty and in a team game can constitute the player being kicked out.

- *Instructional Rules*. Another set of rules exist in an instructional game. These are the rules that you want the learner to know and internalize after the game is played. It is the reason the game is being created in the first place. These rules are the rules that govern the learning within the process of the game. For example, we were creating an online board game to teach inventory managers concepts and ideas to reduce inventory within the organization. One of the rules was that if the player selected a wrong answer, the inventory levels in the factory went up. So the player with the lowest score won the game, not the player with the highest score. This was a conscious choice to reinforce the instructional rule that lower inventory was desirable. The actual game play would not have changed if the score went down, but the instructional lesson may have been diminished if it had." (Kapp 2012, pp. 30–31)

Imagine how student behaviors might change if you change one of the traditional rules of school such as having no grades or the class gets one group grade instead of grades for individuals. If you dare, change a rule in your classroom to see if it plays out like you predicted. Be careful; when I taught high school English, I had a parent complain about giving students a group grade, resulting in me being chastised by my principal. Bucking tradition always seems to invite detractors.

When designing rules, you should follow the KISS principle: Keep It Simple, Stupid: "If the rules of your videogame are so complex that a player can't even form a rough idea of how the game works, they will be overwhelmed and confused. You must make the rules of a complex videogame something that players can discover and understand naturally—not something they have to memorize" (Schell 2008, p. 148). One-way rules can become overly complex is "when you see a ruleset with lots of 'exception cases,' this is generally a ruleset that is [too] complex" (Schell 2008, p. 196). However, I would argue that starting with a simple ruleset and adding "exception cases" to increase the complexity or difficulty of the game as it progresses can help players formulate conditional knowledge. Keep in mind that "very simple ruleset[s] [can] give rise to very complex situations [because they have] emergent complexity" (Schell 2008, p. 196). Take DNA. It has four letters that can be put together in three letter combinations. Sounds simple, yet the possibilities are endless (example from Meadows 2008). A classic example of "emergent complexity" is the game of life. The game of life consists of an infinite grid randomly populated with "alive" and "dead" cells that follow three rules: "A living cell will be alive in the next generation if two or three of its neighbors are alive. A dead cell will be alive in the next generation if three of its neighbors are alive. Otherwise, a cell will be dead" (Salen and Zimmerman 2004, p. 163—game of life designed by John Conway). These three rules create emergent patterns dependent upon the start state. However, technically this is not a game because once set in motion, there are no human decisions; it just runs by itself. Rules by themselves do not make a game. If you designed a game about genetics, having genetic couplings randomly determined and played out does not make it a game. However, interject human decision such as with whom to procreate, add human behaviors impacting epigenetics, and assign a goal (e.g., the longest living species; the strongest species; the smartest species) all within a magic circle, and it becomes a game.

Just like in real life, "Wherever there are rules, there is likely to be rule beating. Rule beating means evasive action to get around the intent of a system's rules—abiding by the letter, but not the spirit, of the law" (Meadows 2008, p. 136). However, you should see rule beating as "useful feedback … to revise, improve, rescind, or better explain the rules. Designing rules better means foreseeing as far as possible the effects of the rules on the subsystems, including any rule beating they might engage in, and structuring the rules to turn the self-organizing capabilities of the system in a positive direction" (Meadows 2008, p. 137). For example, cheating on high-stake tests—and not just by students—is an indication that the "measure has become the target" (Goodhart's Law). Sometimes rule beating is sanctioned,[6] for example, charter schools can bypass union rules, and some card games have "trump" cards that overrule the rules. However, creating systems to subvert the rules might be an indication that we need to restructure the rules. When creating the rules for your game, test for loopholes.

Finding loopholes, however, might be part of the game play. For example, you might design a game with this backstory: Your great aunt's best friend died of cancer because she couldn't afford health care. Your great aunt just recently passed away, and her will directed you to use her estate/money to provide monetary support for those who need cancer treatment. You eagerly began soliciting candidates but early on got burned by someone who claimed to have cancer but did not. You now must become a "cancer detective" to determine which cases are plausible and which are not. Due to HIPPA, you cannot just ask applicants' doctors. Instead, you will examine each case to see if what the applicant describes comports with that particular cancer's symptoms and treatments. The game proceeds from people having obvious discrepancies between the symptoms they describe and cancer symptoms to more subtle ones. With this hypothetical game, there are some cheats. For example, a team could decide to only fund those who sign a HIPPA release form. Or perhaps a team decides to train a cancer-sniffing dog and invite people in for an interview with the dog present. You need to think about whether or not you want to reward students for creative thinking or design the game to prevent such cheats. This all comes down to what your learning goals are. If the learning goal is for students to learn about cancer symptoms, you should discourage shortcuts. However, if your learning goal is for students to learn about how the health-care system operates, perhaps you should encourage students to find loopholes. One common loophole in war games is called spawn camping[7] (from Fullerton et al. 2004, p. 230), hiding out near where players respawn so a player can shoot them immediately. Think of three possible solutions to this loophole before reading on. Here are some: players respawn in randomly generated places; players are invisible when they first respawn until they move; and players can choose

[6] *Illuminati*, a game of deception, offers players an alternative way of playing, a "cheat mode" where players can lie, steal, and do whatever they want to do to win. The instructions state: "We recommend you play the cheating game only with very good friends or with people you will never see again" (Salen and Zimmerman 2004, p. 278).

[7] Some players claim this is not a loophole, but a feature. Some games have created two versions of games—one with and one without (e.g., one version where players can be killed and another where they cannot) or an option of being a player killer with only player killers being able to be killed.

a respawning spot. Now think of problems each of your fixes might have and a fix for them before reading on. Here are some: a randomly generated spot may contain a wall or another player, so design it so it chooses only from available spots; a player could stay still and remain invisible forever, so you could institute a rule where a player must move within a certain amount of time; there still might not be any respawning spots that are safe so have the number of respawning spots equal the number of players so at least one safe one at any given time. Every time you institute a rule, think about potential consequences. If the rule leads to the need for a number of other rules, consider eliminating that rule unless it is essential to game play.

CHALLENGE 5.2: After imagining changing the rules, you realize that when there are rules, people always seem to find loopholes. You challenge yourself to think of loopholes, possible fixes, and fixing any subsequent loopholes—in a game, in the classroom (such as cheating), and in life.[8] **EXERCISE:** Find and try to fix a loophole in a game, in your classroom, and in life.

Balancing rules and interactivity create a sense of "constrained freedom" (Mateas and Stern 2005/2006, p. 656) which leads to a sense of agency in a game world as players have an ability to affect change—to the environment and to themselves. The goal of all games is transformation—transformation of the game world, of the avatar/student as player, and of the student as learner. Keep in mind that the rules serve the greater purpose of helping guide the players in achieving the game goal—both the official game goal of achieving the win state and also your classroom goal of achieving the learning objectives.

Conclusion

Now that you have thought about these various aspects of your game, see how they all fit together. Do they work together as a game? Your goal should be to have a game that is "internally complete, balanced, and fun to play" (Fullerton et al. 2004, p. 196). Play with the variables to see if there are some adjustments you might want to make: "balancing a game is nothing more than adjusting the elements of the game until they deliver the experience you want" (Schell 2008, p.172). Be sure to test for loopholes: "When locking at two problems at once, a common solution often appears more readily" (Reiner Knizia, designer of the *Lord of the Rings* board game quoted in Salen and Zimmerman 2004, p. 26). Do not forget when you make game changes, you might also have to make story change: "Solving a specific design issue should not just address the issue in isolation but should ideally contribute to the overall game play" (Reiner Knizia, quoted in Salen and Zimmerman 2004, p. 27). Tweaking game elements can make a big difference in how players experience your game.

[8] A "life hack" is something that is used to get around the rules of life in order to be more productive. For example, using caffeine to stay awake is a loophole around sleepiness.

Questions to ask about your game include:

- "What skills does your target audience have? What skill level are they at? Within that knowledge, how can you best balance your game for your players' abilities?
- How can you give your players clear, focused goals, meaningful choices, and discernible feedback?
- How can you merge what a player is doing physically with what they need to be thinking about in the game?
- How can you eliminate distractions and fear of failure, i.e., how can you create a safe environment, where players lose their sense of self-consciousness and focus only on the tasks at hand?
- How can you make the game activity enjoyable as an end in itself?" (above questions from Fullerton et al. 2004, p. 86)
- "On which levels of Maslow's hierarchy is my game operating? How can I make my game fulfill more basic needs than it already is? On the levels my game is currently operating, how can it fulfill those needs even better?" (Schell 2008, p. 127)
- "How will players learn to play my game?" (Schell 2008, p. 146)
- "What skills does my game require from the player? Are there categories of skill that this game is missing? Which skills are dominant? Are these skills creating the experience I want? Are some players much better at these skills than others? Does this make the game feel unfair? Can players improve their skills with practice? Does this game demand the right level of skill?" (Schell 2008, p. 153)
- "Do players have the opportunity to take interesting risks in the game?" (Schell 2008, p. 169)

Since all the game elements are dependent upon each other, a change to one means a change to another. You might want to reread parts of this chapter as you work. Once you feel your game is complete, look back at your essential question and ask "What questions does my game put into the player's mind? What am I doing to make them care about these questions? What can I do to make them invent even more questions?" (Schell 2008, p. 30). The questions your game evokes should match your essential question.

Finally, think about what messages your game conveys: "What ideologies are you reflecting, replicating, and promoting in your game? Do you want your game to faithfully depict a particular set of beliefs? Or would you rather question, reverse, or undermine them? Can you incorporate cultural rhetoric into the very experience of your game, encouraging your players to actually play with cultural codes?" (Salen and Zimmerman 2004, p. 522). One of my students initially designed a game where the ultimate goal was to get the atomic bomb first in order to use it. She redesigned the game so that after getting the atomic bomb, each country surveyed the damage and reflected on how World War II could have been prevented in the first place. By changing the final goal, she radically changed the message of the game. Be sure to reflect on what messages your game sends.

Games are the ideal learning environment with their built-in permission to fail, encouragement of out-of-box thinking, and sense of control.

–Karl Kapp 2012, game designer of *Survival Master*

Appendix: Design Quest Worksheet

Possible Title: ____________________

Genre: ________________

Overall Goal: ________________

Core Game Mechanic: ___________________

Starting State: ____

Win State: ____

Rules—answer the following questions to help derive the rules of your game				
Player configuration	How many groups/players?			
	What are their roles?			
	What role will the teacher play?			
	How are players allowed to interact with each other? What is off limits?			
	How are players allowed to interact with NPCs?			
	How are NPCs allowed to interact with players?			
	Any other aspects?			
Game space	Physical boundaries of game			
	Time boundaries of game			
	Can the game be paused? Saved? What happens when the bell rings? If a student has to leave the classroom? If students are absent? When students are late to class?			
	Is it turn-based or real-time or combination?			
	Can players occupy another player's space?			
	Other aspects of game space			
Game objects	Object	Static/dynamic	Function	Rules governing actions/interactions with other objects/ interactions with characters
Resources	Resource	Function	How stored?	Rules governing Resources

(continued)

Scoring	How is progress measured?	
	Can progress be taken away?	
	What else is measured?	
Rules	How are rules used to balance your game?	
	How are rules used to destabilize your game?	
	What are the operational rules?	
	What are the constitutive rules?	
	What are the implicit rules?	
	What are the instructional rules?	
Fixes	What are some potential loopholes? What fixes might take care of them?	

Suggested Design Quest Rubric

Quest	"Wow! I mean, I think this might work" (3)	"Hmm, this is acceptable" (2)	"I need more convincing" (1)	"Go back to the drawing board" (0)
Design quest	Design document shows how all elements come together to create an immersive gaming experience	Design document describes all elements	Design document missing some elements	Very few elements described in design document

Suggested Reading

Alexander, C. (1977). *A pattern language*. New York: Oxford University Press.
Bjork, S., & Holopainen, J. (2005). *Patterns in game design*. Newton, MA: Charles River Media.

References

Aldrich, C. (2009). *Learning online with games, simulations, and virtual worlds: Strategies for online instruction*. Hoboken, NJ: Jossey-Bass.

Baker, E., & Delacruz, G. (2008). Framework for the assessment of learning games. In H. O'Neil & R. Perez (Eds.), *Computer games and team and individual learning* (pp. 21–37). Amsterdam, The Netherlands: Elsevier.

Barrett, K., & Johnson, W. (2010). Developing serious games for learning language-in-culture. In R. Van Eck (Ed.), *Gaming and cognition: Theories and practice from the learning sciences* (pp. 281–311). Hershey, PA: Information Science Reference.

Bartle, R. (1996/2006). Hearts, clubs, diamonds, spades: Players who suite MUDs. In K. Salen & E. Zimmerman (Eds.), *The game designer reader: A rules of play anthology* (pp. 754–787). Cambridge, MA: MIT Press.

Bogost, I. (2007). *Persuasive games: The expressive power of videogames*. Cambridge, MA: MIT Press.

Bransford, J., Brown, A., & Cocking, R. (2000). *How people learn: Brain, mind, experience, and school*. Washington, DC: National Academies Press.

Charsky, D. (2010). Making a connection: Game genres, game characteristics, and teaching structures. In R. Van Eck (Ed.), *Gaming and cognition: Theories and practice from the learning sciences* (pp. 189–212). Hershey, PA: Information Science Reference.
Chatham, R. E. (2011). After the revolution. In S. Tobias & J. D. Fletcher (Eds.), *Computer games and instruction* (pp. 73–99). Charlotte, NC: Information Age.
Coleridge, S. T. (1817). *Biographia literaria*. London: Rest Fenner.
Czikszentmihalyi, M. (1990). *Flow: The psychology of optimal experience*. New York: Harper & Row.
Eisenkraft, A. (2003). Expanding the 5E model: A proposed 7E model emphasizes "transfer of learning" and the importance of eliciting prior understanding. *The Science Teacher, 70*, 56–59.
Fullerton, T., Swain, C., & Hoffman, S. (2004). *Game design workshop: Designing, prototyping, and playtesting games*. San Francisco, CA: CMP Books.
Gagné, R. M. (1985). *Conditions of learning*. New York: Holt, Rinehart, and Winston.
Gee, J. P. (2007). *Good videogames + good learning: Collected essays on videogames, learning, and literacy*. New York: Peter Lang.
Gee, J. P. (2008). Video games, learning, and 'content'. In C. T. Miller (Ed.), *Games: Purpose and potential in education* (pp. 43–53). New York: Springer.
Hodgson, J. (2013). Developing and extending gaming pedagogy: Designing a course as game. In R. Colby, M. S. S. Johnson, & R. Shultz Colby (Eds.), *Rhetoric/composition/play through video games* (pp. 45–62). New York: Palgrave.
Huizinga, J. (1955/2006). Nature and significance of play as a cultural phenomenon from Homo Ludens: A study of the play element in culture. In K. Salen, & E. Zimmerman (Eds.), *The game designer reader: A rules of play anthology* (pp. 96–120). Cambridge, MA: MIT Press.
Hunter, M. (1982). *Mastery learning*. Thousand Oaks, CA: Corwin Press.
Jackson, J. (2009). Game-based teaching: What educators can learn from videogames. *Teaching Education*, 20(3), 291–304.
Johnson, S. (2012). Theme is not meaning: Who decides what a game is about? In C. Steinkuehler, K. Squire, & S. Barab (Eds.), *Games, learning, and society: Learning and meaning in the digital age* (pp. 32–39). New York: Cambridge University Press.
Kapp, K. (2012). *The gamification of learning and instruction: Game-based methods and strategies for training and education*. San Francisco, CA: Pfeiffer.
Keller, J. M. (1984). The use of the ARCS model of motivation in teacher training. In K. Trott (Ed.), *Aspects of educational technology*. London: Kogan Page.
Korbey, H. (2013, March 22). Teachers, students, digital games: What's the right mix? *Mind/Shift*. San Francisco: KQED. Retrieved from http://blogs.kqed.org/mindshift/2013/03/teachers-students-digital-games-whats-the-right-mix/
Kuchera, B. (2011, February 14). How a song from the 2005 *Civilization IV* won a 2011 Grammy. *Ars Technica*. Retrieved from http://arstechnica.com/gaming/2011/02/how-a-song-from-the-2005-civilization-iv-won-a-2011-grammy/
LeBlanc, M. (2004/2006). Tools for creating dramatic game dynamics. In K. Salen & E. Zimmerman (Eds.), *The game designer reader: A rules of play anthology* (pp. 438–459). Cambridge, MA: MIT Press.
Lee, C. (2001). Is October Brown Chinese? A cultural modeling activity system for underachieving students. *American Education Research Journal, 38*(1), 97–141.
MacCullum-Stewart, E. (2011). Stealth learning in online games. In S. de Freitas & P. Maharg (Eds.), *Digital games and learning* (pp. 107–128). London: Continuum.
Mateas, M., & Stern, A. (2005/2006). Interaction and narrative from *Expressive AI*. In K. Salen & E. Zimmerman (Eds.), *The game designer reader: A rules of play anthology* (pp. 642–669). Cambridge, MA: MIT Press.
McGonigal, J. (2011). *Reality is broken: Why games make us better and how they can change the world*. London: Penguin.
Meadows, D. (2008). *Thinking in systems: A primer*. White River Junction, VT: Chelsea Green.
Merrill, M. D. (2002). First principles of instruction. *Educational Technology Research and Development, 50*(3), 43–59.

Morris, C. (2013, May 29). *The one Monopoly rule you shouldn't ignore*. Retrieved from http://games.yahoo.com/blogs/plugged-in/one-monopoly-rule-shouldn-t-ignore-190749670.html
Rabin, S. (2009). *Introduction to game development* (2nd ed.). Herndon, VA: Cengage Learning.
Rieber, L. P. (1996). Seriously considering play: Designing interactive learning environments based on the blending of microworlds, simulations, and games. *Educational Technology Research & Development, 44*(2), 43–58.
Robinett, W. (1984/2006). Adventure as a video game: Adventure for the Atari 2600 from inventing the adventure game. In K. Salen & E. Zimmerman (Eds.), *The game designer reader: A rules of play anthology* (pp. 690–713). Cambridge, MA: MIT Press.
Salen, K., & Zimmerman, E. (2004). *Rules of play: Game design fundamentals*. Cambridge, MA: MIT Press.
Schell, J. (2008). *The art of game design: A book of lenses*. Burlington, MA: Morgan Kaufmann.
Schrier, K. (2007). Reliving history with 'reliving the revolution': Designing augmented reality games to teach the critical thinking of history. In D. Gibson, C. Aldrich, & M. Prensky (Eds.), *Games and simulations in online learning: Research and development frameworks* (pp. 250–269). Hershey, PA: Information Science.
Simmons, A. (2001). *The story factor: Inspiration, influence, and persuasion through the art of storytelling*. New York: Basic Books.
Squire, K. (2011). *Video games and learning: Teaching and participatory culture in the digital age*. NY: Teachers College Press.
Stevens, R., Satwicz, T., & McCarthy, L. (2008). In-game, in-room, in-world: Reconnecting video game play to the rest of the kids' lives. In K. Salen (Ed.), *The ecology of games: Connecting youth, games, and learning* (pp. 41–66). Cambridge, MA: MIT Press.
Swan, R. (2010). Feedforward as an essential active principle of engagement in computer games. In R. Van Eck (Ed.), *Gaming and cognition: Theories and practice from the learning sciences* (pp. 108–136). Hershey, PA: Information Science Reference.
Szalavitz, M. (2012, October 2). Why the teen brain is drawn to risk. *Time Magazine*. Retrieved from http://healthland.time.com/2012/10/02/why-the-teen-brain-is-drawn-to-risk/
Van Eck, R. (2007). Building artificially intelligent learning games. In D. Gibson, C. Aldrich, & M. Prensky (Eds.), *Games and simulations in online learning: Research and development frameworks* (pp. 271–307). Hershey, PA: Information Science.
Wiggins, G., & McTighe, J. (1998). *Understanding by design*. Alexandria, VA: ASCD.

Chapter 6
Fair Game: Designing Quests

> *Your [curricular game] (The original quote uses the word "story", not curricular game.) is the bait. If a fish doesn't bite do you blame the fish? Do you call the fish unmotivated, lazy, greedy? No, you look for better bait ... If your [curricular game] can tap into one of the core human needs that we all share, you've got yourself some pretty good bait.*
>
> *-Annette Simmons, Storyteller, 2001*

Abstract Chapter 6 distinguishes between problems and puzzles and helps the reader think through designing particular ones for his or her game. In doing so, the chapter explores various types of scaffolding and how scaffolding can best be used to support learning so all students can be challenged (Mind in Society, Harvard University Press, Cambridge, MA, 1980), thus keeping students in a state of flow (Flow: The psychology of optimal experience, Harper & Row, New York, 1990). This chapter also discusses different levels within a game and matches them with types of knowledge as well as possible gateways to the different levels.

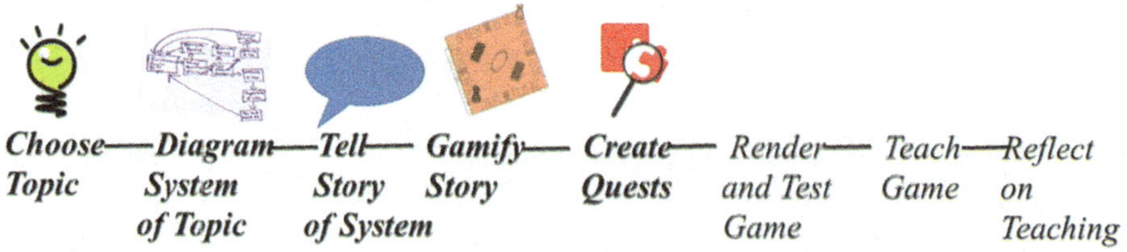

J.J. Kellinger, *A Guide to Designing Curricular Games*,
Advances in Game-Based Learning, DOI 10.1007/978-3-319-42393-7_6

QUESTS QUEST

WHILE the game story does not match the design document, DO revise either the game story or the design document or both UNTIL the game story and design document reflect each other.

As you look over what you have so far, you realize you have a compelling comic strip built on your system with interesting characters and some game rules, but you still do not have a game. "Ok, this is where the rubber meets the road. What sets games apart from a movie?" you ask yourself. Immediately, you know the answer: Interactivity. So how do you make your game interactive? You have built in some interactivity with the decisions users make in the branched narrative version of your story, yet you yearn for more.

"Having options is a privilege," you think. "What if the ability to make a decision rested on the completion of a challenge or solving a puzzle?" You realize that these mini-games, or games within a game, are what make the game experience. If the player were faced with the ultimate challenge at the start, not only would he or she not be prepared, but it wouldn't make for much of a game. You decide the next step is to design some in-game, or in-story, puzzles that in some way serve the larger goal of the game. But how to go about doing so? You think back to a phrase Amy often used, "well-ordered problems" (Gee 2007*, p. 35). You start thinking about how you might go about creating problems that build on each other and busily get to work.*

ACTION: Go through your game story and locate places where the main character faces challenges. Then, design some. When done, check to make sure these challenges afford players opportunities to learn and practice skills, not simply a mechanism to test a player's knowledge.

Part 1: Embedding Challenges

Playing a game is the voluntary attempt to overcome unnecessary obstacles

–Bernard Suits, 1978

When I reflect back on my teaching (almost 25 years!), I can see the seeds of game-based teaching both in the dissatisfaction I had with typical teaching activities and the remedies I devised. For example, the first day of class I used to "go over the syllabus." I finally realized that if I was bored doing so, then students definitely were bored! Not a great way to start off the year. My remedy was to create a syllabus scavenger hunt for the first day of class. I put students in groups and had them search the room and the syllabus for different items, be a hypothetical student and calculate grades, and respond to several scenarios. It got students moving around the class, working together, learning the policies outlined in my syllabus, and set a tone of engagement.

As Prensky (2011) reminds us, "in designing and iterating our high-quality instruction game we would want to focus … not on the 'eye candy' or even the 'story,' but rather on the 'gameplay'—that is, what players actually do—the decisions they make, the ability to go places and do things in the service of the goals, all the various manipulations or 'mechanics' involved" (Prensky 2011, p. 258). What determines the "game play" are the rules that constrain the player from simply walking over and dropping the golf ball into the hole. In this way, games are "goal-driven problem space[s]" (Gee 2008a, p. 49). For our purposes, the cognitive skills required to solve problems in the game should be the same as cognitive skills required to solve real-world problems in that domain:

> Games have content, but they are not about their content. They are about doing, making decisions, solving problems, and interacting. … In good games, content (including story or plot) needs to be a loyal vassal to *game mechanics*, that is, all that players must do and decide in order to succeed. … learning is, for nearly all good games, a core game mechanic. Gamers do not just do things and make decisions. They must learn things and even master them. If they don't, they don't leave the first level of a game. (Gee 2012, p. xvii)

If content doesn't matter, then what does? While the surface structure may differ, the deep structure, or core game mechanic, needs to be the same as the primary performance objective.

A performance objective focuses on what *students* should be able to *do after* an educational intervention and can be stated like this, "As a result of this (lesson, unit, curricular game), students will be able to …." (some teachers use SWBAT for short). It should not be about what the teacher is doing or even a description of what students are supposed to do during the lesson, but rather what the lesson, unit, project, curricular game, etc., prepares students to do. It is outcome based and student centered. Some refer to this as including the "ABCDs" of performance objectives: "A=Audience" (who the objective is for), "B=Behaviors" (what students are expected to be able to do), "C=Conditions" (under what conditions), and "D=Degree" (to what degree) (Sheldon 2011, pp. 191–192). Squire's (2011) questions may help you determine your primary performance objective: "(1) What are the *purposes* for learning that content? (2) What is known about *how* people learn in that domain? And (3) What *strategies* have worked in the past?" (p. 89). Reread your performance objective. If it has the word "understand" in it, it is not a performance objective, but rather a cognitive one. As Wiggins and McTighe (2005) explain, the word understand has multiple meanings ranging from interpreting to empathizing to analyzing to reflecting on self. Substituting a synonym for the word "understand" in each of the following sentences demonstrates the variety of meanings the word "understand" can have:

- *I* understand *what you are going through.*
- *John and Joe have come to an* understanding *about their differences.*
- *I finally* understand *how to figure out standard deviation.*
- *I* understand *what E.E. Cummings meant in his poem "next to of course god america i"*
- *Even though I don't agree with you, I can* understand *your point of view.*
- *I finally* understand *why I've been dating losers my whole life.*

If your objective has the word understand in it, ask yourself how would you know students "understood" the topic? What behaviors would demonstrate that understanding?

Just as the performance objective is what teachers want students to be able to do as a result of a lesson, the core game mechanic is the repeated action that improves throughout the game through practice: in other words, the opportunity for players to enact their learning. The core game mechanic is not "a series of quests" but rather the actions and thinking the students need to do in order to complete the quests. This should match the performance objective—what actions students should be able to do in order to demonstrate they have achieved the enduring understanding. If one of your quests is a word search, unless your performance objective is to find a certain sequence of letters among other letters, you need to rethink your quest. Remember, the learning is in the experience. Think about what the players are experiencing during the game. There should be a tight fit among the enduring understanding, essential question, theme, and core game mechanic. This might involve tearing yourself away from typical classroom tasks like writing a paper or taking a quiz. If the game play does not have the players experiencing the enduring understanding, you need to rethink your quests. Let's call these games where core game mechanics match the performance objective *pedagogically sound* games.

Just like our core game mechanic should mirror our primary performance objective, what we do in education should follow from our larger goal of preparing students for life beyond school:

> By not teaching and pushing our students to develop problem solving skills, we fail to prepare them adequately for life outside of school. We are "preparing" them, in fact, for a world where the questions and answers are pre-packaged and easy to bubble in. And that world does not exist. (Holt 2013)

As Schell (2008) points out, "When problem-solving is removed from a game, it ceases to become a game and becomes just an activity" (p. 35). For example, the goal of checkers is to gather as many of the opponents chips as possible. Strip the rules from it, and it becomes simply the activity of picking up the opposite colored chips and putting them in a pile.

Van Eck (2007) describes problem solving as: "the generation of new rules based on a combination of several prerequisite **Rules** which in turn require the master of different **Defined Concepts** and **Concrete Concepts** which require the ability to make **Discriminations**" (p. 281). This is exactly what happens in playing and in learning: people ask themselves, "What happens when …?" This is also the process behind research and running mental simulations. What drives all of them is curiosity. Ask yourself: "What problems does my game ask the player to solve? Are there hidden problems to solve that arise as part of gameplay? How can my game generate new problems so that players keep coming back?" (Schell 2008, p. 35). Keep in mind that novices solve problems differently from experts: "[Experts] notice patterns in problem spaces; understand a domain conditionally; easily retrieve domain knowledge without expending a large amount of mental resources; [and] approach new situations flexibly" (Adcock et al. 2010, p. 156). Just like we leveled our systems, the problems should build on each other and increase in complexity and difficulty throughout the game.

In order to solve problems, players make decisions or, as Sid Meier, creator of *Civilization*, states, "a series of interesting choices." What makes choices interesting are the trade-offs and uncertain outcomes:

> If we make it our goal, we can easily insert Gameplay into almost everything we do. Want to add Gameplay to a lecture?—just add uncertainty. Begin the lecture by telling people that some of what they are about to hear may not be true. Harvard Professor Ellen J. Langer[14] discovered that when faced with uncertainty, students spend the time actively trying to sort out what is true from what isn't, and are more engaged, with greater retention. Want to add Gameplay to a textbook? Langer has done experiments with inserting "conditional" language. (Prensky 2002, p. 9)

Making decisions based on partial knowledge heightens dramatic tension. Citizens were glued to their television sets as decisions were made about shutting down a whole metropolitan city to try to capture one terrorist in Boston after the Marathon bombing. Everyone held their breath as the police decided to lift their "stay-in-place" order. Why? Because no one knew how it would turn out. Fortunately, the gamble paid off. In terms of video games, not knowing where the enemy is but knowing he, she, or it could be around any corner creates suspense. A first-person view of a maze puts the player in a position of not knowing the layout. If you know you can complete something, i.e., there is a certain outcome, then it is not a challenge. On the other hand, if you know it is impossible to complete something, you also have a certain outcome, and again, no challenge, just frustration. That is why video games adjust to keep players in Vygotsky's zone of proximal development (ZPD).

It is this element of balance that becomes crucial in designing challenging but doable curricular games. You do not want to make the game too uncertain: "In most well-designed games, the element of choice remains dominant. If every choice a player makes results in random effects, they will feel like their choices have no meaning. But keep surprise in mind; used judiciously, it can create a wealth of fun and excitement" (Fullerton et al. 2004, p. 284). Csikszentmihalyi (1990) calls this the "paradox of control": "Only when a doubtful outcome is at stake, and one is able to influence that outcome, can a person really know she is in control" (p. 61). On the other hand, you do not want to make the game too doable: "There is a fine line between granting your players control and burdening them with chores [so game designers make some choices default ones and] leave only the most important decisions … up [to] the players" (Fullerton et al. 2004, pp. 286–287). This is the beauty of the "perpetual running" games. If there is an activity that constantly needs to be done, like running, automate it so the player can concentrate on the core game mechanic.

Remember, uncertain outcomes only need to be uncertain to the learner/player. For example, one of my students designed a branching narrative based on the novel *Mansfield Park* which takes place in the early 1800s. The players did not know the outcomes of their choices, but the designer/teacher knew the historical context and therefore created likely results and, in doing so, taught students about that historical era. A woman choosing not to marry had very different consequences in the early 1800s than today. Having the consequences of the players' choices change the game story made the historical information more relevant and compelling to the players.

In order to be impactful, choices need consequences that "alter the course of the game … you'd be surprised at how many games force the players to make choices that have no impact upon whether they win or lose" (Fullerton et al. 2004, p. 271). However, you may want to include some choices which allow the gamer to "infuse some of his/her personality" by customizing the avatar, setting, and/or game play: "expressive choices are choices that the gamer makes which may have little impact on gameplay, but can improve engagement" (Charsky 2010, p. 202). You can also tie expressive choices to strategy, though, by making the types of strategies available dependent upon expressive choices:

> The traits they emphasize, by distributing points among those traits, would affect the strategies available to them in the game. … The gameplay would lead to situations where the gamer would need to handle a particular situation using the available strategies. With these choices in place it sets up the use of diverse situations: some where the strategies will have great success and somewhere they will not … the expressive choices can be connected to the learning and be seamlessly tied to the content, context, world, and game play. (Charsky 2010, p. 203)

You could even design the game so that players can "purchase" more traits by getting more points.

These choices should occur at nodes where decisions can lead a player down different paths. To identify where these leverage points are, look to your system to find places where "a small change could lead to a large shift in behavior" (Meadows 2008, p. 145). What makes these leverage points interesting is that sometimes what feels like the right decision can "push the change in the *wrong direction*" (Meadows 2008, p. 145) because the decision that helps reach the goal can be counterintuitive. For example, it is very common for schools to punish high school students for being late to school by giving them detention. Too many detentions leads to out-of-school suspension. The end result, then, is less time spent in school when that is what the student is being punished for in the first place. If the goal is for students to be in school, look for the reasons the student was late in the first place and attempt to remedy that.[1] Find the leverage points in your system. These are the places where interesting choices can be made.

In order for the results of these choices to be "interesting," they should have both upsides and downsides. A classic example of creating choices with possible upsides and downsides by holding another factor, or in this case choice, uncertain is the Prisoner's Dilemma. In the Prisoner's Dilemma, two criminals are caught and each

[1] Teenagers not only need more sleep, but their biorhythms are such that they tend to fall asleep later at night, not to mention the time demands of homework, sports, and after-school jobs. Schools who have changed the start time for their high schools to later in the morning have uncovered some positive unintended consequences such as students being more awake and doing better in school even in cases where the overall school day was less time than before. In addition, their communities saw less crime when the high school got out later because there was less "idle time" for teenagers without after-school sports or jobs to be tempted into petty crime (Wahlstrom 2014).

is offered an opportunity to get off if he or she tells, or "rats," on his or her partner unless both rat, in which case both get 2 years in jail. If a prisoner refuses to rat but his partner does, then the refuser gets a 3-year sentence and the "ratter" gets off. If both do not rat, then they each receive a 1-year sentence. To represent all possible outcomes, a "payoff matrix" would look like this:

	Prisoner 1 rats	**Prisoner 1 does not rat**
Prisoner 2 rats	Both get 2 years in jail	Prisoner 1 gets a 3-year sentence; prisoner 2 gets off
Prisoner 2 does not rat	Prisoner 1 gets off; prisoner 2 gets a 3-year sentence	Both get a 1-year sentence

The reason this is a dilemma is because of the uncertain outcome—each prisoner does not know what the other might do.[2]

The results of some decisions are zero sum: one person's gain equals another person's loss. For example, if the person cutting a cake in two cuts one piece larger than the other, the person who chooses the piece gains the difference between the two pieces, which is the same as the cutter's loss. Because of this, the cutter will cut the cake as evenly as possible knowing the chooser will choose the larger of the two pieces, thus minimizing his or her loss. This is the essence of the minimax theorem (example from Poundstone 2006).

In some cases, like the cake division scenario, there is a choice that almost equally benefits all players. These are called saddle points. Salen and Zimmerman (2004) warn that game designers should avoid creating saddle points because all players would make the same choice and then there is no game, or rather no fun in the game, because no conflict is generated (p. 241). However, you could create a game where finding the saddle point is the point of the game—as long as finding that saddle point takes some doing. Examples that come to mind include hostage negotiations, a whole host of congressional or Presidential decisions, a child trying to reach a compromise with a parent, and so forth. The trick is that the saddle point must either involve trade-offs for both parties or, if a win-win situation, must be difficult to figure out.

Because our students will likely only play our curricular game once, finding the "golden path" or optimal solution to your game could be the goal of your game. Of course, you need to trust that students will not pass the solution onto the next generation of students. This is not unlike designing tests where teachers have to trust that students will not pass on the answers. Just like with a test, if they do so with a curricular game, students should suffer the consequences of cheating. To be fair, however, you should make it clear that passing on the answers to your curricular game constitutes cheating and comes with consequences.

[2]An urban legend at the undergraduate institution I attended involved four students partying for the whole weekend at another university fully intending to come back early to study for their upcoming chemistry test on Monday, but staying longer than planned. They all agreed to tell their professor that they got a flat tire coming home and therefore did not have time to study. The story goes that the professor allows them to take the test late, puts them each in a different room, and has as the last question on the test: "Which tire was flat?".

If, however, your goal is not to have a "golden path" but rather multiple paths that end in a variety of consequences, you want to create dilemmas where there are "no optimal answers" (Fullerton et al. 2004, p. 273). The decisions made in these dilemmas can range from having a minor impact on the ultimate outcome to being a critical determinant. As a player progresses through the game, the decisions should move up on the decision scale where at the end "everything [should] hang in the balance" (Fullerton et al. 2004, p. 272). You do want to avoid decisions that have no impact on the outcome, obvious decisions, and arbitrary ones. Of course it is always interesting to create a "butterfly effect"[3] where a seemingly small decision at the beginning ends up playing a large role down the road. Remember that doing nothing and letting the system run its course without interference is also an option that can lead to large consequences. For example, doing nothing about pollution allows pollution to continue to increase and impact the ecological system. The second law of thermodynamics states that systems tend to move from order to disorder. This law always makes me think about the state of my bedroom. If I do not take regular action, it quickly devolves into chaos. Doing nothing can be a choice in your game that leads to interesting consequences.

Even though "the game must present a stream of critical decisions that either directly or indirectly impacts the player's ability to win, … nonstop action can get boring too—it's in the breather between waves of enemies that we can appreciate our accomplishments, anticipate the next wave, and steel ourselves for the battle ahead" (Fullerton et al. 2004, p. 271). This cyclical back-and-forth between action and repose, decision-making and information-seeking, and challenge and reward allows players to analyze their actions and apply their refined hypotheses to the next task. If your game is set to low intensity all the time, players get bored. Ironically, constant high intensity can lead to an analogous feeling: "when the play of a game becomes synonymous with anxiety, the experience is surprisingly similar to boredom" because players need time to "feel an actual sense of accomplishment" (Salen and Zimmerman 2004, p. 352). Cycling between highs and lows creates the rhythm of the game.

Ultimately, the various decision paths should reveal the underlying system that you designed in an earlier chapter. You may be asking yourself, "Why not just share this system with your students and bypass all this gaming stuff?" The answer to this lies in Cazden's (1981) phrase, "performance before competence":

> This isn't a random process; it's the essence of the scientific method. Through trial and error, players build a model of the underlying game based on empirical evidence collected through play. As the players refine this model, they begin to master the game world. It's a rapid cycle of hypothesis, experiment, and analysis. And it's a fundamentally different take on problem solving than the linear, read-the-manual-first approach of their parents. (Reese 2010, p. 232 quoting Will Wright)

[3]The term "butterfly effect" comes from the proposal that a butterfly flapping her wings in one location could change the initial conditions in such a way that it might alter the course or even occurrence of a large weather event such as a tornado in another location.

Gee (2007) uses his own experience playing video games to demonstrate why "reading the manual first" does not work:

> This issue of situated understanding became dramatically clear to me when I started playing video games. Like a good baby boomer, but not a smart young person, when I played my first game, I initially tried to read the manual cover to cover. I understood what the manual was saying as words, but I had no idea what it really meant or how it applied. I felt that I would be unable to play the game, since it all seemed so unclear. But then I put the manual down and played. After a few hours of play, I returned to the manual and now what had seemed so unclear was completely lucid. I even had a hard time recalling why the text had seemed so hard in the beginning. (from the Forward to Selfe and Hawisher 2007, p. ix)

On the other hand, in schools teachers often expect students to be able to read and understand the textbook with little to no context: "It's very difficult to comprehend specialized texts until you've been immersed in situations in which they are useful. … Gee notes that a problem in secondary schools is that we 'give people the book before they are ever allowed to play the game.' In games, you play before you read the book" (Squire 2012, p. 20). This idea of trying before learning bears out in research studies as well:

> "We are showing that exploration, inquiry and problem solving are not just 'nice to have' things in classrooms," said Blikstein. "They are powerful learning mechanisms that increase performance by every measure we have." Pea explained that these results indicate the value for learning of first engaging one's prior knowledge and intuitions in investigating problems in a learning domain—before being presented with abstracted knowledge. Having first explored how one believes a system works creates a knowledge-building relevance to the text or video that is then presented. (Plotnikoff 2013)

When teachers *push* information onto their students, students have no context, no reason, and no motivation to learn the material. Allowing students to explore a domain, try something out, make mistakes, and even fail provides not only a context with which to connect new information but also a desire to *pull* that information in order to make use of it during the next performance cycle.

Puzzles and problems create opportunities for performance. They are what makes the difference between your course being a game instead of "an elaborate field trip" (Jenkins 2011, p. xxiii). While puzzles have single solutions, problems have multiple solutions. Because of this, problems are good for players to "learn the underlying properties of the system," whereas "puzzles are especially good at serving as *choke points* to test understandings" (Squire 2011, p. 91). However, puzzles can be designed so that each player or groups of players solve a different one resulting in players having different pieces of information. It is only when those different pieces of information are put together that players have the information they need to solve a problem:

> This jigsaw design seeks to support engagement and learning. First, it immerses each player in a role with unique abilities, which we hope increases role identification. Second, differentiated roles require players to synthesize what they read. Third, it creates responsibility, as players are accountable to their group for understanding their information. Finally, it creates a cooperative, distributed puzzle-solving game which provides a pleasurable context for meaningful interactions with content. (Squire 2011, p. 184)

I would like to add a fifth dimension, and that is of creating short-term and long-term goals. Schell (2008) uses the example of the JUMBLE puzzle where players have to unscramble words and put them together to figure out the punch line of a joke to demonstrate how having many mini puzzles required to be solved in order to solve one larger puzzle creates what Johnson (2005) calls "telescoping" (p. 41).

If a puzzle is different every time it is encountered, it forces the player to understand underlying mechanics instead of just trial and error and memorizing a solution (Osterweil and Klopfer 2011). This can be done well or poorly. My children play a game where one puzzle, completing a pattern, needs to be done three times in order to open the treasure chest. However, every time the game is played, the puzzle involves the same three patterns in the same order. Designing an algorithm to randomize those patterns is not a large coding stretch so I am not sure why the developers did not do this. However, at the end of the game, the player has to identify the order of three events in the story. This puzzle is randomized every time, thus teaching, or at least testing, the underlying concept of plot sequence. In another game my children play, each "puzzle" involves the same goal—getting Mickey Mouse enough water to supply his lemonade stand—but each round adds a layer of complexity. For example, in addition to digging through sand, in the next level, players must also figure out how to get a cloud to rain the water onto the sand. In this way, the puzzles are not just mere repetition but rather build on one another.

Mateas and Stern (2005/2006) claim that puzzles deflate emotional involvement:

> Puzzles disrupt enactment, breaking immersion in the action and forcing reflection on the action as a problem to be solved. As the player thinks about the puzzle, action grinds to a halt … All the dead ends involved in solving a puzzle introduce incidents that expand time and reduce emotion, thus disrupting intensification. … the form of engagement demanded by the puzzle is disruptive of dramatic properties. (pp. 648–649).

However, I disagree. After all, *Hamlet*, one of the most well-known dramas, is all about Hamlet trying to figure out what to do to avenge his father's death with a constant run-in with dead ends (you could say the same about *Macbeth* trying to solve the puzzle of the oracle proclaiming his destiny to become king and all of the literal "dead ends" he and his wife commit). The trick to maintaining engagement while puzzle-solving is to create the sensation that players/students are solving the puzzle as if they are a character in the game story. In other words, you want players to constantly ask themselves "What would my avatar do?" (WWMAD?), with the knowledge, skills, values, goals, motivations, thought patterns, dispositions, and so forth of their avatar while following the rules and principles of the game world. If truly immersed, players will not be asking WWMAD, but rather will be inhabiting their avatar as they navigate the game world and asking themselves "What should I do?" Certainly, an interesting twist would be to have students (either the same student or different (groups of) students) solve the same puzzle from different character perspectives.

One activity I do in my classes is to have my students solve the same puzzle from different knowledge bases in order to impress upon my students the importance of prior knowledge. To do so, I divide the students into three groups, and each group reads a different piece: one about doctors using stem cells to try to cure a boy with cancer, another about interval training where athletes alternate periods of rest and increasing levels of training, and another about a general who divides his troops to approach an enemy from five different directions so that the weight of the troops will not be enough to trigger the minefields surrounding the enemy. I then present the following problem to the whole class:

> A man has a tumor which needs a 100 g dose of radiation to kill it. However at this level, the force of the radiation would destroy the healthy tissue between the tumor and the ray. A dose of 20 is the maximum that can be used without the healthy tissue being destroyed. How might the doctors treating the man try to help him?" (this problem and the general piece taken from Bransford et al. 2000, p. 64)

Inevitably, the three groups develop three different responses. The group who read the stem cell piece typically proposes extracting healthy stem cells before the treatment and using them to replace the tissue destroyed by the radiation process. The group who read the interval training piece typically proposes that the patient be subjected to incrementally higher doses with rest periods in between. The group who read the piece about the general tends to propose that the doctor give the patient five 20 g doses from five different angles simultaneously so the tumor receives a total of 100 g with none of the doses being strong enough to kill healthy tissue. In this way, students see how prior knowledge, and character perspective, can impact problem solving.

Assessment

Teachers are likely to look at the steps I have outlined so far and ask, "Where's assessment?" Here it is! Read this definition of assessment: "we size up a situation by gathering data, apply some criteria to make inferences that are meaningful to us, and then decide what to do next" (Gibson 2007, p. 309). This sounds exactly like how gamers play video games.

Assessment is in the challenges, problems, and puzzles players must figure out in order to advance: "Every action [in a game] is a test with feedback, and the boss at the end of a level is a 'final exam' for that level" (Gee 2012, p. xvii). One of the most important aspects of game design, and of teaching, is to keep students in their own challenge zone: "The master adjusts the complexity of the task and the degree to which the learner is given responsibility for and control over the undertaking, thereby keeping the work within what Vygotsky (1978) calls the learner's 'zone of proximal development'" (Steinkuehler and Oh 2012, p. 157). Although most video games can adjust to various player levels within a game, they usually do not assess and tailor themselves to the initial needs or knowledge of players,[4] another constraint of commercial off-the-shelf (COTS) video games and another reason for us, as teachers, to design our own. As teachers, we already have practice using diagnostic[5] assessments to tailor our instruction to the needs of students in our classes.

[4] Some do have "initial calibration games" (Magerko et al. 2010, p. 270).

[5] Personally, I am not a fan of the term "diagnostic" because it implies that teachers are trying to "diagnose a disorder." However, it is a term, like classroom management, that is so widely used, I have given up trying to change the tide.

Because learning involves connecting new knowledge to prior knowledge, diagnostic assessments can help identify students' prior knowledge, misconceptions, interests, skill level, and even dispositions in order to make prior knowledge explicit:

> Consider the challenge of working with children who believe that the earth is flat and attempting to help them understand that it is spherical. When told it is round, children picture the earth as a pancake rather than as a sphere (Vosniadou and Brewer, 1989). If they are then told that it is round like a sphere, they interpret the new information about a spherical earth within their flat-earth view by picturing a pancake-like flat surface inside or on top of a sphere, with humans standing on top of the pancake. The children's construction of their new understandings has been guided by a model of the earth that helped them explain how they could stand or walk upon its surface, and a spherical earth did not fit their mental model. Like *Fish Is Fish [a children's book where a frog describes land creatures to a fish and the fish imagines them with fish features]*, everything the children heard was incorporated into that preexisting view. (Bransford et al. 2000, p. 10)

My children know the difference between hot and cold in terms of temperature. When I said that this bowl of salsa is hot (as in spicy), they asked for the "cold" salsa. Because they do not have a reference for spicy hot and mild, they apply what they know, their prior knowledge, to the current situation. However, often teachers do not know the prior knowledge students are applying to the current situations. One of the key aspects of teaching an educational video game is making thinking visible. One of the affordances of developing your own educational game is that you can design one that explores your students' questions about themselves and their world.

Earlier I advocated for performance before competence. Your students' performances on the first puzzle can also serve as a diagnostic assessment. Just as we drew different levels of systems representing our topic, students have their own mental model of the topic before even beginning the game. This mental model could be completely inconsistent with reality, have major gaps in the model, or be a simpler version of reality:

> According to Pelligrino et al. (2001), central to assessment is reasoning from evidence generated through a process consisting of three points: 'a model of how students represent knowledge and develop competence in the subject domain, tasks or situations that allow one to observe students' performance, and an interpretation method for drawing inferences from the performance evidence thus obtained.' (p. 2)" (Dexter 2007, p. 232)

While games may not always assess a player's initial knowledge and skills, they often allow the player to choose the level at which they play, ranging from easy to difficult. Sometimes games even have "fish tanks," defined earlier as an experimentation area where players can get used to a simplified version of the rules of the game world without being in the game itself. Fish tanks are a perfect place to do some stealth assessment (Shute 2011), i.e., tracking data in ways that do not disrupt the flow of the game. Video games can do this by tracking "clickstreams"—where users click on the screen and in what order. Advertisers do this to test their advertising by using eye-tracking devices which tell them where people are looking. You can design your game to adjust to players' levels, but you can also do this through observation. For example, one of my students noticed that her students were taking notes in random order. Based on this, she realized students needed more scaffolding in the form of a graphic organizer. In this way, you can track students' behavior in order to gather evidence.

The evidence you collect then can be used to generate claims or statements about what a learner is able to do. You can then provide scaffolding in the game to support the learning of individual students. However, it is very important to adjust your claims in order for the game to have adaptivity and keep the learner in the flow of the game. Just like teachers see everything as assessment opportunities, "the goal is to eventually blur the distinction between assessment and learning" (Shute 2011, p. 505). In an ideal game world, the challenges are constantly adapting to the player's learning curve based on constant assessment. To do so, tasks or puzzles must be designed to "elicit behaviors that can inform how the system should shape the next steps or courses of instruction" (Baker and Delacruz 2008, p. 27). In other words, formative assessment, or assessment during instruction, or, in our case, game play, should provide data that can be used to determine what feedback to give and which direction to take the player.

Using assessment to elicit evidence in order to make claims about students' abilities is called **evidence-centered design** (ECD), i.e., using assessment as "a machine for reasoning about what students know, can do, or have accomplished, based on a handful of things they say, do, or make in particular settings (Mislevy, Steinberg, and Almond, 2003, p. 4)" (quoted in Gibson 2007, p. 309). In other words, teachers identify what evidence is needed to make a claim about a student's knowledge and skills and then "determin[e] what tasks in the game or simulation will elicit that information" (Dexter 2007, p. 229), much like Wiggins and McTighe's (2005) second step of figuring out what evidence is needed in order to demonstrate that a student has achieved a unit goal. The amount of evidence needed should be strong enough to infer the abilities of the student, much like a sample of a population needs to be large enough to support a generalization about that population. You could even argue that, like samples, evidence should be drawn from random tasks so that each time the player plays a game the tasks are randomly chosen from a pool of tasks. However, another approach would be the use of carefully chosen problems in order to create "daisy chains" where "the fruits of the one … problem leading directly to the task of the next" (Green 2014, p. 120). In some cases, you might even want the solution used to solve one problem lead to an incorrect answer to the next problem, causing the players to revise and refine their strategies.

Once you have determined the claims you want to be able to make about students and the evidence you would need in order to make that claim, the next step is to develop a **task model**. A task model is a narrative description of what tasks are likely to elicit the types of behaviors described in the claim: "Tasks are the most obvious part of an assessment, and their main purpose is to elicit evidence (which is observable) about competencies (which are unobservable)" (Shute 2011, p. 511). A task model is written in terms of instructions for creating items to elicit evidence to support a claim.

Sample Task Model: Student is prompted to identify an item being personified in a text that is written at the target level of complexity.

This sample task model above is typical of a standard assessment. However, we are not designing standard assessments. We are designing tasks in a game world.

Perhaps the player is a detective who finds a clue and has to figure out that a name (such as Rose, Chance, Miles, and so forth) is really the item or abstract concept being personified and not an actual person. Or perhaps an art historian or museum docent has to identify personification in a painting. Or a scientist has to realize that the aliens she is studying have the ability to shapeshift and she has to figure out how to distinguish between actual items and alien creatures who are impersonating, or rather anthropomorphizing, items or a character in a children's book like *Alice in Wonderland* who has to figure out what items are personified by the author and which creatures are real.

CHALLENGE 6.1: You know what Amy would have you do. She would have you practice. You pull the standards out of you satchel, close your eyes, flip through them, and put your finger down. Now that you have chosen a standard in your discipline, you rewrite it in terms of a claim being made about a student's ability and make sure it includes a target level. You then write out a task model, i.e., instructions for designing tasks that would elicit evidence of that claim. Then, you attempt to describe at least three different ways you could construct tasks in a game world that would supply evidence of that claim. Once again, you try to evaluate your own work not from your eyes as an educator but through Amy's eyes as a game designer.

EXERCISE: Design a task model for one of the standards in our discipline. Then think of three different game challenges that could provide evidence that the standard was met.

The challenge above mentions "target levels." You may want to develop tasks in order to determine which level of the claim can be made about various students. In other words, design it to be able to discriminate among players who demonstrate behaviors at different levels, much like an analytic rubric which has descriptors for each level per criterion. This is called the **competency model**, an analytic rubric with criteria and target levels identified for cognitive skills/learning objectives. However, you can make a competency model more complex by giving criteria different weights or even developing a model of how criteria interact with each other. Be sure to consider the labels of the levels and the messages they may send, especially if they are part of the feedback given to students. For example, this model has "unacceptable" for the lowest level, which has very negative connotations. Using "Not Yet," on the other hand, suggests that the player will get there eventually. Earlier I mentioned the importance of using everything to reinforce your theme; here is a perfect chance to label the levels using naming conventions common in the domain. A game about medicine might have the following levels: premed, medical student, intern, resident, fellow, and attending. You can also use these labels as a means of giving in-game feedback from the perspective of a game character, like I did in the rubrics that accompany this text.

	4 Excellent	3 Good	2 Needs Improvement	1 Unacceptable
Technique	Uses a variety of methods such as Boolean operators, quotation marks, and dates to narrow searches	Uses two or less methods to narrow searches	Uses only one method to narrow searches	Cannot narrow searches
Result	Narrows four searches	Narrows three searches	Narrows one or two searches	Narrows zero searches
Time	Completes task in less than 20 minutes	Completes task between 20 and 30 minutes	Completes task between 30 and 40 minutes	Does not complete task
Independence	Works independently	Asks one question for clarification	Asks two questions for clarification	Needs constant supervision

One way to think of the competency model is to use your most complex systems diagram as your "reference frame," i.e., a model of how experts approach a topic. Assessment lies in ascertaining the degree to which a student's mental model (what Shaffer (2012) calls "epistemic frame") matches this reference frame or expert model. You can also think about this in terms of ways in which a student has "adopted the discourse practices of a community" (Shaffer 2012, p. 426). In other words, how much does the student use the jargon, the conventions, and the ways of thinking in your topic area, i.e., the content area literacy skills? In order to do this, assessment must make thinking visible, just like your math teachers probably instructed you to "show your work": "Looking at the choices people make in a course of action devoted to solving problems in a certain area is a much better assessment both of what they know and of how well prepared they are for future learning" (Gee and Hayes 2012, p. 147, quoting Dan Schwartz). Shute (2011) calls these series of choices "action sequences" (p. 511). Loh (2007) calls them "information trails" (p. 329). However, you do not need to track student behavior when looking at the game state can give you enough information to infer where they are in their thinking: "You can look at somebody's city [in *SimCity*] that they've designed at any point and see that it's kind of a snapshot of their current understanding of the model" (Fullerton et al. 2004, p. 135 quoting Celia Pearce's interview with Will Wright). Since the goal of learning is to move students from novice thinking toward expert thinking by reducing the discrepancy between a student's mental model and the expert model, assessment involves revising what is known about the student model based on incoming data and then measuring the difference between where the student is and the ways experts understand a field to determine the progress of that discrepancy reduction.

The **evidence model** "contains the inference rules that relate the task and student model variables into an analysis of what the user knows and can do" (Gibson 2007, p. 312). How the evidence model does this is by describing the evidence needed:

> Evidence rules classify observables into patterns that can then be used to make inferences or claims about the learner ... When we say 'rules' we mean a set of 'IF ... THEN ...' statements that connect patterns or sets of observables into meaningful relationships that allow us to make claims .... All games and simulation assessments that focus on what users have learned have to claim that the evidence created by a user interacting with the application provided realistic evidence of performance in some other context. (Gibson 2007, pp. 313–314)

This sounds complicated, but it can be as simple as those descriptions of what each level looks like, i.e., how a learner would behave, in an analytic rubric. Rubrics can be read as a series of "IF-THEN" statements: "IF the learner exhibits this descriptive pattern, THEN the learner is at a certain level of competence in terms of this criterion." However, an evidence model can be made more complex by making it situational: "Player exhibits A behavior in Y situation but B behavior in Z situation" thus demonstrating the learner has gained conditional knowledge. An example of conditional knowledge in standards language is: "a student is able to adjust diction to different audiences in a persuasive writing piece."

Some common tasks in video games include (from Dickey 2011, p. 143):

- Collecting items (e.g., Pac-Man eating dots)
- Eliminating enemies (this can be other players, NPCs, objects, creatures, and so forth) (e.g., in *Space Invaders*, shooting enemy aliens)
- Avoiding being killed by an enemy or an object (e.g., avoiding ghosts in *Pac-Man*; cars in *Frogger*)
- Managing resources such as money, items needed for survival, etc., or even making intangibles tangible such as a health meter (e.g., acquiring and trading properties in *Monopoly*)
- Racing with another player, NPC, or object (e.g., any racing game)
- Navigating an environment (e.g., *Q*bert* jumping on blocks, *Frogger* crossing roads, any game with a maze)
- Constructing an item (e.g., *Minecraft*, building in *Second Life*)
- Solving a puzzle (e.g., the many puzzles in the *Myst* series)

In order for these tasks to become puzzles or problems where the player needs to figure something out and not merely activities, the game should impose rules or restrictions. For example, "a supply of resources must not only be useful, but also limited in some way. To limit a resource, we can restrict the total supply to a finite amount or restrict the rate. We might instead provide special conditions for their use or employment, or create penalties for their consumption" (Rabin 2009, p. 119). While rules are usually thought of as controlling and limiting, using rules to guide behavior within the context of the game story instead of defining each interaction can lead to the illusion of free will: "Giving each type of object in the world a simple set of rules for interaction, rather than scripting each encounter separately often leads to creative and unusual results" (Fullerton et al. 2004, p. 290). In this way, rules can act as "enabling constraints" (Davis et al. 2000). Rules create the game world. Successful task completion involves learning the rules, operating within the rules, and sometimes using the rules to a player's advantage.

However, sometimes people assume rules that are not there. The classic example of this involves connecting a 3 by 3 grid of nine dots with only four lines. Most people when initially faced with this puzzle assume the lines have to remain within the imagined square formed by the nine dots. The key to solving this puzzle is to literally "think outside the box" by drawing lines that go beyond the boundaries of the square:

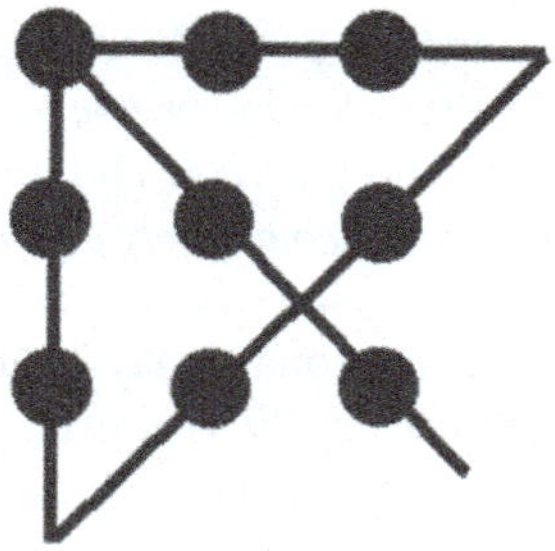

How do people break this "mental set," i.e., using the same incorrect solution without trying something new?

> Insight occurs when learners reorganize or restructure their perceptions in order to really 'see' the solution (Ohlsson, 1992). According to Gredler (2009), there are three possible mechanisms for restructuring a problem: reencoding, elaboration, and constraint relaxation (p. 55). Reencoding occurs when an incorrect or somewhat inaccurate interpretation of a problem or a procedure is corrected. Elaboration involves retrieval of additional information from long-term memory or adding overlooked information to the problem. Constraint relaxation amounts to removing unnecessary boundaries or limitations that learners impose on themselves. (Dempsey 2010, p. 98)

One way to create a puzzle task, then, is to tap into these mechanisms.

Reencoding: Design a puzzle where a common misconception or assumption leads to an unsuccessful solution (these misconceptions are called "distractors" in multiple choice construction). A classic example of this is the surgeon puzzle: *A father and son get into a car accident where the father is killed and the son requires emergency surgery to survive. When wheeled into the operating room, the surgeon exclaims, "I can't operate on this patient. He's my son!" How can this be?* The reason this works as a puzzle is because of the sexist assumption that surgeons are male and that all couples are heterosexual. The solution is that the surgeon is the son's mother or that the son has two dads.

Elaboration: Design a puzzle where the solution requires information given earlier, easily overlooked information, information the player should already have perhaps even from outside the game world, information the player can infer, or information the player needs to acquire such as from an NPC, by finding an object like a journal, by noticing something in the background, or by completing another task.[6] A classic example of overlooked information occurs in the following puzzle (best done orally): *You are a bus driver. At the first stop, you pick up ten passengers. At the next stop, five passengers get off and three get on. At the next stop, no one gets off and six passengers get on. At the next stop, four passengers get off and seven get on. What's the name of the bus driver?* In this case, by not explicitly naming the bus driver but instead using the common construction of "you are …" paired with the assumption that the key information is the number of passengers and that this is going to be a math problem causes people to focus on what turns out to be irrelevant information. The answer, of course, is your name.

Constraint relaxation: Design a puzzle where people are likely to assume a rule that is never stated. Sometimes this involves people assuming that a puzzle has to be solved in a certain way. For example, the following puzzle is best solved when people move from a chronological orientation to a reverse chronological one: *The size of a lily pad doubles every 24 h. The lily pad completely covers a pond in 30 days. On what day does the lily pad cover half the pond?* The easiest way to solve this is backward. If the lily pad completely covers the pond on day 30 and doubles every day, then the lily pad will cover half the pond on day 29. However, people's assumption that solving the problem involves starting on day one will blind them to this simple solution.

Common mistakes, misconceptions, unknown information, and inaccurate or incomplete mental modeling in your field can be a ripe source of puzzles in your game.

CHALLENGE 6.2: You successfully designed some tasks, but still feel like you haven't created the cognitive dissonance that can really motivate and challenge students. You think about the importance of prior knowledge. "How do I figure out what prior knowledge students are bringing to the task at hand?" Right! You remember that professional development you attended on assessment. You look for patterns in student work. Ahhh, just like players look for patterns in games to figure out the rules of the game world. You dig around in your satchel in the hopes that you brought some student work with you so you can practice. You pull out a piece of paper and puzzle over it. It seems like eons ago, and in some ways it is, but you had picked up some litter off the hallway floor earlier on the day you were transported. It looks like some kids' math homework. You try to find the pattern in this student's responses in order to identify his misconception[7]:

33	1091	8	28	90
+99	+ 60	+24	+70	+6
24	17	15	17	15

[6] The reality television show *The Amazing Race* has used this technique a few times by placing an inconspicuous sign somewhere that players must notice in order to complete a task.

[7] Because we know how to add numbers in this way, it makes it difficult to discern that the student is adding all the numbers in each problem. In the first item, the student adds $3+3+9+9$ in order to get 24 and so forth. Looking for patterns also means recognizing that the pattern might not hold true in every case. Note that the student does make an arithmetic mistake in one of the problems. Don't let that throw you off in your search for patterns.

*Example from Bartholemae and Petrosky (***1986***, p. 199)*

EXERCISE: Examine the math problems to try to discover what rule the student was following.

Your ultimate goal is to incorporate these tasks into your storyline, but you can also use your storyline to help generate these tasks. Keep in mind that students should work on individual parts of a task within the context of the whole task. This can be one aspect at a time or cumulative, once a student has mastered one aspect and then has to do that aspect plus another: "keeping the core performance as a small integrated set of modular behaviors allows players to learn them as anticipatory units, to explore possible variations of the skills, and again, frees up cognitive resources for other purposes" (Swan 2010, p. 128). Some call this cognitive task analysis, i.e., separating out the cognitive demands of the task. Cognitive demands have a wide range and can include applying an algorithm, performing arithmetic, circumlocution (being able to talk around an unknown word), translating, converting units of measure, identifying, selecting, providing examples, hypothesis testing, communication, collaboration, planning, self-monitoring, metacognition, critical thinking, applying problem-solving heuristics, and so forth. The point is to separate out all the subskills that are involved in performing a larger task.

It is important to distinguish between how most COTS video games break a larger skill into subtasks and how intelligent tutoring systems, poorly designed educational video games, and sometimes teachers do:

> The focus of instructive interactions throughout the endeavor typically is sequenced so that simpler, more rudimentary subtasks are highlighted before more complex ones; however, the activity remains intact throughout the exchange (Collins, brown, & Holum, 1991; Tharp & Gallimore, 1991) in contrast to more decontextualized 'skill and drill' approaches (which break the target activity down through task analysis and then drill students on each separate subtask)." (Steinkuehler and Oh 2012, p. 158)

If puzzles are not constructed in the context of the whole problem, i.e., the overall success in the game, learners see the subskills as isolated and unrelated to the larger problem space. In other words, subskills need to be learned and practiced within the context of the larger skill. To do so, a game designer can isolate the target subskill and automate the rest of the subskills but still have them present so that the learner not only learns the subskill but also understand how that subskill operates within the larger system.

However, there may be some exceptions. You may want to have learners learn individual skills without a sense of the bigger picture in order to create that "aha" moment later on. For example, in the original movie *Karate Kid*, the mentor has the protagonist learn how to paint a fence, wax a car, and do other seemingly menial chores. Later in the movie the mentor shows his protégé how these skills transfer into fighting skills.[8] You can use this technique in your game as well, but in a way that hints that these will be used as part of the bigger picture in order to inspire curiosity.

[8]Those of us from that generation are now repeating "Wax on. Wax off" in our heads.

Studies have repeatedly shown that the average person can only handle seven plus or minus two chunks of information in their working memory (Driscoll 2005, p. 86). Notice the use of the word "chunk" instead of item. Now say the alphabet out loud. Most people "chunk" the alphabet into "abcd," "efg," "hijk," "lmnop," "qrs," "tuv," and "wxy and z"—seven chunks of information in order to remember 26 discrete items. Chunking is a common mnemonic device: dividing up number sequences such as phone numbers and social security numbers, using acronyms such as FBI and so forth. Fullerton et al. (2004) point out that it is probably not a coincidence that "the game *Tetris* includes seven shapes" (p. 157). Chunking is one of the most powerful learning strategies because it frees up space in people's working memories for other cognitive activities.

The first time a player encounters a task, each element within that task is perceived as a chunk. Once a task or skill is mastered often through practice, the elements are chunked together and the behavior becomes automatic, thus freeing up working memory for more items and skills that require greater attention. Instructional designers are careful not to overburden a learner's "cognitive load." They use the following formula to determine a task's cognitive load:

$$\textit{Extraneous demands} + \textit{intrinsic demands} + \textit{germane demands} = \textit{total cognitive load}$$

Extraneous demands are imposed by the format, i.e., how information is presented. For example, seeing a square tends to be processed more quickly than someone verbally describing a square. Organizing information and looking for patterns tax a working memory. If the objective is pattern detection, then this should be a large part of the cognitive load. If not, it should be reduced, for example, by using tools such as graphic organizers or ways of highlighting patterns.

Germane demands are imposed by the amount of effort it takes to encode information, i.e., to assign meaning and incorporate into preexisting schemas in order to transfer information from working memory to long-term memory. Making connections between new information and prior knowledge explicit can reduce the germane demands. However, if your objective is for students to make these connections themselves, this should comprise a large part of the cognitive load.

Intrinsic demands are the inherent difficulty of a problem and are considered fixed.

Since intrinsic demands are fixed, the goal of an instructional designer is to decrease extraneous load so the learner has an increased capacity for the germane demands. However, this depends on the objective of the task. The upshot is to think about how knowledge can best be represented to enable a learner to encode, or attach meaning, to the knowledge without overloading the learner. This may mean chunking the information and/or employing mnemonic devices. Think about what skill, knowledge, or disposition you want the learner to be able to demonstrate, put the focus on that, and minimize cognitive load of everything else. A prime example of this in the video gaming world is using the control device. If the gaming console involves too much of a learning curve, new players get frustrated because they cannot concentrate on the game itself.

One solution to this mentioned earlier is having the game perform a task that is irrelevant to the objective. Perpetual running games do this by offloading the running onto the game and allowing the player to focus on the tasks at hand, such as ducking, moving side to side, jumping, and turning. You can also make automation an option: "You can give the players ways of automating certain tasks … This provides players with the degree of control they desire" (Fullerton et al. 2004, p. 287). You can even give a choice of automation only after they have mastered a skill. In this way, players can demonstrate an ability to perform a subskill and then have that subskill automated so they can learn new subskills within the context of the larger problem.[9] You might de-automate the subskills, however, for the final challenge or even de-automate combinations of subskills leading up to the final challenge.

One thing to keep in mind is that the task should match the goal. For example, does the evidence supplied need to be recall or recognition to support your claim? "Action selection" ("doing the right thing") or "action expression" ("doing the thing right") (Mateas and Stern 2005/2006, p. 660 citing Sengers 1998)? Process or product? Knowledge (remembering), comprehension (understanding), application (applying), analysis (analyzing), evaluation (evaluating), or synthesis (creating) (from Bloom's Taxonomy)? The claims you want to be able to make about your students determine the evidence you need and how the tasks should be constructed to elicit the appropriate evidence.

Once a player has mastered something, you want to give them a chance to repeat it and show it off, but not to the point of becoming "repetitive or tedious" (Fullerton et al. 2004, p. 286) which can "mask any progress being made" (Fullerton et al. 2004, p. 287). One way to do this is by making the next skill build off of the previously mastered skill. A "bridge to transfer" is to provide opportunities for students to practice the skill in multiple contexts:

> As players move through contexts—each containing similar but varied problems—this helps them to interpret and eventually generalize their experiences. They learn to generalize—but always with appropriate customization for specific different contexts—their skills, procedures, principles, and use of information. This essentially solves the dilemma that learning in context can leave learners with knowledge that is too context specific …, but that learning out of context leaves learners with knowledge they cannot apply. (Gee 2008b, p. 49)

In other words, learning from the game experience allows students to learn declarative knowledge (the *what*) within the context of procedural knowledge (the *how*), but it is the embedding of similar problems in different contexts that allows learners to develop conditional knowledge (the *when*). It also increases the ability of students to be able to transfer, which is really applying and adapting, that knowledge (declarative, procedural, and conditional) to new situations.

Designing a game is designing balance. Using tasks (puzzles, challenges, problems, quests) within a game as assessment allows the game to adjust the individual player's zone of proximal development (Vygotsky 1978):

> A critical aspect of game design is to provide challenges that are hard enough to be demanding, but not annoying, while easy enough to be interesting, but not boring. Since the line

[9] For example, in math students are often discouraged from using calculators when learning addition and subtraction but then allowed to use them later when learning more complex math.

> between frustration and boredom may differ with every user, data on learners' academic motivation and educational abilities may be particularly useful for designing game challenges, as well as creating the algorithms necessary to monitor the behavior of the user to adapt the level of difficulty during game play. (Hirumi and Stapleton 2008, p. 136)

It is this cycle of completing a challenge within a player's ZPD and the subsequent reward, with each challenge teaching a player the skills necessary to succeed in the next challenge, that creates the "pleasant frustration" (Gee 2007, p. 36) that keeps a player's immersion in a game alive. The reward, which can be the chance to explore a new part of the game world or even the success itself, helps cement the learning and motivates the player to keep playing through hormonal changes in the brain. Successfully solving a puzzle or completing a challenge taps into our "achievement motivation" (Driscoll 2005, p. 311) or, as Shute (2011) states: "success is addictive" (p. 507)[10] and plays a large part in motivation. However, the "intrinsic satisfaction of successful play [must be] sufficient to overcome the [degree of] frustration of initial failures" (Osterweil and Klopfer 2011, p. 163). On the other hand, if a player is rewarded for doing something easy, particularly if a player is repeatedly rewarded for doing something easy or completion of an easy task results in a huge reward, players lose motivation because the game is perceived as not challenging and therefore not fun.

While the game adjusts to the user, the user adjusts to the game. Proceeding through different levels is another way of designing for a player's zone of proximal development:

> Intermediate challenges are similar to the device of dramatic tension or 'plot hooks' in literature; as one challenge ends another challenge arises enticing the player forward episodically. Intermediate challenges comprise iterations or cycles of variable challenge that lead up to the final 'confrontation.' Thus, games offer a stream of varying opportunities to develop and test adaptive abilities through *cycles of provocation and resolution.* (Swan 2010 p. 126)

Allowing advanced players to move quickly through earlier, and thus easier, levels of a game until they hit their challenge zone is another way to do this. The speed at which a player advances, how far a player advances, or how long it takes a player to complete a game can be a form of assessment.

Video games often have "choke points," or gateways, in order to advance to the next level:

> In Sim level design, action gates are places where the players have to demonstrate mastery of a single necessary action before they can continue. The action gates are used to help players learn both what abilities are possible and how to engage them using the interface. For example, a player in the first level of a first-person Sim may be trapped in a room and allowed to continue only after demonstrating the ability to open a door. (This skill of opening doors presumably would be required for later success in the Sim.) (Aldrich 2009b, p. 358)

Each choke point must enable a player to demonstrate mastery of that level's system before moving on to the next level of complexity. Of course, you as the game designer need to determine what the cut points are for demonstrating mastery, i.e., how much counts as mastery. A possible formula for this could be:

[10] Gee describes Squire's advocacy for the use of video games in education as "pushing a much stronger 'drug,' one that can, in the right conditions, become addictive to humans: deep and challenging learning" (in Foreword to Squire 2011, p. ix).

First level = diagnostic assessment, i.e., uncover the player's mental model

In-game goal = teaching declarative knowledge, i.e., the *what* that is needed to understand the problem

Gateway to next level = resolving an instance of cognitive dissonance, i.e., present information that contradicts player's mental model and have player resolve that contradiction

Second level = formative assessments, i.e., series of subskills that provide data on player progression

In-game goal = teaching procedural knowledge, i.e., the *how* needed in order to solve the problem

Gateway to next level = a challenge that requires the player to demonstrate ability to combine subset of subskills

Third level = boss level has player combine all subskills

In-game goal = teaching conditional knowledge, i.e., the *when* or "if-then": which conditions call for which set of strategies and solutions to solving problems within the domain but in different contexts

Final challenge: Summative assessment or boss challenge[11] involves skills from all previous tasks applied to a new situation or scenario that requires an adjustment of skills

Replaying of the game from a different perspective

The final boss level should provide "transfer practice" (Prensky 2011), opportunities for students to transfer the skills learned in the game to new domains. The more domains a skill is practiced in, the more likely that skill is to transfer to a new domain (Bransford et al. 2000): "Assessments that require students to actually apply knowledge in a problem-solving transfer task [i.e. "different contexts involving different constraints"] can be a more powerful indicator that meaningful learning has occurred" (Baker and Delacruz 2008, p. 32) than a "retention task" that solely measures amount of declarative knowledge remembered. Performance tasks provide information about how students might perform within a domain; retention tasks only provide information about what information a student knows. Imagine yourself going into surgery and think about which type of assessment you would want your surgeon to have passed.

Ideally, figuring out the final solution to the problem space will allow the players to see the game story, and thus the topic, in a different way and even make players want to replay the game, like in the World War II game described earlier where the final task has countries assess the damage done by using an atomic bomb and then reflecting on how the war could have been averted in the first place. Another student of mine had his students choose a party platform, but did not label them. One was the Nazi platform which he did not reveal until later on in the game. While risky, it

[11] "In a boss level, you face a boss monster (or some equivalent thereof)—a monster so intimidating it requires you to draw on everything you've learned and mastered in the game so far. It's the equivalent of a midterm or final exam" (McGonigal 2011, p. 131).

certainly introduced an element of surprise that caused students to want to replay with this new knowledge. Another student designed a role-playing game about the bubonic plague. While students may initially have thought about how the bubonic plague affected individuals, through the game play this student designed, students come to realize how the bubonic plague also disrupted the global interconnectedness that started happening just before the plague hit. Carefully designed problem spaces, ensuing solutions, and game play can provide students with a new perspective on a topic they may have felt they already understood.

Games teach through assessment and can do so in ways that help remove the judgment that is too often embedded in traditional schooling: "The fact that games are excellent systems for objective judgment is one of their most appealing qualities" (Schell 2008, p. 128). While games may not be completely objective, after all, humans do create and program them, they do provide the sense that the feedback is coming from the game and not the teacher, sometimes in ways that make it feel like any feedback is unknown to anyone but the recipient. This can encourage risk-taking. I give far more honest feedback on student work that I am not grading because when I grade student work, I feel like my feedback must justify that evaluation. When designing in–game assessment, ask yourself: "What does your game judge about the players? How does it communicate this judgment? Do players feel the judgment is fair? Do they care about the judgment? Does the judgment make them want to improve?" (Schell 2008, p. 128). In-game assessment should help the player advance through the game, not discourage them from trying.

> *Educational video games typically fail to populate the dimension of action with choices that are personally relevant, creative, or powerful. That's because contemporary education fails in exactly the same way*
>
> –Brenda Laurel, 2004

SCAFFOLDING SECTION OF THE QUESTS QUEST

WHILE the challenges are merely quizzes of prior knowledge dressed up in game story, revise challenges UNTIL challenges teach instead of test.

"Talk to me. Talk to me. Talk to me!"

Whoah. You wake up drenched in sweat. Shaking your head, you realize you were dreaming that you were trying to get a wall to respond to you. You realize the wall symbolizes the Commander. You feel adrift with no sense of whether or not what you are doing will please her, but you feel the need to soldier on.

You realize you don't want your players to feel the same way. You need to build some life vests, life preservers, and life boats in your game as well as including some navigational tools such as compasses and telescopes to guide their way. A radio would help too, so they can send out a distress signal if necessary.

Sleepily, you write, "soldier, sailor, tinker, tailor" on the sticky notes you keep next to your bed, roll over, and go back to sleep.

The next morning you read what you wrote. "Huh?" you think, and go about your day, but the children's rhyme keeps haunting you.

"Right!" In the middle of your shower you realize that games need to allow players to tinker around, and based on their tinkering, you can provide feedback to tailor the game to their needs! Of course! You need to figure out ways to scaffold

student learning in your game! You look through the puzzles you have designed so far and think about what supports students need to figure them out.

"I really need some scaffolding myself," you think. "If only I had Amy to support me in this process! Do I dare try contacting her again?"

WHILE you decide NOT to text Amy, you struggle endlessly and get nowhere.
UNTIL you say under your breath, "Damn the space-time continuum! I'm going to contact Amy."

ACTION: For every challenge you designed, decide what feedback the player should receive when he or she meets the challenge and when the player does not.

Part 2: Building Scaffolding Through Feedback

> *"Ok, now Mom, let's experiment. What do you think will happen if you start going across the hill and if you press more on the right inside edge of your feet than on the left? How about if you press your toes into the boots and then the heels"*
>
> *"But David, can't you just tell me the right way to do this?"*
>
> *"I don't know the right way, Mom, but your skis and the snow will tell you. They'll write patterns in the snow the same way your hand and the pen write letters on a page. Let's just be curious."*
>
> -Dawna Markova, 2001

Previously, we discussed "performance before competence." However, as the above quote shows, it is the feedback from the performance that develops competence. In the quote above, the son is encouraging his mom to create her own data by "be[ing] curious," i.e., testing out "what happens when …" she "press[es] more on the right inside" or "press [her] toes into the boots and then the heels." In this case the data are the "patterns in the snow." One time when I was on a ski lift, I struck up a conversation with my ski lift neighbor who told me when he was a little boy, his father would get mad at him if at the end of a day of skiing he didn't have any snow on his bottom because it meant he wasn't taking risks in order to find his own boundaries. Falling in the snow is certainly powerful feedback! Learning to ski involves multiple iterations of testing our expectations against our experiences, revising our expectations and adjusting our actions accordingly, and testing again. That is exactly what gamers do and why Swan (2010) prefers the term "feedforward" because the learner uses the results of past actions to predict the consequences of future actions. Swan (2010) points out that feedforward has another advantage as well: "current success engenders expectations of future success" (p. 126), thus providing both the mechanisms and motivation for continued game play.

Ironically, this feedforward cycle of success is fueled by mistakes. We discussed in Chap. 1 how mistakes, like falling in the snow, are powerful learning opportunities. However, it is difficult to learn from mistakes if there is no feedback: "Simulations give the player *permission to fail*, which (aside from being fun) is incredibly educational—because the learner not only sees the failures, but sees why they happened, which leads to significant insight about the workings of the whole system" (Schell 2008, p. 446). In the quote at the beginning of this section, the son provides some guidance to his mother about different things to try and points out the data she needs to read. In traditional schooling, when students simply receive a letter grade at the end of an essay, grades feel like arbitrary rewards and punishments that are done *to* the student. We have all heard students utter "My teacher failed me." This sense of grades being out of one's control can quickly lead to an external locus of control and to learned helplessness. On the other hand, when teachers give meaningful feedback, it sends the message that the teacher believes the student can succeed: "If the player believes failures to be attributable to correctable errors on his own part, he believes the game to be winnable and plays on in an effort to master the game" (Crawford 1984, quoted by Swan 2010, p. 113). Attitudes about learning play an important role in learning itself. The self-fulfilling prophecy can make a difference in how much effort students put in and thus how much students get out of learning. Studies about how people define themselves in terms of being good or bad at math have borne this out (Kimball and Smith 2013).[12]

It is meaningful feedback that helps students develop their skills:

> In one of the most famous early studies comparing the effects of learning a procedure with understanding, two groups of children practiced throwing darts at a target under water (described in Judd, 1908; see a conceptual replication by Hendrickson and Schroeder, 1941). One group received an explanation of the refraction of light, which causes the apparent location of the target to be deceptive. The other group only practiced dart throwing, without the explanation. Both groups did equally well on the practice task, which involved a target 12 inches under water. But the group that had been instructed about the abstract principle did much better when they had to transfer to a situation in which the target was under only 4 inches of water. Because they understood what they were doing, the group that had received instruction about the refraction of light could adjust their behavior to the new task. (Bransford et al. 2000, p. 18)

This concept applies not only to learning in the traditional sense but also to changing behaviors. For example, people with electric meters in their front hall reduced their energy use by one-third during an energy crisis, while those with meters in their basement did not (example from Meadows 2008, p. 109). Squire (2011) points out that games have all sorts of feedback mechanisms, both built into the game but also outside of the game:

> Games are surrounded by walk-throughs, guides, even videos explaining and demonstrating almost every nuance of the game. … In educational terms, there are examples, non-examples, and worked problems for players to analyze to improve their performance. It's as if students had access, not only to the teacher's notes, but also to the guidebook, the Cliff notes, and experts in the field in question. (p. 13)

I have often wondered why students do not get the teacher's edition of textbooks. Perhaps it is because we do not trust our students not to cheat or rather we don't give students reasons not to cheat. Traditional schooling's focus on the product or some-

---

[12]There is a teaching urban legend about a new teacher who receives a list of his students along with their IQs. Thinking his students are incredibly smart, he teaches them this way and achieves great success. At the end of the year, he finds out those numbers were not their IQs but rather their locker numbers.

times not even the product itself but rather the teacher's evaluation of the product or the state's evaluation of standardized tests can discourage learning. When those standardized test scores are used not just to evaluate students but also to evaluate teachers, it can create atmospheres where even the teachers are tempted to cheat, as evidenced in some recent scandals where teachers manipulated test scores.

Why don't gamers cheat? Why don't gamers rely on walk-throughs to take them through the game? "Certainly from the perspective of players, they prefer to 'figure it out on their own;' they tend to seek didactic help as a last resort" (Swan 2010, p. 119). The point of playing a video game is figuring it out on your own, not to get an A. Consulting a walk-through not only takes away this fun but can be personally shameful, even if no one else knows. When feedback is embedded in the game in ways players cannot avoid seeing it, game designers need to be careful about what and how they do so. Allowing players to seek out scaffolding instead of foisting it upon them is one way to attend to this. One of my students called this "choose your own scaffolding."

The form of the feedback makes a difference as well. If you correct a student's writing mistakes without teaching them the general rule, the student only knows how a sentence should look in that instance. Teaching them the rule allows them to apply that rule in other writing situations. However, you can also push students to think about their choices and ask students to reflect on why they worded something a certain way and what they think the effect of that wording might be on the audience. You can even do so while telling them what the accepted convention is. Then ask "what happens when" the student changes the wording. How might that new wording impact the audience differently? This can enable students to understand not only rules and conventions of a system, such as writing, but also when exceptions to rules can be used to achieve a certain purpose. For example, a car company might deliberately use passive voice when writing a letter to customers to inform them about a defect in order to displace the blame. Moving from declarative knowledge to conditional knowledge (how to apply it in different situations) gives students a sense of agency and ownership.

Kirkley et al. (2011) found that "scaffolding was most effective when students first took ownership of the problem and then worked on it, developing an understanding of their learning needs. They were then able to make use of the lecture scaffold to revise or clarify their understanding" (p. 377). Flipped instruction is often done by having students listen to video lectures before class, but flipped instruction needs to be flipped again. Students should first grapple with problems before they access the content and then use their new knowledge to work on the problems again. In this way, students have some context to understand and apply the concepts learned. Otherwise, the content is divorced from both context and purpose. Flipping flipped instruction is similar to the five stages of problem-based learning:

1. *Situation stage*: The problem is introduced to the learners.
2. *Issues identification stage:* The learners develop initial hypotheses about solving the problem and identify what needs to be learned.
3. *Inquiry stage*: The learners investigate to find out more background information and pose more possible solutions as they do so. Facilitators provide scaffolding and feedback to help guide the inquiry process.

4. *Action stage*: Learners decide on the final course of action, provide a rationale, and take action.
5. *Assessment stage*: Learners evaluate whether or not their course of action led to their predicted results and why or why not. If not, learners go back to stage 2.
6. *Debriefing stage:* Facilitators provide space to reflect on the process and bridge to transfer to help students generalize this specific problem to a larger range of problems. This can include providing a subsequent problem that is in a different domain, has an important difference, is of greater complexity (e.g., more variables involved), and so forth.

Problem-based learning provides multiple forms of scaffolding. In stage three, learners seek out scaffolding in the resources they look to, but facilitators also provide scaffolding in the form of guidance. In the fifth stage, learners receive scaffolding in the form of the consequences of their actions. In the last stage, students receive scaffolding in the form of debriefing, both in terms of reflecting on past actions and thinking about future actions.

In the traditional sense, at least in terms of teaching, scaffolding is often thought of as graphic organizers and other written supports, but, as we see in the description above, scaffolding comes in many different forms. There are all sorts of scaffolding that happen that often go unrecognized. For example, wait time[13] is a type of scaffolding as it gives students, particularly those who take longer to process information such as English Language Learners, time to formulate an answer. Spending time in class to field clarifying questions about an upcoming assignment is another. In the realm of video games, there are also several accepted conventions that serve as scaffolding that might not be recognized as such. Many of these we, as educators, can adopt and adapt into our classroom practices, even outside of playing curricular games.

Directions

Directions are important, otherwise learners and players feel lost. Gamers quickly lose interest if at the start of the game they find themselves "roam[ing] around but have no idea where they're supposed to go or what they're supposed to do" (Fullerton et al. 2004, p. 335). However, telling people step-by-step exactly what to do takes away the opportunity to learn: "Traditional instruction tends to tell the students what to do, giving them procedures and directions for each step of the way. However, these directions remove the students' challenge to make sense of and understand the situation" (Kirkley et al. 2011, p. 377). Too much instruction can

[13] "Wait time" is the amount of time between a teacher asking a question and when a teacher calls on a student to respond. Studies (Rowe 1986) have shown the longer the wait time, the more students who can answer and the more developed their answers.

also prevent learning. When my sister taught me how to rollerblade, she did so in the context of how to play roller hockey. If she had told me how to move my feet, I would have focused on that. Instead, I focused on how to play the game and my feet naturally followed:

> A centipede was happy—quite!
> Until a toad in fun
> Said, "Pray, which leg moves after which?"
> This raised her doubts to such a pitch,
> She fell exhausted in the ditch
> Not knowing how to run. (Craster 1871)

When I took surfing lessons, however, I followed the instructions to a T, reciting step one, step two, and step three as I did so. In the home videos, you can see my stiff movements as I force my body between the positions defined by my instructor in each step. On the other hand, my wife naturally and fluidly pops up and balances on the surfboard. You can almost hear her thoughts: "Instructions be damned!"

Perhaps it would be useful for our purposes to distinguish between instructions and directions by defining instructions as telling students what to do step-by-step and directions as providing guidance for student actions. With these definitions, following instructions, then, would be similar to a list of steps: turn left at Main and Elm type of instructions to reach your destination. Using directions would involve employing maps, sign posts, and landmarks to find your way. For our gaming purposes, we want to provide directions, not instructions. I hope you view this book as a set of directions, not instructions, as well since it is intended to provide guidance, not to be used as a strict recipe.

Even with this distinction, however, we do not want to overload our students with directions. Instead, directions should be provided when the learner needs them. If you teach high school students about how to get the best mortgage rates, it will have no meaning to them, will not be stored in long-term memory, and therefore is useless 15 years later when they apply for a mortgage. However, if you teach people how to get the best mortgage rates when they are applying, they end up getting better rates than those people who took financial literacy in high school. But, if you make it a game where students compete for the best mortgage rates and it can mean the difference between foreclosure and success in the game world, students will have the context, and the motivation, to store it in long-term memory. Waiting until the learner needs the information makes that information useful.

In some cases, however, you may want your students to discover their own directions when they are ready. The trick, then, comes in finding the right balance between exploration and guidance:

> A distinction needs to be made between *productive mucking around* and *unproductive flailing about* in a game. *Productive mucking around* involves players developing and testing hypotheses to learn the rules of the game/understand the system. *Unproductive flailing about* occurs when a player engages in random clicks or spends excessive time trying to figure out how to do something in a game that is unrelated to the learning goals. (Squire 2011, p. 93)

We read earlier about Jim Gee's experience finding the video game manual incomprehensible when read before playing the game. Instead, he found it more useful to try his hand at the game first. This experience is not unique to him: "computer games rarely provide[] instructions, and when instructions are present they are usually ignored. Players tend to discover game rules by induction" (Tobias et al. 2011). This is where scaffolding comes into play in order to provide "just-in-time" supports to guide students in discovering rules instead of telling them by asking questions like, "why do you think that happened?" or "what do you think your goal is?" and so forth:

> That "most people get it" is not much comfort to the poor sucker left out. Think of puzzle design like game design. You want to offer your players both challenge and control. Help them to understand the goal, that it is solvable, and how they might go about finding that solution. They should be guessing at the answer rather than the point! A puzzle that displays progress encourages players to keep working at it. Whenever you see a player sitting still, staring into her screen, you are looking at a mounting risk of frustration. It's better to have distinct failure states and let the player try again immediately. Perhaps your puzzle can, through this trial and error, reveal something about its solution. (Rabin 2009, p. 94)

While "many games use animated agents, usually cartoons resembling human or animal figures, for comment or guidance to help players navigate through the game" (Tobias et al. 2011, p. 173), this can be easily done by the teacher in the classroom. This can be especially effective if the teacher role-plays a mentor character in the game story or plants information by giving it to a student role-playing a character.

Directions, particularly directions in the form of story, can be doled out as rewards for successful game play. For example, at the beginning, the game can either provide a general goal or maybe even just hint at the overall goal. An easy way to do this would be to have a nonplaying character (NPC) state, "I dream of a day when … [INSERT GOAL HERE: we could live above ground, we can live in freedom, the aliens are defeated, we can use our knowledge of genetics to cure diseases, and so forth]." Subsequent successful game play (i.e., solving puzzles) can unlock further direction, guidance, or details about the ultimate goal. The game can also help avoid player stagnation by setting time limits or using other indicators of player frustration to judge when to offer scaffolding: "make sure that the game has some way of recognizing when a player is stuck and providing them with just enough assistance to make it past the obstacle without diluting its challenge completely" (Fullerton et al. 2004, p. 288). Teachers do this all the time in their teaching:

> When I feel like I'm talking too much, I feel like I'm shutting [my students] down so I'll immediately stop. And I'll sense that a lot. I'll sense, "Whoa. Wait a minute. Why was I just getting ready to say that sentence?" That's the internal dialogue. "Why was I just getting ready to say that when I could be asking them?" So I think I kind of have a tuning fork for that balance of them versus me in terms of who's giving more, who's interacting more. So, a little buzzer goes off that says, "Whoa, Patrick. Pull back. You're giving too much and they're gonna get tired and they're just gonna zone you out." That's I think the conscious process. When that buzzer goes off, I make a conscious process of, ok, where can I bring them back in? Where can I get them more actively involved in this? (Patrick, from Jackson 2007, p. 162)

When designing your game, think about the "buzzers" you can use to determine when students need scaffolding. This could be hints emerging after a certain amount of time. For example, if the players are supposed to find a hidden item, after a certain amount of time, an NPC can knock something out of the way that partially shows the item or the item might start making a noise or flashing. Or you could even use student choice by having a link to a hint or even a series of hints with each subsequent hint providing more and more specific instructions so students can choose how much support they need.

Saving a Game

Taking risks in thinking is a radical departure from today's high-stakes testing culture, and, perhaps, that's why so many youth today game. I contend that one of the most important educational affordances of games is creating a "risk-reduced" environment where students are encouraged to learn from mistakes[14] and, in some cases, even to make mistakes and are able to do so not only without penalty but with encouragement: "Indeed, *recoverability* is one of the key features that distinguishes computer games from real life" (Swan 2010, p. 119).[15] Ironically, the compelling element of some games is creating over-the-top fantastical goals such as "saving the last family on earth" thus raising the stakes, but this is done in a playful way where risks are raised hypothetically, but lowered in the reality that is created in the game world:

> The role of failure is very different in video games than it is in school. In good games, the price of failure is lowered—when players fail, they can, for example, start over at their last saved game. Furthermore, failure … is often seen as a way to learn the underlying pattern and eventually to win. These features of failure in games allow players to take risks and try out hypotheses that might be too costly in places where the cost of failure is higher or where no learning stems from failure. (Gee 2008a, p. 34)

Being able to save a game state and return to it later, along with other "recoverability mechanisms" (Swan 2010, p. 119) such as healing potions and extra lives, allows people to take risks and learn from their mistakes in ways traditional schooling does not.

There may be instances, however, where you, as game designer, want to force your students to start all over again. You can do this after the game is over and require the player to start at the very beginning (instead of having the game say "Game Over" you could have it say "Game Do-Over"). You could also set it up so that the player restarts at the beginning of a level instead of at the beginning of the game or at some other predetermined point. You also want to make sure players can save a game right after a big challenge has been accomplished. Saving a game is a key feature of video games, but how that saving works is up to you as game designer.

---

[14] Certainly this is a crucial part of learning for several fields, such as pilots in training using flight simulators where their mistakes will not cost lives.

[15] When I was in college, I had a friend who would jokingly use the phrase "Game Over" about a real person dying. He was old enough to know the difference, but younger children may not. It is crucial for young children to understand that when you die in real life, you can't just come back to life like in a video game.

Revise and Resubmit

Why is it that "in the world of gaming, … the very elements of struggle, challenge, and failure that discourage kids in the classroom become the primary drivers of engagement and achievement"? (Barker 2013). I contend that it is primarily because "good games permit the player to undo his last move, or play it over instantly. The quicker and more easily the player can correct a mistake, the safer he will feel and the more exploratory and playful his play will be" (Crawford 2003, p. 32 quoted by Swan 2010, p. 119). Currently the faculty in my department are discussing the merits and minuses of allowing students to "revise and resubmit" the work in their courses. For game designers, the answer to this question was determined long ago. That is because games rely on the notion that learning is effort-based. Too often our schooling assumes talents are either innate or, if not achieved within a predetermined amount of time, impossible. Game designers, and thus gamers, take a "not yet" attitude. Schools and standardized testing, however, too often take a "now or never" attitude:

> Leveling up is a much more egalitarian model of success than a traditional letter grading system based on the bell curve. Everyone can level up, as long as they keep working hard. … if you fail a quest, there's no permanent damage done to your report card. You just have to try more quests to earn enough points to get the score you want. This system of 'grading' replaces negative stress with positive stress, helping students focus more on learning and less on performing." (McGonigal 2011, p. 130)

This idea of "leveling up" sets benchmarks for student achievement without imposing a time limit or punishment for a number of tries. Designing classes in this way enables teachers to live up to the poster adorning many classrooms that says "All children can learn."

Joli Barker (2013) changed the tone of her classroom from a "now or never" one to "not yet" by changing the feedback she gave to students: "I even decided to forgo the usual grading system in my classroom, so that as far as the students knew, they were either 'Leveling Up!' (proficient) or they needed more practice with 'Game Over: Try Again.'" They stopped defining themselves by grades and saw "try again" as an opportunity to do just that. "Revise and resubmit" has become commonplace in my teaching and one of the most praised aspects of my classroom structure on course evaluations.

Rewards

McGonigal (2011) describes rewards in games as giving players an "'I rock vibe" (p. 222). My children play a video game where they literally get this "I rock" vibe when the crab says to the player, "You rock, Iguana Girl!" after successfully being shelled. This extreme positive feedback is referred to as being "juicy" (Gabler quoted by Juul 2010, p. 45). As mentioned in Chapter 1, rewards reinforce learning not just at the cognitive level but also at the neurological level as well: "each time the child is rewarded, his brain secretes such neurotransmitters as dopamine and acetylcholine, which help consolidate the map changes he has just made (dopamine reinforces the reward, and acetylcholine helps the brain 'turn in' and sharpen memories)" (Doidge 2007, p. 71). Because of this, you want to make sure the rewards reinforce what you want them to reinforce: "design reward structures that are tied to the learning goals" (Charsky 2010, p. 203). Otherwise, you may inadvertently reward tangential behaviors or behaviors in opposition to your learning goals. In other words, "create rewards for each experience you want to support" (Rabin 2009, p. 93). For example, teachers often use homework passes to reward student behavior, but homework passes send the message that homework is something to be avoided.

If rewards are so powerful, why not dole out rewards constantly? One reason is because people can get oversaturated with rewards:

> Jay Minn calls the reward loops the "potato chip loop." The game serves potato chips to players periodically, encouraging progress. The chip might be a reward for completing a stage, collecting an object, or some interesting feat. The chip may be bigger or smaller, but the most important thing is the rhythm between one chip and the next. Too few, and the player gets hungry, looking for something else to eat. Too many, and the player gets full and wants to take a break. (Rabin 2009, p. 93)

While "People have a tendency to get acclimated to rewards the more they receive them, and what was rewarding an hour ago is no big deal now" (Schell 2008, p. 191), there are remedies to this: "One simple method many games use to overcome this is to gradually increase the value of the rewards as the player progresses in the game" (Schell 2008, p. 191). Another solution is to make rewards variable instead of fixed: "It's like bringing donuts to work—if you bring them every Friday, people will come to expect them and take them for granted. But if you bring them every now and then on random days, they are a delightful surprise every time" (Schell 2008, p. 191). Indeed, the random-ratio maintenance schedule has been found by behaviorists to be the most effective (Driscoll 2005, p. 51) and is one that *EverQuest* uses (Fullerton et al. 2004, p. 282), which, if you recall from Chap. 1, is commonly called *EverCrack* due to its addictive nature. You can also "allow players to chain rewards together … by using collections of small rewards that lead to huge rewards" (Rabin 2009, p. 93), such as collecting coins which can be taken to town to buy things like better armor. However, "the timing and quantity of rewards is also critical. If you give a steady stream of small rewards, it can become meaningless. Players know the rewards are coming, no matter what they do and they stop caring" (Fullerton et al. 2004, p. 282). Think carefully about when to reward your players.

In my readings, I came across different advice about how often to reward players. One writer claimed that rewarding players every 15 min was the "industry standard" (Rabin 2009, p. 93). Another stated: "According to a top video game developer, video games are designed so that game players are asked to make a critical decision about every one-half to one second and are positively reinforced or rewarded for those decisions every seven to 12 seconds. In contrast, according to a recent research study, students on average receive positive reinforcement in the classroom only about once every 12 hours" (Crockett et al. 2011, p. 90). I suspect that the video game developer this source cites designed first-person shooter-type games because that many rapid-fire critical decisions are a lot. The pacing of the critical decisions should be dependent upon the depth of the critical decision and the rewards on skill mastery. The point is to think about how many critical decisions you want your students make, what kind they are, what kind of reinforcement students get, and how to spread them out over the course of the game so they are not all bunched up in the beginning, middle, or end.

You also want to consider how to reward your players. There are lots of different types of rewards: praise, points, prolonged play (i.e. extra lives), a gateway to a new area to explore or level to complete, a cut scene that reveals more backstory or further directions, more powers, resources, more expressive abilities such as being able to customize more parts of your avatar, and so forth. Rewards are another opportunity to "reinforce your theme" so make sure they are in keeping with the game story:

> The best rewards are those that have utility or value in the game … Rewards that are useful in obtaining victory carry greater weight; rewards that have a romantic association, like magic weapons or gold, appear more valuable' rewards that are tied into the storyline of the game have an added impact… Make each reward count, and if it can both push the player closer to victory and advance the storyline, that's even better. (Fullerton et al. 2004, p. 282)

One of the more fun forms of reward is Easter eggs or "hidden surprises" (Robinett 1984/2006, p. 713). Robinett, the creator of the first adventure video game, invented Easter eggs in response to Atari's insistence on anonymity of game designers. Robinett puts in an invisible dot that, if picked up, allowed entry into a secret room that said, "Created by Warren Robinett" (Robinett 1984/2006, p. 712). By the time a 15-year-old player discovered this and Atari eventually found out, Robinett no longer worked for Atari. There are some famous Easter eggs strewn throughout video games. As mentioned earlier, I have planted some Easter eggs of my own in my curricular games to reward students for exploring the game world. Often they come with extra credit points for finding them.

One in-game reward often overlooked is making changes in the game world after a task or level is completed, what McGonigal (2011) calls "phasing" (p. 59). While "leveling up" does tap into everyone's innate "achievement motivation" (Driscoll 2005, p. 311), seeing (or perhaps even hearing) that achievement reinforces that motivation. One gamer wrote this about phasing: "You feel like your actions are having a significant impact on the world around you" (McGonigal 2011, p. 59). One way you could do this in a no-tech way is to transform your classroom after the class has completed a goal. For example, if the class successfully cleans up the air in a game about pollution, the teacher could adorn the classroom with birds and flowers. Or if the class travels to a new region in a foreign language game, the teacher could decorate the room with items from that region. In a medium-tech way, you can make changes to the visuals on a classroom wiki or learning management system. A parallel way to do this, particularly if you want to reward individuals instead of the whole class, would be to change the attire of players, much like we do in the real world with scout badges or graduation garb. In martial arts, the different colored belts have tremendous significance. I sometimes joke that I got a Ph.D. so I could wear the Ph.D. floppy hat, which, embarrassingly, has a grain of truth to it.

One of the most motivating rewards in real life and game life is peer recognition: "Humans crave acknowledgement for their achievements, and there's little that can motivate us more. … if there's a way for you to make the players, even the ones who aren't winning, feel recognized for their efforts when they do achieve a goal, then you will have a much stronger game" (Fullerton et al. 2004, p. 283). Having an NPC talk about a player's heroic efforts can inspire that player to greater heights. Sometimes, this can be done indirectly. While I am not a fan of the term "gossiping" that Karp (2004) uses to describe having your child overhear you while you tell someone else about their accomplishments, having done this myself, I can testify to its effects. Having NPCs sing your praises can be rewarding, recognition for your efforts from your peers can do so even more. You can think of some of the traditional "praise rewards" given to high school seniors like "most likely to succeed" for inspiration. In a game context, these titles might be "most valuable player," "most improved," "most persistent," "most creative problem solver," and so forth. My father-in-law often points out that people work not for the salary or for the position but rather for the recognition. If the recognition is not there, no matter how much money someone makes or what their title is, a job is no longer rewarding.

A common means of using peer recognition as game motivation are the leaderboards listing who has the "high score." During the 1980s when arcade games came on the scene, you would hear stories of someone unplugging *Pac-Man* or some other arcade game to reset the leaderboard in order to have their name, or sometimes just initials, be at the top of the leaderboard, at least temporarily. I have tried high score recognition in my curricular games but have found that it is most motivating to the person with the highest score who wants to remain on top and to the top two or three contenders for high score. For the rest of the class, however, it can serve as discouragement. Now instead of having a leaderboard, I e-mail the person with the high score to let them know. This leaderboard proxy, though, does not provide the peer recognition, which in middle and high school and, increasingly in elementary school, is more powerful than teacher recognition. It also does not provide the motivation for those close to the high score. Perhaps those are the people I should be e-mailing ("You are just two points shy of having the top score in the class!"). I could e-mail that to everyone in the class even if it was not true, but that would be disingenuous. I do think the best use is for people to try to beat their previous score. Then, they are playing against the game instead of their peers. On the other hand, "Game elements like competition predictably and almost inevitably focus students on getting a high score rather than on learning the material" (Aldrich 2009a, p. 24). Aldrich (2009b) provides a stark example of this: "Here is an actual cheat for *Roller Coaster Tycoon*: To increase park ratings, find all of the guests who are unhappy or angry. Drown them. Eventually your park rating will go up 100 to 200 points" (Aldrich 2009b, p. 269). Think about the best ways you can use a leaderboard-type feature to motivate your students without discouraging them.

Punishment

Behaviorists and game designers agree that "whenever possible, if you need to encourage [someone] to do something, it is better to use a reward than a punishment" (Schell 2008, p. 193). Schell (2008) cites an example from the game *Diablo* where originally players had to gather food to prevent themselves from going hungry but players really did not like that. In response, the game designers changed the game so that "your player never gets hungry, but if they do eat food, they get a temporary boost in abilities" (Schell 2008, p. 193). So, if "rewards is always a better tool for reinforcement than punishment" (Schell 2008, p. 193), then why use punishment at all? Rabin (2009) explains that "reward and punishment forms a language that game designers use to communicate and teach the players the relative values of rights and wrongs in the game's universe" (Rabin 2009, p. 92). If there were no punishments, then players would not know when they violated a game rule.

In addition, punishments, or at least the specter of punishment, add drama to game play. Schell (2008) found this out first-hand:

> We used lighter versions [of punishment in *Toontown Online*], and it made battles boring—there was no risk in them. We tried tougher versions, and it made players too cautious in battles. Eventually we settled on a combination which struck an appropriate balance between encouraging caution and risk in the players. (Schell 2008, p. 194)

Schell (2008) explains why punishment increases drama: "When failure means a punishing setback in the game, the challenge of play increases and giving players a chance to risk terrible consequences makes success much, much sweeter" (Schell 2008, p. 192). However, punishment increasing drama does not just apply to big battles. Smaller aspects of game play can also be made more dramatic through risk of punishment: "You don't want to punish players so much that they stop playing your game. But often, the threat of punishment, if not the actual punishment itself, carries a dramatic tension that can add layers of meaning to even the most trivial choices a player makes" (Fullerton et al. 2004, p. 281). For example, "resources in a game are worth more if there is a chance they can be taken away" (Schell 2008, p. 192). If your game story or game play feels like it is dragging, you can increase engagement by creating risks.

Just like video games come with a variety of rewards, they also come with a variety of punishments including shaming, loss of points, shortened play such as "losing a life" or losing time on a clock, terminated play, suffering a setback by having to go to an earlier point in the game, removal of powers, resource depletion, and so forth. Sometimes these punishments are just temporary setbacks: "to have [powers] taken away may feel unfair to [players so sometimes they are just temporarily lost] … if an opponent hits one of your targets with a tennis ball, your tank goes into an uncontrolled spin for five seconds, and your gun becomes inoperable during that time" (Schell 2008, p. 193). In first-person shooter games, if a grenade goes off near you, often a loud buzzing sound that fades away prevents the player from hearing temporarily or a flash bang can temporarily blur your vision. One of the games my children play issues a "time out" in order to discourage random clicking. Schell (2008) pointed out that the threat of taking resources away, and remember time is a resource, makes them more valuable. Schell (2008) argues the opposite, however, for points: "when players can lose points, it cheapens the value of earned points. Points that can't be taken away are very valuable—points that could be subtracted on the next bad move have less endogenous value" (p. 193). When choosing when and how to deploy punishments, you need to consider the messages they send. A daycare decided to levy fines on parents who were late to pick up their children thinking that would discourage late pickups. Instead, more parents picked their children up late because they saw the fines as paying for teachers' time (Levitt and Dubner 2009). If performing the skill is part of a game story punishment, for example, a character is jailed and has to answer a certain number of math problems in order to escape, math is portrayed negatively. Just like teachers and parents use "logical consequences" in determining punishments for youth, games should do the same. If a building is not built correctly in a game about architecture, instead of losing points, the building should fall down.

If you do employ punishments, "it is crucial that all punishment in a game is for things that the player is able to understand and prevent. When punishment feels random and unstoppable, it makes the player feel a complete lack of control" (Schell 2008, p. 194). You can do this by providing scaffolding through the form of warnings before an event: "A good rule of thumb is to caution your players at least three times before hitting them with anything catastrophic … the bigger the impact, the more of a heads up you should provide. If you follow this rule, the events won't appear arbitrary, and your players will feel like they are in control of their destiny" (Fullerton et al. 2004, pp. 289–290). You can also give players ways to mitigate the damage, for example, an opportunity to purchase an antidote to the plague (example by Fullerton et al. 2004). Players feel "railroaded" when a punishment comes out of the blue: "Players bemoan situations where they are forced into a consequence by the designers, where they are going along playing a game and suddenly are told, 'You had no way of knowing but doing thing X results in horrible thing Z'" (Church 1999/2006, pp. 373–374). Instead:

> Players should always blame themselves for failure. If the game kills them off with no warning, then players blame the game and start to dislike it. But if the game hints that danger is imminent, shows players a way out and they die anyway, then they'll consider it a failure on their part; they've let the game down and they need to try a little harder. When they succeed, and the game rewards them with a little treat—scripted sequence, special effect, and so on—they'll feel good about themselves and about the game. (Birdwell 1999/2006, p. 215, one of game designers of *Half-Life*)

While Easter eggs can be unexpected rewards, you do not want any unexpected punishments.

The flipside of craving peer recognition is despising public shaming. If you decide to incorporate punishments into your curricular game, make them private, humorous, and recoverable. And do not shame. Just like when we discipline students we focus our comments on their behaviors, not on who they are as a person, comments should focus on the player's actions, not who the player is. Even something as subtle as shifting the subject in a sentence can make a difference. For example, saying "Your response time was too slow" focuses on the action, whereas "You are a slow driver" focuses on the person. Schell (2008) suggests asking yourself the following questions: "What are the punishments in my game? Why am I punishing the players? What do I hope to achieve by it? Do my punishments seem fair to the players? Why or why not? Is there a way to turn these punishments into rewards and get the same, or better, effect? Are my strong punishments balanced against commensurately strong rewards?" (p. 194). Punishments should serve a purpose in a game. The punishment should be worthy of the purpose, but the purpose should also be worthy of the punishment.

Sometimes video games do not punish a player for making a mistake. Instead, mistakes produce "amusing failure states" (Squire 2011, p. 142), humor, or surprises when something failed. Experiencing an "amusing failure state" can motivate players to try out different things, sometimes even failing on purpose. For example, my children know that clicking on a certain island on a map moves them forward in a game so they purposefully click on all other islands first to see their "amusing failure states" because if they click on the correct island, they move on in the game and miss out on these. However, you need to watch out for "paradoxical reinforcement contingencies because consequences for wrong answers are often more interesting than those for correct responses" (Tobias et al. 2011, p. 194). Tobias et al. (2011) recommend that "consequences for success [should be] more exciting and interesting than those for failure" (p. 205), but I think "amusing failure states" along with success being the only route to moving on in a game can reinforce learning. Prensky (2011) agrees: "Entertainment games very often *do* do this quite deliberately, because they know that new players first rush to the failure states to see those (fun) consequences before advancing to the game's real goals" (p. 261). For example, virtually mixing two chemical resulting in an explosion can help cement in a player's mind the disastrous results of combining those two chemicals. For those of us who are Harry Potter fans, you can imagine that the surprising results some students experience in Snape's potions class would help imprint the learning. Learning is not just limited to learning how to do something, it also involves learning *not* to do things as well.

Progress Bar

Earlier I mentioned the simple reward of achievement but noted that players need feedback to reflect that achievement. One common way to do this is to have a progress bar. A progress bar lets players know "where they stand in relation to the overall game" (Hirumi and Stapleton 2008, p. 142). It is this knowing that enables players to feel the almost mutually exclusive emotions of motivation and satisfaction: "Nothing is quite as satisfying as seeing the choices you make result in progress. It's part of human nature to derive joy from the act of advancing towards a goal. … Allowing players to feel they are moving forward is the best way to draw someone into a game and keep them engaged" (Fullerton et al. 2004, p. 284). I have experienced this "joy" not only in gaming but in something as simple as taking a survey. Somehow seeing that percentage completed bar get closer and closer to 100 percent gives me both feelings of motivation and satisfaction. When players do not have a sense of where they are in a game, players feel lost:

> While *Balance of the Planet* sports a very large possibility space, the game's controls and feedback system make it difficult for players to keep track of the decisions they have already made and to see the aggregate effects of those decisions. The game is *hard to play*; that is, it is difficult to understand the processes at work inside and the nature of the possibility space those processes create. (Bogost 2007, p. 43)

It is important to "advertise these milestones to the players so that they know what they're striving for, and reward them after each accomplishment" (Fullerton et al. 2004, p. 285). It also helps players in real life judge whether or not they have time to complete a level before dinner, or in our case, lets students know they should save their game before class ends. Progress bars provide in-game and real-life feedback. Teachers have been using "progress bars" in their classrooms for a long time, just think back to the "sticker charts" from your childhood.

You may need more than a bar graph to help players keep track of where they have been. On long car trips, my friend Scott and I used to play the *Kevin Bacon* game where one of us would name two actors and the other would try to connect the two actors through movies they had been in (e.g., "Annabeth Gish was in *Mystic Pizza* with Julia Roberts who was in *Pretty Woman* with Richard Gere"). Inevitably, I would struggle, alternating beginning with one actor and then the other. This would result in me connecting an actor with him- or herself (e.g., "Jodie Foster was in *Elysium* with Matt Damon who was in *Behind the Candelabra* with Michael Douglas who was in *Napoleon and Samantha* with Jodie Foster"). Because my brain could not keep track of where I started, my friend Scott would just shake his head and say, "You did it again." Providing a map or some other way of showing where a player has been can be a tremendous aide, especially if spatial memory is not one of your learning goals.

If possible, institute a status or progress bar so that players can see not only how much they have accomplished but what milestones they have left. In this way, they can gauge how far they are from their goal: "providing a path for the player to follow gives a sense of achievement" (Fullerton et al. 2004, p. 285). In one of my previous curricular games, each time a student achieved a level, a new book would show up on the bookshelf. While this provided rewards, or at least was supposed to be rewarding,[16] because the unreached books were not depicted on the bookshelf, it did not give students a sense of accomplishment. I tried all sorts of workarounds in the learning management system to make future books grayed out, but my university switched learning management systems before I could figure it out. In a way, a syllabus can serve as a progress bar, but syllabi are most often written in terms of time such as weekly or daily class sessions. Because the passing of time is inevitable, i.e., something that students do not have control over, even if students marked off each session, syllabi give very little sense of agency. The ideal progress bar "communicates where the goal is, how it might be achieved, whether the player is making progress toward it, exactly when it was reached and completed, and its impact on future play" (Salen and Zimmerman 2004, p. 354). Progress bars should mark player progress, not the passage of time or some other element not under a player's control.

If you do institute a progress bar or even just a scoring mechanism, keep track of progress by what is intrinsic to game, such as money, health, and so forth, in order to reflect the in-game goals. This is yet another opportunity to "reinforce the theme" (Schell 2008). For example, a game about Kashrut (Jewish dietary laws) might keep score on a scale from treyf to kosher. How you depict progress should be in keeping with the game as well. If your player's goal is to gain knowledge, you could have a lightbulb over their head that gets brighter as they gain more knowledge. Although you could make that lightbulb dimmer if players lose knowledge, Meadows (2008)

[16] While most students responded positively to this, I did have one student in her course evaluation say that every time a new book showed up on her bookshelf, she groaned because the book represented more work to do.

advises to "make [the progress bar] sensitive to the best performances of the past, instead of the worst. If perceived performance has an upbeat bias instead of a downbeat one, if one takes the best results as a standard, and the worst results only as a temporary setback, then the same system structure can pull the system up to better and better performance" (Meadows 2008, p. 123). Revise and resubmit systems should do the same, allowing students to progress by factoring in the highest score, not necessarily the most recent.

Keep in mind that progress bars may not be a good fit for all games. There might be too many paths to the win state to depict or perhaps you want to create mystery and intrigue throughout the game. If your first goal is figuring out the goal, you might not want the progress bar to show up until players figure out the goal.

Data Repositories

While progress bars show general progress through the game, often players need data at a much finer grain size. heads-up displays, or HUDs, enable users to see complex data within their visual field so players can access data during in-game action. For example, a game might have a transparent map overlay or a control panel with gauges showing how much fuel is remaining. However, too much detail all at once can feel overwhelming. If you have ever glanced inside an airplane cockpit and you are not a pilot, you have a sense of what this feels like. Ironically, not displaying all the feedback can be a form of scaffolding:

> [Progressive disclosure] is a technique in which a computer program, in this case a game, displays information in small 'chunks' a little bit at a time. The technique is used so that a player is not overwhelmed by the amount of information displayed on the screen. As the player becomes more comfortable with the level of display, more information is provided. This is evident in *World of Warcraft*. A lower-level player has a much less complex user interface screen than a higher-level player. (Kapp 2012, p. 67)

Although we do not call it a "heads-up display," teachers have HUDs in their classrooms. For example, having today's objectives, agenda, and homework written on the chalkboard puts all that data within a student's visual field. One piece of advice I received when I was a new teacher was to adorn my classroom walls with educational materials. That way, if students' minds wander, at least they will be learning when they look around the classroom.[17]

Keeping in mind that our curricular game serves as a means of assessment, however, heads-up displays may not serve our purposes since we do not have a way to record what students look at, that is unless we have an eye-tracking device: "Process data may be the best way to capture proficiency" (Baker and Delacruz 2008, p. 30); therefore, "embedding features into the game to capture intent, such as requiring the learner to

[17] I experienced this as a student. I was sitting in ninth grade history class not paying attention at all, when I noticed a photo on the wall. It was a replica of the famous photo of a white man jabbing an American flag at a black man. When I saw the date, April 5, 1975, I realized that the Civil Rights Movement was not a part of history but rather a part of my present, as I would have been 5 years old at the time.

perform an explicit action to access information [such as "clicking on a button to see the time remaining"], can yield useful information about problem-solving strategies" (Baker and Delacruz 2008, p. 30). Keeping track of how many times and when students access data can provide powerful data for you both as game designer and as teacher.

One common form of data tracking in video games is an inventory of resources. Sometimes this involves displaying the inventory the player has picked up on his or her journey. Other times it can be of inventory that the player needs. Do not forget that information itself is a resource. Journals, either ones already written in or ones players can write in or even ones already written where players can add their own annotations, can serve as rich data sources. Cameras that capture screenshots and store these "photos" are another means of storing data. Some games even employ graphic representations of information through concept modeling. Notice that all of these video game apparatuses are also real-life data capturing tools which can be used in the classroom.

When talking about role-playing earlier, we talked about giving students roles as different professionals. However, "just telling the player that he or she is an investigative reporter is not convincing or believable unless he or she also believes that he or she has the expertise [and resources] to take on that role meaningfully" (Barab et al. 2012, p. 321). As game designers, we can provide those resources. We can even provide relevant and irrelevant details or reliable and unreliable information forcing students to learn and use information literacy skills: "The game was designed to elicit misconceptions, a key step for using games for assessment. Through carefully placing red herrings in the game, we were able to understand which sources of evidence students used and which they did not, and to what extent they understood the texts" (Squire 2011, p. 200). However, we need to think carefully about information dissemination: "New information is provided to the learner not in advance of the activity, as a prerequisite to participation, but within the actual context of use—what Gee (2007) and others call just-in-time information" (Steinkuehler and Oh 2012, p. 158). Just like heads-up displays can be overwhelming if all the data are presented in the beginning, confronting a new player with a character's entire 150-page journal would do so as well.

While we do not want to overwhelm students to the point of frustration, there may be instances when we want to expose students to the hugest inventory of information of all—the Internet. Doing so opens up a world of information that requires all sorts of information literacy skills such as identifying keyword bias, digesting large amounts of information, navigating hyperlinks, etc.:

> Games could easily be designed to include features requiring students to get further information from printed resources in order to continue in the game. Furthermore, Internet links to relevant information could be built into games so that students would automatically be branched to those resources. Re-entry into the game could be made contingent on students' obtaining and comprehending the necessary data from external sources. (Tobias et al. 2011, p. 204)

Requiring students to use information from the Internet to solve a puzzle can serve as a gateway to further game play. Of course, these should be done in the context of the game story. In addition to software tools that enable users to keep track of useful websites, there are also software tools that allow people to capture the contents of webpages and even to mark them up or put virtual sticky notes on them. Keep in mind, though, that webpages are ephemeral. If you want students to discover a webpage, you might want to use screen capture to copy and paste it into your game. You could even have students collect webpages to store in their own portfolio. In these ways and others, students can create their own inventories of information.

A glossary serves as an inventory of vocabulary. You can provide a glossary or have students construct one of their own or even have a combination of teacher and student-generated glossaries. With software tools like wikis and Google docs, glossaries and other information repositories can be co-constructed by the whole class. You can even use "progressive disclosure" so that only words already encountered in the game world appear in the glossary. However, students need more than just a glossary to understand concepts. To learn vocabulary at a deeper level than just memorizing definitions, students need to experience them in context:

> Miller and Gildea (1987) showed that when young people learn vocabulary words within the context of every day cognition the gains are rapid and successful. Yet when vocabulary is learned in an abstract way, in other words, taken out of context, learning is slow and many errors are made. People learn languages and their associated ways of thinking best when they can tie the words and structures of those languages to experiences they have had (Gee, 2004). (Barrett and Johnson 2010, p. 284)

Ideally, curricular games would also require students to use vocabulary words in context as well.

Feedback

While we often think of feedback in terms of providing a response to a user's attempt at a puzzle, in-game objects need to provide players with feedback about what they are. For example, Squire (2011) describes how "walls [in his game] were translucent, which meant novice users had no idea what they were. As one asked, 'What is that thing? A warp shield?' Through playtesting, we learned that walls must communicate their 'wallness'" (p. 93). In addition, any time a player performs an action, a player needs to know if that action was registered. People have double-paid for an item they purchased on the Internet because there was no indication that their first attempt worked so they tried again:

> In design, it is important to show the effect of an action. Without feedback, one is always wondering whether anything has happened. Maybe the button wasn't pushed hard enough; maybe the machine has stopped working; maybe it is doing the wrong thing. Without feedback, we turn equipment off at improper times or restart unnecessarily, losing all our recent work. Or we repeat the command and end up having the operation done twice, often to our detriment. Feedback is critical. (Norman 2002, p. xii)

If the response takes a while, there should be some indication like a ticking clock or an hourglass. One of the initial problems with the healthcare.gov website was that there was no indication that information entered was being processed so people kept clicking or abandoned their efforts. Even if there is an action a player cannot take at that moment, there should be an indication that it will be actionable in the future. For example, if a player tries to open a door he or she is not able to at that point in the game, the handle could turn while the door remains shut. This way the player knows opening the door is possible, just not at that time. In this way, the game communicates a future goal to the player and sets the player off on another task to find the key. On the other hand, if the door handle does not turn, the player keeps clicking to see if his or her action registered, eventually decides that the door is not supposed to be opened, and wanders off aimlessly, wondering what to do next. This type of action feedback has a psychological effect as well: "the game world must acknowledge players every time they perform an action. … if the world ignores the player, the player won't care about the world" (Birdwell 1999/2006, pp. 215–215—one of game designers of *Half-Life*). These action responses are what Doug Church calls "perceivable consequences" (Church 1999/2006, p. 373). Players need to feel like what they do makes a difference, just like people in real life desire as well.

In designing this type of feedback, games should be consistent. Hallford and Hallford provide an example of a player pushing a button that opens a secret door the first time. Later, when the player pushes a similar looking button, a fireball comes out of the wall:

> If the designer hasn't provided some kind of clue about what sets this button apart from the door-opening variety, they've just violated a rule that's already been established by the game. The value of choice has been taken away from the player because they have no way of knowing whether pushing the button opens a door or whether it will do some catastrophic amount of damage. While this would certainly add a heightened degree of tension to the pushing of any buttons in the game, it really is nothing more than a way of arbitrarily punishing the player for being curious. Even worse, the value of the things that the player has learned are now worthless, making the winning of the game more a matter of chance than of acquired skill. (quoted in Salen and Zimmerman 2004, p. 367)

It is the consequences of these in-game actions that provide the most immediate and visceral feedback: "*functional*, or *pragmatic*, way of knowing, because we make meaning through interacting directly with the world and observing our actions' consequences" (Squire 2011, p. 143). The game response informs the player of whether or not the consequences they predicted occur (e.g., the patient heals). The trick to educational games is to move this away from trial and error (e.g., randomly picking treatment equipment to see if it works) to intentional hypothesis testing. Limiting the number of tries and instituting a time limit are some ways to do this. You can also have an NPC or the teacher constantly asks "why" just like 3-year-olds do ("why did you select that treatment equipment? Why did the patient scream in pain when you applied salt to the wound?"). Dunwell et al. (2011) outline several types of performance feedback:

- *Evaluative* = score (measurement of a variable) (e.g., 120/200)—sometimes simply being evaluative is desirable so a player explores on his/her own what makes a score go up in order to uncover underlying rules of the system.
- *Interpretive* = score plus reason (e.g. 120/200 because your response time was too slow).
- *Supportive* = score plus suggestion to improve (e.g. 120/200, perhaps you need to practice your reaction time).
- *Probing* = score plus questions to user about why they may have gotten that score (120/200, was this because you had difficulty identifying the equipment you need

or difficulty locating the treatment equipment you needed to load onto the truck or because you had difficulty figuring out where to put the equipment on the truck?).
– *Understanding* = score plus background knowledge explaining possibly why (e.g. 120/200, because the emergency involved a burn patient, you needed antibiotic cream to prevent infection and gauze to protect the burn while it heals).

Some claim explanatory feedback (feedback that explains why the response did or did not work) is better than corrective feedback (feedback that just tells the user if something worked or not) (Leemkuil and de Jong 2011, p. 361). For example, my ear, nose, and throat doctor initially told me to use a nasal rinse daily. Instead, I did so sporadically. However, the next time I went to see him, he explained to me why I needed to do the nasal rinse daily. Because I understood why, this time I followed his instructions religiously. However, if the goal of the game is for the player to figure out the reasons why, then giving players an explanation denies them this opportunity: "In many cases, the computer game does not tell the player that what they did was right or wrong; it simply plays out the natural consequence of the action within the game. The evaluative function is most often left to the player" (Swan 2010, p. 118). Natural consequences can promote players to think of their own explanations and test them out. People have an innate drive to think of explanations, as the Greeks and Romans used mythology to explain their world and my children are constantly posing "maybes" (e.g., to try to explain why someone wouldn't have a television in her apartment, my twins said, "maybe her television got stolen," "maybe she gave it to someone else," etc.). You want to be prudent about supplying explanatory feedback, especially when you want your students to generate their own hypotheses.

Scaffolding can range from direct instruction to constructivist questions, from reactions by objects to text explanations (for both correct and incorrect actions), from explicit modeling to worked examples, from various amounts of background information and availability before, during, or after game play, and from scaffolding/guidance being system-initiated (e.g., after so many failed tries) or user requested. However, one type of scaffolding that is often not considered is giving the answer:

> Give the Answer! No, seriously, hear me out on this one. Ask yourself this question: What is it that is so pleasurable about solving puzzles? Most people answer that it is the "Aha!" experience you get when you figure out the answer. But the funny thing is that experience is triggered not by solving the puzzle, but by seeing the answer. Sure, it's a little sweeter if you solved it yourself, but if you have given serious consideration to a problem, your problem-solving brain is primed for a rush of pleasure at merely seeing or hearing the answer. Think about mystery novels—they are just big puzzles in book form. And sometimes readers guess the ending ahead of time, but more often, they are surprised (Oh! The butler did it! I see now!), which is just as pleasurable, or weirdly, *more* pleasurable than if they had figured it out themselves. (Schell 2008, p. 218)

Sometimes, when players figure a puzzle out themselves, they feel the answer was obvious. For me, if I think I should have figured out the answer on my own when given the answer, it makes me remember the answer better—"Duh! Of course! Why didn't I think of that?" For example, when reading the book *Catching Fire*, I was kicking myself because I felt that if I had spent more time thinking about what the game world was, I could have realized it was a (spoiler alert) clock. Because of

Table 6.1 Matching scaffolding and feedback to goals

Goal	Visual or audio scaffolding	Inquiry scaffolding	Explanatory scaffolding	Indirect feedback	Direct feedback
Identifying salient features	Highlighting features using visuals or sound or both (can range from subtle to blatant)	Asking "what do you think that feature means?" and "does the presence of X make a difference?"	Pointing out features, identifying their degree of relevance, explaining their relevance, opportunities for students to list salient features	Clicking on or identifying a feature elicits a subtle response such as lighting up or pointer changing to a hand	Clicking on or identifying a feature provides new information or allows player to perform another action
Distinguishing among objects, events, conditions, scenarios	Highlighting differences using visuals, sound, or both (can range from subtle to blatant)	Asking "what is different?"	Pointing out what is different, explaining differences, opportunities for students to describe differences	Selecting correct object for condition or category highlights object	Selecting correct object for condition or category provides explanation
Classifying objects/events/ conditions/ scenarios	Highlighting similarities (can range from subtle to blatant)	Asking "what is similar?"	Pointing out what is similar, explaining similarities, opportunities for students to describe similarities	Selecting more than one object highlights both	Selecting all objects in a category shows relationship among them or provides explanation
Responding to events	Tutorials, demonstrations, worked examples (can range from full to partial; if partial, leave out last/later steps instead of first steps; helps to "chunk" steps into subgoals; can also range from just how to how + why), menus of set responses	Strategy suggestion "what do you think would happen if you did X?"; "what do you think will happen next?"	Strategy explanation including sequence order (by student, game, or instructor)	An error produces undesired consequences, while correct response leads to desired consequences, player strategy explanation "why did you do X?" Player outcome explanation "why do you think X happened?"	An explanation of why error produced undesired consequences and why correct response led to desired consequences
Understanding concepts	Highlights words or objects representing concept	Asking "what do you think that means?," "how does that work?"	Glossaries	Applying concept correctly leads to desired consequences	Applying concept correctly provides new information or explanation

(continued)

Table 6.1 (continued)

Goal	Visual or audio scaffolding	Inquiry scaffolding	Explanatory scaffolding	Indirect feedback	Direct feedback
Understanding rules	Responses from in-game objects or characters	"Why do you think X happened?," "what do you think would happen if … ?"	List of rules, explanations of rules, opportunities for player to explain rules	Applying rule correctly leads to desired consequences	Applying rule correctly provides new information or explanation
Understanding relationships among objects, events, scenarios	Use of analogies	"What happens when?," "how does that relate to other concepts?"	Graphic organizer or diagram (completed, partially completed and student completes rest, student designs)	Selecting objects in correct sequence or in relation to each other leads to desired consequences	Selecting objects in correct order or in relation to each other elicits explanation or diagram
Handling increasing complexity	Initially making some variables set internally by the game then increasing variables player can control	"What happens when new variables are added?"	Diagram or visual showing new variables	When player's actions account for new variables, desired consequences occur	When player's actions account for new variables, an explanation or diagram shows how new variables play into the system
Setting nested goals (short term and long term)	Goals explicitly stated by NPCs, in storyline background, or revealed gradually based on player mastery	"What do you need to do next?," "what is your ultimate goal?"	Suggesting goals, student identifying goals	Actions lead to desired consequences; achieving smaller goals leads to bigger goal	Achieving a smaller goal reveals a piece of the larger goal
Pattern recognition	Highlighting pattern in order	"What pattern do you see?" "In what order do the objects occur?"	Explanation of reasoning behind pattern	Being able to continue pattern leads to desired consequences	Being able to continue pattern elicits explanation of pattern
Completing transfer tasks	Highlighting analogous task already completed	"Where have you seen something like this before?"	Explanation of similarities and differences between tasks	Successfully performing task in new condition leads to desired consequences	Successfully performing task in new condition elicits explanation of conditional knowledge
Collaborating	Sociogram of potential collaborators	Asking, "who could help you with this?"	Explaining who might have what information	List of "friends"	Sociogram of collaborators

Seeking, identifying, evaluating information sources	List of potential sources	Asking, "what could help with this?"	Explanation of different sources	Sound or other indicators letting user know if information source is useful	Use of information source provides access to new paths
Synthesizing information sources	Concept web	Asking, "what happens if you put this information together in a new way?"	Explaining how items might fit together	Highlighting all items in same group	A new item created that is more than sum of parts
Navigating environments	Maps (with current location or not; can also have NPC locations)	"Where are you?" "Where is X?" "How do you get to X?"	Explaining where essential items are located	Trail on map depicting where player has been	Indication of where user needs to go; new environment to explore
Metacognition	Elements that might go into a concept map	Asking, "what are you thinking?"	Explanation of thinking	Active listening by NPC	Concept map

Note: I am differentiating between scaffolding (before or during action), feedback (after game response to action) this "duh" moment, this memory likely sticks with me more strongly than if I had figured out it was a clock on my own. Textbooks, particularly math textbooks, often have the answers in the back. The reason they are in the back and not on the page is so you can check your answers when you choose, presumably after you have done the work. If you do employ this technique, it is important to make the answer feel obvious, whether it was or not, but not in a condescending way where the player ends up feeling stupid. Table 6.1 gives suggestions for types of feedback and scaffolding depending on your goal.

Modality

Various studies have been conducted about the impact of using various modalities for feedback. Because touch in the real world often results in a noise, "the human mind easily maps sound to touch" (Schell 2008, p. 241) so having audio feedback to let the player know the results of his or her actions can simulate touch in a player's mind. For example, the sound of a doorknob jiggling can make a player feel like he or she is actually touching a door handle. Feeling like an animated agent is present requires only a voice. However, it is better to have a human voice than a computer-generated one (Tobias et al. 2011). Sound and music are particularly useful to evoke mood and therefore help your students experience the material: "audio feedback can also establish the rhythm of interaction for the player" (Michael Sweet, Creative Director at AudioBrain quoted by Fullerton et al. 2004, p. 309). When music speeds up, the player's heart starts racing and he or she transitions into action mode. When music slows down, players relax and move into a more reflective mode. In *Space Invaders* "the marching invaders made a sort of heartbeat noise, and as they sped up, the heartbeat sped up, which had a very visceral effect on the player" (Schell 2008, p. 45). I have often thought it would be useful if my life had a soundtrack, letting me know when to anticipate danger and when the person I was dating might be true love.

While audio feedback is best for letting players know the immediate results of their actions, visual feedback is better for providing ongoing data. Tobias et al.'s (2011) meta-analysis suggests that pictorial feedback is more successful than text alone, particularly if that pictorial feedback is of something easily recognizable: "Since we can notice facial expression in our peripheral vision more easily than we can discern numbers [the designers of Doom put a small picture of the avatar's face on the bottom of the screen] and made the facial expression correspond to the health meter, so that players got a sense of how injured they were without having to take their eyes off of their enemies" (Schell 2008, p. 326). Make sure you place two sets of data that a player is likely to need to view at the same time close together in a HUD as splitting a novice's attention visually between two sources places a greater cognitive load when the learner tries to integrate the two in his or her mind. This is called the split-attention effect. Instead, text and graphics can be put together in one diagram or a game can provide an audio explanation as learner looks at a graphic model (Jin and Low 2011). Adcock et al. 2010 found that "'animation + narration' presentation had higher retention scores than those given an 'animation + text' presentation" (p. 175) and worked best when the audio and visual needed to be mentally integrated for comprehension. Keep in mind that providing a means for replaying and pausing narration is crucial for all players, but particularly for English Language Learners, as well as providing closed captioning. However, when information can be completely comprehended through one channel, a redundancy effect occurs causing players to devote some cognitive load to cross-checking information. It is important to note that "techniques that are effective for novices may be quite counterproductive as expertise increases" (Adcock et al. 2010 p. 177). With advanced learners, integrating scaffolding into text is distracting and unnecessary, what is called the expertise reversal effect. The best way to find out what works best for your game and your students is through playtesting—having people think out loud while they play your game—a step that will be explored in more detail later.

Who Scaffolds?

So far I have repeatedly mentioned the possibility of NPCs providing feedback. However, in a classroom situation, not only can you, as the teacher, be an NPC doling out advice, but you can also have your students role-play and have them as PCs (playing characters) provide scaffolding by "planting" information and questions. For example, you could e-mail your students or just hand out slips of paper at the beginning of each gaming session (i.e., class) that directs them to ask other PCs questions, provide certain feedback, and so forth. Remember, however, to have them do so (and have what they say and do) be in character. To help with pacing, you can also have students who have completed a task act as advisors, or even gatekeepers, for those still working on a task. This might also help with logistics. For example, if your players have to say a certain phrase in a foreign language while chatting with an informant at a café, you as the teacher could play the informant for the student who makes it to that point first, responding, of course, with a "je ne comprends pas" until the student says the correct phrase. Once that student has passed, though, that student can turn into an informant for the next student to come through. Since they have passed that challenge, they should be able to judge that next student's performance. You then generate more and more "judges" until all students have passed the challenge, hopefully before the bell rings.

In one of the classes I teach, my students role-play high school students. I use index cards with certain demographics (the proportionality is based on the demographics of the student population of Boston Public Schools) that students select and can then trade. However, every student gets a "wild card" with a student situation such as "father is in jail" that they cannot trade with each other, but they can trade in for another wild card if they like. My students then create their own character's stories to create Facebook-like pages. Based on the characters they create, later in the semester I assign students "zingers," things that they say or do that would be in keeping with their student character that they act out while another student is practicing their teaching. For example, one of my students was role-playing a pregnant teenager, so her assigned zinger was to pretend to throw up while another student was teaching. While technically these assignments are tasks, or really surprises thrown at students while they complete a task, I see them also as scaffolding learning by providing students an opportunity to think about what they might do if that happened to them when they are a high school teacher and not just pretending to be one. During debriefing, those who were practicing teaching got peer feedback, including feedback on how they responded to any zingers that occurred while they were teaching. In early stages of the class, students who are teaching can "pause" the lesson and consult others teaching that same lesson (for the sake of time, students tag teach—each student teaches a 10-min segment of the same lesson). Later on, the pause feature is removed. In a very low-tech way (e-mail communication), I use NPCs (when they are role-playing their student, technically they are NPCs since the goal is to help prepare them to be teachers) to scaffold learning.

When using characters to scaffold, you can have the different characters play different roles:

> By embedding help systems in pedagogical agents,[18] we provide social aspects of learning when humans cannot be present, and we do so without violating the environmental context. These animated pedagogical agents can take on different roles, or persona, in computer-based instruction, including assistant, pedagogical expert/mentor, learning companion (Baylor, 2001), and motivators (Baylor & Kim, 2005). … Agents in games can provide the necessary content in the context of any of several different roles or personas within the game including as co-investigators, mentors, team members, or peers with content knowledge. (Van Eck 2007, p. 289)

Not only do characters need to respond "in character," but their responses also need to be in keeping with the game world:

> So it is not enough for a pedagogical agent to be merely thematically tied to the game (e.g., a trainer with the game world); the agent must be a character who is engaged in advancing the goals and story of the game world according to the same motivations and constraints as other characters in the game. They must present any instructional content as contiguously as possible to the events in the game that require the application of that content. What we need to integrate agents into games, then, is a pedagogical approach that is compatible with this constant cycle of player action and game feedback, the 'conversation' between player and game. (Van Eck 2007, p. 290)

An interesting way to do this might be to have one NPC responsible for declarative knowledge, one for procedural knowledge, and one for conditional knowledge. Is this realistic or, rather, plausible? I knew two coworkers who other coworkers would often seek out for advice. If someone needed just a quick answer (declarative knowledge), they would ask one coworker in particular, but if they wanted to learn how to do something (procedural knowledge), they would go to the other one.

[18] Agents are computer-programmed characters (versus avatars which are controlled by humans). However, for our purposes, you might want to use "teacher-controlled students" as agents by assigning them different things to say and do.

One potential problem with using NPCs to provide guidance is if an NPC knows the answers or how to solve the problems, why don't they do it themselves? There are several ways to solve this problem in your game story. It could be that the NPC has a different goal or motivation. The NPC could be acting as a co-learner or player, similar to Hermione Grainger in the Harry Potter series who would do things like go to the library to learn about something and report back. Perhaps it could even be a game decision whether or not to send an NPC to the library or to the chemistry lab. You can also have a Mr. Miyagi[19]-like NPC, i.e., someone who knows the answers or how to do something but withholds them in order to encourage growth or a Professor Dumbledore-type NPC, someone who withholds certain information in order to protect the main character from danger. Perhaps the NPC has been sworn to secrecy. Or the NPC could be someone ancient, like Yoda, who has done something similar before but lacks the physical prowess to do it now or a ghost who cannot physically move objects. You can also have the NPC display their full knowledge of how to do something: "NPCs [can] model correct skills and knowledge for the player" (Gee 2008b, p. 25). Of course, you can also do the opposite: "Letting players see other characters make mistakes that they'll need to avoid is an effective way to explain your puzzles and add tension and entertainment value" (Birdwell 1999/2006, p. 219). The possibilities are endless, but whatever you come up with, make sure it is plausible within the game story.

You also want to make the character's responses plausible as well: "A character who comes up to me as part of the game … and instead of answering questions in a forthright manner begins to quiz me, evades my direct questions, and provides long didactic statements is likely to receive the same response I would give to a co-worker who did the same thing" (Van Eck 2007, p. 290). As with every aspect of the game, the more feedback appears true to the game world, the more immersive the experience: "Embedded helps, in general, should be non-intrusive and non-didactic; they should appear as if they arise naturally out of the interaction wherever possible. The quality of appearing to be natural parts of the environment preserves participants' sense of accomplishment" (Swan 2010, p. 119). Van Eck (2007) notes that "players would quickly become irritated with an agent who continually responded with suggestions for them to think more about the material, or who gave them hints and prompts instead of direct information relevant to solving the problem at hand" (p. 293). He suggests instead to use "shorter interchanges" that are "distributed (among agents and within the game environment itself) fashion" (Van Eck 2007, p. 294). A long lecture will make a player feel like he or she is a student in class. Shorter exchanges, particularly if they are from several places, will feel more like authentic conversation.

Adcock et al. (2010) describe three different types of feedback that can feel natural: *critical* or informing learners of mistakes, *positive* or "reinforce[ing] the learner's efforts and offer[ing] advice and/or just-in-time guidance," and *anecdotal* or "com[ing] from experts that offer additional information in the form of stories and/or similar cases" (pp. 193–194). You could even use interactions between or among

[19] Mr. Miyagi was the martial arts mentor in the movie *Karate Kid* who would have his protégé do seemingly unrelated tasks like paint a fence and then later would reveal why.

NPCs to create plausibility: "The various NPCs might be argumentative, constantly offering alternative perspectives, characters that offer a different cultural perspective, and others" (Adcock et al. 2010, p. 194). This might be a way of injecting uncertainty into game play as players have to choose which NPC or which parts of the arguments to believe.

You can also add a dimension of plausibility by making the NPCs' responses dynamic so that each time a player interacts with an NPC, the interaction changes in some way. For example, the NPC could offer more details as the NPC grows to trust the main character. Or perhaps the NPC at first politely answers questions, but then gets annoyed as the player asks more questions. Or perhaps the NPC learns from interactions with the main character or even other NPCs and changes responses accordingly.

If one of your NPCs plays the role of "cheerleader," you might have them employ a mental trick my sister taught me when we were playing tennis. Instead of saying to yourself when you make a mistake, "Oh, that was so dumb of me. Why do I do that every time?" say, "Gosh, I usually make that shot. That was unusual of me to miss it." What this does is to frame yourself as successful instead of as a failure. In keeping with this advice, you could have an NPC say something like, "that's unusual for you to fail." According to Dweck's (2006) research, a better statement would be: "Your efforts usually lead to success." Dweck (2006) found that the type of praise given can shift people from a "fixed mindset" to a growth or mastery mindset, similar to external locus of control versus internal locus of control. The goal of those with a fixed mindset is to avoid failure; those with a growth mindset aim to learn: "craft feedback to focus on ways the learner can improve, rather than on labeling the person a 'success or failure' (Dweck 2006)" (quoted by Magerko 2010, p. 261). It is important to realize that for people with a fixed mindset "both positive and negative labels can mess with your mind. When you're given a positive label, you're afraid of losing it. When you're given a negative label, you're afraid of deserving it (Dweck 2006, pp. 75–76)" (Magerko et al. 2010, p. 261). However, those with growth mindsets see criticism as constructive. Sometimes mindset may vary depending on task (e.g., someone may have a "fixed mindset" in terms of school and a "growth mindset" in terms of skateboarding); sometimes it changes over time. I certainly have been hurt initially by criticism but, after time has given me some distance, have learned from it. Keep Dweck's (2006) research in mind when you determine the labels of your different levels. The labels "apprentice" (learning from someone), "journeyman" (performing some of the tasks on your own), and "master" (performing all of the tasks at once) focus on the actions of the character within those different roles. The labels "Freshman, Sophomore, Junior, and Senior" focus on growth (although in the US system, these are based largely on seat time and not on mastery). Dork, Dweeb, Nerd, and Geek, however, focus on who the person is. Even Ace, Genius, and Champion tend to presume fixed innate talent. As with other aspects of your curricular game, you need to consider what messages your game sends.

Some games measure "effort" not by what the gamer does but by what the protégé of the gamer does:

> Teachable agents are an assessment tool where kids teach a digital character how to solve a particular problem. In other words, Betty is a software program designed to know less than [the student]. And it's [the student's] job to 'teach' the program, by demonstrating solutions and working patiently with Betty until she gets it. At Quest, these teachable agents replace quizzes, easing the anxiety associated with having to perform under pressure. With a teachable agent, you're not being tested to see if you've really learned something. Instead, you're mentoring someone because you really have learned something, and this is your chance to show it. There's a powerful element of naches[20]—vicarious pride—involved here. (McGonigal 2011, p. 132)

Just like we, as teachers, use feedback from our students to determine how we are teaching, teachable agents give players feedback through their responses. If a player does not understand or explain a concept well, the teachable agent will not learn it well: "garbage in, garbage out." Being forced to clarify your own understandings in order to teach another person can foster a truly deep understanding of the material.

Teachers themselves can also play a character in the game: "plant instructors in the game so that they can manipulate the game space to provide more instruction or create learning opportunities. The instructor could be allowed to enter the game in various roles to scaffold, guide, and coach in a manner that would be consistent with the fantasy, context, and narrative of the game world" (Charsky 2010, p. 200). Playing a role such as an advisor or mentor can allow you to perform that function in the game. However, you could also be another character whose responses provide feedback or even act as a "teachable agent" in order to reflect back to the student his or her understanding of the material or a sidekick who asks seemingly naïve questions to prompt critical thinking. Because students often have a heightened awareness that as their teacher, you eventually have to assign them a grade, it can be difficult for your students to forget your role as teacher. Be sensitive to your identity as teacher potentially disrupting game play. If you are going to play a character, props and costumes might help distinguish that you are playing a role other than teacher.

Feedback does not always have to happen within the context of the game world. Barrett and Johnson (2010) use what they call "inner loop feedback (immediate feedback to learner actions during game play)" and "outer loop feedback (feedback between gaming episodes and other activities)" (p. 288). The inner loop operates "so that learners understand clearly the consequences of their actions and can learn from their mistakes" (p. 289) and does not interrupt game play (e.g., comments by NPCs, reaction or non-reaction by gaming elements) because it is a part of the game play. For example, if a player uses the informal pronoun in French, like in one of my student's games, the NPC might respond "I am not your pal." On the other hand, the outer loop can be "virtual coaches [that are] polite, encouraging, and supportive" (p. 289) in order to provide reflection or skill-building outside the game environment

[20] "Naches, a Yiddish word for the bursting pride we feel when someone we've taught or mentored succeeds" (McGonigal 2011, p. 87).

itself. Exit tickets, responses to questions asked at the end of class handed to the teacher on the way out the door, or reflective homework assignments might even enable students to come up with their own feedback and scaffolding.

Timing of Scaffolding

Timing is especially crucial in the beginning of a video game because this is when you are either going to hook your players or lose your players. The same is true in the classroom. The big difference, though, is students cannot put down the classroom and walk away like they can with a video game. They have to suffer through (not your class, of course!). If a player does not experience early success, the player is likely to get frustrated. In addition, people remember what happens at the beginning the most and the best. Cognitive scientists call this the primacy effect (Driscoll 2005, p. 88). If a player experiences frustration at the beginning of a game, this is what he or she remembers and, potentially, how he or she defines himself or herself in terms of being a player in that game. This is one reason why scaffolding is so crucial at the beginning of a game and of a class.

According to Squire (2011), "players should experience new successes after 5 minutes, 15 minutes, and an hour" (p. 164). Keep in mind that success doesn't mean solving a challenge; it could be just figuring something out and getting a response/reward. Squire (2011) uses an example from *Lure of the Labyrinth* where players are likely to figure out that disks are coins that can be dragged into a vending machine and that different combinations release different items within the first 5 minutes even though figuring out the whole puzzle of how to release certain items (and which items are needed) will likely take longer. Squire (2011) calls this the "orchestration of time" (p. 6), where short-term goals should take about 60–90 seconds, medium-range goals 45–60 minutes, and long-term goals 3–4 hours. These goals, however, do not have to be linear. Part of the decision-making process might be deciding which goals to pursue when. Interestingly, those medium successes should occur approximately every hour, which happens to be both the average gaming session and a typical class period. Part of scaffolding, and the "flow channel," is providing time for players to reflect on their game play to produce their own feedback. Schools have their own natural ebb and flows with in-class work and out-of-class work. You can take advantage of this by structuring homework to give students the opportunity to reflect on their game play.

Scaffolding should occur before taking action (an invitation to action), during action consequences (an indication that the action was registered), and post action (consequences of the action). Badly designed objects tempt users with incompatible actions:

> The surest way to make sure something is easy to use, with few errors, is to make it impossible to do otherwise—to constrain the choices. What's to prevent people from inserting batteries or memory cards into the cameras the wrong way, thus possibly harming the electronics? Design them so that they fit only one way, or make it so they work perfectly regard-

> less of how they were inserted. … Rule of thumb: when instructions have to be pasted on something … it is badly designed. (Norman 2002, p. xii)

A door handle that suggests it should be pulled frustrates users when it actually needs to be pushed, something that happens so often it is the subject of a well-known *Far Side* cartoon. Well-designed objects make the actions obvious and compel the user to take such action: "A good designer makes sure that appropriate actions are perceptible ['perceived affordances'] and inappropriate ones invisible" (Norman 2002, p. xii). For example, a teapot with a handle makes it clear how the user should lift it. Well-designed objects make the user think he or she has free will, but actually the user is fulfilling the will of the designer:

> For a game to be truly immersive, more subtle means [of getting a player back on the golden path] should be explored. One method employed by theme parks is to place highly visible, intriguing items that draw the players in and interrupt them from their aimless wander. This way, players are guided toward the item, but are still moving toward it of their own free will. Another subtle method is to keep primary objectives on a wider physical path, while side quests are placed, literally, off to the side, with smaller roads leading to them. The size of the road can cue a player consciously or subconsciously where the important things will be found. Whatever methods are employed, they should be as unobtrusive as possible. (Rabin 2009, p. 152)

You should time your hints so that the least obvious occurs first, with the more and more obvious hints occurring only as the player needs them. For example, you may have nothing to indicate that the player needs to click on a teapot, then you might have the teapot start whistling, then you might have the teapot start rattling on the stove as if it is about to explode if you do not do something with it. Goals, whether large or small, should "*seduce* players into pursuing them" (Squire 2011, p. 7). Think about "How is the possibility of choice conveyed to the player" and "how is the result of the choice conveyed to the player?" (Salen and Zimmerman 2004, pp. 64–64). By doing so, players should be able to see how that result leads to further choices.

Most of the time you want well-designed objects. However, there are times you might want objects whose ways they can be acted upon not so obvious or, better yet, not immediately obvious, so that once the player discovers the action, the player has a "duh" moment where it feels obvious. A box may hide a trapdoor. A pile of leaves may hide a dead soldier (from one of my student's games). There also might be cases where you want to lead your player into performing an incompatible action or have unexpected consequences of an action to teach a lesson, perhaps to dispel a common misconception. Players would likely be attracted to a tree in the middle of a field during a thunderstorm, but gathering under the tree could cause their demise as lightning strikes the tallest object around. Temptation can lure players into learning valuable lessons through their mistakes.

To determine what scaffolding should occur when, Schell (2008) suggests asking yourself the following questions:

> What do players need to know at this moment? What do players want to know at this moment? What do you want players to feel at this moment? How can you give feedback that creates that feeling? What do the players want to feel at this moment? Is there an opportu-

> nity for them to create a situation where they will feel that? What is the player's goal at this moment? What feedback will help them toward that goal? (Schell 2008, p. 230)

The key to scaffolding is assessing a student's ZPD and adjusting the scaffolding accordingly. If a student is operating in the:

- Independent zone, no scaffolding.
- If they are in the ZPD, ask *what* they notice (including patterns); *now what?* How they think they should proceed and why; ask what background information they need and ask how they can find that out; *so what?* What they think something means, provide incomplete worked examples, etc.
- If they have reached the frustration zone, ask leading questions, point out specific cues or patterns, provide resources with key background information, provide an explanation, model the skill through tutorials, worked examples, etc., and then have them do it on their own.

To determine a student's ZPD level, though, you need performance feedback to first assess his/her success. Salen and Zimmerman (2004) call this process "dynamic difficulty adjustment" (p. 222), a process essential to keeping players in the flow zone.

One of the most touted pedagogical affordances of video games is their ability to deliver immediate feedback. However, sometimes delaying scaffolding can be its own form of scaffolding by operating like wait time, giving students time to wrestle with the problem and figure something out on their own. If a student asks a question by e-mail I think they can figure out on their own, I won't answer it right away. Most of the time I get a "never mind" e-mail a short time later. I did this one time with my department chair who called me with a technology question at 9:00 at night. If I had logged on right away and solved her problem, I might have created a dependency where she would continue to call me immediately whenever she ran into a technical problem: "Perfectly smart people may ask you questions that you know they could figure out by themselves. If you give them an answer. … you perpetuate their dependence" (Simmons 2001, p. 65). I waited instead until the next morning. By then, she had figured it out herself, which I suspect then gave her the confidence to continue to figure other things out before asking since she has not asked me any technical questions since.

Whenever a birthday card is passed around the office, if I read what other people wrote before I sign it, I find thinking of my own birthday wish nearly impossible as I fixate on the witty wishes written by my peers. The same can also be true of scaffolding, particularly with exemplars, worked examples, and student samples. Encourage students to develop a solution first, no matter how basic, before providing students with an example. By doing so, you might have a student come up with an elegant solution that would have been inhibited by looking at the sample first: "When you decide to awaken sleeping wisdom rather than to convince others you are right, you will produce a much more powerful experience for both of you" (Simmons 2001, p. 50). Even if the example ends up inspiring a student, at least he or she would have wrangled with the problem first.

Amount of Scaffolding

As mentioned above, providing no scaffolding can be scaffolding in and of itself because you are "scaffolding" players into figuring something out themselves: "the subtlety of good simulation design lies in knowing when to do something (scaffold) or create an absence (disequilibrium)" (Barton and McKellar 2011, p. 248). In voluntary games:

> players instinctively seek out the least amount of help necessary to advance them through the game, intuitively implementing a scaffolding approach to keep themselves in the ZPD. Making this guidance and scaffolding process a more regulated feature of the game would lessen the extra steps players must now take outside the game environment to get assistance. Indeed, many games provide these kinds of resources through lists of questions the player can choose from when speaking with a character in the game, or through agents in the game who can provide limited hints. (Van Eck 2007, p. 288)

Sometimes in mandatory schooling, as mentioned earlier, students have been conditioned to regard getting an A by whatever means necessary the only goal of schooling. School-based gaming is confronted with this second day of creation effect. Some ways to counter this is to deduct points for using hints, although perhaps it would be better to give students extra points for using less help. You could also institute a three-hint free rule and then deduct points to discourage an overreliance on hints. This would force players to be strategic about selecting hints. You could also have unlimited hints on the first level, three freebies for the second level, and a point deduction or no hints allowed on the third level. You could also try the game first to see if students over-rely on them before implementing a deduction system. Another consideration is whether or not students are using hints for learning or simply to get through the game.

Feedback has different amounts of "density." Some feedback can be very parsimonious, such as my wife telling me my pasta was "undercooked." Not only does this tell me that I did not cook it right, it also tells me why and how to fix it. Contrast that with my friend who grew up with her father speaking Arabic but did not know it herself. When her husband decided he wanted to learn Arabic, she could only tell him when something "sounded wrong." She could not tell him why or how to fix it, she just knew it did not sound right. However, you may not want your feedback to be dense. You may want to dole out feedback on an "as-needed" basis starting with the fact that something did not work and then give the player a chance to fix it. If it still does not work, you might want to supply an explanation. The "how to fix" feedback might only occur when the student is in the frustration zone for too long, thus blocking learning. You need to think carefully about how to do this so students do not get into the habit of just clicking three times (or the physical/classroom equivalent) until they get to the "how to" hint. Even when my twins were three, they would prompt me to press play when I pause a television show to ask them what a word is on the screen when they know the show will provide the answer. Some ways to prevent this include imposing a time delay between hints, having a "hint penalty," or even some sort of ritual or having to ask someone or some acknowledgement that the student is asking for hints.

Showing a replay of action , particularly if you can do a slow motion one or an annotated one or one from a different perspective or even a "sports-casted" one can also be a form of feedback. When Bobby Hurley played basketball for Duke University, he was criticized for sulking on the court when in fact he was upset with himself for a bad play. When his coach showed him a montage of these reactions, he realized that to the world it looked like he was a sore loser. Like what Duke's coach did, you can have students use action replays to develop their own feedback. I do so in my classes by videotaping my students teaching and then have the students annotate the videos with their reflections, including discussing what decisions they made and why. Some video games allow players to record their own game play and even edit it with different camera angles. For example, game play might be first person, but the recording might be third person. Any time you can mirror back to a student his or her actions or his or her thinking, particularly if you have prompts that get them to think about their decision-making, you help build their metacognition or awareness of their own thinking.

Tailoring Scaffolding

One aspect of metacognition is an awareness of your preferred mode of learning: "giv[e] the player the power to choose the learning mode they prefer. This approach would essentially allow players to self-diagnose their individual differences and decide what kind of game would be best for them" (Magerko et al. 2010, p. 259). However, sometimes teenagers, and even adults, lack metacognitive awareness, particularly about a topic that is new to them. In these cases, you can use a questionnaire, record their activities in an exploratory game mode (a "fish tank"), or use a diagnostic assessment to find out about their learning style. What may be more relevant, though, than traditional learning styles (visual, auditory, kinesthetic) is the type of game player they are. Earlier I mentioned four different types of players: achievers, explorers, socializers, and killers.[21] Explorers "need time to explore and 'tend [to] be more aware of a wide range of phenomena, while giving careful attention to complexities, inconsistencies, novel events, and unexpected possibilities. They need time and freedom to make choices, to gather and process information' (Beswick, 2007, p. 1)" (quoted by Magerko et al. 2010, p. 260), whereas achievers desire focused challenges with clear outcomes. Socializers need opportunities to collaborate, and killers, well, these are really just a specific type of achiever whose goal is to defeat "enemies." A fifth kind is validators (Magerko et al. 2010), players who need validation to allay their insecurities. I would argue that like Gardner's Multiple Intelligences, we have all of these aspects, just to differing degrees that also differ according to task, context, and even people involved. For example, someone may be a "killer" when they play tennis against a certain opponent, but a

[21] Some game scholars divide these categories up even further.

socializer with another opponent. I also maintain that it is good for people to be pushed to try out different aspects of their gaming style. An achiever may need to be encouraged to explore more and so forth.

Socializers welcome collaboration as a source of feedback and scaffolding, while achievers see talking to others as a waste of time and prefer in-game scaffolding that expedites their trajectory through the game. Validators also seek in-game tutorials and hints, but do so in order to build their confidence. On the other hand, explorers prefer minimal scaffolding and even seek out side quests, quests that are not required to complete the game. However, be sure to make it clear that these side quests are optional, otherwise achievers will get frustrated and validators overwhelmed. When designing your scaffolding, think about how you can provide supports for these different types of players.

Taking Down Scaffolding

Remember that the point of scaffolding is for it to eventually be taken away. For example, a game designer could provide worked examples early in the game, examples for the student/player to work on their own in the middle of the game, and then have students/players come up with examples later in the game. This can be either a part of the game play itself (e.g., choke points so they have to be able to do this before moving on to the next level) or part of the class, small group, partner, or individual discussion about the game. If scaffolding is never taken away, then the game risks "shifting the burden to the intervener" (Meadows 2008, p. 132), in this case, the student learning to rely on the scaffolding instead of being weaned off of it. Meadows (2008) supplies an example of this with modern medicine: "in general [it] has shifted the responsibility for health away from the practices and lifestyle of each individual and onto intervening doctors and medicine" (Meadows 2008, p. 132). Overreliance leads to dependency. Teachers should teach so that they are eventually not needed.

One goal of teaching should be having students learn how to learn or "strengthen the ability of the system to shoulder its own burdens" (Meadows 2008, p. 134). Meadows (2008) goes on to contend that "the secret is to begin not with a heroic takeover, but with a series of questions" (p. 134). Instead of pulling a "heroic takeover" where the red pen corrects every mistake, ask questions: "If you are the intervener, work in such a way as to restore or enhance the system's own ability to solve its problems, then remove yourself" (Meadows 2008, p. 135). Instead of constantly reminding my children when they were being potty-trained to go to the bathroom, I would ask them what we do before going out or sometimes intentionally "forget" and have them remember for me. Both these tactics increase their willingness to go because they feel like they thought of it on their own. Sometimes I will give them a choice such as asking if they want to sit or stand, go here or at the store, and so forth, which gives them a sense of ownership. The goal is to eventually remove yourself as the source of scaffolding. We would think it weird if a parent reminded her college-aged kid to go to the bathroom, although I am sure it does happen out of habit.

Conclusion

Why is scaffolding important? One reason is because it addresses some common ways games can fail identified by Salen and Zimmerman (2004): "feeling as if decisions are arbitrary"; "not knowing what to do next"; "losing a game without knowing why"; "not knowing if an action had an outcome" (pp. 65–66). Meadows (2008) claims that "missing information flows is one of the most common causes of system malfunction" (p. 157). Certainly more information can make being a spectator more enjoyable. For example, having a computer-generated streak follow the puck on television increased the audience of ice hockey because viewers could better make sense of the action.

While scaffolding helps prevent games from failing, it also allows players to experience what McGonigal (2011) calls "fun failure" (p. 65): "Positive failure feedback reinforces our sense of control over the game's outcome. And a feeling of control in a goal-oriented environment can create a powerful drive to succeed … If failure feels random or passive, we lose our sense of agency—and optimism goes down the drain" (McGonigal 2011, p. 67). Why is failure important? Because:

- "Victory often short-circuits critical analysis" (Chatham 2011, p. 82).
- "Winning tends to end the fun. But failure? It keeps the fun going … Because being really good at something is less fun than being *not quite good enough—yet*" (McGonigal 2011, p. 68).
- "Success is a lousy teacher. It seduces smart people into thinking they can't lose" (Bill Gates).
- "Those who succeed are those who failed more often."
- "Failure is feedback."
- "F is the new A."

The true source of self-confidence is that you can recover from your mistakes.

[When you give students directions, they focus on] understanding the directions rather than understanding the problem.

-Kirkley et al. 2011, *p. 377*

Appendix

QUESTS QUEST WORKSHEET

Topic: ______________________

Twitter Storyline (140 character synopsis): ____

Primary Performance Objective (At the end of this curricular game, students will be able to …)	
Core Game Mechanic (repeated action that is improved upon through practice--should mirror the performance objective)	
Claim (statement about students' ability—should match performance objective)	
Task Model (instructions for how to design tasks to elicit evidence to support claim)	
Competency and Evidence Model (analytic rubric with criteria, levels-rename based on theme, and descriptors)	(see rubric below)
Task Integration- describe how the tasks might be integrated into your storyline	

Criteria	Level 1	Level 2	Level 3

Levels	Name	Function	Description
Level one		Diagnostic Assessment	How level one uncovers a student's mental model:
Gateway task to level 2		Resolve cognitive dissonance	
Level 2		Teach subskills; Formative Assessments	How level two prepares the learner for the boss challenge:
Gateway task to level 3		Combinations of subskills	
Level 3		Combine all subskills	How level three is cumulative:
Boss challenge		Applies skills to a new scenario	
Scaffolding	*Challenge*	*Scaffolding before action*	*Feedback after action*

Suggested Quests Quest Rubric

Quest	"Wow! I mean, I think this might work" (3)	"Hmm, this is acceptable" (2)	"I need more convincing" (1)	"Go back to the drawing board" (0)
Quests' quest	Quests require critical thinking	Quests at the comprehension level	Quests at the knowledge level	Quests' core game mechanics do not match learning objectives

Suggested Reading: Nonfiction

Shute, V. (2011b). Stealth assessment in computer-based games to support learning. In S. Tobias & J. D. Fletcher (Eds.), *Computer games and instruction* (pp. 503–524). Charlotte, NC: Information Age Publishers.

References

Adcock, A., Watson, G., Morrison, G., & Belfore, L. (2010). Effective knowledge development in game-based learning environments: Considering research in cognitive processes and simulation design. In R. Van Eck (Ed.), *Gaming and cognition: Theories and practice from the learning sciences* (pp. 152–168). Hershey, PA: Information Science Reference.

Aldrich, C. (2009a). *Complete guide to simulations and serious games : How the most valuable content will be created in the age beyond Gutenberg to Google*. Hoboken, NJ: Pfeiffer.

Aldrich, C. (2009b). *Learning online with games, simulations, and virtual worlds: Strategies for online instruction*. Hoboken, NJ: Jossey-Bass.

Baker, E., & Delacruz, G. (2008). Framework for the assessment of learning games. In H. O'Neil & R. Perez (Eds.), *Computer games and team and individual learning* (pp. 21–37). Amsterdam, The Netherlands: Elsevier.

Barab, S., Pettyjohn, P., Gresalfi, M., & Solomou, M. (2012). Game-based curricula, personal engagement, and the Modern Prometheus design project. In C. Steinkuehler, K. Squire, & S. Barab (Eds.), *Games, learning, and society: Learning and meaning in the digital age* (pp. 306–326). New York: Cambridge University Press.

Barker, J. (2013). How I turned my classroom into a "living video game"—And saw achievement-soar. *eSchoolNews*. Retrieved January 8, 2016, from http://www.eschoolnews.com/2013/03/12/how-i-turned-my-classroom-into-a-living-video-game-and-saw-achievement-soar/

Barrett, K., & Johnson, W. (2010). Developing serious games for learning language-in-culture. In R. Van Eck (Ed.), *Gaming and cognition: Theories and practice from the learning sciences* (pp. 281–311). Hershey, PA: Information Science Reference.

Bartholomae, D., & Petrosky, A. (1986). *Facts, artifacts and counterfacts*. Portsmouth, NH: Boynton/Cook.

Barton, K., & McKellar, P. (2011). From Master to Games-master: Managing disequilibrium and scaffolding in simulation-based learning. In S. de Freitas & P. Maharg (Eds.), *Digital games and learning* (pp. 226–251). London: Continuum.

Birdwell, K. (1999/2006). The Cabal: Valve's design process for creating Half-Life. In K. Salen & E. Zimmerman (Eds.), *The game designer reader: A rules of play anthology* (pp. 212–225) Cambridge, MA: MIT Press.

Bogost, I. (2007). *Persuasive games: The expressive power of videogames*. Cambridge, MA: MIT Press.

Bransford, J., Brown, A., & Cocking, R. (2000). *How people learn: Brain, mind, experience, and school*. Washington, DC: National Academies Press.

Cazden, C. (1981). Performance before competence: Assistance to child discourse in the zone of proximal development. *Quarterly Newsletter of the Laboratory of Comparative Human Cognition, 3*, 5–8.

Charsky, D. (2010). Making a connection: Game genres, game characteristics, and teaching structures. In R. Van Eck (Ed.), *Gaming and cognition: Theories and practice from the learning sciences* (pp. 189–212). Hershey, PA: Information Science Reference.

Chatham, R. E. (2011). After the revolution. In S. Tobias & J. D. Fletcher (Eds.), *Computer games and instruction* (pp. 73–99). Charlotte, NC: Information Age Publishers.

Church, D. (1999/2006). Formal abstract design tools. In K. Salen & E. Zimmerman (Eds.), *The game designer reader: A rules of play anthology* (pp. 366–380). Cambridge, MA: MIT Press.

Craster, K. (1871). Centipede's dilemma. *Pinafore Poems*. Ann Arbor, MI: G. Wahr.

Crockett, L., Jukes, I., & Churches, A. (2011). *Literacy is not enough: 21st century fluencies for the digital age*. Thousand Oaks, CA: Sage Publishing Company.

Csikszentmihalyi, M. (1990). *Flow: The psychology of optimal experience*. New York: Harper & Row.

Davis, B., Sumara, D., & Luce-Kapler, R. (2000). *Engaging minds: Learning and teaching in a complex world*. Hillsdale, NJ: L. Erlbaum Associates.

Dempsey, J. V. (2010). Elemental learning and the pyramid of fidelity. In R. Van Eck (Ed.), *Gaming and cognition: Theories and practice from the learning sciences* (pp. 82–107). Hershey, PA: Information Science Reference.

Dexter, S. (2007). Educational theory into practice software (ETIPS). In D. Gibson, C. Aldrich, & M. Prensky (Eds.), *Games and simulations in online learning: Research and development frameworks* (pp. 223–235). Hershey, PA: Information Science Publishing.

Dickey, M. (2011). Murder on Grimm Isle. In S. de Freitas & P. Maharg (Eds.), *Digital games and learning* (pp. 129–151). London: Continuum.

Doidge, N. (2007). *The brain that changes itself: Stories of personal triumph from the frontiers of brain science*. New York: Penguin Books.

Driscoll, M. (2005). *Psychology of learning for instruction*. Boston, MA: Allyn and Bacon.

Dunwell, I., de Frietas, S., & Jarvis, S. (2011). Four-dimensional considerations in serious games. In S. de Freitas & P. Maharg (Eds.), *Digital games and learning* (pp. 42–62). London: Continuum.

Dweck, C. (2006). *Mindset: The new psychology of success*. New York: Ballantine Books.

Fullerton, T., Swain, C., & Hoffman, S. (2004). *Game design workshop: Designing, prototyping, and playtesting games*. San Francisco, CA: CMP Books.

Gee, J. P. (2007). *Good videogames + good learning: Collected essays on videogames, learning, and literacy*. New York: Peter Lang.

Gee, J. P. (2008a). Learning and games. In K. Salen (Ed.), *The ecology of games: Connecting youth, games, and learning* (pp. 21–40). Cambridge, MA: MIT Press.

Gee, J. P. (2008b). Video games, learning, and 'content'. In C. T. Miller (Ed.), *Games: Purpose and potential in education* (pp. 43–53). New York: Springer.

Gee, J. P. (2012). Foreward. In C. Steinkuehler, K. Squire, & S. Barab (Eds.), *Games, learning, and society: Learning and meaning in the digital age* (pp. xvii–xx). New York: Cambridge University Press.

Gee, J. P., & Hayes, E. (2012). Nurturing affinity spaces and game-based learning. In C. Steinkuehler, K. Squire, & S. Barab (Eds.), *Games, learning, and society: Learning and meaning in the digital age* (pp. 129–153). New York: Cambridge University Press.

Gibson, D. (2007). simSchool and the conceptual assessment framework. In D. Gibson, C. Aldrich, & M. Prensky (Eds.), *Games and simulations in online learning: Research and development frameworks* (pp. 308–322). Hershey, PA: Information Science Publishing.

Green, E. (2014). *Building a better teacher: How teaching works (and how to teach it to everyone)*. New York: W.W. Norton and Co.

Hirumi, A., & Stapleton, C. (2008). Applying pedagogy during game development to enhance game-based learning. In C. T. Miller (Ed.), *Games: Purpose and potential in education* (pp. 127–162). New York: Springer.

Holt, T. (2013, April 19). The ultimate education reform: Messy learning and problem solving. *Powerful Learning Practice*. Retrieved January 8, 2016, from http://plpnetwork.com/2013/04/19/ultimate-education-reform-messy-learning-problem-solving/

Jackson, J. (2007). *Unmasking identities: An exploration of the lives of gay and lesbian teachers*. Lanham, MD: Lexington Books.

Jenkins, H. (2011). Foreword. In S. de Freitas & P. Maharg (Eds.), *Digital games and learning* (pp. xxiii–xxvi). London: Continuum.

Jin, P., & Low, R. (2011). Implications of game use for explicit instruction. In S. Tobias & J. D. Fletcher (Eds.), *Computer games and instruction* (pp. 395–416). Charlotte, NC: Information Age Publishers.

Johnson, S. (2005). *Everything bad is good for you: How today's popular culture is actually making us smarter*. New York: Riverhead Books.

Juul, J. (2010). *A casual revolution: Reinventing videogames and their players*. Cambridge, MA: MIT Press.

Kapp, K. (2012). *The gamification of learning and instruction: Game-based methods and strategies for training and education*. San Francisco, CA: Pfeiffer.

Karp, H. (2004). *Happiest toddler on the block*. New York: Bantam books.

Kimball, M., & Smith, N. (2013, Oct. 28). The Myth of I'm bad at math. The Atlantic. Retrieved from http://www.theatlantic.com/education/archive/2013/10/themyth-of-im-bad-at-math/280914/

Kirkley, J. R., Duffy, T., Kirkley, S., & Kremer, D. (2011). Implications of constructivism for the design and use of serious games. In S. Tobias & J. D. Fletcher (Eds.), *Computer games and instruction* (pp. 371–394). Charlotte, NC: Information Age Publishers.

Leemkuil, H., & de Jong, T. (2011). Instructional support in games. In S. Tobias & J. D. Fletcher (Eds.), *Computer games and instruction* (pp. 353–369). Charlotte, NC: Information Age Publishers.

Levitt, S., & Dubner, S. (2009). *Freakonomics: A rogue economists explores the hidden side of everything*. New York: HarperCollins.

Loh, C. S. (2007). Designing online games assessment as 'information trails'. In D. Gibson, C. Aldrich, & M. Prensky (Eds.), *Games and simulations in online learning: Research and development frameworks* (pp. 323–348). Hershey, PA: Information Science Publishing.

Magerko, B., Heeter, C., & Medler, B. (2010). Different strokes for different folks: Tapping into the hidden potential of serious games. In R. Van Eck (Ed.), *Gaming and cognition: Theories and practice from the learning sciences* (pp. 255–279). Hershey, PA: Information Science Reference.

Mateas, M., & Stern, A. (2005/2006). Interaction and narrative from *Expressive AI*. In K. Salen & E. Zimmerman (Eds.), *The game designer reader: A rules of play anthology* (pp. 642–669). Cambridge, MA: MIT Press.

McGonigal, J. (2011). *Reality is broken: Why games make us better and how they can change the world*. London: Penguin Books.

Meadows, D. (2008). *Thinking in systems: A primer*. White River Junction, VT: Chelsea Green Publishing.

Norman, D. (2002). *The design of everyday things*. New York: Basic Books.

Osterweil, S., & Klopfer, E. (2011). Are games all child's play? In S. de Freitas & P. Maharg (Eds.), *Digital games and learning* (pp. 152–171). London: Continuum.

Plotnikoff, D. (2013). Before reading or watching videos, students should experiment first. *KQED/Mindshift*. Retrieved January 8, 2016, from http://blogs.kqed.org/mindshift/2013/07/before-reading-or-watching-videos-students-should-first-experiment/

Poundstone, W. (2006). Game theory. In K. Salen & E. Zimmerman (Eds.), *The game designer reader: A rules of play anthology* (pp. 382–408). Cambridge, MA: MIT Press.

Prensky, M. (2002). The motivation of game play, or the REAL 21st century learning revolution. *On the Horizon, 10*(1), 5–11.

Prensky, M. (2011). Comments on research comparing games to other instructional methods. In S. Tobias & J. D. Fletcher (Eds.), *Computer games and instruction* (pp. 251–280). Charlotte, NC: Information Age Publishers.

Rabin, S. (2009). *Introduction to game development* (2nd ed.). Herndon, VA: Cengage Learning.

Reese, D. (2010). Introducing flowometer: A CyGaMEs assessment suite tool. In R. Van Eck (Ed.), *Gaming and cognition: Theories and practice from the learning sciences* (pp. 227–254). Hershey, PA: Information Science Reference.

Robinett, W. (1984/2006). Adventure as a video game: Adventure for the Atari 2600 from Inventing the Adventure Game. In K. Salen & E. Zimmerman (Eds.), *The game designer reader: A rules of play anthology* (pp. 690–713). Cambridge, MA: MIT Press.

Rowe, M. (1986). Wait time: Slowing down may be speeding up. *Journal of Teacher Education, 37*(43), 43–50.

Salen, K., & Zimmerman, E. (2004). *Rules of play: Game design fundamentals*. Cambridge, MA: MIT Press.

Schell, J. (2008). *The art of game design: A book of lenses*. Burlington, MA: Morgan Kaufmann.

Selfe, C., & Hawisher, G. (2007). *Gaming lives in the twenty-first century: Literate connections*. Gordonsville, VA: Palgrave Macmillan.

Shaffer, D. W. (2012). Models of situated action: Computer games and the problem of transfer. In C. Steinkuehler, K. Squire, & S. Barab (Eds.), *Games, learning, and society: Learning and meaning in the digital age* (pp. 403–431). New York: Cambridge University Press.

Sheldon, L. (2011). *The multi-player classroom: Designing coursework as a game*. Herndon, VA: Cengage Learning.

Shute, V. (2011a). Stealth assessment in computer-based games to support learning. In S. Tobias & J. D. Fletcher (Eds.), *Computer games and instruction* (pp. 503–524). Charlotte, NC: Information Age Publishers.

Simmons, A. (2001). *The story factor: Inspiration, influence, and persuasion through the art of storytelling*. New York: Basic Books.

Squire, K. (2011). *Video games and learning: Teaching and participatory culture in the digital age*. New York: Teachers College Press.

Squire, K. (2012). Designed cultures. In C. Steinkuehler, K. Squire, & S. Barab (Eds.), *Games, learning, and society: Learning and meaning in the digital age* (pp. 3–31). New York: Cambridge University Press.

Steinkuehler, C., & Oh, Y. (2012). Apprenticeship in massively multiplayer online games. In C. Steinkuehler, K. Squire, & S. Barab (Eds.), *Games, learning, and society: Learning and meaning in the digital age* (pp. 154–184). New York: Cambridge University Press.

Swan, R. (2010). Feedforward as an essential active principle of engagement in computer games. In R. Van Eck (Ed.), *Gaming and cognition: Theories and practice from the learning sciences* (pp. 108–136). Hershey, PA: Information Science Reference.

Tobias, S., Fletcher, J. D., Dai, D., & Wind, A. (2011). Review of research on computer games. In S. Tobias & J. D. Fletcher (Eds.), *Computer games and instruction* (pp. 127–221). Charlotte, NC: Information Age Publishers.

Van Eck, R. (2007). Building artificially intelligent learning games. In D. Gibson, C. Aldrich, & M. Prensky (Eds.), *Games and simulations in online learning: Research and development frameworks* (pp. 271–307). Hershey, PA: Information Science Publishing.

Vygotsky, L. (1978). *Mind in society*. Cambridge, MA: Harvard University Press.

Wahlstrom, K. (2014). *Examining the impact of later high school start times on the health and academic performance of high school students: A multi-site study*. Center for Applied Research and Educational Improvement. Retrieved January 6, 2016, from http://conservancy.umn.edu/bitstream/11299/162769/1/Impact%20of%20Later%20Start%20Time%20Final%20Report.pdf
Wiggins, G., & McTighe, J. (2005). *Understanding by design*. Alexandria, VA: ASCD.

Fiction

Any of books in the *Encyclopedia Brown* series.

Chapter 7
Game Changer: Rendering and Testing the Game

A game isn't automatically fun just because it's about pirates ... The difference between good and bad games is more in the polished game experience than in the content.

-Kurt Squire, 2011

Abstract This chapter dives into the specifics of creating the physical game with varying levels of technology. The chapter provides ways the reader can create a no-technology version of the curricular game. This no-tech version is then used to playtest the game with peers and with potential students. Once this feedback has been used to revise and refine the game, the chapter then discusses ways to repurpose technologies the reader is likely to be familiar with, such as PowerPoint, in order to make a low-technology version of the game. How to do this with medium technology, or technology readers may be unfamiliar with, and with programming, or high technology, is also explored.

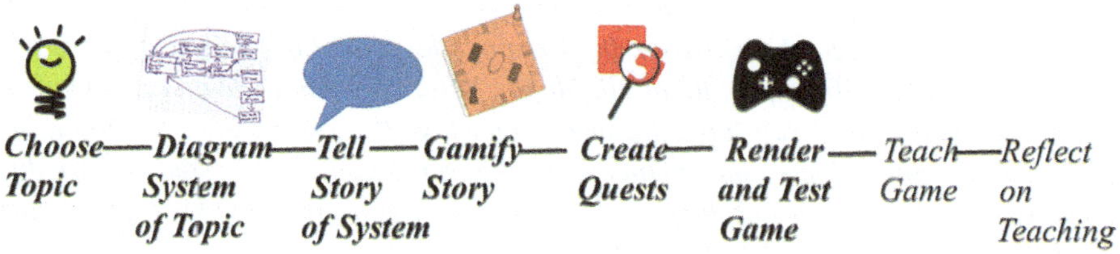

J.J. Kellinger, *A Guide to Designing Curricular Games*,
Advances in Game-Based Learning, DOI 10.1007/978-3-319-42393-7_7

RENDERING QUEST

IF the primary performance objective has the word "understand" in it, THEN replace "understand" with a concrete action verb.

ELSE WHILE primary performance objective does not match core game mechanic, DO revise one or both UNTIL they match.

WHILE quests do not match core game mechanic, DO revise quests UNTIL they match.

WHILE game story does not incorporate quests, DO revise game story and/or quests UNTIL all quests are embedded in the game story.

Day 90 is quickly approaching. After telling Amy you are designing a game for your class, running your ideas by her, and incorporating her feedback, you have finally gotten Amy's approval—something you have always longed for in your friendship with her. Excitedly you run to the Commander with your design document and description of quests, eager to hear her feedback. Instead, she glances at it quickly, stating, "What is this? This isn't a game. I can't play a word document. Don't come back to my office until you have a game I can play!"

Dejectedly you return to your living quarters. Your body is physically wrecked. Lack of sleep and lack of exposure to the sun has depleted your resources. You crash on your bed, resigning yourself to losing the Commander's game. There is no way you can program a video game in the time remaining. If only you could bring Amy into the future. Typically you would cry yourself to sleep over something like this; however, you are too weak to even do that. You fall into a deep slumber.

You dream that you are a pawn in a game of chess. You move around the board until you encounter a knight who quickly beheads you.

You wake up, shaking your head. Remembering your dream, you groan. You realize the knight is the Commander and you, just a pawn in her game. You have easily been defeated. You go through your routine of putting on your clothes and head to breakfast. As you chew on your institutional eggs, you reflect on your dream: "If that were the message of the dream, the Commander would be the queen. Perhaps that is not what the dream meant at all. Maybe I don't have to code an actual video game! She said, 'until you have a game I can play.' Chess is a game that can be played that is not a video game. I can create a learning game where students are the chess pieces, the elements of the game! I don't have to program a video game. I can create a game without any technology at all!"

You barely swallow your eggs as you abandon your breakfast and run at a full sprint back to your room.

ACTION: First, run your curricular game idea by some of your students or by people in that age range and get their feedback. Then, design a no-tech version of your game that does not rely on anything with an on/off switch. Playtest your game by playing it yourself, having a peer play it and give you feedback, and having students—or people in the age range of your intended audience—play it and give you feedback. After reflecting and revising based on that feedback, create a low-tech version of the game using software you are already familiar with. Then, if time, create a medium-tech version using software that is a stretch for you. Then, if time, create a high-tech version using game design software.

One evening I was out with a teacher friend who said she needed to go home to prepare her lesson for the next day. I wanted to stay out longer, so I asked her what the lesson was about, thinking I'd never be able to help her since she taught science. She said her students had to review for a test. I said, "Easy Peasy! Put them in groups and have each group design a sample test. Then, have the groups exchange tests, grade each other's tests, and give back the results. See, your planning is done." This was a generic curricular plan I came up with (I'm sure I wasn't the first) that had no time investment and a big pedagogical payoff. Students often feel tests are something done to them and do not even think about what goes into designing a test, let alone grading one. This plan allows students to think about what might be on the test, get exposed to what their peers think as well, think about what the best format is for assessing that information, and how to evaluate different possible answers (what counts as right? do you give partial credit?). In other words, it gets students to role-play the teacher and, in doing so, become better students because they learn how to play the "game" of test-taking by being a test-designer and evaluator. By focusing on what students do when test-taking instead of what students need to know, I was able to create a successful lesson.

As the quote at the beginning of the chapter suggests, you want to create a "polished game experience." You might be thinking, "How am I going to do THAT in my classroom?" Don't panic. What's most important are the four compelling game elements identified by Malone and Lepper (1987), all of which can be done without any technology:

> Malone and Lepper (1987) define four characteristics of games that contribute to increases in motivation and eagerness for learning. These are challenge, fantasy, curiosity, and control. Challenges in a game … keep [students] engaged with the activity by means of adjusted levels of difficulty. Fantasy in a game increases enthusiasm by providing an appealing imaginary context, whereas curiosity offers interesting, surprising, and novel contexts that stimulate students' needs to explore the unknown. Finally, the control characteristic gives learners the feeling of self-determination. (Akilli 2007, p. 6)

This might sound daunting, especially if you think about the amount of time that might be involved in creating a curricular game that embodies these four characteristics. As a teacher, I know firsthand that time is the biggest constraint in teaching. I have often said that teaching is like a goldfish—it grows to fit the size of its container. In other words, teaching is never done—there is always be more to do—so planning expands to fit the amount of time you allow it. I have spent hours and hours and hours preparing a lesson that completely falls flat. On the other hand, there have been times I have spent just a few minutes on a lesson plan that is a tremendous success. The point here is that designing an engaging lesson, even a game-based lesson, unit, or course, does not have to take a tremendous amount of time. It can even be a time-saver if you design a game where students contribute to the content. However, sometimes the time investment does pay off. After all, you get to play, I mean your students will get to play, your curricular game year after year.

Below is an example of a game-based weekly course about teaching that I designed in less than half an hour while writing this chapter (refinements and creating the materials which are not included took longer):

Day 1 Observation Quest—INTRO and develop teacher and student profiles, and watch teacher video and annotate until annotation matches teacher annotation.

Day 2 Tutoring Quest—pair up to teach a "language," study profile of tutee, must pass language quiz to move on, and if not, teacher must teach some more.

Day 3 Small Group Discussion Quest—lead a small group discussion on a topic of your choice. Each teacher will be given a secret goal you cannot explicitly name. Once goal is reached, you pass (5 goals for each group: a student challenges another student, a student refers back to what another student said, a student asks a question of another student, a student changes his/her mind, and have an exchange among three students in a row without teacher intervention).

Day 4 Rubric Quest—reverse engineer a holistic rubric for a set of essays by dividing into A, B, and C piles and describing each, convert to an analytic rubric, and use to grade new essays until a score that matches those given is reached.

Day 5 Feedback Quest—give feedback on a series of revisions to a college essay, and only get the next version after specific feedback is given.

Days 6–8 Branched Unit Quest—in small groups, plan a branched unit and execute parts of it with diagnostic assessment to determine first decision point; choose topic and initial planning, design diagnostic assessment, and give for homework.

Day 9 Analyzing Data Quest—score the diagnostic assessment, determine a plan of action, and plan a hook lesson.

Day 10 Hook Quest—tag teach (each student in a small group teaches 10 min of the same lesson); hook (must get every single student to contribute, have an option to pause, to consult, and to rewind).

Day 11 Objective Quest—plan a hidden objective lesson OR teach another hook.

Day 12 Objective Quest—tag teach a hidden objective lesson and do not say the objective of the lesson; if at least 75 % of students identify the objective, move on OR plan a hidden objective lesson OR teach another hook; they can have an option to pause and consult, but cannot rewind.

Day 13 Zinger Quest—plan zinger lesson OR teach or plan previous lessons not passed.

Day 14 Zinger Quest—teach zinger lesson (OR do past lessons) which will be videotaped with no pausing/consulting.

BOSS LEVEL: video commentary on your part must include classroom management, content, and pedagogy comments, and each type must have positive and negative comments with evidence and negative comments must have suggestions for the next time which include zingers

Day 15 Debrief class-group reflection on process/what was learned/what should have been done differently the next time the class can share and discuss as a whole.

Notice how each quest has a specific goal the player/student has to achieve before moving on to the next one, with each subsequent goal requiring a greater level of teaching skill, thus maximizing *challenge*. Students are role-playing students when they are not role-playing themselves as the teacher, thus engaging in the *fantasy* element. I embedded "zingers"—actions given to students based on their student character profiles that they would act out and teachers would have to respond to, and the student role-playing aspect lent itself to natural surprises, thus engendering *curiosity* as to what might happen next. For example, one "student as student" came out as gay during a teaching session, forcing the current "student as teacher" (as well as others) to think about what he/she might do if this happened in an actual classroom. Lastly, students are *controlling* their behaviors—as teachers and as students—in reaction to other characters' behaviors and to the game goals, both immediate goals and the overall goal. In less than half an hour, I constructed the outline of a game-based course that embodies all four engaging elements identified by Malone and Lepper (1987).

In addition to these four elements, this course configuration allows for "play," or "the free space of movement within a more rigid structure" (Salen and Zimmerman 2004, p. 304), an element I would argue should be added to Malone and Lepper's (1987) original four. Bogost (2007) describes this "possibility space" in a video game as "the myriad configurations the player might construct to see the ways the processes inscribed in the system work. This is what we really do when we play videogames: we explore the possibility space its rules afford by manipulating the game's controls" (pp. 42–43). This is what I did in the first version of the course outlined above. Students in groups designed a unit plan and taught it by role-playing teachers and students for their fellow students as teachers.

However, this new iteration adds, or increases, the "game" element by setting specific goals (as opposed to the old version which just had a general "design a unit and teach it" goal). These goals are fun for students to attain, I hope, and students must achieve these specific goals in order to move on to the next level. For example, having "students as teachers" try to get the "students as students" in their small discussion group to exhibit a certain behavior without explicitly saying it is similar to the premise of several party games. I toyed with the possibility of having students do the small group discussion challenge in front of an audience who knows the target behavior to make it more like a game show; however, I did not want to frustrate, embarrass, or make a student cry. Plus, putting it in front of an audience not only creates logistical issues with time but also requires me to come up with a lot more target behaviors. Note that there is still "play" in this—"play" in the sense of "play in a steering wheel" in that students choose how to achieve these goals. It is important to also note that these goals are embedded in larger contexts—both the hypothetical one created in my class and students' own goal of wanting to get licensed to teach. I added an element of realism by having the student profiles based on the demographics of the local school system, in this case, Boston Public Schools. This version, by the way, garnered me one of the highest course evaluation scores in all my years of teaching college (average of 3.968 on a 4-point scale, compared to an average of 3.3 for the times I taught this particular course in a more traditional manner).

Promotyping

Before you even begin to build your game, first you should "promotype" (Hirumi and Stapleton 2008, p. 134). Before investing the time and expense of building a prototype, designers will promotype—"test" their idea by floating it by potential consumers to see what people think. Look over your worksheets. One asked you to write a Twitter description of your game, another a title, and a third a two-word phrase to advertise your game. Put those together to develop an elevator pitch. An elevator pitch is a short descriptive promotion that can be said in the length of an elevator ride. Use your elevator pitch to promotype your game. This means pitching your game to your students and asking them what they think about playing such a game in class. This can give you a sense of the likelihood your students will find your game engaging. Maybe a student will even have a good suggestion that you can incorporate into your game. By promotyping before building your game, you can make major changes, or even ditch an idea and start over, before you get too far in the design process.

No Tech

There are several reasons to create a no-technology game. As teachers, we know that if something can go wrong, it will. Designing a "no-tech" version gives us a backup plan in case something does go wrong, such as the Internet going down. A no-tech version also might be most feasible for your first time teaching a curricular game. A no-tech version might be all you need to teach your curricular game. Sometimes, technologies can get in the way! I have a class set of clickers students can use to answer multiple choice questions, but by the time I get them distributed, deal with exchanging ones whose batteries have run out, and explain how to use them, I could have just used a show of hands or have students write their answers on a sheet of paper and hold up their answers. Therefore, I only use them if I have a large class or I have a need to get accurate data. Think carefully about how much technology is truly necessary to run your curricular game. You may find that your no-tech version is sufficient or, in some cases, even superior.

When I talk about creating a game with "no technology," I do not really include old technologies we take for granted in my definition of technology: "Technology is anything that was invented after you were born" (Alan Kay, late 80s). Unless you have students pantomime your game, it is hard to truly design a "no-tech" game as paper and pencil, chalk and chalkboard, and so forth technically are technologies. Technology is really just tools that humans use to accomplish goals. However, some technologies are so "old school" they are rarely considered technology any more. For our purposes, I will use the definition of technology given by flight attendants: "anything with an on/off switch." For our no-technology version of our game, we will design one only using technologies that lack on/off switches.

Combining some "no-tech" technologies can create some interesting affordances. For example, when I taught high school, I discovered that my chalkboard was magnetic. I went to a craft store and bought a roll of sticky magnets, found some sentence strips (thick paper with lines on them), put magnets on the back, and wrote on the sentence strips. These magnetic sentence strips allowed me to randomize elements in a sequence to create some one-shot games where students had to put the sentence strips in the proper order (usually with two teams competing against each other). For example, students had to put together the punctuation and elements in an MLA citation properly. While this one-shot competition does not constitute the type of curricular game you are developing, it is an example of repurposing common items to create a mini-game. Think about what "no-tech" technologies you already have or can create in your classrooms that you could repurpose for your game. For example, a no-tech version of the Odysseus Order sequencing game I described earlier could involve rearranging magnetic sentence strips, each with a different adventure from the *Odyssey*.

CHALLENGE 7.1: You find yourself staring at the shoe you are using to prop open your bathroom door because you were getting so tired of scanning your finger every time you needed to run into the bathroom to receive a text from Amy. You think about the items in your old classroom you used to "repurpose"—use in a way other than its intended use. **EXERCISE**: Find an item in your classroom or in your life and "repurpose" it.

Words can be one of the most effective ways of creating realism. One of my students wrote such realistic dialect in her curricular game, and at first I thought she was quoting a book! Another student used real-life Presidential campaign examples in his campaign simulation game to explain the results of each decision. Yet another student had his players get a "phone call" from a gruff police chief by recording his own voice. You supply the framework, "the player, through imagination, supplies whatever else is necessary to complete the 'construction' of the setting" (Swan 2010, p. 115). Remember, that creating a sense of realism does not have to be flashy graphics: "the goal of graphics is not aesthetic excellence or stunning realism, … the goal of graphics is first and foremost, to communicate" (Swan 2010, p. 116). Given enough scaffolding, we conjure up the rest of the mental image in our minds:

> If I tell you a short story: "The mailman stole my car yesterday,' I have actually told you very little, but already you have a picture of what happened. Weirdly, your picture is full of details that I didn't include in my story. Take a look at the mental image that formed, and answer these questions: What did the mailman look like? What kind of neighborhood was my car in when he stole it? What color was the car? What time of day did he steal it? How did he steal it? Why did he steal it? … This ability to automatically fill in gaps is very relevant for game design, for it means that our games don't need to give every detail, and players will be able to fill in the rest. The art comes in knowing what you should show the player, and what you should leave to their imagination. (Schell 2008, pp. 124–125)

Indeed, it is reader's ability to make inferences that allowed Ernest Hemingway to win a contest by writing a short story in six words: "For sale: Baby shoes, never worn."

Although some of the appeal of commercial video games are the graphics, and video game companies spend a lot of money on this, "Research suggests that there is no difference in motivation and learning in either low immersion or high immersion environments (Moreno & Mayer, 2002)" (Green and McNeese 2011, p. 99). Indeed, some of the first "video" games that I played were text-based adventure games where the player would type in commands like "turn left" and the computer would reply, "you are facing a fireplace." One of the "pleasant frustrations" (Gee 2007) of those games was the ability to spatially create the space in your imagination. Schell (2008) points out that "you don't need to perfectly replicate real experiences to make a good game. What you need to do is to capture the essence of those experiences for your game" (Schell 2008, p. 20). Begin by asking "What experience do I want the player to have? What is essential to that experience? How can my game capture that essence?" (Schell 2008, p. 21). For example, when designing Wii Sports, the designers

> realized they wouldn't have time to simulate every aspect of baseball as well as they wanted. So, they made a big decision—since swinging the controller was the most unique part of the game, they would focus all their attention on getting that part of the baseball experience right—what they felt was the essential part. They decided that other details (nine innings, stealing bases, etc.) were not part of the essential experience they were trying to create. (Schell 2008, p. 21)

Jesse Schell (2008) uses an example of finding the essence of a snowball fight by listing elements of a snowball fight and drawing a line through anything that was nonessential—that you could remove and still have it capture that experience (p. 20). Take those essential elements and think about how you can represent them. For example, if you decide that being cold is an essential part of a snowball fight, think about what represents being cold. Perhaps just having characters wearing scarves is enough to signify being cold.

Keep in mind that people can be used in different ways as well. For years I would think, "Wow. Wouldn't it be great to create a video game for my pre-service teachers to play to practice being teachers?" but then I would think about the complexity of designing a game to replicate something as unpredictable as human interaction in a classroom setting. I then realized, why design a video game when I have a class of students every year who can role-play middle and high school students! Similar to having students design their own tests to review for a test to learn how to think like a teacher, by role-playing middle and high school students, my students have reported to me that this has allowed them to better understand their students. One way to add realism is to have students dress up as their role to create human avatars. This does not need to be elaborate; a simple prop such as a Viking hat can conjure up a whole culture. Do not forget, you should dress up as your character as well.

CHALLENGE 7.2: Now that you have realized you do not have to code a video game, you realize you need to practice "no-tech-ing" a video game to get into the mindset. You take a video game and design it as a game without any materials (just verbal/physical), then as a card game, then as a ball game, and then as a board game. For example, verbal Angry Birds *would have the teacher say the height of the tower and the distance between the tower and the birds ("Instructor as game-engine" (Hodgson 2013, p. 57)), and the students would have to state the angle of their slingshot. As a card game, students would draw from the Height card pile and the Distance card pile to determine these variables. As a ball game, students could actually throw a ball to try to knock over the towers. And as a board game, students might have to build a tower in the middle of a checkerboard. Students would roll a die to determine their position on the checkerboard. They would then have to calculate the trajectory.*

EXERCISE: Think about how you might redesign a video game without any materials, then as a card game, then a ball game, and then as a board game.

Even though your curricular game does not have to be photorealistic, you can use audio and visual details to convey meaning. When I played *MYST*, I was as drawn in by the music as much as I was by the visuals. Just hearing the introduction song playing would get me excited. Think about how often people use the *Jaws* theme to allude to fear and suspense or how compelling the *Star Wars* theme music is. I know, technically playing music requires something with an on/off switch, unless you are willing to sing. However, using a familiar technology to play music can be a powerful way to create mood.

Decorating the classroom is another way to create context. Imagine how excited students would get walking into a classroom decorated as the interior of a haunted mansion. I mentioned earlier putting masking tape on the floor to design the game space. Although admittedly this also involves on/off technology, if you can get a hold of four LCD projectors and four laptops, you could darken the classroom and project four pictures on your four walls to create the sensation of being in a video game and change the setting as play progresses. You could even have decorating/designing the room be the first quest of their mission. For example, in a game about ecology, students would have to decorate room like the ecology the game is enacting. To help determine what details you need, ask yourself: "What must the player understand to play my game? Can some element of imagination help them understand that better? … What details I provide inspire imagination? What details I provide stifle imagination?" (Schell 2008, p. 201). Earlier I described phasing—signaling progression in a game through objects. You can do this by changing the decorations in your classroom or by giving students certain props. In the stolen painting game two of my students designed, they described using props and decorations to transform their classroom into a train station one day, a café the next, and so forth. Imagine how exciting that would be for students to walk through a classroom door and enter a new world. Having a progress bar on the wall would make the game space even more meaningful as each change would clearly signal progression through the game.

Of course there is also good old poster paper. For example, if you wanted to create a Facebook game where students play animals (and/or plants) in an ecosystem, or fictional characters from a novel (or several novels), or historical figures, you can draw a Facebook template on several sheets of poster paper, post them around the room, and have students post their picture, update their status, "friend" each other, and post on each other's "walls." You can then introduce certain events such as a natural disaster or human intrusion that students have to react to in their Facebook statuses. Poster paper is a safe way to tap into students' personal technologies without facing potential consequences of having students go on the Internet. Be aware, though, of how characters are depicted and the messages that might send. In his storyboard, one of my students used animals to depict slave owners. Here is my response: "When I first looked at this strip, I wondered why the slaves were depicted as people and the white people as animals. Someone might read that as you trying to hide/blur the historical fact that slave owners were white people. But then I thought it actually turns slavery on its head as slaves were treated like animals, but it was really the white people who were acting like animals in the ways they treated slaves. If done well in the classroom, this could be used as a teachable moment." Having students design their own characters can also introduce conflicting messages. In the game where my students role-play middle and high school students, I worry about stereotyping; so in class we discuss how to realistically portray people without going overboard. While you do not want to interrupt the flow of the game, if a student says or does something disruptive, do not be afraid to pause game play for a teachable moment.

In her book *Reality is Broken*, Jane McGonigal (2011) describes several no-tech games. One is *Bounce*, where players call someone at least 20 year older than themselves and get points by finding similarities between themselves and their senior stranger. Another is *Cruel to be Kind* where players play a kind of rock, paper, scissors game with kindness acts such as smiling and complimenting others. Salen and Zimmerman (2004) describe a game created by a History teacher (Alfred Leonardi) in 1980 to simulate WWII dogfighting. He did so by creating two books, each page with an illustration of the current action from that player's perspective and the player's choices along the bottom. Both players announce their choice at the same time, and the grid along the bottom identifies which page the players then turn to (p. 425). We have become so wedded to technology that sometimes we forget that we do not need technology to do things[1] like have fun!

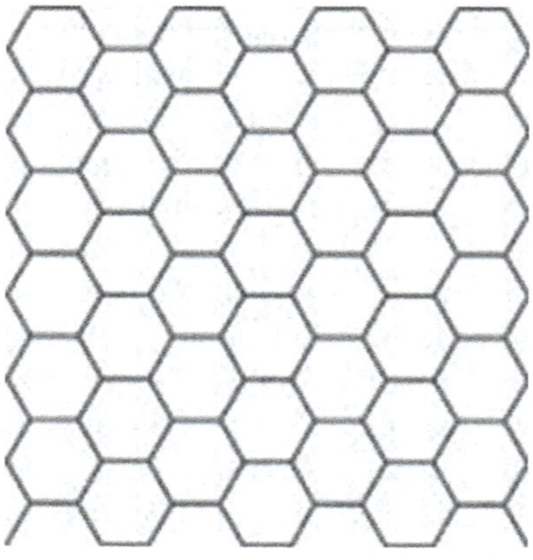

However, we can take cues from real video game designers on how to create no-tech games. Believe it or not, video game designers create no-tech versions of games in development to test them out. One game designer (Eric Zimmerman of SiSSYFiGHT 2000) describes his first prototype as being "played with post-it-notes around a conference table" (Fullerton et al 2004, p. 203). Video game designers even create a no-tech version for playtesting real-time war games. They do so by

[1]After 9/11, some felt the need to create "bomb-proof" trashcans but lamented the cost of the technology. Boston's subway system, however, created "bomb-proof" recycling bins by using very flimsy, transparent trash bags, making it impossible to hide a bomb in them since any bomb placed in there would be obvious to any passerby.

using HexPaper as the game board so characters can move in multiple directions, including diagonally. They then use something with a directional like an arrow to represent the players to indicate which way each player is facing. Something moveable like folded index cards is used to represent any barriers like walls or boundaries so they can test out different configurations. Even if the real game will be real time, in order to see how it might play out, the prototype is turn-based with a die, spinner, or turn cards to regulate game play. For initial playtesting, only the essential rules are used such as designating where players start, how turn taking is determined, how many spaces/which direction a player can move on a turn, how actions are determined, how scores are kept, how to know when a win state is achieved, and so forth.

You could use your classroom to create your own HexPaper game space by putting masking tape on the floor or purchasing hexagonal shaped floor tiles that can be mixed and matched. Desks or tables could be used to designate boundaries. Students, of course, are the players with their own directional built in—their faces. The rules can be written out on the board along with keeping track of turn taking. This, however, may not work for your game. Your game might be better built by repurposing an existing board game, say by changing the rules and printing up your own turn cards. You may not even need a game board at all. You could have students close their eyes as you describe a scenario, have students discuss it, and then vote on a decision with a show of hands. How you create your no-tech version is up to you, but keep in mind that your no-tech version is a great way to work out any kinks in your game and can be part of your playtesting process.

PLAYTESTING QUEST: You have designed a no-tech prototype of your game but you are unsure of your next step. You think you might need to test out your no-tech version, but maybe you should wait until you ramp up the technology. You recall Amy dreading the playtesting process but always being glad she did it afterward. You used to tease her, claiming that teaching was your playtesting process. "Used to," you think. "I'm acting like Amy is dead. Well, I guess she probably is in a way since I am in the future, but then again, perhaps I appear dead to her?" Thinking about the logistics of time traveling hurts your head. You remind yourself that Amy is alive in the sense that you can communicate with her, but decide to do so only as a last resort. For now, you need to figure out what to do.

IF your no-tech version can be playtested as is, THEN read/do the playtesting section next.

ELSE

simplify your no-tech version so it can be playtested and read/do the playtesting section next

OR

skip to the low-tech version section, read/do that, and then

RETURN to the playtesting section.

Playtesting

Playtesting is when you get various people to try your game to gather feedback in order to revise your game. Although one of my students said playtesting "was my favorite part of the experience, because I actually had the opportunity to see my game in action and talk through it with others", playtesting can be a painful process. Jesse Schell (2008) admits he hates playtesting—he says it is like sending out an engraved invitation that says, "You are cordially invited to tell me why I suck. Bring a friend—refreshments served" (p. 391). However, the same can be said about teaching as students constantly evaluate you. I have a friend who told me about a religious guru you can pay a lot of money to in order to sit down with him and have him "call you on your shit." When she told me this, I laughed out loud and said, "I'm a high school teacher. I get paid to be called on my shit every day!" Now, of course, being "called on your shit" is even available online through websites like "Rate my professor.com."[2] Teaching is vulnerable, and the more nontraditional your teaching is and the more passion you put into it, the more vulnerable you feel. However, the payoff can be much bigger as well.

Not playtesting can be dangerous. When Massachusetts rolled out their initial health-care reform, they playtested their website interface extensively by having state workers role-play different possible applicant situations. On the other hand, when the federal government rolled out their health-care website, very little playtesting was done, resulting in the federal government having to majorly overhaul the website after it had been made live. Diane Ravitch roundly, and justly, criticized the Common Core standards for not being field tested in order to "find out how the standards worked in real classrooms with real teachers and real students" (Strauss 2014). I will not bore you with my long list of pedagogical strategies that worked in my head but failed in the classroom. Fortunately, as teachers, we have built in opportunities to field test every day as we can use formative assessments to adjust our teaching midstream and summative assessments to make changes for the next time. The key, however, is to know when and how to solicit data and what to do with that data. I worked with a teacher who clearly did not do any playtesting in her classroom. When her students complained that her class was boring, her response was, "You think you're bored. I've been teaching this same material for twenty years." If you ever find yourself saying that, you know it is time to get out of teaching.

[2] If you ever do look yourself up on one of these websites, keep in mind that the unhappy students are usually the only ones motivated enough to post—and they are usually unhappy because they did not do well in your class. To counter this, keep your own "smile file" of positive things students say about your teaching. Teaching is emotionally hard and we all need to look at a "smile file" every once in a while to keep us going.

Gray Box Testing

A black box is a term used to describe something where the inner workings are unknown. My television set is a black box to me. I know how to use it as a user, but I do not understand how it works inside. Sometimes I turn it on and the screen is pink. When that happens, I just turn it off and hope when I turn it back on that it returns to normal. A white box is something where you do understand the inner workings, particularly if you designed it. Gray box testing, then, refers to a designer (white box view) interacting with their product as a user might (black box view) and using that feedback to revise. If you have ever designed a test and then taken it yourself before administering it to your students, you have gray box tested. A new learning management system adopted by my university had a student view for professors, but that student view was only available once the class was live, making gray box testing beforehand impossible. Fortunately, in the wake of multiple complaints, they have since changed that. Gray box testing should be the first step in testing the actual product. Your first goal in playtesting is fixing any flaws. After gray box testing, one of my students posted "my reaction was disbelief at my inability to notice these flaws while I was creating the game." As much as you think everything is perfect, it hardly ever is.

Next is to make sure your game is engendering the types of experiences you want your players to experience. Placing the tasks in a play matrix (Fullerton et al. 2004, p. 209) with one axis being "skill-to-chance" and the other "mental calculation-to-physical dexterity" can help give you a sense of the types of experiences your players might have. Sometimes there are activities that you think will involve skill, but actually are largely determined by chance. In these cases, "the solution might be to change a variable determined by chance into a variable determined by player choice" (Fullerton et al. 2004, p. 210). Two of my students discovered that while they thought "free reign" would require a lot of skill, they found that too much free reign and not enough guidance resulted in students using trial and error, i.e., chance. Once again, balance is key for designing games that teach. Clearly for academic reasons, you want your game to mainly fall into the skill box. As for mental calculation versus physical dexterity, that clearly depends on the type of skills you game is designed to teach.

When you gray box test, "if it feels unnatural, it is" (Dempsey 2010, p. 100). Anything that feels contrived to you will feel really contrived to your players. If so, think about how you can change the story or the game to make the game play feel more natural. Remember our content-swapping test. If part of the game is to answer three questions posed by a monster in order for it to step aside to let you move on to the next level, all you have done is dressed up a quiz as a game. You do not want your game to be "Alex Trebek[3] wearing a mask" (Amtzis 2014). Make sure the learning is in the content, and the context, of your game.

[3] Host of the trivia game show *Jeopardy*.

The next step is to make sure your game is engaging. Over a decade ago, a game designer said "When you add an instructional designer to a game design team, the first thing they do is suck the fun out" (quoted in Prensky 2011, p. 261). By creating a fantastical story where the player is the hero and embedding puzzles and challenges in it, your game will not suck. However, sometimes it is hard to break free of old patterns of didactic teaching. While you play your game, ask yourself "What sucks?" and removing anything that sucks (Prensky 2011). You will know something "sucks" if you find your mind drifting off. Anything that too closely resembles traditional classroom assignments might also suck. To flip around the teacher statement I quoted earlier, if you are bored, you know your students will really be bored.

Of course this is more complicated than simply removing everything that sucks. Often removing one thing means making adjustments elsewhere. As teachers, we know that we cannot teach everything about a subject. An important component of teaching is selecting what to include, which means leaving some things out—and makes teaching, by its very nature, political. I recognize that in today's day and age, teachers feel beholden to cover the curricular content dictated by the state—especially knowing that this content will be on high-stakes tests which are becoming more and more not just high stakes for students but high stakes for schools and for teachers. However, if done well, leaving certain content out can actually motivate students to learn more. As Prensky (2011) puts it, "the engaged student is a lot more likely to find any missing content than the bored student is to remember any content covered in an uninteresting way" (p. 272). Alluding to the heated rivalry between Tesla and Edison or the tragic end to Alan Turing's life might inspire students to find out the details.

Prensky (2011) argues that teachers focus too much on "covering the content" and not enough on "keeping students engaged" (p. 271). A major mistake I make (and still make) as a teacher is to assume that students cannot learn something unless I tell it to them. However, what is closer to the truth is that students probably have not learned something if *they* have not said it, thought it, or done it. The goal of your curricular game should be to get students to say, think, or do, i.e., enact, the material. If you find as a user of your game that the game and/or the teacher does the thinking for you, you need to overhaul your game.

Besides assuming that students learned something just because I said it, another common trap I have fallen into as a teacher is the "father [or, in this case, teacher] knows best" syndrome where I, as the teacher, am the "decider." When in this mode, I decide what content gets covered, how it gets covered, how it gets assessed, and leave very little decision-making up to the students. The little decision-making left is voluntary, i.e., raising hands to answer a teacher-initiated question. This allows students to mentally check out. Because of my fear of the potential emotional damage of "putting students on the spot," I have short-circuited the Kolb Learning Cycle (1984) of decision-action-feedback-reflection by making the only student decisions be whether or not they should answer a teacher-posed question. By only calling on those who decided in the affirmative, I had no sense of whether or not non-volunteers were following the lesson. As Prensky (2011) points out, "we have left decision making out of most of our instruction, letting our students slide by with volunteering decisions (i.e., raising their hand) only when the feel like it. We typically leave the *required* decision making to the testing, where it comes with no feedback at all, or until generally too late to be useful for learning" (pp. 272–273). Games, on the other hand, should be "a series of interesting decisions that lead to a satisfying conclusion" (Sid Meier, designer of *Civilization*, quoted by Prensky 2011, p. 272). As you play your game, think about who, or what, is making the decisions.

You should play your game several times. At least one time you should play your game as if you are an average student in your class to assess the "usability" of your game. How user-friendly is your game? How intuitive is it? Are the decisions being made and the thinking being done in service of the learning or does the player have to think too much to figure out something that is irrelevant to the learning objectives. Then, you should play your game several other times from different perspectives to adjust for accessibility. Accessibility means making your game playable by a range of players including those with visual, hearing, physical, and cognitive impairments as well as English (or other) Language Learners. If you attended a teacher preparation program, you most likely took classes on accommodating a range of students, commonly called inclusion. For a glimpse into ways the video game industry strives to do this, read *Includification: A practical guide to game accessibility* (Barlet and Spohn 2012). If your game requires players to measure something, how will those with visual impairments accomplish this? Will your students from other cultures know what a yard is? Should you use the metric system for everyone? Or should you allow your students to choose? One of my students described an example of a math word problem on a standardized test using the phrase "tennis racket." He pointed out that even if language learners are allowed to use a dictionary, this is what they might find in their dictionary if they look up the word "racket" (from dictionary.com):

1. A loud noise or clamor, especially of a disturbing or confusing kind; din; uproar: *The traffic made a terrible racket in the street below*
2. Social excitement, gaiety, or dissipation
3. An organized illegal activity, such as bootlegging or the extortion of money from legitimate business people by threat or violence
4. A dishonest scheme, trick, business, activity, etc.: *the latest weight-reducing racket*

None of these even come close to what a tennis racket is. Think about cultural assumptions you might be making. When I was a high school teacher, I designed some unit tests for the district I worked for. When these tests were field tested, teachers pointed out several of the cultural assumptions I had made. For example, asking students to identify which fairy tale the plot of a short story resembled. When testing for accessibility, remember the principle of Universal Design for Learning (UDL): an accommodation for one student often can help other students as well. When you have students playtest, you should also have a range of students, including average students, test it, but you can at least start thinking about how to make your game both usable and accessible at the gray box testing stage by putting yourself in your students' shoes.

Alpha Testing

Why not just end at gray box testing? For the same reasons you get someone else to proofread what you write. Alpha testers are peers you get to test your product before you test it with people from the target demographics, in this case, students. My students were very thankful for the feedback they got from their alpha testers. I am eternally grateful to my alpha tester, my sister, for catching my many mistakes and making innumerable suggestions, most of which I incorporated into this book. One of the major problems with proofreading your own writing or stopping at the gray box stage of testing is that we tend to see what we expect to see. This is called the Stroop effect (Driscoll 2005, p. 85). Look at the statement in the triangle below. Quickly, what does it say?

Now reread it. What does it actually say? We see what we expect to see and, as teachers, we know that students often hear what they want to hear. When we read our own writing or play our own game, we know what we intended and therefore see that:

> Nothing is quite as humbling as being forced to watch in silence as some poor play-tester stumbles around your level for 20 minutes, unable to figure out the "obvious" answer that you now realize is completely arbitrary and impossible to figure out. (Birdwell 1999/2006, p. 219)

As teachers, a dangerous trap we can easily fall into is playing the "guess what the teacher is thinking game." I know a teacher who used to teach by dropping the last word of every sentence and expecting her students to fill in that word.[4] She was literally playing the "guess what the teacher is thinking" game. Right now I have a college essay written by a high school student that underwent several major transformations partially due to feedback I gave her. I would like to incorporate a quest into my English Methods class where students have to read the first version and only get the second version after providing specific feedback and so forth until the hypothetical student "gets into college." I am excited about giving my students practice providing feedback on written essays—a large part of being an English teacher and something I was never taught. However, I am concerned that this will easily turn into a "Guess what I was thinking" puzzle, particularly since feedback on college essays can be so subjective. The solution? I will wait for you to think of it. Yes, of course! Scaffolding! I will design it so that students will get a series of lessons about

[4] Like the economics teacher in the movie *Ferris Bueller's Day Off.*

giving feedback on writing, guidelines, suggestions, and hints (feedback on their feedback!) with each iteration. However, I also do not want students to think there is only one way, my way, to give feedback. Ideally, I would have this puzzle branch where certain feedback would lead to different versions with multiple paths to writing the final essay that gets the student into college. This, of course, will not account for every possible path, but for this type of puzzle, that would be impossible, and at least branching would convey that there are multiple ways to give feedback.

When gray box testing, as you played the game you knew what you were thinking when you designed the game. A common classroom activity in teacher preparation programs is to have one student give instructions about fixing a peanut butter sandwich to another student. Following the exact directions often results in the peanut butter ending up anywhere but between two slices of bread because of the number of assumptions the instructor makes. When someone else tests your game, "We never truly see the output of our work, since it is an experience had by someone else and, ultimately, unsharable. This is why deep listening is so essential for game design" (Schell 2008, p. 11). Not only should you look to their behaviors—Where do they look? What do they do? What is the sequence of their "clickstream" (in a computer world, where they click; in a classroom world, where they take action)?—you should have your playtesters think out loud: "We are bound by believing that to understand the meanings of game play we can simply look at the rules when we, in fact, need to look at players' performance and understand *their* understandings of them" (Salen 2008, p. 15). Have your playtesters verbalize their decision-making, tell you what they are looking at, and report their emotions.

You should instruct your playtesters to be brutally honest including stating when they are bored or identifying things that "suck." However, you need to think about how you can hear critical feedback without breaking into tears:

> Ignore your ego. If you're going to gain anything from a playtesting session, you have to transform yourself. Imagine that you are someone else. You are no longer the designer of this game. Instead, you are an analyst hired to uncover the truth. Your job is not to have these people love the game or you, it's to discover what they don't want to tell you or know how to tell you … [and then] embrace the criticism … remind yourself that you need to hear the problems because you cannot fix the problems if you don't know what they are. (Fullerton et al. 2004, p. 206)

Just like with any assessment where you look for patterns in the data to identify what your students are thinking, look for patterns in your testers' game play to infer what they are experiencing:

> The most common mistake is for the game designer to sit down and begin reading off the rules and describing their vision for the game. … Remember, people learn by playing, not by listening. Let them start playing allow them to make mistakes. … let your testers figure it out. You will tend to learn more the less you speak. … Remind playtesters they are testing the game, not their skills. Any difficulties in playing the game will help you to improve your design … Ask them to talk out loud throughout the game about what they are thinking, questions they may have. Warn them that you won't be able to answer their questions, you just want to know what they are. You are just an observer here. You won't be stepping in to help them, not because you don't want to, but because you need to see where problems exist with the game and how they solve those problems. (Fullerton et al. 2004, p. 201)

You should have all your playtesters think out loud. You could even think out loud while you gray box test and record it so you can capture all your thoughts. However, you should especially have your alpha testers think out loud so their thinking can help shape the expert model you use as the benchmark for assessment. In other words, this testing process provides data you can use to model how an expert approaches the game, how an intermediate approaches the game, and how a novice approaches the game. Since your goal is to move novice thinking toward expert thinking, data from alpha testing can then inform your assessment criteria.

Beta Testing

Why not stop at alpha testing? After all, these are the experts who have been weighing in:

> Testing with friends and family may feel like it works, and it does in the early stages, but it won't suffice once the game matures. The reason is that your friends and family have a personal relationship with you, and this obscures their objectivity. You'll find that most of them are either too harsh or too forgiving. It all depends on how they're used to interacting with you. Even if you believe that your confidants are providing balanced feedback, it's best not to rely too heavily on a small group of individuals. They will never give you the objective, broad criticism that you require to take your design to the next level. (Fullerton et al. 2004, p. 198)

Beta testers are playtesters drawn from the target audience, your students. They may not be your exact students, but should be from about the same age range and skill. As a matter of fact, you may not want a current or a prospective student since your role as teacher involves giving them a grade and so may influence their feedback:

> It is only through the process of inviting total strangers into your office or home and allowing them to fiddle around and criticize your creation that you will gain the fresh perspective and insight you require to improve your design. This is because outsiders have nothing to lose or gain by telling you honestly how they feel. (Fullerton et al. 2004, p. 199)

Beta testing is the most important part of the playtesting process since beta testers represent your audience. For example, a couple of my students discovered that while the word "research" did not bother their alpha testers, it was a complete turn off for their beta testers.

When you solicit and select your beta testers, you want a range of testers to help you balance your game so that it is a challenge for advanced players without being frustrating for beginners, i.e. a low floor and high ceiling. Video game designers use the phrase "tissue testers" to refer to newbies because "like a Kleenex tissue, they can only be used once" (Schell 2008, p. 394) before they are no longer "virgins" to your game. As teachers, we get "tissue testers" constantly—except that they can be tainted by the snot of previous players or even students in classes earlier in the day. On the other hand, by keeping the same testers while you make changes to your game, "You may even find that features which you removed or changed don't work as well, and these testers will be able to point that out. But don't become too dependent on a handful of testers. It's still smart to keep fresh recruits streaming in throughout the process. There's nothing like a pair of virgin eyes" (Fullerton et al. 2004, p. 200). A combination of veteran testers and new testers as you go through your testing cycle can best help you refine your game. Whether new to your game or old-timers, players will crawl all over your game like spiders, finding hidden spaces and things you did not think players could do. It can make you feel very vulnerable, but better to find these things out with playtesters than a class full of students. However, even if you end up being pressed for time and have your first set of students be your beta testers, I have found students to be very forgiving largely because they recognize the effort you are putting into their learning.

When designing puzzles, keep in mind that while the designer "sees" the answer, it is often much harder for others to see it. In the case of students, they might lack the background knowledge needed. Students too, by virtue of the generation gap, come from a different set of experiences. Olson (2007) provides an example of an English teacher who read that the rabid dog in *To Kill a Mockingbird* symbolized the town of Maycomb. He decided to have his students discuss the book and come up with this themselves. This is not even an instance of "guess what the teacher is thinking"; it is "guess what the teacher read about the book and did not even come up with himself." Predictably, he got frustrated when his students did not arrive at the answer. As one of my research participants said, "No student is going to discover the Pythagorean Theorem on their own." On the other hand, we can scaffold student learning to help students figure something out. For example, to help students make the connection between the rabid dog and the town of Maycomb, the teacher could have had students fill out this analogy: "If Maycomb were an animal, it would be ____________ because ____________" (Olson 2007, p. 140). Students might not think of the rabid dog, but it would stretch their thinking and could be the first step in leading them to that answer. On the other hand, sometimes we design something that we think is really hard, and students get it immediately. Yet another reason to playtest!

While your beta testers play your game and think out loud, you want to ask them key questions. However, you do not want to ask them questions constantly as that will distract them from playing your game and may lead them to thinking about things they typically would not: "remember, it's not the number of questions you ask but the quality of the responses" (Fullerton et al. 2004, p. 214). Questions you ask during game play should not direct their thinking, but help make their thinking visible such as "Why did you do that?" Wait until playtesters finish playing before asking questions about overall game play like: "What is the goal of the game? What did you learn? What makes it fun? What detracts from learning? What detracts from fun?"

While playtesting, look for plausibility, being internally complete, a sense of balance, dead ends where players get to an unwinnable game state, loopholes that "allow players to circumvent the intended conflict" (Fullerton et al. 2004, p. 131), confusion where players end up arguing over the rules, a sense of fairness where "all players [have] an equal opportunity to achieve the game goals" (Fullerton et al. 2004, p. 132), and fun and challenging game play. How will you know when these things happen? Will Wright and Katie Salen identify key moments that indicate a well-designed game (Salen 2008, pp. 11–13):

- "Can I try?" indicates not only a willingness but a confidence that one can play.
- "Can I save it?" indicates an investment and sense of ownership.
- "Want me to show you?" indicates a willingness to convey understanding which means a sense of understanding of the rules/system of the game has occurred.
- "How did you do that?" indicates a "community of practice" has developed—a willingness to ask and receive.

Ideally you would have the opportunity to beta test your curricular game multiple times as you engage in the iterative process of soliciting feedback, revising, and soliciting more feedback on that revision: "in the hopes of solving one problem, introduces a host of new problems. … Games are fragile systems, and each element is inextricably linked to the others, so a change in one variable can send disruptive ripples throughout" (Fullerton et al. 2004, p. 7). Because of this, if possible, make only one change at a time between cycles: "If you change two or more variables at once, it becomes difficult to tell what affect each of those changes has on the overall system" (Fullerton et al. 2004, p. 253). Keep in mind that playtesters, particularly veteran ones, do not have to play the game from the beginning every time:

> You can have [playtesters] experience a particular feature/situation/condition by having them start at a "control point"—somewhere in the middle—and play something out. This is one of the reasons that cheat codes exist for electronic games. They are tools that the game developers use so that the team can test controlled situations. (Fullerton et al. 2004, p. 217)

You can also make playtesting cumulative where every time you test, you add a new rule or a new feature. You can also have each playtesting session designed to answer a particular question. However, make sure these questions are not solely from you, but that you also playtest for questions that come from your playtesters.

Schell (2008) calls this iterative process "looping": "The Rule of the Loop: The more times you test and improve your design, the better your game will be" (Schell 2008, p. 80); therefore, "the work is never finished—only abandoned" (Schell 2008, p. 94). As teachers, even though, we have the advantage of constant playtesting since every time we teach a class, we get another group of playtesters, we do want to playtest prior to implementation in a classroom setting to work out the major kinks. However, video game designers warn against changing the game for every playtester's whim. If I changed my teaching based on what every single student wanted, my teaching would be in a constant state of flux since what one student likes another one hates. When we as teachers look at course evaluations or any solicitation for student feedback, we have to look across all of them and dismiss the outliers. Even having a consensus, though, does not mean we should necessarily make a change, otherwise we would be showing movies all day! Keep in mind that often teaching is not appreciated until later:

> Before a game is completely finished, playtesters may reject an unusual idea. They sometimes need to see it completed before they can really appreciate it. If you don't trust your own feelings about what is good and bad, you may, at the advice of your playtesters, throw out an 'ugly duckling' that could have grown up to be a beautiful swan. (Schell 2008, pp. 16–17)

I had a former high school student come to me and say, "I know I was a knucklehead when I was in your class, but what you taught me about writing has been invaluable." Students may not appreciate your teaching at the time. The ultimate test for your game is not whether or not students like it, but rather whether or not students are learning.

How do you know what feedback to consider and what feedback to throw out? Part of it comes from gut instinct, which you should not discount. After all, your gut is drawing on your experiences teaching *your* content to *your* students. You can also, though, follow the advice of Chris Crawford (2006), who has designed 14 computer games, his first in 1978:

> Most suggestions are additions; some are embellishments, some are corrections, and some are consolidations. The additions are new features; those I dumped instantly. You don't add new features to a game during playtesting. If the game needs major improvement, then it should be redesigned; if it doesn't need major improvement, you shouldn't go adding features this late in the design cycle. Embellishments are improvements on existing elements in the game; these got a few seconds' consideration. Again, the burden of proof falls on the embellishment; if I can't see a compelling reason for adding the embellishment, then I don't want to mess around with it. Corrections fix clumsy aspects of the design; these I relish. My only concern in hearing such suggestions is that they constitute genuine corrections, that they really do fix a problem in the design. If they do, then there's nothing to discuss; it's a go. Lastly, consolidations are ways of bringing two dissonant aspects of the game into harmony; these I also embrace. It's rare that a playtester sees some deeper connection that escaped me, but when they do, I grab the idea and run with it as if it were my own. (p. 723)

Use the feedback to adjust your game in ways that support student learning, not to make a cool game for your students. Keep in mind your agenda is for your students to achieve the learning objectives. Your playtesters and students may have a completely different agenda of just having fun.

As you go through these cycles of playtesting, your game should go from a rough prototype where major changes are made to an almost finished game where just the details are tweaked, what Robinett (2006), designer of first graphic adventure game *Adventure*, calls "tuning" your game:

> The length of recoil between biting and swallowing is quite important. If it is too long, it is trivial to avoid being eaten, and players can ignore the dragon and do whatever they want. If the interval is too short, players never succeed in recoiling, and their cursors get eaten every time. There is a middle ground between "trivial" and "impossible" called "challenging." Trying out the game with various players and watching how well they do is the best way to adjust a game's timing. … Varying the length of the recoil interval turned out to be an effective means of varying the games difficulty. (Robinett 1984/2006, p. 702)

Posing problem statements about your game allows you to "make every loop count" (Schell 2008, p. 80) by seeing the effects of these subtle adjustments. Because we, as teachers, have the advantage of built-in looping, after playtesting we can continue playtesting by using the no-tech version the first time we teach our curricular game; then building a low-tech version, playtesting, and teaching it; then building a medium-tech version; and so forth.

Low Tech

For your low-tech version of your game, you are going to repurpose a technology tool to branch your narrative. In other words, students will be offered a series of decisions, will choose a decision, and then be directed where to go from there. You can have students do this individually, in partners, in small groups, or as a whole class. I suggest using either small groups or a whole class so that students have to deliberate before making a decision. Having students do it as a whole class allows you to ask guiding questions and hear student thinking. Requiring unanimous decision-making will likely engender even livelier discussion but also could result in a stalemate. Using whole-class decision-making also solves a common problem of not having enough technology in the classroom and of students randomly clicking through your game, getting through by trial and error.

In order to branch your narrative, you will create internal links—links within your product that lead to alternative paths. You can even generate conversations between the player and NPCs by using a dialogue tree where the player chooses from a menu what to say to an NPC, the NPC responds to the player's choice, the player is then given another menu of choices, etc. Go back to the branched narrative you designed in the story building chapter. You should have identified key leverage points and mapped out the results of various choices. In addition to storyboarding, video game designers create wire frames, a blueprint for each type of screen, and then story board the different actions that might take place within that wire frame. When designing your branched narrative, you might want to do the same by creating templates for different scenes or simply copying and pasting or duplicating a slide if you are using a presentation tool. By using the same format or similar formats, not only do you cut down on the time players need to figure out what to do so they can concentrate on the game, it also conveys to the players that they are in the same game, program, or website. This is important generally, but particularly important if you use a lot of external links such as having players do research on the Internet.

CHALLENGE 7.3: *Frustrated with your lack of technology skills, you decide it is worth the risk to contact Amy again. You text her to ask how to create links so students can choose to go to different slides in a presentation. Her response infuriates you: "Performance before competence: Open up whatever software tool you use to create presentations. Try to create a link that users can click to take them to another slide, or frame, that is not the next one in the sequence.*[5]*"*

"Does she not realize the pressure I am up against?" you say out loud, not thinking about the fact that your voice might travel outside the bathroom walls and into any "bugs" that might be planted in your room. Once you calm down, you realize

[5] To do this, you need to create at least three slides. Number them 1, 2, and 3. On the first slide, type in "link to 3," highlight it, and go to insert link (or hyperlink) to see if there is an option of linking to another slide in that same document (in PowerPoint, you need to go to "Place in this document"), and select the third slide. To test out the link, it must be in presentation mode and not edit mode (to know if it is in presentation mode, the slide should take up the whole screen). Click the link to see if it takes you to the slide labeled "3."

Amy is just being Amy. Plus, she has no idea about your situation. You know that outside of this context, she would be right. Better to learn it by figuring it out on your own than by slavishly following her instructions. You laugh at yourself as you remember dropping a friend off at her destination and then realizing you had no idea how to get back because you just followed the friend's step-by-step directions for getting there without thinking about where you were going or how to get back.

EXERCISE: Try to figure out how to create an internal link, a link from one slide to another one that is not the next slide, in a presentation.

You probably learned a few things by doing the above challenge. First, you may have encountered presentation software that does not allow you to create internal links. If you were unable to create an internal link, search the Internet to see if it was you or the software. If it is the software, find another tool (PowerPoint is one that has this feature). If you did discover your presentation software tool does allow for internal links, you quickly learned that you cannot link to something that does not exist. You will either have to design it completely backward—creating all the end points, the links to those end points, the links to those links, and so forth OR by "swinging" back and forth between the starting point(s), creating the next set of paths, and going back to the starting point to insert the links. You also learned by doing the challenge that once you linked to the other slide, you had no way of getting back to the original slide. This is called "orphaning your user." Think about whether or not you want your players to return to previous points in the game or even a Table of Contents slide that they can use as a home base to explore a number of options. If so, include a return link. Remember, these links do not have to be exponential—you can have links that dead end, multiple links that go to the same path, and so forth. For most presentation tools, internal links will only work when in presentation mode, not when in edit mode.

What I Recommend

Because of their ability to easily create visual and audio effects, as well as their branching capability (for most of them), I recommend using a presentation tool (versus a wiki, a website, or a site designed for designing branched narratives such as Twine). Not all presentation tools have the option of linking to different slides, so make sure your presentation tool does have this option before diving in. Most software tools will change the color of a text link once it has been chosen. This can be useful if you need your users to keep track of where they have been. It will be reset, however, once the document is closed and reopened. Sometimes the color scheme that is automatically chosen makes it hard to distinguish the followed link from the background. If you want to change the color of the links—both followed and not followed—you can customize the color scheme.

Internal links: You can also hyperlink from a picture or a shape. Some programs allow you to create "action buttons" that allow you to do things like ending the slide show, link to other slides, have a sound effect play, and other things both for clicking on the action button or for mousing over the action button. You can even cover a whole slide with an action button, make it transparent,[6] and program it to do what you want—forcing the user to take a certain action. For example, you might have a dead end but have more slides after it that are on another path so you can use a transparent action button to end the slideshow. If you do not do this, your users will encounter the next slide after the "Game Over" one.

You can also use hyperlinked transparent shapes or action buttons to demarcate a section of a picture as clickable. You might do this so your player can click to go to an island on a treasure map, cause an action to happen, or allow the player to take a closer look at something. For example, one of my students pasted a painting on a slide and then had different areas link to other slides with a close-up of that section. This allows the user a closer look at what is reflected in the mirror, the shoes under the chair, the artist's autograph, and so forth. To do so, she took a screenshot[7] of the painting from a website and then pasted the whole picture linked to slides, selected the crop tool to select the close-up section, and then stretched that section to fill the whole slide. She then went back to the original slide, pasted the painting there, and put action buttons over those sections that linked to the corresponding close-up slides.

[6] Or mostly transparent. When items are completely transparent, some programs think they are not there. I discovered this when I upgraded to a new version of PowerPoint. My old version could make action buttons completely transparent. I could not for the life of me figure out why my transparent action buttons were not working in this new version. I only figured it out after searching online for the answer. In PowerPoint, you can right-click on the action button, select "Format Shape," and move the transparency slider button.

[7] This means to take a picture of what is on the computer screen which then can be pasted elsewhere. Typically you can use CTRL+Print screen on PCs and Command+CTRL+3 for Macs, although my latest laptop uses a different combination of keys, which I had to use Google to figure out.

You can also use this technique to create "Easter eggs," or hidden items, by creating clickable areas that are not demarcated for the user. One of my students placed several Easter eggs in a picture of a coral reef so her students could learn about coral reefs by "exploring" one. Clicking on the ocean linked to a slide that revealed the shark lurking in the distance. Clicking on the sea anemone exposed the clownfish hiding within and so forth. Telling her students there are ten Easter eggs (which you might want to wait to do until after they discover the first one) gives her students a goal and allows those achievers to know when they have found everything while also satisfying explorers need for discovery. You do need to make sure the action button, hyperlinked shape, hyperlinked picture, or hyperlinked text is on top of everything by clicking on it and choosing bring to front or bring forward, otherwise you can have a picture or other object blocking the action. This means every time you edit a slide or a picture covered by an action button, you have to move the action button, do your editing, and slide the action button back onto that slide or picture. You can also put action buttons on top of other action buttons. If you do, make sure the smaller action buttons are "on top" by bringing them to the front. This can be one way to mask where the clickable areas are. In the coral reef example, students could discover where the clickable areas are by scrolling over the picture to see when the arrow turns into a hand, what is usually used to indicate something that is clickable. However, if you want to force your users to figure out what they need to click on on their own, you can place a transparent action button over the whole slide and either set it to end the show or to link to itself and then place the other transparent action buttons on top.

Visual effects: There are lots of ways to create visual effects. Different presentation tools have different options so there may be some described here that are not available in the tool you are using. Some visual effects are not special effects, but simply used to make the picture more realistic. For example, when combining images, you can make a color on an inserted picture transparent, in this case making white transparent, so that the background shows through.

Something as simple as a line can create more of a 3-D effect

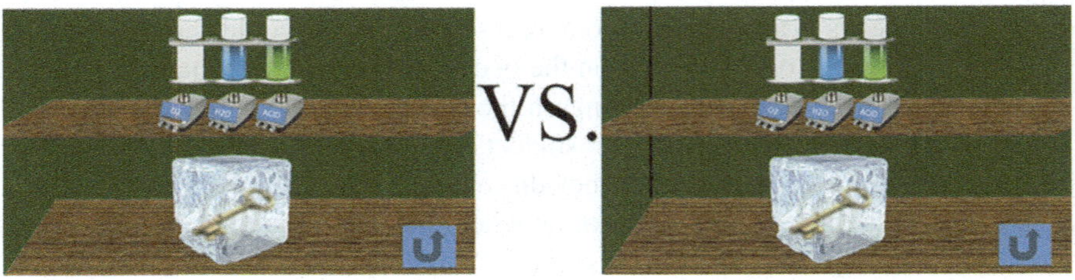

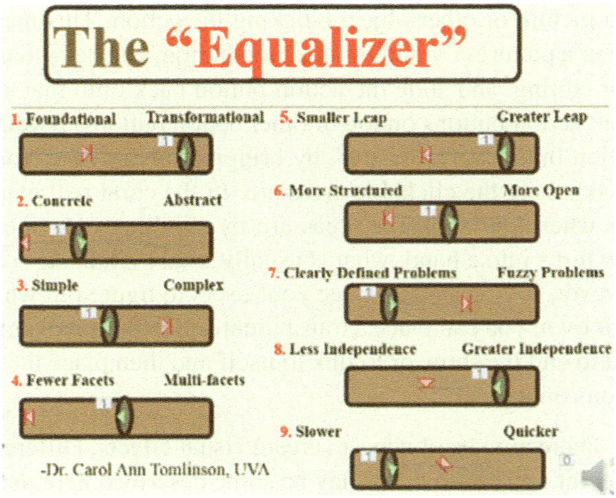

In some presentation tools, you can use what is commonly called animation to make objects appear and disappear. Having something "disappear" is a great way to have a player click to look under something to make a discovery. Do not forget, you can also hide text and objects by making them the same color as the background or place a shape over something that is the same color as the background that disappears when clicked to create an Easter egg in the same slide. You can also have objects follow certain trajectories. You can even design your own motion path for objects to follow. For example, I wanted to create the effect of sliders being moved on an equalizer so I drew horizontal rectangles and used an oval shape to indicate the slider. I then assigned each oval shape its own path moving back and forth so when I click, all the sliders move back and forth at the same time. You can even assign sound effects to your animations, control the timing, and determine if it happens automatically or after a click.

Although using animation is probably the most common way to create visual effects, you can also use transitions to create certain visual effects. For example, you can have a picture of a set of blinds take up the whole screen and then use the "blinds" transition so it looks like blinds are opening to reveal whatever you have pictured on the next slide such as a person wielding a knife! You can also use transitions to open a set of double doors, make it look like a page is turning, or even like a package of food is being peeled open. Play around with transitions to see what effects you can create.

You can also use a lack of transitions to create certain effects. If you want something to appear, instead of using animations, you can duplicate the slide and put the new item on the second slide. You can even create your own animated cartoon by creating a "flip book"—each slide containing a slight variation on a picture—and insert timing so that it appears as though the item is moving. You can also record narration and sound effects as well as inserting music to make your animation more complete.

Audio effects: Transparent action buttons placed over pictures can create certain effects, including sound effects. For example, I just inserted a picture taken from a recent trip to Disney World, covered it with a transparent action button, and clicked "Play Sound" under the Mouse Over tab so it makes a "cha-ching" sound every time a user scrolls over the Disney picture. Remember, sound is easily mapped to touch, so doing something like having an object that when clicked causes a buzzing sound can give the player the impression of being shocked. Sound effects are a great way to add realism to your curricular game and to convey meaning:

> From environment to interface, games present visible and audible experiences. Recorded effects and voices bring games to life. But it is easy to overlook the importance of strong audio cues in your interface. Audio is that underappreciated tool that gets players through menus and options with a minimum of confusion or need for a manual. Beeps, pops, clicks, and other abstractions communicate to users when their controls have made an appropriate choice such as a selection, or an inappropriate one, like trying to use a deactivated button. Your interface should offer a small vocabulary of audio effects, standardized sounds for things like selections, advancing (start), return (back), and errors in input as well as warnings and confirmations. As a general rule of thumb, if an element of the interface (button, slider, window) produces a visible reaction to player input (pressing, closing), there should be an accompanying sound effect to reinforce the action. (Rabin 2009, p. 105)

The more senses that are involved, the more "real" your game will feel. However, if a sound does not match the visual, this can jar a player out of his or her "suspension of disbelief." Use sounds to reinforce actions, let the player know his or her input has been recorded, to create mood, and to provide hints and guidance. Sound should complement game play, not disrupt it.

Cutscenes: Even though you technically can create a cutscene using the "flip book" method described above, there are several free tools on the web you can use to create a cutscene by making a cartoon. When choosing your cartoon-making tool, beware of ones that fall into the "uncanny valley" realm.[8] The term "uncanny valley" comes from people reporting an increase in empathy as creatures approach human looking but when an animated human is too realistic, there is a dip in empathy that then rises again when viewing real people. When an animated character resembles real human beings too closely, people report feelings of discomfort, revulsion, and even nausea, as it throws off their sense of what is real and what is not: "The cause of this uneasy feeling may be that when we see things that almost

[8] For me, the characters in the movie *The Polar Express* fall into the "uncanny valley" category.

look like people, our brains register them as 'diseased people' who might be dangerous to be around. Zombies are a canonical example of the creepy things that live at the bottom of the uncanny valley" (Schell 2008, p. 328). Regardless of why "almost human" animations jar our senses, you want your players to be challenged by your quests, not by how they regard your computer graphics.[9]

You can insert these cutscenes into your presentation as a video or link to them externally. If your software tool does not have the option of downloading (or you have to pay for that option), try using a free video download application. Also, your presentation tool might have an add-in which will allow you to display a webpage within a presentation slide.

You can also create your own video—either by recording or using a video editing tool which allows you to not only edit video but also use images to create a movie by stringing them together. If you have watched the video *White Teacher* by Candance Doerr-Stevens, you probably felt like you were watching a video. If you watch it again carefully, you will see it is actually a series of pictures, i.e., a slideshow, with the feel of a movie. This is because the editor used the Ken Burns effect of camera movement such as zooming out of a picture makes what is essentially a slide show feel like a movie. In some presentation tools, you can even save a slide as a picture and insert it into your movie. If you do use a video editing tool, make sure you use a version that allows you to record your own narration. Otherwise you'll have to record it in a separate tool, import it in, and sync it with your images.

Animated GIFs: You can also create animated GIFs that you then insert into your presentation. Animated GIFs are graphic images that move. You create them using the flipbook technique I described above—small changes cycled through rapidly to create the illusion of motion. For example, my wife and I took surfing lessons on our honeymoon and; as part of the package, they took rapid fire photos of each of us learning to surf. I put the photos of my wife in order to create an animated GIF so it looked like a little movie. However, I did have to convert JPEG files (JPEGs are great for photos because they code for every pixel and therefore show nuances in colors) into GIFs (GIFs, on the other hand, code for blocks of color, e.g., make a ten by ten block of pixels yellow, and thus take up less file space but also look like graphics and not photos). My students have found several free animated GIF tools online, including one that creates water effects (imagine creating a scene in PowerPoint where your waterfall looks like it is flowing!). To create a series of slightly different GIFs, you can use an image editing tool to make each sequential change to the image. You can also create slides in your presentation tool, duplicate the slide, and make the slight change and then use Save As to save the slides as GIFs. Do not forget to save each one separately and to save them as GIFs. I tend to just number them so I know I am putting them in the right order. You can then insert the finalized GIF into your presentation just as you would a picture.

[9]This advice is a variation on the advice given to me by my dissertation chair, Dr. Marilyn Cochran-Smith, who said, "You want your readers to be challenged by your ideas, not by your writing."

Some examples: Previously, I described creating a game based on the *Odyssey* where the story changes depending on the order of the episodes. To do this in a presentation tool, you could create a map of the islands/locations Odysseus visits and have the players choose the order. Some presentation tools can "remember" the links you visited by color coding followed links; however, none that I know of remember the order in which you visited them. So, if you want order to matter, you would have to have multiple maps for the various paths and, as we know from the section on scaffolding, the locations marked with the order in which Odysseus has visited them. This does create a huge presentation from the designer's perspective, but you can duplicate slides so you do not have to recreate each from scratch. You can also cut down the number of options by chaining, making some episodes have to follow others or by including only some of episodes.

If, however, you are creating something where order does not matter but you still want the map to indicate which locations the player visited by placing Xs over the locations, you can animate the Xs so they appear only after a location on the map has been selected by that picture as the trigger. You can then have that slide link back to the map. When it does, the X will be there since it was triggered by clicking on that location.

I had one student create a curricular game in a PowerPoint where the game appeared to remember where the player had been. I could not figure out how my student did that until I investigated the internal links and discovered he used action buttons to return to "the last viewed slide." Often when you want to do something, if you investigate enough—either by playing around with menu options or searching on the web to see how others did it—you can figure it out. As one of my students said, "reverse engineering[10] [is] a great way to learn how a system works."

CHALLENGE 7.4: While eating dinner, you suddenly feel your pocket buzz. You look up to make sure nobody noticed. Thank goodness you set your cell phone to vibrate! You sneak off to the bathroom to find an unsolicited text from Amy: "Take a presentation created by someone else that has a lot of special effects and 'reverse engineer' it. Reverse engineering means you take apart something in order to figure out how it works."

"She thinks I failed the last challenge she gave me and now she's trying to help me out. I'll show her," you think. You realize you might even have one of her presentations on a flash drive in your satchel back from when you were roommates. After dinner you go back to your room and do just that—reverse engineer her presentation. **EXERCISE**: Take a presentation, game, website, video, or any other product created by someone else that uses technology beyond your ability and "reverse engineer" by examining it in edit mode to see if you can figure out what the creator did.

I created a *Can you escape?* type puzzle in a presentation tool by hijacking an idea from one of my students who created a *Can you escape*? game by designing physics puzzles that must be solved in order to escape from each room. I thought I might

[10] Reverse engineering, or "looking under the hood," is different from Backward Design. Reverse engineering starts with an end product that has already been developed. Backward Design is developing something from scratch by imagining what the end product should look like.

create a chemistry version for an upcoming presentation I am doing on game-based teaching. My chemistry is rusty, so the solution to the puzzle is rather simple, but it demonstrates how presentation tools can be used to create puzzles. I first pasted in a picture of the room. Clicking on the lab on the table shows you the lab close-up which has a key frozen in a block of ice and three vials above it labeled "O2," "H2O," and "Acid." Clicking on the O2 vial makes a breeze sound to indicate the oxygen is just released into the air. Clicking on the H2O shows water being poured onto the ice but nothing happens. Clicking on the acid makes the vial pour acid onto the block of ice and disintegrating the block of ice and the key. The trick is that the player has to realize that the objects with the labels are actually Bunsen burners. Turning on the Bunsen burner below the oxygen and the acid causes an explosion, but turning on the Bunsen burner below the water causes bubbles to float around along with a blue flame that dances. Only then, when you click on the water does the hot water pour over the block of ice, melting the ice but not the key. Using motion paths, action buttons, and animations, I was able to do all this in PowerPoint.

Presentation tools can be used to do much more than present. By taking advantage of internal links, visual, and audio effects, you can create a powerful curricular game with a lot of player interaction in ways that immerse players in the game play.

Other software tools you can use to branch:

Word processors: A surprising number of software tools also have internal links that will allow you to branch your story. Even word processing programs have what are known as "bookmarks" that allow users to click on a link that will take them to a specified section of the document.[11] However, I would caution against using a word processing program as users are very used to simply scrolling down which would make all options visible. A tool that is a collection of discrete pages as opposed to one long document of pages allows you to control what users see based on the links a user clicks. Of course you could create a whole bunch of individual word document files, but if you move them around at all—say from one computer to another—the link will be pointing to somewhere that the document used to be and no longer is. Using cloud storage can help take care of this, but there are better tools out there for branching.

Survey tools: Commonly survey, quiz, and form software tools allow for branching. For example, you could write your narrative in the prompt area, select multiple choice for the question type, and select "Go to page based on answer" or whatever the branching prompt is. In order to do this, you would have to create multiple pages. While you can insert images and even video into a lot of survey tools, they do not offer the most options in terms of visuals and user interaction.

Wikis: Using a website or a wiki is another option. A common convention in websites is that anything underlined is a link. To make your wiki or website more

[11] For example, if you had a long list of alphabetized items, you might want to have the alphabet across the top of the document so users can link directly to the section of items that begin with that letter. You have to insert the bookmark first, name it, and then go back to where the decision is made to insert a hyperlink to that bookmark (in Word you go to "Place in this document").

user-friendly, only underline links. Another common convention is to have links to another page in your wiki or website open up in the same window, while links to external websites open up in a new window. Websites have two types of internal links—ones that go to a specific spot on a page and ones that go to another page. The ones that go to a specific spot on the page are analogous to Bookmarks in word documents except in web lingo, and these are called "Named Anchors." More commonly, you would be linking to other webpages. In a wiki or a WYSIWYG (What You See Is What You Get) HTML[12] editor, you would use the toolbar to insert a link to another page within that wiki. Do not forget, you have to create that other page first! If you are writing out the HTML, you would use the tag <a href="link"> text on the page </a>. If the "linked to" page is in the same folder as the "linked from" page, you just need to name the file. If it is in another folder, you would have to indicate the path using a backslash for a subfolder and double dots to go up a level. If you are linking to an external site, add target="blank" as an attribute to the "a href" tag so it opens in a new window: <a href="link" target="blank"> text on the page </a>. "Why is she talking about programming in the low-tech section?" you are probably asking yourself. It is because HTML, while it can get complicated, at its core is an easy language to learn.

CHALLENGE 7.5: *"Another text from Amy! She is getting way too into this. All right. What does she want me to do now?" You read the following text: "Open up the text editor on your computer*[13] *and type the following:*

```
<HTML>
<head>
<title> This is the title of my webpage</title>
</head>
<body>
<center> <strong> This book rocks!</strong> </center> </br>
</body>
</HTML>
```

Now look for patterns."

"Really?" you think. You remember one of the issues you had with Amy as a roommate was how bossy she was. Still, she was usually right. Sighing, you do what she says. You notice that this has a "head" and a "body." You get yet another text:

[12]HTML stands for HyperText Markup Language. Markup languages are what publishers use to indicate how a page in a manuscript should look when printed—for example, indicating how much the text should be indented. HTML tells web browsers how to render a webpage. However, each browser translates the HTML instructions slightly differently which is why webpages will look different in different browsers.

[13]Do not use a word processing program—it embeds its own meta-language behind what you write—instead for PCs, most likely you will have Notepad or Wordpad; for Macs, you'll likely have TextEdit although you may have to change some settings. Things change quickly so you may need to look this up on the Internet for the settings for your Mac, but you can try this: under "New Document" tab, select Plain Text for format and deselect wrap text; under "Open and Save," select "ignore rich text comments" and deselect "Add .txt extension for Plain Text files."

"Go to cnn.com. Right-click and choose 'View Page Source.' You will see the HTML for that page. In the head, you will see a description of CNN. That description does not show up on the page itself. The head contains the 'meta data'—data about the webpage that does not show up on the page. You will also see a list of keywords. Search engines used to rely on those keywords so web designers would choose them very carefully. Now, however, search engines also search the content of webpages. The body contains the instructions for how the content of that page should show up on your computer screen."

You do what she says, discovering that CNN still exists in the future and HTML is still used. That was informative, but that still doesn't explain how the HTML instructs the browser to display the page. On closer inspection, you notice that most of the text is encased in angle brackets. Again, another text from Amy! It is like she is reading your mind, or really, anticipating what patterns you will see: "The angle brackets designate 'tags.' Like stage directions, tags tell the browser what to do, but the words in the tags do not actually appear on the screen. Most tags have follow-up tags, indicated by a back slash. Now save your document as a text file but in the filename, replace the file extension .txt with .html. Now click on the filename. It should open up in your default browser. Notice that the text that is not enclosed by angle brackets is what actually shows up on the webpage. Now go to a website that has a basic list of HTML tags and play around with your HTML code. See what happens. Create a second page and try linking to it from your first page."

After following her instructions, you think, "Wow!! That was crazy. I am ashamed to admit that I had absolutely no idea how websites were coded. I can't believe that worked!"[14]

One more text from Amy: "Now pat yourself on the back! You just coded your first website!" You smile as you recall how sweet praise from Amy could be, especially because she was so stingy with it, although not as stingy as the Commander, apparently. **EXERCISE**: Go to www.cnn.com and view the source code. Then, open notepad (PC) or textedit (Mac) and type in the HTML code from this challenge. When you save it, change the extension (letters after the dot) with html. Then, close the file and open it again. The words "This book rocks!" should appear in your default browser. Find a website that lists common HTML tags and what they do and play around with the original HTML by changing the background color, the text, inserting images, etc. Don't forget to refresh the webpage each time to see the changes. Then, create a website by creating a second page and linking to the first using <a href="filename.html"> text</a> (with filename being the name of the first webpage). Test your link to make sure it works.[15]

---

[14] This quote is from a discussion post by one of my students after doing this challenge.

[15] Don't worry. Your new website is not visible to everyone on the web. It is just on your computer. However, if you want to make it visible to others, you can always put the .html files in cloud-based storage and provide others with the link. Be sure to store everything in the same folder, including any images you want in your website, because those links are "relative," meaning they depend on where you start (like in these directions: "walk three blocks, turn left, and it is the second house on the right"—where you end up depends on where you begin), and not absolute (as in 36 Elm St. Smithville, NY which is the same spot no matter where you start, just like a URL).

If you want players to interact with each other online, I suggest you use a wiki. Wiki is Hawaiian for fast because users can quickly upload content. Not only can users edit the page itself, a lot of wikis have the ability for users to comment on a page or even create a backchannel discussion. Wikis are also designed, or at least should be designed, so it is easy for people to create websites. However, this interactivity can create a problem if your students edit something you do not want to be edited. Do not worry, most wikis keep track of the history of the document, allowing you to recover any previous version, but you do not want to have to do this if you do not have to. Wikis often have the option of "locking" certain pages so only the designer can edit it, but sometimes you have to pay money for this option. If you do decide to pay money for any software, look to see if there is an educator discount.

You may also be able to design templates, such as a Facebook template, for your students to use in a wiki. Depending on the wiki site you use, this template may or may not be locked. Wikis are a great alternative for designing social media games if you do not, or cannot, use social media in your teaching. While using social media taps into literacies most students are already using, it also comes fraught with problems ranging from schools restricting access; to opening yourself up to students see something age-inappropriate on the site or students posting something inappropriate; to certain sites, including Facebook, limiting access to people over 13 years old due to COPPA (Children's Online Privacy Protection Act); to sites, including Facebook, having rules about only creating accounts for real people (thus limiting having students creating accounts as Thomas Jefferson and so forth); and to subverting parental rules limiting their child's social media use. Because of these reasons, wikis can be a safe alternative, particularly if you password protect it or at least make it unlisted, i.e., so it is not searchable on the web. You can also use what I call "closed circuit" educational social media sites. These are sites designed specifically for educational purposes where students can only interact with other students in their class. Thanks to the TEACH (Technology, Education and Copyright Harmonization) Act, one advantage of these sites is that because they are password restricted, you can post copyrighted material as long as it is for educational use, you can use only the amount necessary (and not a whole book!), and students only have access to it while they are in your class.

Video: You can also create a completely video-based branched narrative by using YouTube's video editing tool. There may be others, but this is the only one I have found that allows users to insert hyperlinks directly onto a video. First, create the all the videos for all the paths on your flowcharted storyboard. Then, upload them into YouTube. Under the privacy settings, make them unlisted. Then, go to the first branch and copy the URL to that video. Go to the starting video and when you get to the decision point (either the end or if one of the decisions allows the video to continue playing wherever that decision point is), insert an annotation. In that annotation, put the text of that decision point and click the "link" box. You can then insert the URL of the video that decision links to. You may also want to insert a pause, although you can also not pause the video in order to give the player only a certain amount of time to make a decision.

Spreadsheets: You can also use a spreadsheet to "branch" your narrative. In the medium-tech section, we will get into ways you can use a spreadsheet to do some calculations for you, but for now, let's see what we can do just using some basic functionalities of a spreadsheet. One nice thing about a spreadsheet is that you can create a board game effect by coloring the cells that trace the path(s) and then turning off the gridlines (usually just by clicking Gridlines under View). Unlike a page in a word document, a wiki page, or a presentation slide, spreadsheets allow an (almost) unlimited canvas horizontally and vertically. However, you could create something similar to a children's book I loved as a child where users follow a path which branches at the end of a page (in a spreadsheet, where you determine that is—although if you end up printing it out which is always a good idea in case you have technology problems, you may want to use Page Break view to do it), and then users click on their decision which takes them to another sheet or, if you want users to see the alternative paths, both (or all) could take them to the same sheet, but different cells with new paths that branch. You can also use a spreadsheet to create a circular or rectangular path like *Monopoly* or *Sorry!* or a linear path like the game of *Life*. Paths do not just have to be a series of cells filled in; you can also insert pictures so your path has bridges, stops along the way, and so forth. You could program your spreadsheet to generate random numbers in a certain range to simulate rolling a die, OR you could just have players roll an actual die!

Scaffolding

One of my students discovered that the predominant feedback he got from playtesting was the need for more scaffolding. In some programs, mousing over external or internal links produces a comment box. If your software has this option, when you create a link, you will likely see a button that allows you to type in this mouseover text (sometimes called a "screen tip"). This is a handy way to insert some scaffolding into your curricular game, especially because it allows the user to choose which hint to see. If you want a balloon with text to pop up only when a user scrolls over something but you do not actually want to link anywhere, you can create a bookmark and then put the link to that bookmark in the same location as a workaround. Another way to control the amount of scaffolding shown is to use a selection pane which has a picture of an eye either open or closed that you can use to make items visible or not. You can even group items together and name those groups in the selection pane so the user can choose what to see. For example, you might group all the vocabulary definitions together and name them vocab. The user could then click the eye to make the vocabulary scaffolding visible or not. You can do something similar with comments and use keywords in place of the reviewers' names. However, you would need to include directions so students know to and how to do this. Just as we are "repurposing" software tools designed to do other things in order to make our game, there are lots of functions within those software tools we can "repurpose" to do what we want. Often, it just takes playing around to see what is possible.

CHALLENGE 7.6: "Enough!" you think, as you feel your phone buzz once again: "Take a software tool you are relatively familiar with. Go through all the tabs, menus, and toolbars. If you see something and you do not know what it does, click on it to find out." Your one question has led to a flood of directives from Amy. You feel like she has wanted to teach you these things all along and was just waiting for an invitation to do so. **EXERCISE**: Explore the menus in a software tool you think you are very familiar with. See if you can discover anything new.

Hybridization

Perhaps you want both special effects and interaction among players. A presentation tool is best for creating special effects, but wikis allow for communication among players. You can always link to a wiki from your presentation. It would be even better if you had an add-on so the live wiki page is displayed within a slide. Don't forget, not only can you combine software tools, for example, landing on a certain cell may link to a cutscene video or even a puzzle, you can also use no-tech elements as well. If your game uses turn cards, you can write them out on index cards OR you can use a flashcard quiz site to create turn cards that will be chosen at random. Blending no-tech and low-tech options can help create a powerful curricular game. As one of my students said, "low tech does not mean low quality."

Medium Tech

In our medium-tech version, you will do some "mini-programming" in order to perform calculations. Remember when the Commander said she cannot play a word document? This is not true. You can create mini-programs in word processing programs and other software tools so that one action sets off a series of other actions. These mini- or microprograms are, ironically, called "macros." To do so, you record a macro by assigning shortcut keys (you might have to try different combinations to find ones that are unassigned) and then perform the actions you want the program to do automatically. Press stop recording when you are done. The program will "record" these actions and "play" them automatically when that shortcut key is typed. For example, you could write the first part of your game story and then instruct players to type one shortcut key or another depending on which decision they make. The program will then execute the series of actions you programmed it to based on the shortcut key pressed. Of course it might be easier to use a presentation tool with links to different slides that are animated. Remember to follow the technology version of KISS (Keep It Simple Stupid)—use the simplest technology you can use to create the effects you want.

What I Recommend

Spreadsheet programs can also be used to "program" your game. Some even connect to the Internet to provide real-time data. You can have players input data, have the spreadsheet perform calculations on these data, and produce a result. This might be particularly useful for puzzles within your game, but also for simulations of systems where players can test their hypotheses by adjusting one variable to see the impact on the whole system. For example, perhaps you have a game where players have to decide whether to buy a house or rent an apartment. Players could then adjust the salary input to see how much money they would need to earn to afford a house payment including, of course, how long it would take to save for the down payment. This can be made even more complicated by having players choose geographic location as well as other expenses. You could even have players choose different occupations and have salary determined by average starting salary for that occupation. The big advantage of spreadsheets is that you can do much more complex and nuanced calculations based on student input than branching does. You can even "carry the work forward" by using Paste Special to paste formulas onto the next worksheet so if a change is made on a previous worksheet, it then changes the subsequent worksheets. You can also have your calculations done in hidden cells or sheets so your players only see the interface.

Although spreadsheets are known as data crunchers, data are not necessarily numbers. For example, foreign language teachers could use if-then-else statements to compare student input with the expert model to see if students translated or said something correctly.

Ex: =IF (A2="Bonjour tout le monde", "Bonjour étudiant", "Je ne comprends pas")

If I remember my French correctly, this statement says: If the player typed "Bonjour tout le monde" (Hello, world) into cell A2, then print "Bonjour étudiant" (Hello, student) in this cell, otherwise, print "Je ne comprends pas" (I don't understand). Keep in mind that every spreadsheet has its own conventions, so you might have to do some online searching or just plain old trial and error to see exactly what format your program requires. I was really getting frustrated one time when working in a database because it seemed to be random which statements it would accept and which it rejected. Because the box in the database program was so small, I had been writing some statements in a word processing program and others right into the database. I finally figured out that the word processing program used curly quotation marks and the database required straight quotation marks. The vast majority of the time if you are having a problem, someone else has had that same problem and you can find the solution—or sometimes even find out that the program does not do what you want it to do—on the web.

You could even use a spreadsheet to create a text adventure game. Perhaps when a player encounters a door, the player can only open that door if the player has first found the key. You could program the spreadsheet to check the player's inventory for the key which is only stored there if the player moved aside a rock previously. First you would need to program the spreadsheet so that when the player typed "move rock," another cell in the inventory (which can be a separate worksheet named inventory so the player can check to see what she has stored) outputs "key" (IF (B6="move rock", "key", "")). When the player gets to the door, the door is only opened (IF (Inventory!A3="key", "open", "closed"). You can even create more complicated if-then statements by using Boolean operators (AND, OR, NOT) and nested if-then statements which are if-then statements within if-then statements. For example, you might want to say IF (C8="move rock" AND Strength>20, "cave entrance open", (IF (C8="move rock" AND Strength >10, "cave entrance partially blocked", (IF (C8="move rock", "cave blocked", ""))).

CHALLENGE 7.7: As your phone buzzes again, you find yourself hoping this is the last time Amy texts: "Program a spreadsheet to play Jotto where players try to guess a target word and the spreadsheet indicates how many letters in their guessed word match the letters in the target word." Although you are eager to get back to designing your game, once again you comply with Amy's directive partially because of the hold she has over you and because her exercises have been so enlightening. **EXERCISE**: Use a spreadsheet to design the game Jotto by choosing a secret target word and then comparing the words a player inputs to the target word, outputting the number of letters that are the same. Be sure to program a congratulatory message when the player figures out the target word.

So far I have been talking as if spreadsheets have little to no visuals. However, as mentioned at the end of the low-tech section, you can insert pictures into most spreadsheets and create clickable sections by inserting transparent shapes and hyperlinking them. For example, I used Excel to create a Jotto game with three different levels. The first level was a picture of an attic with a hole at the bottom for players to exit the attic. However, clicking on the hole did not link to the next level unless the Jotto puzzle was solved.

The typed letters were displayed on one treasure chest and the number of letters that matched the target word on another using the camera tool. Once the three-letter Jotto puzzle is solved and the player clicks on the exit, the player is taken to the next level (a separate Excel file) which is a bedroom which requires guessing a five-letter target word to be able to leave through the door. That door takes you to a third level (another Excel file) with a picture of a living room. Players have to guess a seven-letter target word in order to escape from the house by leaving through the front door.

High Tech

There are a lot of free and not so free gaming software programs out there that range from ones that do the programming for you to ones that are programming intensive. There are several game creation tools such as *Scratch* by MIT that utilize drag-and-drop software programming. Before you get involved in programming a game, however, you should create an "ugly" software prototype that is text only so you can do the "tuning" before the programming. This can be as simple as creating a spreadsheet to do the calculations or drawing out a flowchart. Below are some suggestions for building an "ugly" prototype from Nikita Mikros, lead programmer of *I-Spy Challenger:*

1. "Everything is a variable."
2. "Try to avoid any literal constants in your code, in other words a code snippet that looks like this: totalOutput=15*2 should look like this: totalOutput=rateOfProduction*numFactories."
3. "Expose as many variables in the interface as possible."
4. "Litter your prototyping tool with editable text fields; any value that has a remote possibility of changing should be editable through these fields. Your tool will be as ugly to look at as your high school yearbook picture, but you'll be happy when you don't need to recompile or go rifling through your code looking for a variable in the middle of a playtesting session."
5. "Don't even think of reusing this code" (Fullerton et al. 2004, pp. 167–168).

When programming the game, think about how the player will interact with the game: "the goal of an interface is to make players feel in control of their experience" (Schell 2008, p. 222). The goal of the game is for the players to learn the content and skills, not how to use a controller or interact with computer, so "Keep It Simple Stupid" (KISS). Crawford (2006) calls an interface that is "simple" yet allows players to be "expressive" (Swan 2010, p. 116), "elegant controls":

> A qualitative criteria for elegant controls is that using the controls should recede into the background of the player's consciousness, while player action in the game moves into the foreground (Rollings & Adams, 2003). … Ideally, using the controls should become like walking, or riding a bike; they can be done without consciously thinking about them, freeing up the conscious mind to deal with other matters—like winning the game. (Swan 2010, p. 117)

Do not get too caught up in trying to emulate commercial video games. Those designers work with a team. Often, each member of the team has their own team of specialists. It is worth reiterating what I said in Chap. 2 that Squire (2011) found that the "floor" was the point of comparison:

> Kids compared [*Supercharged!*—the educational video game Squire helped create] to 'what they did at school' rather than 'the games they played at home'. We saw no evidence of kids rejecting *Supercharged!* Because it wasn't *Grand Theft Auto*. There was not one complaint about the graphics or lack of violent content. We presented *Supercharged!* As a game, and students played it. (Squire 2011, p. 96)

However, Squire and his team did find that:

> These kids *were* critical of bad design. … As kids grow up awash in software, their expectations evolve. Twenty years ago, when I was a kid, the computer was so interesting it really didn't matter what we did with it. We were happy just to be on the computer. Now, almost every kid has access to an iPod touch, gaming console, and personal computer. They are sophisticated consumers who expect good design. (Squire 2011, p. 96)

What I did not include earlier were some of the criticisms students had of Squire's game:

> Poorly arranged levels that didn't match the ship's controls (e.g., levels that were too big or too small) were criticized. Likewise, when the pacing was off—when new levels did not introduce new challenges or challenges graduated too quickly, students tuned out. Finally, sometimes the collision detection clipped or players got stuck near a wall, which was deadly for engagement. … Kids don't expect educational games to be *Grand Theft Auto*, but they *do* expect good design. This means clear, compelling objectives; intuitive controls; clean interfaces; aesthetically pleasing worlds; and difficulty curves that ramp well. (Squire 2011, p. 96)

As you read through these criticisms, you will see that these are the type of design issues that will bubble up during playtesting.

Conclusion

Game designers sometimes get stuck thinking there is only one way to render their game. This can be extremely frustrating to novice game designers who think they lack the skills to make their game playable. I hope this chapter has shown you that not only are there multiple ways to create your game, you can also repurpose and combine a number of tools, including ones without on/off switches, to create your game. I also hope this chapter has taught you new features of familiar software tools and introduced you to some new software tools. Most of all, though, I hope this chapter has encouraged you to take risks with technology. Just like I wrote about replicating your system in a spreadsheet so players can "play" with the variables to see what happens, technology is a system where you can "play" with various menu options and features to accomplish your goals. Lastly, I hope this chapter has impressed upon you the importance of playtesting. It can feel very vulnerable, but like my alpha tester sister said of her husband who is a gaming aficionado and therefore someone I am a little intimidated to show a rough draft of this book to, he is going to read this book someday, it might as well be when I can take action on his suggestions and criticisms.

> *Design is really an act of communication, which means having a deep understanding of the person with whom the designer is communicating.*
>
> -Donald Norman, former VP of Apple's Computer's Advanced Technology Group, 2002

Appendix

RENDER QUEST WORKSHEET

Title: ____________________

Elevator Pitch: ____

Promotyping	Feedback	
	Revisions	
No Tech description		

Graybox testing	Play Matrix—place the different tasks in your game in the appropriate quadrant	Skill Physical Dexterity ——— Mental Calculation Chance
	What feels unnatural?	
	What sucks?	
	Revisions made	
Alpha testing	Description of expert thinking	
	Feedback	
	Revisions	
Beta testing	Description of novice student thinking	
	Description of intermediate student thinking	
	Description of advanced student thinking	
	Feedback	
	Revisions	
Low tech version	Link or attach	
Medium tech version	Link or attach	
High tech version	Link	

Suggested Curricular Game Rubric

Criteria	"Wow! I mean, I think this might work" (6)	"Hmm, this might be acceptable" (4)	"I need more convincing" (2)	"Go back to the drawing board" (0)
Compelling storyline	Multiple compelling storylines engage players, use second person, and are doled out to create suspense and just-in-time learning	Story furthers pedagogical goals and encompasses quests	Little to no connection between story and pedagogical goals	Lack of a storyline or storyline unclear or confusing
Engaging quests	Quests require critical thinking	Quests at the comprehension level	Quests at the knowledge level	Little to no quests OR core game mechanics of quests does not match learning objectives
Supportive scaffolding	Tiered scaffolding comes just in time	Student chooses type of scaffolding	Scaffolding supports learning	Little to no scaffolding
Making thinking visible/ audible	Game is designed so students have to constantly make thinking visible and/ or audible	Multiple prompts for students to critically reflect on their decision-making throughout	Opportunity for students to reflect on their decision-making at the end	No opportunities for students to reflect on their decision-making
Playtesting	Description of how results of gray box, alpha, and beta testing used to revise product	Three levels of testing described	Only two levels of testing described	Only one level of testing described
Techie (2 extra points)				
Both low-tech and medium-tech versions turned in				
Tech savvy (4 extra points)				
High tech—uses drag-and-drop game creation software like Scratch				
Tech guru (6 extra points)				
Even higher tech—codes own game				

Suggested Reading

Fullerton, T. (2008). *Game design workshop: A playcentric approach to creating innovative games*. Burlington, MA: Elsevier.
McGonigal, J. (2011b). *Reality is broken: Why games make us better and how they can change the world*. London: Penguin Books.
Rushkoff, D. (2011). *Program or be programmed: Ten commands for a digital age*. Berkeley, CA: Soft Skull Press.
Schell, J. (2008b). *The art of game design: A book of lenses*. Burlington, MA: Morgan Kaufmann.

References

Akilli, G. (2007). Games and simulations: A new approach in education? In D. Gibson, C. Aldrich, & M. Prensky (Eds.), *Games and simulations in online learning: Research and development frameworks* (pp. 1–20). Hershey, PA: Information Science Publishing.
Amtzis, A. (4/2/2014). Personal communication.
Barlet, M., & Spohn, S. (2012). *Includification: A practical guide to game accessibility*. Charles Town, WV: Ablegamers Foundation.
Birdwell, K. (1999/2006). The Cabal: Valve's design process for creating Half-Life. In K. Salen & E. Zimmerman (Eds.), *The game designer reader: A rules of play anthology* (pp. 212–225). Cambridge, MA: MIT Press.
Bogost, I. (2007). *Persuasive games: The expressive power of videogames*. Cambridge, MA: MIT Press.
Crawford, C. (1982/2006). Eastern front (1941). In K. Salen & E. Zimmerman (Eds.), *The game designer reader: A rules of play anthology* (pp. 714–724). Cambridge, MA: MIT Press.
Dempsey, J. V. (2010). Elemental learning and the pyramid of fidelity. In R. Van Eck (Ed.), *Gaming and cognition: Theories and practice from the learning sciences* (pp. 82–107). Hershey, PA: Information Science Reference.
Driscoll, M. (2005). *Psychology of learning for instruction*. Boston, MA: Allyn and Bacon.
Fullerton, T., Swain, C., & Hoffman, S. (2004). *Game design workshop: Designing, prototyping, and playtesting games*. San Francisco, CA: CMP Books.
Gee, J. P. (2007). *Good videogames + good learning: Collected essays on videogames, learning, and literacy*. New York: Peter Lang.
Green, M. E., & McNeese, M. N. (2011). Using digital games and virtual environments to enhance learning. In M. S. Khine (Ed.), *Learning to play: Exploring the future of education with video games* (pp. 79–105). New York: Peter Lang.
Hirumi, A., & Stapleton, C. (2008). Applying pedagogy during game development to enhance game-based learning. In C. T. Miller (Ed.), *Games: Purpose and potential in education* (pp. 127–162). New York: Springer.
Hodgson, J. (2013). Developing and extending gaming pedagogy: Designing a course as game. In R. Colby, M. S. S. Johnson, & R. Shultz Colby (Eds.), *Rhetoric/composition/play through video games* (pp. 45–62). New York: Palgrave.
Kolb, D. (1984). *Experiential learning: Experience as the source of learning and development*. Upper Saddle River, NJ: Prentice Hall.
Malone, T., & Lepper, M. (1987). Making learning fun: A taxonomy of intrinsic motivation. In R. Snow & M. Farr (Eds.), *Aptitude, learning, and instruction* (Conative and affective process analyses, Vol. 3). Hillsdale, NJ: Lawrence Erlbaum.
McGonigal, J. (2011a). *Reality is broken: Why games make us better and how they can change the world*. London: Penguin Books.
Olson, C. B. (2007). *Reading/writing connection*. Upper Saddle River, NJ: Pearson.

Prensky, M. (2011). Comments on research comparing games to other instructional methods. In S. Tobias & J. D. Fletcher (Eds.), *Computer games and instruction* (pp. 251–280). Charlotte, NC: Information Age Publishers.

Rabin, S. (2009). *Introduction to game development* (2nd ed.). Herndon, VA: Cengage Learning.

Robinett, W. (1984/2006). Adventure as a video game: Adventure for the Atari 2600 from Inventing the Adventure Game. In K. Salen & E. Zimmerman (Eds.), *The game designer reader: A rules of play anthology* (pp. 690–713). Cambridge, MA: MIT Press.

Salen, K. (2008). Toward an ecology of gaming. In K. Salen (Ed.), *The ecology of games: Connecting youth, games, and learning* (pp. 1–17). Cambridge, MA: MIT Press.

Salen, K., & Zimmerman, E. (2004). *Rules of play: Game design fundamentals*. Cambridge, MA: MIT Press.

Schell, J. (2008a). *The art of game design: A book of lenses*. Burlington, MA: Morgan Kaufmann.

Squire, K. (2011). *Video games and learning: Teaching and participatory culture in the digital age*. New York: Teachers College Press.

Strauss, V. (2014, Jan 18) Everything you need to know about Common Core—Ravitch. The Answer Sheet Blog, *Washington Post*. Retrieved January 9, 2016, from http://www.washingtonpost.com/blogs/answer-sheet/wp/2014/01/18/everything-you-need-to-know-about-common-core-ravitch/

Swan, R. (2010). Feedforward as an essential active principle of engagement in computer games. In R. Van Eck (Ed.), *Gaming and cognition: Theories and practice from the learning sciences* (pp. 108–136). Hershey, PA: Information Science Reference.

Chapter 8
Let the Games Begin! Teaching Your Game

In the most carefully constructed experiment under the most carefully controlled conditions, the organism will do whatever it damn well pleases.

—Morningstar & Randall, game designers of Habitat, the first large-scale virtual multiuser environment, quoting "some wag"

Abstract This chapter explores pedagogical and logistical aspects to teaching the game by walking the reader through different steps and ways to implement the game. Certain scenarios such as how to deal with "cheaters" and those resistant to "playing games" in school are discussed. This chapter stresses the importance of the role of the teacher in putting into place the structures around the game in order to leverage learning, including exploring teachers playing a role in the game story (Digital games and learning, Continuum, London, pp. 226–251, 2011). It also encourages teacher research, or systematically collecting data to answer questions and to use these answers to further develop the curricular game. Finally, it proposes the idea that students can learn by designing, creating, and teaching their own curricular games by drawing on Papert's (Mindstorms: children, computers, and powerful ideas, Basic Books, New York, 1980) notion of constructionism.

J.J. Kellinger, *A Guide to Designing Curricular Games*,
Advances in Game-Based Learning, DOI 10.1007/978-3-319-42393-7_8

TEACHING QUEST

"Done! I can't believe it! And with a day to spare! Thank goodness Amy mentored me through. The Commander is going to love it—I think. Who knows what that lady is thinking? Well, here goes."

You step into the Commander's office, eager to show off your new creation. You start walking her through it, and almost immediately, she stops you.

"Remember our deal? You can't just talk the talk. You have to walk the walk. I have a room full of 'students' waiting to be taught with me among them. Let's go use your game to teach."

"To teach! Dammit! That's right. I forgot she told me I'd have to teach with it! I was so focused on making the game, I forgot about the teaching simulation. Well, I think I thought it through enough that it should teach itself."

You stride into the classroom, computer in hand. You are faced with a room full of about 20 "students" of all ages ranging from the Commander as the oldest down to a kid who looks to be around eight. The age range doesn't concern you, as much as what is missing—computers. None of them have a computer. You set yours up in the front of the classroom facing your students, but of course, the screen is too small to be seen even by those in the front row. You ask them to crowd around and you start showing them your game. As they jostle around clearly uncomfortable and not learning a thing, you ditch the computer and try to move into your no-tech version. However, you don't have any of the props, situation cards, or dice. This is an unmitigated disaster. The Commander is clearly angry. She storms out of the room saying to herself, "I knew this was going to be a waste of my time." Dejectedly you return to your room. You put too much time, effort, and creativity into this to let it fail.

IF you give up, THEN you return to your time period defeated.

ELSE you return to her office to beg for forgiveness, but she says, "No dice" and rejects you. You GO TO your ROOM.

In your ROOM,

WHILE the Commander is angry, you WAIT for a while UNTIL you think the Commander has cooled off. You realize you shouldn't do nothing (well, you aren't doing "nothing", you are really kicking yourself for forgetting about the teaching part), you should 'busy-wait'—a phrase you have heard Amy use. You aren't sure what it means, but for this situation, you decide it means assuming she'll give you one more chance so you take advantage of this time to prepare.

You take a deep breath and start thinking about all the different aspects of teaching—hooking your students with a catchy beginning; whether students should work individually, with a partner, or in groups; how to configure the classroom; and so forth. You find yourself struggling to decide which will be more effective—your no tech or your tech version of your game. Each has its own affordances and constraints. You realize you are repeating the mistake of generations of educators—assuming something has to be either/or! You decide to merge your no tech and low tech versions, taking advantage of the affordances of each. Excitedly, you feel it start coming all together when you hear a soft knock on the door.

"Come in!" you instinctively say, then realize that no one has knocked on your door in months. You have no idea who it could be. Your Engineering Elder 'friend' saunters in with a big smile on his face which makes you think that maybe he wanted you to fail. In stereotypical engineering style he skips introductions and jumps right in.

"Do you know how the Commander came to be commander?" Not waiting for a response, he continues, "To determine who would be the best leader, the Survivors held a massive video game contest to see who could win Lead or Bleed. *Very few people know this, but she was initially failing very badly and her avatar actually died. However, she figured out how to hack into the code to mod the game to give herself another life. Us Engineering Elders figured out what she had done, but we also figured someone smart enough to be able to do that and determined enough to survive would make a good leader anyway so we decided not to say anything. In her second life, she learned from her original mistakes and emerged triumphant by making a very bold final move." Without any further explanation, he exits the room. You ponder this new information and decide it's time to talk to the Commander.*

IF you use this new information to blackmail the Commander,

THEN she orders her guards to take you to the time machine and "disappear" you. GAME OVER.

ELSE you walk into her office with your head held low. You confess that you were so busy building your game that you forgot about the teaching simulation. You ask for a second chance, a "second life", you say, "just like in good video game fashion, allowing players to learn from their mistakes." She eyes you suspiciously, but then begrudgingly says, "Five days. Now go."

You rush back to your room and continue working.

ACTION: Teach your curricular game, solicit feedback from your students, and make revisions.

One year when I was teaching high school, I had student complain that she was not learning anything because all we did was play games. It turns out she was disappointed she had not gotten into Advanced Placement English, a class with a teacher who had a reputation for college-style lecturing. Sometimes "your first step may be to listen to their story. … When old beliefs crowd new ideas out, the new ones wither and die. Listening to people helps them pour out a little of their current thinking so they can make room for new thinking" (Simmons 2001, *p. 180–182). In the case of my student who wanted lectures, me listening to her concerns and her witnessing her peers having fun and learning won her over.*

Because you did rigorous playtesting, you have a sense of what your organisms, i.e., your students, might do, but, as you know from teaching, it is impossible to predict everything they might do. I have had some doozies in my own teaching ranging from a student taking his pants off in class to another one coming to class in a skimpy bikini—all with his or her own "explanations" for the behavior. In terms of game play, Steinkuehler and Oh (2012) call this the "*mangle of play*—a mangle of designer's intentions (represented by rules) and players' intentions (represented by emergent shared practices of the in-game community) and the broader economic, legal, and cultural reality in which this interplay take place" (p. 155). However, the more you think through how to respond to what might happen, the better prepared you are for the unexpected. One way to prevent your game into devolving into an "anything goes" atmosphere is to set clear structures for your game, establish game rules, have clear directions even for "figure-it-out" activities, anticipate some potential student reactions and misconceptions, and provide enough scaffolding so that students are not in the frustration zone too long along with enough challenge so that students are not in the independent zone for too long.

Reading over this list, you may be asking yourself, "why not build these into the game itself and thus eliminate the need for a teacher?" While of course you should build all of this into the game itself; however, "It is a common misperception that once created, the simulation will run itself" (Barton and McKellar 2011, p. 245).[1] Since every set of students is unique and somewhat unpredictable, it is almost impossible to anticipate every action a student might take in a curricular game. I have found through teaching online classes, particularly game-based ones, that students will find all the nooks and crannies, including items I did not realize they could access, and will employ them in ways I did not anticipate. It is also impossible to predict every thought students will have, which is where teacher guidance can play a crucial role:

> Mayer (2004) and Sweller (1999, 2004) have pointed out that discovery-learning environments impose a heavy cognitive load on learners, and would therefore be expected to interfere with learning of subject matter. … without guidance, students carried out series of actions that produced results they found confusing, causing them to erroneously doubt or modify previously correct portions of their understanding of the subject matter [therefore] conventional game experiences alone are unlikely to promote effective and efficient learning. … Guidance and instruction can be used to ensure that students are rapidly exposed to crucial concepts, important features, effective procedures, and other important information about the subject matter, rather than being left to 'discover' these facts for themselves. Active guidance results in better learning in less time. (Munro 2008, p. 58)

"Active guidance" means teacher scaffolding: "Far from being sidelined, teachers were required to take a central role in scaffolding and supporting students' learning through games" (Edvinsson 2008, p. 56). While scaffolding is of course built into the game, no matter how explicit or how much in-game support is provided,

[1] This was a lesson learned by the creators of *Sesame Street* who discovered that children learned a lot more from their show when they watched it with their parents.

there will always be cases where students need specialized support. Even the military, who has almost perfected the use of games and simulations for learning, has instructors present in order to provide scaffolding:

> Simulators are typically used in the presence of human instructors. … These instructors often provide introductory demonstrations and other orienting experiences. When they judge that the cognitive task load imposed by the simulation is not too great, they may recommend actions, point out salient features, or ask pointed questions about the simulated environment in order to guide the student's understanding of the simulated task. In almost every case, instructors participate in a post-simulation debriefing for the student, sometimes including a simulation replay with commentary and discussion. (Munro 2008, p. 59)

I have found in my teaching that some students will find a way to misinterpret something, sometimes in the face of contradictory evidence. No matter how much I stress the importance of critical thinking, I still have students who are preservice teachers who create curricular products that are just drill and skill worksheets dressed up in technology, probably because it has been ingrained in them that that is what teaching is. My colleague Dr. Arthur Eisenkraft, author of *Active Physics*, cites an example of a science teacher asking students for evidence of the Big Bang theory. A student replied, "Because the textbook says so." Upon further questioning, the teacher discovered that the student's idea of evidence came from his English class where students were told to support their claims with "textual evidence." Teachers will always be needed because there is always the possibility of unanticipated student misconceptions.

CHALLENGE 8.1: As you work on hammering out the details of teaching your game, you find yourself having the same thought loop over and over again: wishing you could ask Amy for help and then realizing that she's not a teacher, you are, you should have the answers. You finally break out of your loop when you realize that Amy is a teacher too! "She teaches through video games," you think, "and in some ways, does a much better job than I do! My students don't stay up all night doing my homework like they do playing her games." You text her: "How do you scaffold your games?" Her response puzzles you: "I write a skeleton outline of the code." You realize she must not know what scaffold means in the education sense. You text back, "How do you make sure players don't misunderstand what you want them to do?" She texts back "Sometimes that is the fun of game playing—misunderstanding and then figuring it out. Of course there are ways we help our players if they get too frustrated along the way. Begin a class by standing in front of the room and don't say anything. Place 'sign posts' around the classroom informing students of what they should be doing. See how long it takes students to notice these signposts and how they respond to them. If your students don't notice the signposts, how long do you wait until providing them a hint? You could start by staring at the back of the classroom. If they don't notice the signposts you can change your gaze to one of the signposts. If that still doesn't work you can face your body to the signpost. If that still doesn't work then you could point. Then finally as a last resort then tell them to look around the room." Well, you don't have a classroom—and you might not want to start your teaching simulation that way, or maybe you should? However, you could experiment at breakfast. You decide to place a sign in the dining room sending people to various clues hidden around the room and ending at your table just to see what will happen.[2] **EXERCISE**: Place a signpost or signposts in your classroom, office, or home, remain silent, and observe how long it takes others to find and follow them. Try to judge when someone is about to enter the "frustration zone" and give them a signal before they do.

The *Proposal Quest* in the beginning of this book asked you to play and analyze three video games for their affordances and constraints, yet the product of the quest mainly focused on affordances. Countering the constraints is where good teaching comes into play. Studies have shown that media and technology usage by children—whether that be television or iPads—requires adult guidance in order to optimize their pedagogical capabilities (Bransford et al. 2000). The same is true for video games (Leemkuil and de Jong 2011):

> It does not promise to replace traditional pedagogy, but rather reinforces the necessity of discussion guided by the teacher. Role-playing games place the teacher in a new role as facilitator in the students' process of collaborative learning. The machine handles the more mechanical tasks of distributing information, and the teacher handles the more intuitive tasks of interpretation and synthesis required for students to translate gameplay into [academic] understanding. (Brown 2008, p. 124)

Video games do not replace teaching; rather video games can be used as a teaching tool. Teachers are needed to leverage the pedagogical affordances of video games and also to accommodate the pedagogical constraints: "The facilitators … were like big brothers in that they guided interactions, enforced rules, and sometimes imposed justice. … Levi steered the game in ways so that it's rewarding for everyone" (Squire 2011, p. 170). By serving as game master, teachers can manipulate the game to have reinforcing feedback loops when necessary or balancing ones in order to maximize game play and learning for all students.

---

[2] One of my students who is a science teacher reported that he had a lot of fun with this activity because he was able to make parallels with the content of his lesson: "After the activity, we talked about what traits were advantageous in this activity. Students decided that desirable traits included being observant, knowledgeable, and social. We compared this to organisms having specific desirable traits in various environments, depending on the type of environment it is, in order to survive and reproduce. They needed to be observant to see the directions posted in the room and answer some of the questions. They compared this to organisms finding/hunting food or avoiding predators. They needed to be knowledgeable in order to answer some of the content questions. They compared this to parents passing down prior knowledge to offspring so that they don't make a fatal mistake in the wild. And they also needed to be social in order to form initial groups of three. In some classes where the student number was not a multiple of three, one or two students were eliminated at the start. Other students were held up by the random group making process. They compared this to organisms forming social groups for the betterment of the 'pack.' We compared the winning group to organisms in the environment that had the best balance of these traits that were able to obtain food, and survive, as opposed to other losing groups, that represented organisms that may not have survived. We also compared the actions of some students to competition for resources, since some students were bartering for answers or asking each other for paper, etc. This activity ended up going exceedingly well and I had the students hooked for the rest of the class—so thank you for the inspiration! One student even said, 'Can we do something like this as the "Do Now" every class??' :)"

One of the biggest pedagogical constraints of most videogames is that they often lack opportunities for reflection and tools to make thinking visible: "Most commercial games fall short as platforms for learning because they do not help people articulate and connect their evolving intuitive understandings to more explicit formalized structures that would support transfer of knowledge to other contexts" (Clark and Martinez-Garza 2012, p. 279). However, more and more video games are building these into the game mechanics with journaling capabilities, the ability to converse with computer agents and human avatars, and even thinking maps. In addition, players are creating their own ways to make thinking visible through online communities and even online "schools" to teach players how to play certain video games, what Gee and Hayes (2012) call "nurturing affinity spaces." Teachers, can also construct opportunities to make thinking visible and to create "nurturing affinity spaces." When students make in-game decisions, they often do not take the time to reflect on their motivations or the values their decisions express. Teachers can turn in-game decision-making into teachable moments: "Videogames, they have found, need not replace teachers. In fact, they give teachers new importance as guides for counterfactual inquiry, helping students to examine their motives in making decisions and framing the contrast between game events and historical events as lessons in contingency" (Brown 2008, p. 135). Building in opportunities for students to articulate their decision-making also deflects another potential constraint—the possibility of students simply using random trial and error (versus purposeful trial and error) to proceed through a game.

One common constraint of technology is the novelty effect. Novelty effect, or "hype cycle" (Schell 2008, p. 409), refers to increased motivation, attention, and even learning because something is new. The problem with the novelty effect is that novelty wears off quickly. The first time I used PowerPoint in my teaching, my high school students had never seen a PowerPoint presentation before (yes, I have been teaching that long). They were riveted! I had never had such rapt attention in my class! I thought I had found the Holy Grail of teaching and vowed to use PowerPoint every day. Of course, you can guess what happened. The next day when I broke out the PowerPoint, my students reverted back to their normal selves. The novelty effect applies to almost every pedagogical technique that comes along, even to just changing a rule. One of my students found this out when he made the rule that students could not sit in class to see what would happen, "I think this subtle rule change sort of removed [my students] from the norm of day-to-day routines, so they were making sure to pay attention to what they needed to do since there was an uncertainty of what would happen next." There is the danger that any increase in learning and motivation with any new educational trend is due to a novelty effect that quickly wears off. A well-designed game, however, "provides the same consistent structure each time but a different experience and outcome every time it is played" (Salen and Zimmerman 2004, p. 340), thus keeping the novelty effect constantly alive. As one of my student's students said of his gamified class, "this was literally the most fun I've had this whole year."

However, do not confuse student enjoyment with student learning: "games themselves are not sufficient for learning, but there are elements in games that can be activated within an instructional context that may enhance the learning process"

(Munro 2008, p. 59 quoting O'Neil et al. 2005, p. 465). To teach observation skills, I often show my students a video of a teacher using a teaching format based on the television show *Who Wants to be a Millionaire*. I stress that observers should use student behaviors as evidence for their conclusions. However, in this case, the students in the video are excited to be in a classroom structured like a familiar television show. Initially my students tend to praise the teacher. When questioned further, however, they see that the majority of the questions are at the knowledge or recall level of Bloom's Taxonomy[3] and that, with the exception of a "phone a friend" lifeline, only one student in the class is part of the lesson. Excitement does not always translate into learning. That is where good teaching comes into play.

Jenkins (2011) observed that "institutional practices of schools impose their own constraints on these activities and in some cases, crush the play out of the game" (p. xxiv). Osterweil and Klopfer (2011) point to four "freedoms" of play that are often at odds with traditional schooling: "freedom to fail," "freedom to experiment," "freedom to fashion identities," and "freedom of effort" (p. 156). In the following chapter, I hope to help you situate your curricular game into the context of your classroom and, in doing so, leverage the affordances of a typical classroom while minimizing the constraints. One thing I always try to keep in mind in my teaching is that classroom time is precious; therefore, I try to take advantage of it as much as possible. One of the big advantages of a typical school is that it brings students together into the same space, or, in our case, the same game space. If my students are doing something in class that they could be doing at home, I know I need to rethink my teaching. As you plan how to implement your curricular game, think about what can be done at home and what must be done in a classroom setting.

Selling Your Game Through Engagement

One of the appeals of playing video games is that they are interest driven. I choose to play adventure games because I love exploring the immersive environments and solving puzzles. I choose not to play first-person shooter games because virtual killing upsets me. Barab et al. (2012) ask, "What happens when we start inserting our educational aspirations and making participation required?" John Holt (1964) and other members of the "unschooling" movement argue that making learning mandatory results in little to no meaningful learning as students resist what is chosen for them. However, Barab et al. (2012) found that "engaging in classroom

[3] Bloom's Taxonomy is a hierarchy of learning goals that begins with the knowledge level, i.e., just recalling something from the text to comprehension, application, analysis, synthesis, evaluation, and creativity. Angel Green, an instructional designer with Allen Interactions—a company who designs video games for business training—has created a "Taxonomy Alignment for Gaming" which describes a type of game that corresponds with each level of Bloom's Taxonomy (recall, judgment, consequence, strategy, exploration, and simulation); however, I have found that good games incorporate many different levels of Bloom's Taxonomy.

[games] comes to have value in itself because it gives rise to experiences of mastery and accomplishment" (Barab et al. 2012, p. 322). While hopefully your curricular game will appeal to all your students, it is important to think about the various reasons people play games: for progress (development), fate (games of chance), power (bragging rights), identity (exploration), the imaginary (escapism), the self (relaxation), and frivolity (Sutton-Smith 1997/2006, pp. 304–305). As much as I am for diversity, there are certain types of game play that foster learning more than others. For example, some play to win as quickly as possible: "One kid even spiked the controller afterward, declaring, 'Ha! I beat your game!'" (Squire 2011, p. 96). This student did not get the point of the game, which is not to win, "but to understand" (Squire 2011, p. 97). The students who played to understand "replayed levels and sought more elegant solutions" and "played reflectively" (Squire 2011, pp. 96–97). Therefore, it is important for teachers to stress that the joy is in the journey, i.e., the game play, not in the destination.

We explored different types of players earlier; however, Bartle's (2006) analogy with playing cards can help you remember the basic types that show up in all classifications: "achievers are Diamonds (they're always seeking treasure); explorers are Spades (they dig around for information); socializers are Hearts (they empathize with other players); killers are Clubs (they hit people with them)" (p. 757). Bartle (2006) notes, though, that these are stereotypes as most players exhibit more than one type of game play. Squire (2008) provides a very stark example of this:

> Honovi [A 12 year-old African American player of *Grand Theft Auto: San Andreas*] seemed to use the game as a way of participating in a discourse of masculinity … For Honovi, the game was a sandbox, a set of representations and behaviors with which he could play and which he could use to express himself. Game play itself was a performance, one that arose in context, shaped—in part—by the other participants in the gaming experience … When played alone, the iconography and experiences presented allowed Honovi to perform an identity of an automobile designer, an identity that affords status within his community and ties to identities to which he aspires. When played socially, the same iconography was leveraged to display other aspects of his identity. These experiences suggest that, for players, there is no *one* game that is played. Different game-play models and experiences are activated by play in different contexts. Similarly, discussions of game play are activated by different discourses. … it is critical that we remember that games are not texts, but contexts that emerge from the intersection of representations in the game, players' goals, and the social contexts in which they are embedded. Significantly, *how* people talk about their game play depends on these variables as well. (p. 175)

As teachers, we can survey our students to get a sense of what types of play they like in order to better understand their behaviors within a game. We can also make students aware of the motivations behind different styles of play in order for them to better respect and understand the game play of others. However, there may be some types of game play we discourage, such as that of "killers." Bartle (2006) suggests that killers are actually "imposers." As such, he classifies those who are overly helpful also as "killers" because they are imposing their will on others. While I am not sure I agree with expanding the killer category that far, it does point to a possible way to channel the behavior of killers into a more productive manner. Having "killers" also points to the need to teach empathy and ethics. When you have a killer in your game, treat it as a teachable moment—an opportunity to explore the differences between killing and dying in a game and in real life, discussing the ethics of killing in a game, and analyzing the effects of violent game play. As mentioned earlier, youth can find ways to repurpose almost anything—for example, using sticks as guns. You may have constructed what you think is the most innocuous game, but "killers" can find ways to make it about death and destruction. One huge advantage of having teachers moderate game play is so they can pause game play when the need arises.

When finalizing your game, you also want to consider the developmental needs of your students. According to Piaget, children go through three stages of understanding game rules: (1) no fixed rules, (2) religious adherence to rules, and (3) viewing rules as a social contract (cited in Salen and Zimmerman 2004, p. 474). According to Salen and Zimmerman (2004), how adults approach a new game parallels child's development, going from a "vague sense of the game's operation" to "mechanisms of game seem fixed and the player's attention is focused on learning how to play," and then, "the more that a player plays a game the more she sees the game as a system open to manipulation" (p. 475). Squire (2011) suggests creating your game for three different levels of players—newbies, players, and elders. He uses an Easter Egg Hunt as an example of leveled game play: preschoolers (newbies) have separate hunt where eggs are placed conspicuously similar to a fish tank in a video game, elementary aged players have eggs hidden well, whereas tweens (elders) would hide the eggs. For our purposes, your students are probably all at similar levels—both in terms of Piaget's rule development and in terms of knowing your game, but this might be helpful in terms of thinking about how to design the different levels of your game.

While students may be at roughly the same developmental level, it is likely that they will come to the game with different sets of prior knowledge both in terms of playing games and in terms of the content of the game. We already discussed the impact of prior knowledge in the chapter about designing puzzles as well as the importance of diagnostic assessments[4] in terms of game design. While it would be ideal to build the diagnostic assessment into your game, it might be easier to use a traditional diagnostic assessment to find out what your students know and can do before the game as well as find out their interests. Before you do so, though, see if you can change the game story to come up with a plausible reason for a diagnostic assessment within your game, such as interviewing for a position in the game.

Gaming scholars talk about the "metagame," the intersection of the game world and the outside environment, and delineate four metagaming categories: "1. What a player brings *to* a game. 2. What a player takes away *from* a game. 3. What happens *between* games. 4. What happens *during* a game other than the game itself" (Garfield 2000 quoted in Salen and Zimmerman 2004, p. 482). Translating this to a traditional school structure might look like this: (1) prior knowledge/skills/values, (2) learning

[4] I was reminded of my distaste for the term "diagnostic assessment" recently when I was at a poster session and saw a poster that used the word "dosage" to refer to how often the educational "intervention" occurred.

outcomes, (3) homework, and (4) the hidden curriculum.[5] Up until this chapter, we have been focusing on the game itself. However, the game is played within a context. In our case, the context is our classroom. Students do not come to our classrooms as blank slates, nor do they come to our classrooms just as slates with different things written on them, i.e., different sets of prior knowledge. They also bring with them conceptions of what they think teaching and learning should look like.

All students come to your class with preformed notions of what good teaching looks like, which often does not include gaming:

> Many students bring with them a cultural model that says: "Learning is a matter of mastering a set of facts." They may bring, as well, a model that says: "Learning is a matter of memorizing information from teachers and books." ... if students are to adopt different models of content learning in school, teachers need to know that these unfortunate models exist. Students need to think about them, why they have them, where they do and do not work, and new and different models and why they might want to adopt these in word and deed. (Gee 2003, p. 171)

Violating these traditional notions about school learning can create backlash—not just from students but also from parents, administrators, department chairs, and other teachers:

> gaming violates most students expectations of what it means to go to school and learn. ... Students expect direct instruction while games mainly feature learning through direct experience and from the experience of peers. In many instances, peer sharing information about how to complete work (quests/assignments) would be considered cheating in a regular classroom. Also, the idea that the content must be delivered by the instructor, rather than through the efforts of the learners, is at the heart of assumptions of many classroom students. (Travis and Young 2011, p. 162)

Documenting evidence of student learning is the best way to counter any backlash you may encounter from those who are not in your classroom; however, you also have the ideas you fleshed out in your initial proposal as well.

If parents complain that the game is a waste of time and suggest spending time on test problems, you can also use the motivation card. Here is a suggestion for what you might say: "In my experience, I have found that students are much more likely to be motivated to learn the material when presented in a game format (or maybe just 'this way' to avoid the trigger word 'game') than a series of worksheets. Once they have learned the material, then they see how it translates into a test question. Giving students a series of test questions does not teach the material, it only tests if they know the material." At the risk of making a snide remark, you could even add: "there are very few jobs where people get paid to take multiple choice tests". You can also show them this book and point out the lengthy reference section full of academic support for your new game-based pedagogy.

---

[5] Hidden curriculum refers to all the implicit messages of school. For example, no one tells students that the subjects should be treated separately, yet they get that idea from the fact that they go to math for 50 min, then English, and so forth with little to no interdisciplinary connections.

However, you also have to deal with the resistant student in your classroom at the time of the resistance. You should be prepared for this: "Traditional instruction tends to tell the students what to do, giving them procedures and directions for each step of the way. However, these directions remove the students' challenge to make sense of and understand the situation" (Kirkley et al. 2011, p. 377). Because students are used to being told what to do, you may encounter some resistance in the form of "Just tell me what to do!" or you may even get the "But you're the teacher! You are not doing your job if you don't tell me what to do." Powers and Kirkpatrick (2013) found when they gamified their course that "since most students are accustomed to assuming a passive role in class, our teaching methods initially produce insecurity and anxiety in some" (p. 67). You need to be prepared to respond by saying something like, "The learning is in figuring it out" or "My job is to teach you how to teach yourself" followed by a constructivist statement like: "Tell me what you think you should do next and why?" Of course there is also the story about teaching a man to fish instead of just giving him the fish that you can pull out as well.

You also may get resistance from students, and parents, concerned about scoring high on your state's high-stakes test. Aligning the standards with your game objectives and highlighting specific game tasks that address these standards and having it handy are worth your time in case you encounter this type of resistance. One of my participants in a study about gay and lesbian teachers said that administrators never like to be surprised and suggested couching your plans, in that case to come out, in terms of the school's mission. If you suspect you might encounter resistance, you should tell your administrators what you are planning on doing and come armed not only with how your curricular game furthers the school's mission but also with alignment to any standards you are expected to teach. That way you can help your administrators be prepared for any student or parental resistance as well as getting them on your side.

Another type of resistance can take the form of a student who intentionally ruins the game. Huizinga (1995/2005) calls these players who "shatter the play world" "spoilsports" (p. 106). Gamers call these players "griefers"—those who take advantage of the game world to harm others: "the griefer sees himself as higher status than the other players because of the power he can wield over them by spoiling a game that they care about and he doesn't" (Schell 2008, p. 368). An immediate response might be to institute an anti-griefing rule. With classroom rules, you need consequences, and the natural consequence would be to punish the griefer in some way: "Some games have created 'anti-griefing policies' that ban griefers from the game … but it creates the ugly situation of having to police griefing, and then having to maintain a 'court of law' to decide which griefing was intentional abuse, and which was just 'fooling around'" (Schell 2008, p. 368). Instead, Schell (2008) suggests limiting situations where griefers might cause grief, such as not allowing players to steal. However, another way around this would be to allow players to steal and make that part of the game play, particularly if stealing was part of the actual "system," such as a game about the Great Depression. By making stealing part of game play, you can then set regulations about stealing.

To prevent obscenities from being used, some games have blacklists, words that are forbidden, and some games have white lists, listing the words that can be used and banning all others—but griefers try to get around this. Schell (2008) claims the best remedy is to filter the game so only the griefer sees his or her own obscenity, but the rest of community does not so the griefer does not know if community heard his obscenity. However, this might not be realistic in a classroom game. For example, if the game is played by writing on the poster paper Facebook "walls," all students would see the obscenity. Since a "blacklist" has already been built into rules of school with its own means of enforcement, it also might not be necessary to make this explicit since you do not want to plant ideas into your students' heads. A gray list might be best. For example, you might make a rule that players can only use Shakespearean language or language that scientists would use or whatever fits your content. That way you can police language by including it on your rubric and in other ways that help reinforce your game's theme: "When a student acted up [the teacher] would ask, 'Would a scientist speak that way?'" (Squire 2011, p. 199). You can also ask if a scientist would think that way in order to promote scientific thinking. Squire (2011) observed that "Tina used the game's fiction to enforce classroom rules. Using the game to set high expectations was an unexpected benefit of the unit" (p. 203). One difference between video games and teaching is that players can be anonymous in video games, but a teacher knows all his/her students. Allowing students to be anonymous can be a gateway to griefing. Take advantage of knowing students' names. People do not realize the power of knowing people's names until they become a teacher or someone in authority. I remember my first-year teaching encountering a student I did not know fooling around in the hallway and threatening him with a trip to the office. He of course just ran off, and I was helpless because I did not know his name.[6]

For griefers, asking them to take the lead on something can tap into their desire to dominate. When I was a high school teacher, I learned that I would lose any power struggle that took place in front of students because just engaging in a power struggle with a student signaled that I had lost my authority in the classroom. One time I had a student who accused me of stealing something of his because I had confiscated it and told him I would turn it into the office. Instead of immediately getting defensive, I was able to mentally disengage and just let him rant. When he was done, I simply said, "You can pick up your Walkman from the office at the end of the day" (yes, I have been teaching that long). By disengaging, I got the rest of the students on my side because allowing him to tell his story showed how irrational he was being. It also let him vent and then calm down once he was done:

> To listen is to bear witness and validate someone's fear, sadness, or anger at injustice in a way that allows the individual to move past these paralyzing emotions and regain their power and will to act anew. Listening invites a group or individual to reflect, to examine

[6]There is an urban teaching legend about a college student taking a timed essay exam who refused to turn in his essay at the end of class. Instead, he kept writing while the professor was telling him he would not accept his essay. When done, the student walks up to the professor's desk and says, "Do you know who I am?" The professor says, "No, and quite frankly, I don't care who you are." The student replies, "Good," lifts up half the stack of turned in essays, puts his essay in the middle, and walks away.

> their thoughts and perceptions for incongruities or trouble spots [but] … You will have to ask the good questions and coach them into telling their *story* instead of their conclusions. (Simmons 2001, p. 187)

After teaching high school for a while, I finally learned the trick of saying, "See me after class." It allowed me to address the situation in the moment without having a public confrontation. The other students would all say "ooohhhh" as they imagined the worst. Instead, after class I would give space for the student to tell his or her story and then try to redirect their actions to something more productive: "People will often examine their line of reasoning when given the space to do so. It is when you crowd them into a corner that they tighten their hold on existing beliefs and justifications" (Simmons 2001, p. 187). Confronting a student in class makes a student defensive; talking to a student after class gives him or her space to reflect on his or her actions.

"Hackers," on the other hand, are not "griefers." They are players who try to game the system to their advantage: "Possibly the [hacker]'s greatest joy is to find a loophole in a game system that lets them do something that they shouldn't be able to do … particularly if other players don't know how to do it" (Schell 2008, p. 369). One thing that I have found works most of the time as a teacher is to tap into that person's abilities to get them onto my side and give them the attention they are seeking, but in a positive way. For example, you can say to a hacker, "You obviously have a strong understanding of game systems. Can you help me design this so others can't hack or grief in the future?"

Another tactic is to take preventative measures by designing a "good sport" contract that all players, including the teacher, must sign before entering the game. A contract that contains clear performance expectations of students and of the teacher as well as tiered natural consequences[7] when students do not adhere to those expectations can go a long way to help prevent or mediate a student revolt, particularly if those consequences are within the context of the game and part of the game play. For example, if a student is playing a blacksmith apprentice and curses in front of his or her boss, he or she would be fired. If a student refuses to sign a contract, they can play a different game—a game of reading the materials and taking quizzes. Establishing the rules/expectations in your classroom is a social contract, "A social contract, a commitment to a shared set of behaviors and values, is a social frame for understanding what it means to enter into the magic circle [of a game]" (Salen and Zimmerman 2004, p. 473). Koster (2000/2006) who wrote a "Declaration of the Rights of Avatars" states: "having a clear code of conduct for both players and administrators has been shown to make running the space go much smoother overall" (p. 806). It is advisable to include language about safety and trust in the contract: "players must feel a sense of safety and trust to be comfortable enough to enter into the social space of a game" (Salen and Zimmerman 2004, p. 473). Ideally, you would build signing the contract into the

[7] By "tiered natural consequences," I mean having consequences that are tied to the infraction and increase as the number of infractions increase with the exception, of course, of a major infraction which might have the most drastic consequence for a first-time offense.

game story. For example, in a game where students are doctors, they might sign a "Hippocratic Oath." Any other occupational game might have students sign a job contract. However, all games come with a set of rules, and including rules about acting in a manner and using language appropriate to the role-playing role can also help ward off spoilsport behavior. The faster you can get students personally invested in the game world, for example, by having students choose their role, design their avatar, or even take a personality quiz in order to match students with their role, the less likely you will have a spoilsport. Signing an in-game contract can be a way to immediately get students invested.

No matter how much you anticipate, however, games have the potential for conflict to arise. Some game theorists argue conflict is essential to game play[8]; however, conflict can be the competition between the player and himself or herself trying to beat his or her own best score. In this case, however, I am talking about conflict among players. When conflicts do arise, if you can handle the conflict within your game role or manipulate the game to handle the conflict, do so. You might also opt to designate "guild leaders" (Sheldon 2011, p. 62) charged with enforcing the rules; however, in an elementary, middle, or high school classroom, I would rotate leadership either within or among games so all students get a chance to learn leadership skills. There may be some situations, though, where you need to break out of your game role and play teacher to mediate a conflict. It is essential in either case that students perceive the game, the rules, and the outcome as fair: "establishing a sense of fairness is crucial to successful game play" (Salen and Zimmerman 2004, p. 262). One of the most consistent praises students said about me when I was a high school teacher was that I was fair, often couched with language about me being tough. If there are ways the game has advantaged some students or some students get more support, for example, English Language Learners, and students object, I find the following explanation helpful:

> If you have two children, one with diabetes and one without, and one vial of insulin, to be equal, you would give each child half the vial of insulin. To be fair, you would give the whole vial to the child with diabetes.

One way to ensure a game feels fair is to have the whole class compete against the game or against the teacher. Other ways are to establish clear rules, make sure you build in balancing feedback loops, and address any perceived unfairness during debriefing or reflection time. For example, one of my students is creating a game about the Underground Railroad. I suggested he rig the game so the number of students who reach and retain freedom is proportionally equal to estimates about how many actually did. In this case, it would be vital to point that out during the debriefing and to discuss how having so many students "fail" felt. The game play might even foster some "survivor guilt" among those who did make it. In this case, having the game be "unfair" in the sense that some students succeed and others do not is essential to creating the intended experiences of the game.

---

[8]The New Games Movement, however, created cooperative games. But you could argue that these cooperative games still have conflict in terms of the players versus the game world, i.e. trying to achieve a goal within the constraints established by the game.

If the game feels unfair, you might have not just one student rebel, but a group of students or even the whole class revolt. You may have a game where this is what you want to happen, for example, a game about the American Revolution. But, if you do not, you will have to find ways to address a student revolt. Your first temptation might be to impose or reinforce the rules; however:

> When faced with an impasse situation, the worst thing you can do is to give directives. … Directives can result in malicious obedience—technical compliance with a request with the spirit of intent that makes it work. In fact, many people can technically comply with a directive in a way that ensures its failure. Even when you have formal authority over a group, too clearly 'telling them what to do' may create a passive/aggressive nonresponse or even sabotage. Story is better at communicating your wishes in a respectful way that requests rather than demands. Story avoids a power struggle. (Simmons 2001, p. 73)

Even better than a metaphorical story or a story about someone else, telling a personal story can help diffuse a situation, particularly if you then give students the opportunity to tell their own stories:

> Your curiosity about whomever you wish to influence is the cornerstone of your ability to hold another's interest. Only genuine curiosity can reveal to you the kind of story that will earn their attention. There is a world of difference between being 'curious' about someone and 'trying to understand' someone. Curiosity is more egalitarian, full of wonder, ready for surprises, and seeks permission. Trying to understand implies superiority, a finite framework of logic, and frankly, carries connotations of resentment about having to make the effort. (Simmons 2001, p. 211)

When facing cynics, those who do not believe your sincerity or competence, your story must provide evidence of your sincerity because "cynical people are immune to good intentions" (Simmons 2001, p. 167). If your story makes yourself vulnerable in some way such as revealing a personal flaw, it invites your students to share their own stories. Stories can be a powerful means to deflate conflict.

I had a student revolt one time because some students perceived my actions as being discriminatory.[9] The next class, I shared my own story of how my understandings of race and racism have evolved and continue to evolve. By making myself vulnerable in this way, my students then felt safe to share their own stories, and we had the most honest discussion of race and racism that I have ever had in one of my classes, which students expressed gratitude for in their course evaluations. This was a case where student revolt became productive: "a student revolt can be useful. It provides an opportunity to vent, and is an opportunity for coach or facilitator to show progress, restate goals, and map out the rest of the formal learning program" (Aldrich 2009, p. 489). Do not ignore a student revolt. Instead, embrace it as an opportunity to explore the intersection between the game world and students' lives.

---

[9] I taught this particular teacher education class in an elementary school. We were watching the *Color of Fear*—a movie where a group of people discuss race and racism. Out of respect to the elementary students still in the building who might overhear, I turned down the volume before one of the people in the movie expressed his anger very loudly and with several obscenities. Unfortunately, I turned the volume down prematurely so it appeared as though I was trying silence one of the black members of the discussion in the movie.

Grouping Your Players for Learning

Earlier we talked about player configuration from the perspective of a game designer, but now I want us to think about player configuration from the perspective of a teacher. Some games may be specifically designed for individual, partner, team, or whole-class participation, but most games are probably open to any of those configurations. When you had your game designer hat on, you thought about the consequences each type of player configuration would have on game play. However, now you need to think about the consequences on learning as well as different conditions for why you would choose different configurations. For example, one year you might have several English Language Learners at various levels of English proficiency who could feel lost if the game was played as a whole class. In that case, partners might work best. You could have the native English speaker be the navigator[10] and the English Language Learner the driver for the first few quests but then switch so that the English Language Learner gets practice using academic oral language.[11] If a parent complains that you are using his or her child as a tutor for an English Language Learner, explain that research shows that teaching increases learning. In addition, pairing forces students to convert tacit knowledge into explicit knowledge as they explain and justify their actions to their partner. The driver/navigator pairing and other forms of grouping are also useful if you do not have a one-to-one student-computer ratio.

Another year, you might have several expert video game players. If you base your game on another game like *World of Warcraft*, students might feel that those students who have played the COTS version have an unfair advantage. In this case, you might want to assign groups, or in gamer language "guilds," so that each group has a seasoned player: "Game cultures value learning by diving in, mucking around, and joining people who know something about that topic. …a novice can participate in communities of practice that lead toward authentic participation in complex activities. 'Professionals' and 'amateurs' work side by side, enabling enculturation into communities of practice … and producing new knowledge" (Squire 2012, p. 26). Although not as organic as Squire (2012) describes, you will be creating what Gee (2007) calls "affinity groups" with "distributed intelligence." This replicates, and helps prepare students for, the world of work: "In the real world we rarely work independently on problems. Rather, we work with others either formally in teams or informally as colleagues because knowledge and skills are distributed rather than concentrated in one person or position" (Van Eck 2007, p. 276). If students do not know how to articulate their needs, their thinking, or their questions, they will struggle as workers. Education should give them opportunities to practice these skills:

---

[10] In a navigator/driver partnership, the navigator tells the driver, the person controlling the computer, what to do.

[11] Using "academic oral language" and "social written" language can act as bridges from "social oral" to "academic written" language for English Language Learners and other students (Brisk et al. 2008).

> Students who are trained to ask good questions become better learners. In fact, one finds that question asking in one form or another is a part of most effective learning strategies. For instance, problem-based learning requires that students formulate questions as part of the process. The problem is presented and students are expected to formulate their own questions to guide their acquisition of the knowledge needed to solve that problem. (Delisle, 1997) (Van Eck 2007, p. 286)

Just like we talked about how game-based teaching should promote "pulling" information instead of "pushing" it onto students, students need practice learning how to both "pull" information from others by learning how to listen and ask questions but also how to "push"—explain and promote—their ideas to others as well. Working in groups means students will need to synthesize the knowledge, including contradictory and conflicting knowledge, from multiple people before making a game move.

Even if you have students playing in groups or teams, you can still have the technology for the whole class and the teams play as individuals (each team is one player in the game). This is particularly useful if your technology is limited. For example, one of my students is designing a game where each team plays a different country in World War II. I suggested that each team play a political consultant to a world leader during World War II. To give each team a chance to choose which country they work for while ensuring that each country got chosen only once, I described a scenario where each team/political consultant is vying to work for a world leader so the world leaders set up a contest to see who would get to pick first. Yes, that is unrealistic, but why that would be unrealistic can be debriefed after the game. This way, as teacher, you can have the contest be your diagnostic assessment in disguise. Whichever team wins the contest gets to pick first, second place picks second, and so forth. Even though there is competition, because it is done in teams, it blunts the blow for the team in last place. You can also have the team who had to pick last get the first move. Then, I suggested that she have descriptions of the platforms of each country without the name of the country and that she could use screentips in PowerPoint so that the platform description pops up when a team scrolls over the platform either with a short title that does not give away the country or just a number. In class, each team in rank order would go to the front of the class, view the platforms, and discuss their decision, making their thinking audible to the whole class. Once they decide, they click on the platform link which takes them to their workspace (perhaps a googledoc or a wiki) with the name of that country and its world leader. Imagine the suspense as each team finds out which country they have chosen![12] When each subsequent team comes up to the front of the classroom to make their choice, the followed links will be a different color making it clear which platforms are still available to choose from. In this way, teams are playing individuals, but their decisions are played out in front of the whole class.

Both the literature about learning:

[12] In my head, I picture this much like Sorting Day in the Harry Potter book series.

> having people (including novices and experts) engaged in joint problem solving—is considered by learning theorists such as Annemarie Palincsar and Ann Brown (1984) to be perhaps the 'best' form of learning. (Squire 2011, p. 12)

and the literature about gaming:

> There are many ways to [use games effectively], but letting kids sit and play games individually is not one of them. The best, complex games require specialized teacher knowledge, interest and skills to use effectively. (Prensky quoted by Korbey 2013)

expound upon the importance of collaboration. Working in groups or pairs promotes several of the twenty-first-century skills discussed in Chap. 1 including communication, collaboration, and cultural competence, and I would argue creativity: "Innovation is a team sport" (Hill et al. 2014). Both Squire (2011) and Schrier (2007) found greater involvement, engagement, and learning when students were paired together over playing a video game individually:

> I recommend pairing up students when games are played in class because it (1) prompts players to reflect in action as they discuss moves; (2) requires students to vocalize their intentions, providing insight into what they think; and (3) gives students someone to share struggles with. We saw far less frustration than in our earlier study. (Squire 2011, p. 166)

> Almost all of the participants enjoyed playing the game with a partner because they could share ideas and tasks, engage in mini-debates, remember information better, practice decision-making skills, and reflect more deeply on evidence they gathered. For example, one participant noted that she liked playing with a partner because she 'could exchange ideas, notes, plan what to do next,' while another participant noted that, 'It was fun to play with others, one to have someone to help with the handheld/taking notes, and two, just to have someone to bounce ideas/theories off.' Because the game play and collaboration necessitated dialogue and the sharing of evidence, the participants needed to reflect on the evidence and their interpretations, formulate and offer hypotheses, and collectively decide on next steps—all activities related to developing critical thinking, collaborative, and problem solving skills. (Schrier 2007, p. 259)

Working with a partner not only pushes students to formulate their own thinking and consider the thinking of someone else, it also helps stave off the helplessness and temptation to use just trial and error students sometimes feel when learning is in the frustration zone.

Pairing students together should be strategic. Depending on the learning task, you might want to pair students together who have similar interests or you might want to pair a stronger student with a struggling student. You can even make choosing a partner part of game. For example, in a game designed to teach a foreign language, learners might have a scenario where students have half a phrase and have to find their partner with the other half of the phrase. Do not forget, partners do not have to partner up for the duration of the game; you can also have tasks where partners switch. This allows students to work with several different students like in a small group but with the advantages of working one on one with a partner.

Grouping students, however, can get much more complicated. You might immediately think of grouping students by the types of players we explored earlier. This is tempting and might work, but I found out the hard way that grouping students by similarities can be dangerous. I used to use a personality self-assessment to group my students. According to this personality self-assessment, there were four personality types which also defined how people learned: blues were nurturers, greens were logical thinkers, golds were organizers, and oranges were socializers, i.e., class clowns. You can imagine the chaos that erupted when I put all the class clowns together in one group. I do think that heterogeneous grouping done well can result in different player types complementing each other and encourage students to view the game from different perspectives and hopefully to even try out different types of playing. Magerko et al. (2010) describe a category of players, "validators," who "seek easy challenges where positive validation is likely and avoid hard challenges so as not to risk failure" (p. 264). According to Magerko et al. (2010),

> Validators face a vicious cycle when it comes to digital games for learning. Validators who try playing an unfamiliar entertainment game genre and fail in their early attempts would probably avoid this genre. Overall, Validators probably play easier games for entertainment or choose easier levels within a game, so that playing and winning becomes rewarding validation of self-worth. … Validators are the player type most at risk for not learning from a learning game. (p. 264)

Here is a clear example of a player type who would benefit from working in a well-designed group because any struggles a group faces are faced as a group so failure is less likely to be seen as an indicator of an individual's self-worth. However, careful attention would need to be paid to make sure the Validator does not give up and let the rest of the group take over. One time when I was assigning groups as a high school teacher, I kept reconfiguring them and finally thought I had my final configuration. I then realized that I had placed a quiet female student in a group of rambunctious male students. I almost reconfigured one more time, but then I thought, why not see what happens? That "quiet girl" transformed into a taskmaster! Somehow, that configuration brought out leadership qualities that I did not know existed, and she made sure that everyone did their fair share.

One caution is to avoid MATY groups. MATY stands for More Awesome Than You. It comes from a site for experts at *The Sims* game who pride themselves on hazing newcomers and is about individual competition (Gee and Hayes 2012, p. 150). Sometimes these MATY groups even use "leet speak" (as in "elite") (Squire 2011 p. 152), using words they made up in order to exclude others. A MATY group can develop when one group dominates a game. This can be avoided by having rules that create balancing feedback loops. However, you can also employ "robust role-playing rules [to] make it easier for a [class] to achieve … stability" (Bartle 2006, p. 781). Bartle studied different types of game play that occurred in multiuser domains (MUDs). He found that there were different combinations of players that created stability: "killers and achievers in equilibrium; a MUD dominated by socializers; A MUD where all groups have a similar influence (although not necessarily similar numbers)" (p. 781).[13] One way to replicate these stable forms would be to

[13] Bartle (2006) does emphasize that there may be other forms of stable MUDs out there as well.

create roles for students that mimic these types of players. Having clear roles can also help prevent one player from doing all the work as it allows teachers to evaluate what individuals contribute to group work.

Not only do you need to ward off instability among groups; you also need to prevent instability within groups. Groups should foster interdependence where "students … move beyond the success or failure of the individual and must instead focus on the success or failure of the group. By believing that achievement is a team effort, rewards and resources are allocated in such a manner that can be used to support such group behavior" (Egert and Phelps 2011, p. 140). The features of productive affinity spaces that Gee and Hayes (2012) describe can serve as a model for classroom groups:

1. "A common endeavor for which at least many people in the space have a passion is primary."
2. "Affinity spaces are not segregated by age."
3. "Newbies, masters, and everyone else share a common space."
4. "Everyone can, if they wish, produce and not just consume."
5. "Content is transformed by interaction."
6. "The development of both specialist and broad, general knowledge is encouraged, and specialist knowledge is pooled."
7. "Both individual knowledge and distributed knowledge are encouraged."
8. "The use of dispersed knowledge is facilitated."
9. "Tacit knowledge is used and honored; explicit knowledge is encouraged."
10. "There are many different forms and routes to participation."
11. "There are many different routes to status."
12. "Leadership is porous, and leaders are resources."
13. "Roles are reciprocal."
14. "A view of learning that is individually proactive but does not exclude help is encouraged."
15. "People get encouragement from an audience and feedback from peers, although everyone plays both roles at different times." (pp. 134–144)

Despite the name ElitistJerks, the rules they list are instructive for thinking about "rules of engagement" for groups:

- All posters are to make an effort to communicate clearly.
- Do not post unless you have something new and worthwhile to say.
- Whining in any form is forbidden.
- Is your shift key broken?[14] (Choontanom and Nardi 2012, p. 206)

However, I think it is Jesse Schell's (2008) number one tip for creating community that is most important: "For a community to form, players must be able to speak to each other freely" (p. 359). This is something teachers, ok I, often forget. I often feel like I have to control every moment and that time spent talking freely is wasted time. Sometimes this is the case. But class can be structured to make it more likely

[14]This refers to the practice of capitalizing every letter in an e-mail to indicate "shouting."

that students are on task: "If the game isn't interesting enough, the community doesn't have anything [productive] to talk about" (Schell 2008, p. 360) and so they end up talking socially.

How can you make sure your game is interesting? Of course you are going to playtest. One of my students discovered that her students found some of her quests "boring" from her beta testing. I suggested she make sure her quests require students to "pull" information in order to make meaningful choices. I pulled from another student-designed game to provide the example of having the players who are playing escaped slaves having to choose between going to a Contraband Camp, an Underground Railroad safe house, or a plantation. The students have to know meanings of these phrases to make the right choice; otherwise, they will be captured. This creates a much more interesting quest than being quizzed on the terms by making imperative that groups find out what each term means before making their decision. Another way to boost interest is to involve conflict. Remember, this can be conflict against the game, i.e., trying to beat the game, or even trying to beat your own personal best. However, "forc[ing] players to depend on each other" (Schell 2008, p. 365) also generates interesting conversations as students need each other. Schell (2008) provides the example of *Toontown Online* where "players can only heal other players," they cannot heal themselves, so players had to ask for a "Toon-up" (p. 366). Promoting both conflict and cooperation creates interesting game play and can help prevent situations where one person does all the work.

Using Assessment to Pace Your Game

Whether you have players play as individuals, in pairs, or in teams, you face the dilemma of pacing. As teachers, we have all been in that situation where some students finish a test or a reading or an activity really quickly and have to sit and wait for the rest of the class, or sometimes that poor lone student, to finish. Having the students make decisions as a whole class is one way to solve this problem; however, your game might call for something other than whole-class play. One way to handle pacing is to have several side quests that are not essential to playing the game but offer those who work faster an opportunity to challenge themselves in other ways. Scaffolding is not just for students who struggle; you also need to scaffold learning for those who need more challenge. One of my students had a beta tester who stated that he knew everything about the topic already, but when he got to the side quest about black holes which he did not know about previously, he was mesmerized. Having a practice arena, or area, at the different levels in your game can also provide a place for both students who struggle and those who do not to practice their skills. You can also have "a space for synthetic performance" (Bogost 2007, p. 336), i.e., spaces within a game where players can plan their strategy similar to half-time during a sporting event. I cited an earlier example of having students who have finished a task then play a role where they judge the students still completing the task, thus solving the problem of not enough teachers and giving students even more practice from a teacher's perspective. Students who finish early, or even students whose characters die in a game, can come back as advisors or mentors as ghosts or in dreams or teachers or judges whatever form fits the game story.

One concern, though, might be that students do not finish the game in time, particularly if you face a deadline like the end of the semester or simply have to move on with your curriculum. One way to solve this is to have the number of quests students complete determine their grade. Students who complete all quests receive an A, all but one a B, and so forth. Completion of side quests could turn those grades into plus grades. For this to work, each quest must be completed before students can move on to the next quest. By having the whole game "timed" this way along with having side quests, you solve the problem of pacing, but introduce other problems, particularly if the last quests contain essential skills and this presents a disadvantage for students who do take longer. However, even traditional schooling disadvantages slower students. One way to solve this is to have the final quest in your game be mentoring those still playing. That way no new skills are learned so students who do not reach that point are not missing out on learning something essential but are still learning. Hopefully by adjusting the game so that all students are likely to succeed within the given timeframe and by providing opportunities for early finishers, which can include the opportunity to replay the game from a different perspective or even just replay with the knowledge gained, the pacing will promote engaging game play instead of being a problem.

Formative assessment is crucial for adjusting the pacing of your game, but I encourage you to think of assessment as a by-product of gaming. If you see it as the focus of the game, your game might turn into a dressed up quiz. However, you do want to pay attention to ways you can capture progression in thinking. There are of course standards you and your students may be beholden to, but if you think in larger terms, for example, that you are assessing historical or scientific or literary or mathematical problem-solving skills, that sets you up for designing your curricular game to teach these skills: "Imagine the transformation in schools if learning in school became about how to make good choices in science, mathematics, art, and civic participation" (Gee and Hayes 2012, p. 147). Because playing is about making choices, according to Plato, "you can learn more about a man in an hour of play than a year of conversation" (quoted in Schell 2008, p. 473).

Making Thinking Visible

In order to assess student thinking, you have to make student thinking visible. Remember when the Commander said video games are mere entertainment? That is how they appear if tacit knowledge is not moved to explicit knowledge. Making thinking visible is how this move happens. In a previous study I conducted with gay and lesbian teachers, one of my participants discussed the importance of making tacit knowledge explicit: "If you can't really articulate it, you can't get your hands around it, you can't really plan it, you can't really control it, own it as a tool. And so I feel like I have more tools to use now" (Jackson 2007, p. 183). I have been advocating having students work in teams because that forces students to make their thinking visible, audible, or both in order to collaborate. The one situation where teamwork might not work is if students are producing something that is individually tailored to them. For example, in this book/game, it does not make sense for partners or groups unless students teach the same thing because the end product should be something that students can use in their own teaching. However, by embedding discussion boards for each challenge and quest and by having students upload their worksheets, even though my students work individually for the most part, they still make their thinking visible and can comment on the thinking of others. Squire (2012) provides the example of "During Action Reports" from the game *Civilization* to describe how experts model for novices and experts comment on novice thinking in order to create what he calls "cognitive apprenticeships" (p. 18). By making thinking visible, these discussion boards in my class have served a similar function as students often read others' posts before attempting a challenge and benefit from advice given by students who are further along in the class.

Previously I described evidence-centered design where the student model is compared to the expert model. Lots of modeling systems have been proposed with intimidating names like "Artificial Neural Networks," "Bayesian Nets," and "Hidden Markov Modeling." All of these try to capture what the student is thinking through their moves in video games by using past data to predict what patterns of strategy-switching students will follow. Instead of trying to learn how to do this sophisticated modeling, you can just ask students to reflect on the choices made during game play. If you do all your assessment behind the scenes by trying to model, i.e., guess, at student thinking, you are missing an opportunity to promote metacognition. By getting students to transfer knowledge from tacit to explicit, students can then examine their own thinking and so can the teacher: "For example, if [student thinking] during a mission showed evidence of a widespread misconception, the teacher could turn that into a teachable moment, or may choose to assign struggling students to a team with more advanced students" (Shute 2011, p. 519). Beck and Wade (2004) describe these reflection opportunities as "going meta," or "taking a step back from the immediate situation, analyzing the choices and the odds, and finding the right strategy" (quoted in Bogost 2007, p. 240). However, I would add understanding "how people made those choices" is just as important: "people learn better from games when they are asked to explain their actions" (Mayer 2011, p. 294). Multiple studies have found that reflection on game playing increases recall and transfer (Tobias et al. 2011).

One way to do this is to have students keep a "click or clunk" journal (Klingner et al. 2001) as they play, describing how some things "clicked" for them as they made connections, had insights, or even related game play to their own lives, and how some things "clunked" for them as they struggled, had questions, or just did not understand something. Having students reflect on choices made also makes trial and error less likely. One researcher had students rate their confidence level in their actions and then reflect on the outcome. This allowed him not only to track when students were guessing; it also allowed him to see that students spent the most time reflecting on "high-confidence, wrong answers" (Dempsey 2010, p. 100). Student reflection also serves as further beta testing for you to use to improve your game. In addition, any time you can do this in the context of the game can make the game more engaging and immersive. For example, students can keep a character diary, be required to take field notes if they are playing a researcher or a detective, or have to create reports complete with charts, graphs, and diagrams for their boss. If the game is multicharacter, students can then share these artifacts after the game in order to compare and contrast their character's experience with the experiences of other characters. However, there is also benefit to stepping out of the game story to reflect on the game at large:

> agency is a first-person experience induced by making moment-by-moment decisions within a balanced … interactive system, while transformation as variety is a third-person experience induced by observing and reflecting on a number of interactive experiences … In order to support the total experience, the system must support both first-person engagement and third-person reflection; must provide agency and transformation as variety. (Mateas and Stern 2005/2006, p. 658)

This can be during the game such as having students fill out exit tickets with questions like: What problems did I overcame today? What changes did I make and why? What problems do I still have? What evidence do I need to solve that problem? Where would I find that evidence? One of the most important questions you can ask is to have students make predictions as this involves hypothesis formation and then allows game play to serve as the hypothesis testing and feedback. Of course this then leads to the next question of why something happened or did not happen which then allows players to revise their predictions. It is important to note that "when immersed in time-sensitive gameplay, players can be annoyed by [a teacher's] questions, but when playing in a more relaxed mode, they are usually proud to discuss their strategies and show off their accomplishments" (Osterweil and Klopfer 2011, p. 164). Building in reflective spaces in the game creates time needed for consolidating learning.

Most crucial, however, is the debriefing after game play, or "after action review." One way to structure this is to use the DIE formula where students describe their gaming experiences (what did you do), interpret those experiences (how did you feel and why?), and evaluate those experiences (what did you learn at personal, interpersonal, and societal levels) (Bennett and Bennett 2008 cited in Powers and Kirkpatrick 2013, p. 54). Both oral debriefings for students to share experiences and ideas coupled with writing a reflection so students can express private thoughts, consolidate ideas, and depart from the norm can counter two assumptions they found that professors make—that students understand an idea once it has been discussed and that all students have shared all ideas, thoughts, and feelings during debriefing (Petranek et al. 1992 cited in Powers and Kirkpatrick 2013, p. 65). Both the collective and individual reflection can provide valuable beta-testing feedback.

Debriefing can also be an opportunity to compare the system presented in the game to reality. Squire (2011) describes an example of this: "When I teach with *Civilization*, I use this missing feature [disease] as a teachable moment to discuss the size of Native American civilizations (which most people underestimate) and the importance of diseases" (p. 25). This is particularly important if your game involves "counterfactual analysis," i.e., exploring what might have happened if history played out differently, but also for most other games as well since simulations are simplified versions of reality. When players ask why something would not happen in real life that happened in the simulation or vice versa, this can provoke insightful thinking about how reality works. In a way, debriefing is another level in your game as it adds complexity to the student model of the system.

Asking what is realistic and what is not can reveal a lot about your students as well. Squire (2008) describes a response from a black student when he was asked what is unrealistic about *Grand Theft Auto: San Andreas*: "A black man can't just save a few dollars and go buy a house in a white neighborhood" (p. 177). If a student said this during debriefing, this would be a really rich site for interrogation. Asking questions like "Why not? Why would someone think that? Who thinks that? Who doesn't? What does that say about our society?" could incite an insightful discussion. You could also make connections with other texts, in this case the play *A Raisin in the Sun* by Lorraine Hansberry, which tells the story of a black family buying a house in a white neighborhood. Another revelatory question is what players did during a game that they would not do in real life. When Stevens et al. (2008) asked this of a player, she said she wouldn't clear trees or sell newborn animals in real life, but did in *Zoo Tycoon* because it made her money, the goal of the game, adding that there should be a cost, an ecological cost, to cutting trees (p. 60). You can also ask students how they would play the game differently if they had the chance and why as well as how they would design the game differently.

No matter what your game, a discussion of values it engenders including "counterfactual analysis" questions such as "what values would be implied if these changes were made to the game?" can enable students to view all games, including the video games they play at home, as texts[15]: "the logics that drive our games make claims about who we are, how our world functions, and what we want it to become" (Bogost 2007, p. 340). The win state is one way of conveying a set of values: "For example, what are the winning conditions of your game? Amass the most resources? Destroy the enemy's units? Arrive at a balance of powers? Each of these victory conditions implies a particular set of values, fleshed out through the game rules, materials, and experiences of play" (Salen and Zimmerman 2004, p. 517). One of my students designed a World War II game where students race as countries in order to get the bomb so they can decide which country to bomb. While this makes for exciting game play, I suggested she move the "getting the bomb" part to the middle of the game with subsequent quests about the impact. Her students can then reflect on how the war could have been averted by analyzing the causes. Not only does this allow the game play to be different every time depending on which country gets the bomb first and who they bomb, but it also shifts the goal from getting the bomb to preventing war.

---

[15] In one of my classes, I try to enlarge students' concept of texts beyond the printed word. One of my students tried to stump me one time by throwing out boogers as something that could not possibly be a text. I countered by telling him about my visit to my ear, nose, and throat doctor who "read" my snot by analyzing the color, amount, and thickness.

Games can also serve to promote or tear down stereotypes and other assumptions. Salen and Zimmerman (2004) provide several examples of stereotypes video games reify: "Previous characters such as Smurfette in *Smurf Rescue* and Princess Toadstool in *Super Mario* were merely damsels in distress, helpless females waiting to be rescued at the end of the final level. These characters are synonymous with the end of the game, acting as passive objects of desire, the carrot held out to entice the player to finish" (p. 524). However, video games can also challenge people's stereotypes. Salen and Zimmerman (2004) provide the example of the end of *Samus Aran*, when the protagonist takes off the helmet to reveal that she was a woman all along "This clever design decision reveals the rhetorical presumptions players make about game character gender" (p. 526). As mentioned earlier, one of my students created a storyboard for his game about slaves escaping to freedom where the slaves were depicted as people but the white plantation owner and the bounty hunter as different animals. At first I thought this might upset some students because it hides the historical fact that white people were the owners, but I then thought about how it flipped history around as slaves were treated as animals, but it was actually the white people who were acting like animals. It turns out this was the creator's intent, but it is important to keep in mind that people will read something in completely different ways. For example, when one of my children set up his Legos so that both a hippo and a crocodile had the same fish in their mouths, I said, "They are fighting over the fish." My son replied, "No. They are sharing the fish" which of course made me feel like the worst parent ever, but also reinforced a lesson I should have known which is that it is better to ask questions than to assume (which makes an ass out of "u" and me). Remember this during debriefing.

Whether it be small group discussion, whole-class decision-making, or individual journaling, or any other method of making thinking public such as thinking maps, reflection helps move students from novice thinking to expert thinking (Bransford et al. 2000) in several ways: peer modeling, metacognition, teacher, and peer feedback. A study of students playing the game *Enigmo* where objects in the game react based on laws of physics found that "while *Enigmo* provides students with a strong intuitive 'feel' for physics concepts, it doesn't appear to help students make the leap from tacit understanding to more formalized knowledge" (Clark and Martinez-Garza 2012, p. 281) because the game did not have any affordances that allowed players to articulate their working knowledge. The same could be said of soccer, playing pool, and any other number of games where the learning is literally embodied, or, as Clark and Martinez-Garza (2012) put it, "in the player's 'thumbs'" (p. 284). Therefore, teachers need to provide "supports for metacognition" such as having students "predict[] and explain[] what was happening in the game and reflecting on connections" (Clark and Martinez-Garza 2012, pp. 281–282). This involves moving students from "constraint-based reasoning," or using heuristics to solve a localized problem without examining how actions impact the larger system to "model-based reasoning" where students "create[] a mental model of the whole scenario … and mentally run the model to reason about the … situation" (Clark and Martinez-Garza 2012,

p. 282). While it would be nice to think that students automatically reflect on their thinking, reality is that they often need prompting, support, guidance, and space to do so.

Revise and Resubmit

When the game is done, it is time for some R&R. Yes, it is time for some rest and relaxation as designing and teaching curricular games is hard work, but after allowing enough time for some distance so you are not too emotionally involved in that iteration of game play, use the feedback from teaching the game to adjust the game: "a task that, in our work, *always* has involved multiple iterations of design" (Barab et al. 2012, p. 322). As mentioned earlier, teachers have the perfect set up for iterative design with new rounds of playtesters every year. Unless your game requires an immediate fix to get it to work while being played, keep your fixes, embellishments, additions, etc., to between playtesters. If you need to do a fix during play, keep in mind Farmer and Morningstar's (1990/2006) advice (designers of *Habitat*, an early virtual world): "Work within the system." They compare two examples when a regular player picked up a weapon one of the game operators playing DEATH accidentally dropped—an operator-only gun that can kill in one shot. The first designer demanded the gun back and threatened to disable the user's account if he didn't comply. As you can imagine, "The player gave the gun back, but was quite upset about the whole affair, as were many of his friends and associates on the system. Their world model had been painfully violated" (p. 749). In a sense, this designer was acting as a spoilsport—someone who disregards the "magic circle" and thus bursts the fragile bubble of the game world. In the second instance, the operator (who also was one of the designers) negotiated a deal with the player where DEATH would pay to get the gun back:

> An elaborate arrangement was made to meet in the center of town to make the exchange, with a neutral third Avatar acting as an intermediary to ensure that neither party Cheated. Of course, word got around and by the time of the exchange, there were numerous spectators. We played the role of DEATH to the hilt, with lots of hokey melodramatic shtick. The event was a sensation. It was written up in the newspaper the next morning and was the talk of the town for days. The Avatar involved was left with a wonderful story about having cheated DEATH, we got the gun back, and everybody went away happy. (Farmer and Morningstar 1990/2006, p. 749)

Sometimes you may have to step out of your game role and into your teacher role, but keeping that to a minimum helps create immersive game play.

CHALLENGE 8.2: Inspired by the success of the last "Amy experiment," in fact, you even made some friends in the process, you text her again: "Tell me what happened when you had to change a game—revise and resubmit so to speak?" In typical Amy fashion, she doesn't respond with a straight answer. Instead, she texts back: "Try changing one of the rules in your classroom. See what happens." Well, you can't exactly do that, but you think back to times when you did. **EXERCISE**: Change one of the rules in your classroom or workplace without violating any of the school or office rules and observe what happens.

Students Create Their Own Games

One way to "revise and resubmit" is to have students create their own games on the topic or similar topics after having played your game. You can even use this as a way to generate curricular games that you can use in your future teaching. Having older kids create the games for younger kids can also work really well (Harel and Papert 1990; Kafai 1995) and has the added benefit of developing empathy as the older students need to be able to tailor the material to the younger audience by thinking about their interests, the level of difficulty, and so forth. Do not, however, fall into the trap of having "more advanced" students creating games and "regular ed" or "remedial" students playing them because that deprives those students labeled "remedial" the creative and constructionist opportunity to design their own games and serves to replicate and amplify differences. However, it would be interesting to have the students placed in lower classes create games for other students to play, giving them a chance to be the expert on something, to create something of value, and to "play," i.e., have fun learning, in school. It even can give students a chance to play with the system of school: "When I was a teacher my elementary students once designed a level for *AVATAR* (an online game) based on their school and found a real joy in creating the 'teacher's red pen,' an epic weapon that caused enemies to quiver once they were in its presence" (Squire 2012, p. 28). As teachers, we know that teaching forces a deep understanding of the content, but making all the design decisions of creating a game can foster an even deeper intimacy with the material. This does not mean we, as teachers, should give students free reign. We have an important role as facilitators to make sure students are giving deep thought to the choices they make and how those choices can reinforce the content.

If you were reading closely, you noticed that the studies I cited of teachers having older students create games for younger students were published in 1990 and 1995. You probably thought these were board games, card games, or some other type of no-tech game. However, you would be wrong. These teacher researchers had their students program video games, yes, program video games. Published in 1990 and 1995, the actual projects occurred in 1987 and 1991. Unfortunately, the Instructional Software Design Project (Harel and Papert 1990) and the Game Design Project (Kafai 1995) were anomalies to teaching at that time and even now. Projects like Kafai's (1995) and Hare and Papert's (1990) where students are invested in the purpose, have a sense of ownership, and use programming as a tool for "personal expression" (Kafai 1995, p. 18) encourage spatial thinking, language development, logical thinking, computational thinking, and systems thinking (Coulter et al. 2012, p. 340) in ways that promote transfer. Fortunately, there has been a recent resurgence of teaching computer programming through video game design and a multitude of programming languages that range in difficulty and modality to do so.

Earlier the stages players go through when playing a video game were delineated as "involvement," "immersion," and "investment" (Davidson and Lemarchand 2012). Squire (2008) adds two more advanced stages, that of "tinkerer," or the desire to modify the rules of the game, and "designer," being inspired to create one's own game. Coulter et al. (2012) found that following these stages in teaching worked to build the foundation for students designing their own games: "Using a continuum from playing to modifying and then designing original games, we have scaffolded students as young as fourth grade in the creation of original AR [Augmented Reality] games" (Coulter et al. 2012, p. 339). Modding (modifying an existing game) is popular among gamers and ranges from built-in modding such as choosing or designing your own avatar when those choices impact game play (e.g., choice of armor or weaponry) to soft modding, or using "user authoring tools" such as level editors that allow players to make changes such as constructing new scenarios or changing the settings, to hard modding where the user alters the game by revising the code. Doing so can change the feel or purpose of the game: "Perhaps the most famous modder is Minh 'Gooseman' Le. He took the popular [First Person Shooter] *Half-Life* and modded it to create a version with more team-oriented gameplay. The result was *Counter-Strike*. … Gooseman and the *Counter-Strike* team released the mod online and it became an instant hit. The game has won dozens of awards for gameplay and … many folks buy *Half-Life* just so they can play *Counter-Strike*" (Fullerton et al 2004, pp. 169–170). Some games have even been modded to the point where only the game engine remains the same such as "the use of the *Quake* game engine as a movie-making tool" (Salen and Zimmerman 2004, p. 305). Just as creating curricular games can be done with ever increasing levels of technology, modding can be done with ever increasing levels of transformation.

Construction and management simulation (CMS) games have modding as their core game mechanic, tapping into people's desire to "tinker" and allows player and game designer to co-construct the game, or really the players to construct the game within the platform the game designer provides:

> "By moving away from the idea that media is something developed by the few," [Will] Wright [creator of *SimCity* and *The Sims*] explains, "we open up a world of possibilities. Instead of leaving player creativity at the door, we are inviting it back to help build, design, and populate our digital worlds. More games now include features that let players invent some aspect of their virtual world. … And more games entice players to become creative partners in world building, letting them mod its overall look and feel. … For these players, games are not just entertainment but a vehicle for self-expression." According to Wright, they also foster a more critical, more creative kind of education. Students who use games as learning tools will "treat the world as a place for creation, not consumption." (Brown 2008, p. 165 quoting Will Wright)

While thinking about "tinkering" with game code can be intimidating, particularly to people who are afraid they might accidentally hit an imagined "self-destruct" button on a computer, there are ways to modify nontechnical games. For example, a teacher could bring in a board game and have students mod the game to teach content. Certainly, the number of different versions of *Monopoly* speaks to the ability, and popularity, of doing so. Having students mod existing games teaches students flexibility in thinking as they reconceive the game as having a different purpose; promotes design thinking as they have to redesign the physical game pieces for their purpose; and fosters systems thinking as students change the rules to fit their needs.

When students design their own games from scratch, they experience the creation skills of conceiving and giving birth to an idea. Doing so can develop expertise:

> Often experts can identify the most significant elements of their domain, isolating dynamics and general rules ... In this context, expertise generally is considered to be an understanding of a domain that can be abstracted and adjusted dynamically to suit new problem sets. It is about understanding the underlying systems and rules at play beneath the surface. In essence, game designers—like teachers—must become 'miniexperts' on a subject because they need to parse and reverse engineer the subject's underling systems in order to generate procedural representations of them within the structure of their game. (Macklin and Sharp 2012, p. 385)

Having students design their own games moves teaching from constructivism to constructionism where students "learn through design" by creating "objects to think with":

> Constructionism—the N word as opposed to the V word—shares constructivism's connotation of learning as 'building knowledge structures' irrespective of the circumstances of the learning. It then adds the idea that this happens especially felicitously in a context where the learner is engaged in constructing a public entity, whether it's a sand castle on the beach or a theory of the universe. (Papert 1980, p. 1)

Building knowledge by building objects, including virtual ones, allows the student to receive "production feedback" (Okita and Schwartz 2013), or feedback on their learning through how a product they have created reacts. Educators talk about student ownership over their learning. Constructionism offers a true ownership over learning as students "own" their products and thus the learning that occurs through the feedback and revision process. Having "maker-spaces" in schools where students get to design and build their own products is becoming more and more popular, particularly as the cost of 3-D printers has decreased.

Promoting these ways of thinking through constructionism can be, and has been, done with no-tech games, for example, having students design their own board games about a topic. Doing so through programming, however, teaches a more powerful twenty-first-century literacy[16]:

> In addition to using video games to teach kids how to write computer programs (procedural literacy), we can use them to teach kids how to write computer arguments (procedural rhetoric). When kids program, just as when they write, they can learn to make their own claims about the world in the form of processes. Such a practice reframes video game development as a rhetorical practice, not just a craft practice or a technical practice. By actively teaching kids to mount arguments in procedural form—even simple ones like models of their every-

[16] See Douglas Rushkoff's (2011) book *Program or Be Programmed* for powerful arguments about the importance of learning to code.

> day life—video games can become a carrot medium for both programming and expression. (Bogost 2008, p. 137)

There are more and more gaming software tools that are geared toward beginners and even youth. Drag-and-drop gaming tools such as *Scratch* mentioned earlier are usually simple enough for children to use, but powerful enough to make useful educational games.

Ideally, student game design could be done in an interdisciplinary way wherein English students work on the storytelling and character development, the graphics in art class, the logic of the rules in math (or, in my ideal world, the computer science class all students are required to take), and so forth, promoting yet another twenty-first-century literacy of making connections among disciplines.

However, do not assume that just because students play a lot of video games, they will design good ones. Teachers must facilitate moving tacit knowledge, i.e., "knowing a good or a bad video game when I see one" to explicit knowledge, i.e., being able to list and give examples of distinguishing characteristics. One way to do this is to have students themselves generate lists of good and bad video games and then delve into what makes them good or bad to co-construct abstract general principles for what makes a good video game. A concept diagram can be useful for this where students list examples and non-examples of good video games and then determine what characteristics are always present, often present, sometimes present, and never present. Of course the same can be done with bad video games as well.

Like designing curriculum and teaching it, designing a pedagogical game invites students to come to understand a topic inside and out. I purposefully used the verb "invites" because students might not always take these steps. Unless you walk them through a design process, such as the one outlined in this book, there is a risk that students might produce "edutainment" where the core game mechanic does not match the learning objective. However, with your guidance, designing a video game can be a powerful educational tool:

> We view the process of designing a game as one possible lens through which youth can explore a subject, find its underlying systems, and then create a game for others to play that, in turn, provides some level of experience with the subject domain. The systemic nature of games serves as a gateway and model for the importance of systems thinking to understanding our world. The design and production of games also expose youth to applied contexts for developing and honing skills as varied as mathematics, technology use, programming, logic, communication, iteration, sound and visual design, and conceptual thinking. (Macklin and Sharp 2012, p. 382)

In the experiences of Macklin and Sharp (2012), having students design video games promotes the following literacies:

- "**Issues**: Understanding the subject and its underlying system(s)."
- "**Game design**: From a basic game literacy to an understanding of the dynamics of rules, rewards, aesthetics, and mechanics."
- "**Technology**: Choosing a platform and learning how to create assets and program and use game-development tools."
- "**The iterative process**: Prototyping, testing, and refining games."

- "**Systems thinking**: Understanding the systemic nature of both games and issues."
- "**Storytelling**: Taking difficult-to-understand concepts and creating a tangible representation of them."
- "**Visual art**: Learning how the visual representation and animation lead players through the experience, as well as drawing and rendering skills."
- "**Sound design**: Learning to record and create sounds and how sound serves to cue players and generate a sense of game space." (p. 386)

While all these literacies listed above are useful, particularly in this day and age, it is developing the inside/outside understanding of a system that can be the most powerful outcome of game design. Being able to see an overall system and empathize with an element or elements within that system moves students to a higher level of understanding, which they can then use to foster such empathy in their players.

However, Macklin and Sharp (2012) found that when students designed video games, "tool learning dominated all other concerns, pushing systems thinking and game-design methodologies to the background. And while the locus of the curriculum was on the subject domain of the given group of issues, the participant focus was on basic tool skill development" (p. 387). One way to avoid this would be to have students follow the steps outlined in this book where they first design a no-technology version so they can concentrate on a systems-level understanding of the topic, then repurposing familiar software so the cognitive load of the technical aspects of technology is low, allowing room for students to increase their conceptual understandings of technologies, and then moving on to medium tech to develop the literacies Macklin and Sharp (2012) list, and finally, once a solid foundation in those foundational skills has been established, students can learn to code by building the high-tech version of their game.

Just like good game designers who learn from playtesting, Macklin and Sharp (2012) who developed game design curricula for the boys and girls club and other after-school programs specifically for social awareness games took steps to avoid the pitfall of students focusing on learning to code instead of the game design. For example, they had students develop a game and submit their proposal to a hypothetical game designer which is then evaluated based on a rubric: "By stopping short of having participating youth produce the games, *Playing for Keeps* manages to keep the focus on the development of miniexperts capable of ideation and design conceptualization of form-appropriate serious game concepts" (p. 394). They also used the "Grow-a-Game Deck" developed by Mary Flanagan with five types of cards "*challenges* (social issues or conflicts such as racism), *games* (from board games such as *Monopoly* to video games such as *Tetris*), *values* (ideals such as "loyalty"), *verbs* (action words such as smashing), and *vote* (for giving points to the players with the best ideas)" (Macklin and Sharp 2012, p.389) to help students generate a variety of games. One student pulled the cards that challenged her to design a game about singing human rights. She subsequently designed a game called *Hush* where a mother in Rwanda has to sing to her children so they do not cry and alert the soldiers to their presence. While the idea of allowing students freedom in designing a game they come up with all on their own to reflect their own interests, sometimes these "enabling constraints" (Davis et al. 2000, p. 193) produce the most creative games by providing students structures to channel their interests in a productive way.

On the other hand, giving students full freedom can also lead to creative games and give teachers a glimpse into students' own realities:

> The instructor, Al Doyle, was surprised to see that one of the student's games involved a dark journey through a world filled with dangerous obstacles and enemies. Thinking that the student has misinterpreted the assignment, he asked her what happened to the birthday party. She explained that in order to get to the party, the player needed to make it through the tough streets of the city first. Sure enough, the final level was the bright and cheery world of the birthday party. She had designed a game exploring the contrast between navigating dangerous urban streets and finding safety and friendship. (Macklin and Sharp 2012, p. 398)

The hypothetical Odysseus Order game is likely to prompt students to explore the interaction between plot and character development in ways that leading students through a close reading or other types of projects probably would not. Think about how much more intimately students would understand not just the *Odyssey* but also story construction, if they had to design this themselves. Shapiro (2013) cites multiple students that speak to the types of learning that occur when students code their own games; however, perhaps the most critical skill is one that can be learned without coding: to think about how other people might experience their game. Keep in mind too how much fun the creative process is for students. I have found that the only thing that is more fun than playing a good game is designing one.

In all of these levels of game-based teaching—having students play a curricular game, mod an existing game, or create their own game—teachers are "mission-critical adults" (Horn 2013). Just as this book served as a guide for creating your own curricular game by providing steps, examples, worksheets, and warnings, teachers serve as guides for students by providing the structures, guidance, scaffolding, encouragement, and gentle nudges when students stray off the golden path.

> *Learning and teaching are not inherently linked. Much learning takes place without teaching, and indeed much teaching takes place without learning.*
>
> -Wenger, 1998

Appendix

TEACHING QUEST WORKSHEET

Title: ____________________

Background of students: ____

____
____

Context of classroom/school: ____

____

Merging	What to keep from No Tech	
	What to keep from low/medium tech	
Player configuration	Individual/Partners/ Small groups-how to determine grouping (random, heterogeneous, homogeneous, etc.)	
Rules	Classroom rules to make game run smoothly	
Classroom configuration	Room/desk arrangements	
	Decorations	
	Any other considerations	
Materials Needed	In the classroom	
	By students at home	

continued

Game Schedule	Typical class routine	
	What's done at home	
Making Thinking Visible	Before playing the game (diagnostic assessment)	
	During the game (formative assessments)	
	After the game (summative assessment)	
	After the game (debriefing guiding questions)	
Possible Teacher Scaffolding	For early advancers	
	For students who struggle	
	For English Language Learners	
Accommodations for students on IEPs (Individual. Education Plans)		
Possibilities beyond the game		
Any other considerations		

Suggested Teaching Plan Rubric

Criteria	"Wow! I mean, I think this might work" (3)	"Hmm, this might be acceptable" (2)	"I need more convincing" (1)	"Go back to the drawing board" (0)
Teacher role	Teacher plays an NPC or multiple NPCs as part of game play	Teacher serves as a mentor or guide but not as part of game play	Typical teacher role described	Teacher role not described
Student role(s)	Students interact with each other in different roles	Students design their own avatar	Students take on the role of a character	Student role not described
Connections with learning theories	Learning theories used to shape game	Multiple references to learning theories	References a learning theory	No connection to learning theories
Logistics	Unique leveraging of available resources	Detailed description of implementation (e.g., how to group students)	General description of implementation	Little to no thought given to practical matters of implementation
Revision cycle	Unique means of collection and analysis	Description of how feedback will be used to revise game	Description of how feedback will be collected	No mention of revision
Techie (1 extra point)				
Blends no-tech and low-tech versions				
Tech Savvy (2 extra points)				
Implementation involves students using game to teach others				
Tech Guru (3 extra points)				
Deigned so students can mod game				

Suggested Reading

Hinn, M. (2009). Include players with accessibility issues. In C. Bateman (Ed.), *Beyond game design: Nine steps towards creating better video games* (pp. 157–189). Herndon, VA: Cengage Learning.

Kafai, Y. (1995b). *Minds in play: Computer game design as a context for children's learning*. Hillsdale, NJ: Lawrence Erlbaum Associates.
Koster, R. (2000/2006). Declaring the rights of players. In K. Salen & E. Zimmerman (Eds.), *The game designer reader: A rules of play anthology* (pp. 788–813). Cambridge, MA: MIT Press.
Pitaru, A. (2008). E is for everyone: The case for inclusive game design. In K. Salen (Ed.), *The ecology of games: Connecting youth, games, and learning* (pp. 676–88). Cambridge, MA: MIT Press.
Salen, K., Torres, R., Wolozin, L., Rufo-Tepper, R., & Shapiro, A. (2011). *Quest to learn: Developing the school for digital kids*. Cambridge, MA: MIT Press.
Sheldon, L. (2011b). *The Multi-player classroom: Designing coursework as a game*. Herndon, VA: Cengage Learning.
Shute, V., & Ventura, M. (2013). *Stealth assessment: Measuring and supporting learning in video games*. Cambridge, MA: MIT Press.

References

Aldrich, C. (2009). *Learning online with games, simulations, and virtual worlds: Strategies for online instruction*. Hoboken, NJ: Jossey-Bass.
Barab, S., Pettyjohn, P., Gresalfi, M., & Solomou, M. (2012). Game-based curricula, personal engagement, and the *Modern Prometheus* design project. In C. Steinkuehler, K. Squire, & S. Barab (Eds.), *Games, learning, and society: Learning and meaning in the digital age* (pp. 306–326). New York: Cambridge University Press.
Bartle, R. (1996/2006). Hearts, clubs, diamonds, spades: Players who suite MUDs. In K. Salen & E. Zimmerman (Eds.), *The game designer reader: A rules of play anthology* (pp. 754–787). Cambridge, MA: MIT Press.
Barton, K., & McKellar, P. (2011). From Master to Games-master: Managing disequilibrium and scaffolding in simulation-based learning. In S. de Freitas & P. Maharg (Eds.), *Digital games and learning* (pp. 226–251). London: Continuum.
Beck, J. C., & Wade, M. (2004). *Got game: How the gamer generation is reshaping business forever*. Cambridge, MA: Harvard Business Press.
Bogost, I. (2007). *Persuasive games: The expressive power of videogames*. Cambridge, MA: MIT Press.
Bogost, I. (2008). The rhetoric of video games. In K. Salen (Ed.), *The ecology of games: Connecting youth, games, and learning* (pp. 117–139). Cambridge, MA: MIT Press.
Bransford, J., Brown, A., & Cocking, R. (2000). *How people learn: Brain, mind, experience, and school*. Washington, DC: National Academies Press.
Brisk, M., Horan, D., & MacDonald, E. (2008). A scaffolded approach to learning to write. In L. Stoops Verplaetse & N. Migliacci (Eds.), *Inclusive pedagogy for English language Learner: A handbook of research-informed Practices* (pp. 15–32). New York: Lawrence Erlbaum Associates.
Brown, H. (2008). *Videogames and education*. Armonk, NY: M.E. Sharpe.
Choontanom, T., & Nardi, B. (2012). Theorycrafting: The art and science of using numbers to interpret the world. In C. Steinkuehler, K. Squire, & S. Barab (Eds.), *Games, learning, and society: Learning and meaning in the digital age* (pp. 185–209). New York: Cambridge University Press.
Clark, D., & Martinez-Garza, M. (2012). Prediction and explanation as design mechanics in conceptually integrated digital games to help players articulate the tacit understandings they build through game play. In C. Steinkuehler, K. Squire, & S. Barab (Eds.), *Games, learning, and society: Learning and meaning in the digital age* (pp. 279–305). New York: Cambridge University Press.

Coulter, B., Klopfer, E., Sheldon, J., & Perry, J. (2012). Discovering familiar places: Learning through mobile place-based games. In C. Steinkuehler, K. Squire, & S. Barab (Eds.), *Games, learning, and society: Learning and meaning in the digital age* (pp. 327–354). New York: Cambridge University Press.

Davidson, D., & Lemarchand, R. (2012). Uncharted 2: Among Thieves—How to become a hero. In C. Steinkuehler, K. Squire, & S. Barab (Eds.), *Games, learning, and society: Learning and meaning in the digital age* (pp. 75–107). New York: Cambridge University Press.

Davis, B., Sumara, D., & Luce-Kapler, R. (2000). *Engaging minds: Learning and teaching in a complex world.* Hillsdale, NJ: L. Erlbaum Associates.

Dempsey, J. V. (2010). Elemental learning and the pyramid of fidelity. In R. Van Eck (Ed.), *Gaming and cognition: Theories and practice from the learning sciences* (pp. 82–107). Hershey, PA: Information Science Reference.

Edvinsson, B. (2008). Game-based learning: Teacher and student perspectives. In M. Pivec & M. Moretti (Eds.), *Game-based learning: Discover the pleasure of learning* (pp. 46–56). Lengerich, Germany: Pabst Science Publishers.

Egert, C., & Phelps, A. (2011). Motivating science education through games. In M. S. Khine (Ed.), *Learning to play: Exploring the future of education with video games* (pp. 129–151). New York: Peter Lang.

Farmer, F. R., & Morningstar, C. (1990/2006). The lessons of Lucasfilm's Habitat. In K. Salen & E. Zimmerman (Eds.), *The game designer reader: A rules of play anthology* (pp. 728–753). Cambridge, MA: MIT Press.

Fullerton, T., Swain, C., & Hoffman, S. (2004). *Game design workshop: Designing, prototyping, and playtesting games.* San Francisco, CA: CMP Books.

Gee, J. P. (2003). *What videogames have to teach us about learning and literacy.* New York: Palgrave Macmillan.

Gee, J. P. (2007). *Good videogames + good learning: Collected essays on videogames learning, and literacy.* New York: Peter Lang.

Gee, J. P., & Hayes, E. (2012). Nurturing affinity spaces and game-based learning. In C. Steinkuehler, K. Squire, & S. Barab (Eds.), *Games, learning, and society: Learning and meaning in the digital age* (pp. 129–153). New York: Cambridge University Press.

Harel, I., & Papert, S. (1990). Software design as a learning environment. *Interactive Learning Environments. 1*(1), 1–32.

Hill, L., Brandeau, G., Truelove, E., & Lineback, K. (2014). *Collective genius: The art and practice of leading innovation.* Cambridge, MA: Harvard Business Review Press.

Holt, J. (1964). *How children fail.* Lanham, MD: Pitman Publishing Company.

Horn, M. (2013, May 16). What we can learn from a dinner controversy in the desert. *Forbes.* Retrieved January 10, 2016, from http://www.forbes.com/sites/michaelhorn/2013/05/16/what-we-can-learn-from-a-dinner-controversy-in-the-desert/

Huizinga, J. (1955/2006). Nature and significance of play as a cultural phenomenon from Homo Ludens: A study of the play element in culture. In K. Salen, K. & E. Zimmerman (Eds.), *The game designer reader: A rules of play anthology*, (pp. 96–120) Cambridge, MA: MIT Press.

Jackson, J. (2007). *Unmasking identities: An exploration of the lives of gay and lesbian teachers.* Lanham, MD: Lexington Books.

Jenkins, H. (2011). Foreword. In S. de Freitas & P. Maharg (Eds.), *Digital games and learning* (pp. xxiii–xxvi). London: Continuum.

Kafai, Y. (1995a). *Minds in play: Computer game design as a context for children's learning.* Hillsdale, NJ: Lawrence Erlbaum Associates.

Kirkley, J. R., Duffy, T., Kirkley, S., & Kremer, D. (2011). Implications of constructivism for the design and use of serious games. In S. Tobias & J. D. Fletcher (Eds.), *Computer games and instruction* (pp. 371–394). Charlotte, NC: Information Age Publishers.

Klingner, J. K., Vaughn, S., Dimino, J., Schumm, J. S., & Bryant, D. (2001). *From clunk to click: Collaborative strategic reading.* Longmont, CO: Sopris West.

Korbey, H. (2013, March 22). Teachers, students, digital games: What's the right mix? *Mind/Shift*. San Francisco: KQED. Retrieved January 10, 2016, from http://blogs.kqed.org/mind-shift/2013/03/teachers-students-digital-games-whats-the-right-mix/

Koster, R. (2000/2006). Declaring the rights of players. In K. Salen & E. Zimmerman (Eds.), *The game designer reader: A rules of play anthology* (pp. 788–813). Cambridge, MA: MIT Press.

Leemkuil, H., & de Jong, T. (2011). Instructional support in games. In S. Tobias & J. D. Fletcher (Eds.), *Computer games and instruction* (pp. 353–369). Charlotte, NC: Information Age Publishers.

Macklin, C., & Sharp, J. (2012). "Freakin' hard": Game design and issue literacy. In C. Steinkuehler, K. Squire, & S. Barab (Eds.), *Games, learning, and society: Learning and meaning in the digital age* (pp. 381–402). New York: Cambridge University Press.

Magerko, B., Heeter, C., & Medler, B. (2010). Different strokes for different folks: Tapping into the hidden potential of serious games. In R. Van Eck (Ed.), *Gaming and cognition: Theories and practice from the learning sciences* (pp. 255–279). Hershey, PA: Information Science Reference.

Mateas, M., & Stern, A. (2005/2006). Interaction and narrative from *Expressive AI*. In K. Salen & E. Zimmerman (Eds.), *The game designer reader: A rules of play anthology* (pp. 642–669). Cambridge, MA: MIT Press.

Mayer, R. (2011). Multimedia learning and games. In S. Tobias & J. D. Fletcher (Eds.), *Computer games and instruction* (pp. 281–303). Charlotte, NC: Information Age Publishers.

Munro, A. (2008). Software support of instruction in game contexts. In H. O'Neil & R. Perez (Eds.), *Computer games and team and individual learning* (pp. 55–74). Amsterdam, The Netherlands: Elsevier.

Okita, S. Y., & Schwartz, D. L. (2013). Learning by teaching human pupils and teachable agents: The importance of recursive feedback. *Journal of the Learning Sciences, 22*(3), 375–412.

Osterweil, S., & Klopfer, E. (2011). Are games all child's play? In S. de Freitas & P. Maharg (Eds.), *Digital games and learning* (pp. 152–171). London: Continuum.

Papert, S. (1980). *Mindstorms: Children, computers, and powerful ideas*. New York: Basic Books.

Powers, R., & Kirkpatrick, K. (2013). Playing with conflict: Teaching conflict resolution through simulations and games. *Simulations and Gaming, 44*(1), 51–71.

Rushkoff, D. (2011). *Program or be programmed: Ten commands for a digital age*. Berkeley, CA: Soft Skull Press.

Salen, K., & Zimmerman, E. (2004). *Rules of play: Game design fundamentals*. Cambridge, MA: MIT Press.

Schell, J. (2008). *The art of game design: A book of lenses*. Burlington, MA: Morgan Kaufmann.

Schrier, K. (2007). Reliving history with 'Reliving the Revolution': Designing augmented reality games to teach the critical thinking of history. In D. Gibson, C. Aldrich, & M. Prensky (Eds.), *Games and simulations in online learning: Research and development frameworks* (pp. 250–269). Hershey, PA: Information Science Publishing.

Shapiro, J. (2013, July 9). Are kids who make their own video games better prepared for the digital future? *Forbes*. Retrieved fromhttp://www.forbes.com/sites/jordanshapiro/2013/07/09/are-kids-who-make-their-own-video-games-better-prepared-for-the-digital-future/

Sheldon, L. (2011a). *The Multi-player classroom: Designing coursework as a game*. Herndon, VA: Cengage Learning.

Shute, V. (2011). Stealth assessment in computer-based games to support learning. In S. Tobias & J. D. Fletcher (Eds.), *Computer games and instruction* (pp. 503–524). Charlotte, NC: Information Age Publishers.

Simmons, A. (2001). *The story factor: Inspiration, influence, and persuasion through the art of storytelling*. New York: Basic Books.

Squire, K. (2008). Open-ended video games. In K. Salen (Ed.), *The ecology of games: Connecting youth, games, and learning* (pp. 167–198). Cambridge, MA: MIT Press.

Squire, K. (2011). *Video games and learning: Teaching and participatory culture in the digital age*. New York: Teachers College Press.

Squire, K. (2012). Designed cultures. In C. Steinkuehler, K. Squire, & S. Barab (Eds.), *Games, learning, and society: Learning and meaning in the digital age* (pp. 3–31). New York: Cambridge University Press.

Steinkuehler, C., & Oh, Y. (2012). Apprenticeship in massively multiplayer online games. In C. Steinkuehler, K. Squire, & S. Barab (Eds.), *Games, learning, and society: Learning and meaning in the digital age* (pp. 154–184). New York: Cambridge University Press.

Stevens, R., Satwicz, T., & McCarthy, L. (2008). In-game, in-room, in-world: Reconnecting video game play to the rest of the kids' lives. In K. Salen (Ed.), *The ecology of games: Connecting youth, games, and learning* (pp. 41–66). Cambridge, MA: MIT Press.

Sutton-Smith, B. (1997/2006). Play and ambiguity from The Ambiguity of Play. In K. Salen & E. Zimmerman (Eds.), *The game designer reader: A rules of play anthology* (pp. 296–313). Cambridge, MA: MIT Press.

Tobias, S., Fletcher, J. D., Dai, D., & Wind, A. (2011). Review of research on computer games. In S. Tobias & J. D. Fletcher (Eds.), *Computer games and instruction* (pp. 127–221). Charlotte, NC: Information Age Publishers.

Travis, R., & Young, M. (2011). Operation KTHMA-reign of the demiurge: Game worlds, Greek history, and situated learning. In M. S. Khine (Ed.), *Learning to play: Exploring the future of education with video games* (pp. 153–166). New York: Peter Lang.

Van Eck, R. (2007). Building artificially intelligent learning games. In D. Gibson, C. Aldrich, & M. Prensky (Eds.), *Games and simulations in online learning: Research and development frameworks* (pp. 271–307). Hershey, PA: Information Science Publishing.

Chapter 9
End Game: Passing It On

> *In theory, there is no difference between theory and practice, but in practice there is.*
>
> -Attributed to multiple people including Yogi Berra, Karl Marx, and computer scientist Jan L. A. van de Snepscheut

Abstract This chapter explores the potential, or "transformational possibilities" (Digital games and learning, Continuum, London, 2011), of game-based teaching and what scaling it up might mean for education. It revisits the themes of the first chapter such as teaching for transfer and developing novice thinking into expert thinking in order to encourage readers to think about what happens beyond their curricular game. It also encourages readers to mentor other teachers to help them develop their own curricular games. Finally, it concludes by proposing that game-based teaching can radically alter the path of education by transforming teaching and learning in a way that brings a new approach to thinking in the twenty-first century by exploring what it means to take a gaming stance.

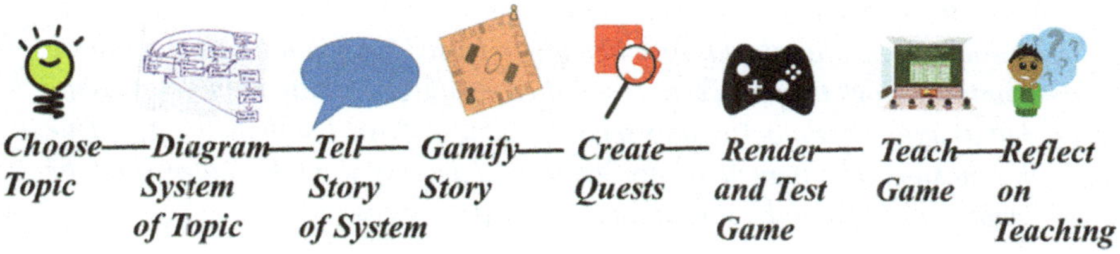

J.J. Kellinger, *A Guide to Designing Curricular Games*,
Advances in Game-Based Learning, DOI 10.1007/978-3-319-42393-7_9

MENTORING QUEST

Success! The second time around after turning your curricular game into a teaching tool, you win the Commander over! At one point in the game play, you even caught her laughing! Even she is capable of having fun! You become the hero of the future! How are you going to go back to your ordinary citizen past after such adulation?

After a well-deserved celebration and rest, the Commander calls you into her office.

"Well played!" she declares. You bask in the glow of her admiration. "Now," she continues, "you need to teach others since you cannot do all of this alone. Besides, I suspect you might have a life to return to in the past. You can "level up"—hone your mentoring skills—by working with one Elder of your choosing. Then, two, then four, and so forth. However, make sure you also mentor your mentees on how to mentor so we can have a ripple effect."

"'We,' she said 'we'! Finally, acceptance!" you think to yourself. You decide to begin with your friend, the Engineering Elder who slipped you the text time traveling device. And so the game of teaching curricular game design begins. Pass it on!

ACTION: Help someone else design a curricular game.

While I have many automatically graded activities throughout my courses, the major assignments usually require me to grade them manually. I discovered that requiring students to earn a certain number of points before moving to the next level meant that students were stuck until I got a chance to grade their assignments. This created frustration among students as they had to wait for me to grade something before they could move on. Initially, I made it clear to students that they could always use the syllabus, which laid out the assignments and the readings, to work ahead. But then I figured out ways to troubleshoot this dilemma within the structure of the game. One way I did this was by having two tracks that covered two different, but interrelated, aspects of a course. This way, while students were waiting for one assignment to be graded, they could move forward in the other track. However, I did create certain points along the way where students had to have made a certain amount of progress in both tracks before moving ahead. Another tactic I used was to have turning in an assignment unlock the next section and then earning a certain number of points on that assignment unlock a later section. In these ways, I managed to stay true to the mastery component of my game-based classes while addressing the pragmatic problem of the time it takes to grade assignments.

Games have served lots of functions throughout the history of mankind. Jane McGonigal (2011) in *Reality is Broken* tells the story of Herodotus to demonstrate the ability of games to help people survive:

> When Atys was king of Lydia in Asia Minor some three thousand years ago, a great scarcity threatened his realm. For a while people accepted their lot without complaining, in the hope that times of plenty would return. But when things failed to get better, the Lydians devised a strange remedy for their problem. The plan adopted against the famine was to engage in games one day so entirely as not to feel any craving for food … and the next day to eat and abstain from games. In this way they passed eighteen years, and along the way they invented the dice, knuckle-bones, the ball, and all the games which are common. (pp. 5–6)

She goes on to say, "Games made life bearable. Games gave a starving population a feeling of power in a powerless situation, a sense of structure in a chaotic environment. Games gave them a better way to live when their circumstances were otherwise completely unsupportive and uninhabitable" (McGonigal 2011, p. 6). There are other "transformational possibilities" (de Freitas and Maharg 2011) as well. Games have also been a way to play out strategies by running simulations to try to predict results:

> Claims that the game [*Kriegspiel*] was behind Prussia's military victories stimulated interest internationally. Prussia's *Kriegspiel* dry runs of war with Austria supposedly led to a strategy that proved decisive in the Six Weeks' War of 1866. After that, the Austrian Army took no chances and began playing *Kriegspiel*." (Poundstone 2006, p. 384)

This technique is also being used today in sports: "Silberman (2009) studied athletes and video games and found that players ranging from the University of Wisconsin baseball team to the Boston Red Sox use them as visualization tools. It helps them see the playbook, identify patterns, or generally just keep their heads in the game on off days" (Squire 2011, p. 11). However, our original goal in gamifying the curriculum is not for survival or strategy, but rather to move our students from novice thinking toward expert thinking and, in doing so, to build to transfer.

The first chapter laid out the argument that people learn primarily through experience. Indeed, Fullerton, et al. (2004) argue that this is why games have been a part of every culture throughout history: "It's important to remember that what has made games such a long-lasting form of human entertainment is not intrinsic to any technology or medium, but to the experience of the players" (p. 1). Recent studies in various fields including neurosciences (Doidge 2007), learning sciences (Bransford et al. 2000), and cognitive psychology (Stavenga de Jong et al. 2006), have supported this claim:

> Newer work argues that people primarily think and learn through *experiences* they have had, not through abstract calculations and generalizations. … There are conditions experiences need to meet in order to be truly useful for learning. First, experiences are most useful for future problem solving if the experience is structured by specific goals. Humans store their experiences best in terms of goals, and how these goals did or did not work out. Second, for experiences to be useful for future problem solving, they have to be interpreted. Interpreting experience means thinking—in action and after action—about how our goals relate to our reasoning in the situation. It means, as well, extracting lessons learned and anticipating when and where those lessons might be useful. Third, people learn best from their experiences when they get immediate feedback during those experiences so that they can recognize and assess their errors and see where their expectations have failed. It is important too that they are encouraged to explain their errors and why their expectations failed, along with what they could have done differently. Fourth, learners need ample opportunities to apply their previous experiences—as interpreted—to similar new situations, so they can 'debug' and improve their interpretations of these experiences, gradually generalizing them beyond specific contexts. Fifth, learners need to learn from the interpreted experiences and explanations of other people, including both peers and more expert people. Social interaction, discussion, and sharing with peers, as well as mentoring from others who are more advanced, are important. Debriefing after an experience—that is, talking about why and how things worked in the accomplishment of goals—is important. Mentoring is best done through dialogue, modeling, worked examples, and certain forms of overt instruction, often 'just in time' (when the learner can use it) or 'on demand' (when the learner is ready). One way to look at what is going on here is this: When the above conditions are met, people's experiences are organized in memory in such a way that they can [run] simulations in their minds that allow them to prepare for action. They can test out things in their minds before they act, and they can adjust their predictions after they have acted and gotten feedback. They can play various roles in their own simulations, seeing how various goals might be accomplished. (Gee 2008, pp. 21–22)

Based on this theory of learning, Gee (2007) asserts that learning best takes place when "performance" occurs before "competence":

> It dawned on me that school books—for example, a high school biology book—are like those manuals. Both are technical documents. Just like the game manual, the biology book makes no real sense unless and until students have gotten to play the game, the game of biology in the case of the biology book. Things will get easier still if they get to understand the genre of the activities they are involved in by engaging with multiple examples. They will get yet easier if they get to participate in dialogue with people affiliated with and devoted to biology in some substantive, yes, even passionate, way. If all kids have in school are verbal understandings and not situated ones, then, while some of them may pass paper-and-pencil tests, few of them will be able to solve real problems in the world. (p. xi)

However, I would argue that "performance" begets "competence" which begets "performance": "The whole game changed my life" (a quote by a student in one of Squire's CivCamps who ended up volunteering for the Obama campaign, Squire 2011, p. 176). In fact, "games researchers like Dmitri Williams (2006) have found empirical evidence that gamers are more likely to be civically engaged than nongamers" (cited in Squire 2011, p. 196). Squire (2011) offers his theory as to why this is: "Once a person has had profound learning experiences in a world that is noticeably 'designed' (or 'socially constructed'), there is a tendency to ask, 'Why is our world designed the way that it is?' and 'Could it be designed differently?'" (Squire 2011, p. 195). In other words, games promote not just content and skill transfer, but an attitude transfer as well.

Earlier I said that you know you have achieved a gaming stance when you see games in everything and everything *as* a game. You also know you have achieved a gaming stance when you realize everything *is* a game. All our business, educational, governmental, and other structures consist of rules that humans made up. Success involves learning how to play those games well. However, how people define success can differ. Realizing that different people have different "in-game" goals in terms of real life can help diffuse insecurities and false senses of competition. Ideally, it would also give people a sense of playfulness toward life.

When done well, game-based teaching not only teaches students the content and skills, but transforms students' identities. Not only does this mean taking on the characteristics of experts in the field: "[students] had become the kind of person who asks questions about history and marshals resources to find answer questions" (Squire 2011, pp. 177–178), but also taking on characteristics of gamers. These characteristics include measured risk-taking, exploration, and playfulness. It is worth reprinting the quote from chapter one about gamers' stance:

> Surveys of gamers show that they have an increased appetite for risk, a greater comfort with failure, a stronger desire for social affiliations, a preference for challenges, a capacity for independent problem solving, and a desire to be involved in meaningful work when compared with nongamers (Beck & Wade, 2004). Underlying Beck and Wade's argument is a notion of changing literacies. Gamers have grown up with a medium built on assumptions unlike those in print cultures (e.g., a game engine can be tinkered with, a text is not necessarily print based or defined by book covers); game players are coauthors along with game designers, co-constructing the game-as-text through their own action (cf., Robison, 2005). Gamers have grown up in simulated worlds, worlds where anything is possible, and where learning through trial and error is expected, information is a resource for action, and expertise is enacted through both independent and collaborative problem solving in self-directed tasks (Simpson, 2005). (Squire 2008, p. 658)

This cultivation of a playful mind means asking hypotheticals, exploring "what-if?" scenarios, the ability and desire to try things out by running mental simulations, and exploring alternative solutions.

Studies on the learning effects of gaming for learning have shown an increase in expertise in the content. For example, students playing *Civ3* went from viewing history as a series of events to seeing "world history as a pattern of interactions" and that "history could be represented through rules" (Squire 2011, p. 137). What this can mean is that even if game players do not end up going into a field that has the same content as the games they play, it impacts how they view the world. For example, Squire (2012) cites an example of an interview where a *Civ* player applies *Civ* terms to frame his take on the Iraqi war; then Squire (2012) states:

> Thus, playing *Civ* didn't inspire one particular read of history or politics but instead provided a language for thinking about it. ... Steve used *Civ*'s model, it's [sic] grammar and lexicon, to think through historical questions. *Civ* gave Steve a symbol system and interconnected set of rules to use in analyzing historic scenarios. Steve's interpretations are quite flexible. *Civ* doesn't provide one 'answer' or interpretation but is instead a set of possibilities for thinking through the problem. ... To a player such as Steve, *Civ* is a *game* to play, a *framework* to think with, and a *tool* to author with. (p. 22)

Game-based learning can give players the language and the concepts and promote ways of thinking used by experts in the field.

Studies have also suggested that game-based learning promotes transfer to real-world settings. Chatham (2011) found that army enlistees that played military-designed video games were better prepared. Players who become "virtual medics" in *America's Army* used those skills to administer first aid/save lives (p. 91). However, no simulation is perfect; when these "virtual medics" were doing "room clearing" for the first time in the real world, some "slipped on the blood" (Chatham 2011, p. 94). Tobias et al. (2011) in their "examination of a wide range of games and simulations used in instructional and training settings" found that "they do facilitate transfer" (p. 167). This skill transfer is not just in the content itself, but also the skills involved with playing with technology: "Some worry that all this intellectual effort and all these skills [put into games] will not 'transfer' to the real world. But the reality is that games—which today, for the most part, involve real people collaborating and working and playing socially with each other—are the real world. ... The evidence that the cognitive surplus devoted to games transfers to other aspects of the real world is the large number of game players, modders, and designers who have moved on to other technical, artistic, and entrepreneurial enterprises" (Gee 2012, p. xix). Because of the vast array of skills involved, the interdisciplinary connections, and the attitudes needed, games can "transfer" in lots of ways.

Beyond expertise and transfer, game-based learning also improves general cognitive skills as well. Researchers found adults older adults than 60 had a "dose-related effect" where more time spent playing *Rise of Nations* improved both specific game-related skills ("switching between tasks") and general cognitive skills ("working memory and reasoning ability") (Basak et al. 2008 cited in Chatham 2011, p. 90). Because of the problem solving involved in playing well-designed games, it is no surprise that seeing alternative solutions, questioning the taken for granted, and hypothesis testing become real-life skills as well.

Game-based learning, however, also changes people. Pro-social games have been found to increase pro-social behaviors (Tobias et al. 2011). Shaffer (2012) contends that it is these changes in values and identity that go hand in hand with transferring content and skills. He argues that in order for transfer to occur, someone has to be enculturated enough into a community of practice so that the various epistemic elements (ways of knowing, thinking, and being) within that community are connected enough to be stable when that community setting is not present. When this happens, when the learning is powerful enough to become a part of one's identity, players carry this learning outside of the gaming community into the real world. McGonigal (2011) cites multiple examples of games that changed people's habits of mind and thus real-world habits:

- "I really mean it when I say *WWO* [*World Without Oil*] changed my life. I really have been using my cloth bags at the stores, walking more/driving less, turning off lights, and, yes, recycling. My friends, family and co-workers have all noticed the difference. In all seriousness, this entire thing has made me a different person" (p. 310)
- "As a result, at the end of the game [a dispatcher at a General Motors plant] decided to go back to school in real life to prepare for a new career in a post-oil economy" (p. 306)
- "a video game called *EVOKE* prompted people from around the globe to collaborate in coming up with solutions to problems led to a pilot program in South Africa designed to teach people how to grow their own food" (p. 338)

Will Wright, designer of *Sims* and *Spore*, claims that "most of the really bad stuff that's happening right now is the result of very short-term thinking" (McGonigal 2011, p. 301). McGonigal (2011) argues that games can be a way of changing that mindset: "We can break free of the cognitive chains of short-term isolated thinking, with games that direct our collective attention to the future and challenge us to take a global perspective" (McGonigal 2011, p. 301). One way games lengthen our range of thinking is through delayed gratification: "pleasure [from games] is an effect of submitting to the rules of the game, that pleasure delayed and constrained is pleasure enhanced" (Salen and Zimmerman 2004, p. 33). However, games also change mindsets by requiring both short-term and long-term goal-setting.

Games can also "act as a tool to help us imagine and invent the future together" (McGonigal 2011, p. 302). Indeed, the tagline for the game *World Without Oil* (*WWO*) was "the best way to change the future is to play with it first" (McGonigal 2011, p. 304). There is one more ingredient, however, in turning people into change agents, and that is hope. Jamais Cascio coined the term "super-empowered hopeful individual" or SEHI for someone who "feels not just optimistic about the future, but also *personally capabl*e of changing the world for the better" (McGonigal 2011, p. 315) thus developing an internal locus of control not just about your own life, but about the life of the planet. A mother who played *I Love Bees*, a massive multiplayer alternate reality game, with her son said to one of the game's designers:

> It is really important to me that you, and other people, understand the differences that alternate reality gaming has made in our way of thinking. It has powerfully affected our attitudes about what is possible. The game for me has been about gathering a first-hand knowledge of how a large community can function, including the role of technology. I know that large scale communities can work and be extraordinarily effective. I am not afraid of the complexities. (McGonigal 2008, p. 223)

The skills plus the knowledge plus the mindset plus the hope equal changing the world.

Choontanom and Nardi (2012) contrast game playing with traditional schooling and noticed that school is not collaborative, the student products are only read by the teacher, the students do not care about the word problems because they have no meaning in their lives, and subsequently students cannot apply the answers to a situation (p. 187). Games, on the other hand, inspire: "There are a lot of guitar and drum teachers in this country now who are seeing steady business because people started with *Guitar Hero* or *Rock Band* and then developed a taste for the real thing" (LoPiccolo et al. 2012, p. 114). As a matter of fact, "in a 2008 study of more than seven thousand *Rock Band* and *Guitar Hero* players, 67 % of nonmusicians in the group reported that they had been inspired to pick up a real instrument since they'd started playing the video game" (McGonigal 2011, p. 75). Barab et al. (2012) argue that "unless we begin to engage youth in rich situations that add meaning to disciplinary concepts—as part of the learning process—the content of schools will be perceived as a thing to be acquired and exchanged for a test score (having *exchange value*) and not as a useful tool that has direct functional value in the world or to the learner" (p. 306). However, transfer does not happen automatically: "Mayer and Johnson (2010) found significant gains on a transfer task following game play for participants in the self-explanation condition in comparison with the control condition" (Clark and Martinez-Garza 2012, p. 287). Teachers must structure curricular games in ways that prompt reflection in order for students to move tacit knowledge to explicit knowledge.

There is some evidence, however, that the curricular game itself can inspire student reflection inside and outside of classrooms:

> One teacher shared this comment with us about the Virus game: ''I was amazed at the kids' ability to problem-solve … these incredibly low kids who are generally disengaged. I had a look through the post-virus questionnaire … without exception … every single kid said that the game was fun and I know from being out in the hallways between classes that the kids were talking to each other about the game, about who is getting everyone sick and so the kids were very engaged. From that perspective I think the game was incredibly successful." Another teachers stated about the Tit-for-tat game: "But a lot of times you find them getting into what they have to do. And how often do you go into a math class and see a bunch of kids sitting around a table arguing no it's really this, no I swear, look what I did and then the other kids saying no it's this way. And they just kind of like duke it out and sort it out and it's really cool to watch."(Klopfer 2008, p. 86)

With all knowledge available at our fingertips, perhaps it is this kind of curiosity that should "become a top educational priority … Could it be that shifting our educational system toward more play-based models might be the best possible way to prepare children to thrive in the 21st century?" (Schell 2008, p. 448). This book argues that playing and creating curricular games promote not just content learning, not just skill development, and not even just habits of thinking and doing, but also a gaming stance that transforms how students see themselves, see others, and see the world. As one of my students said of his game-based teaching class: "Participation went from zero to fun … in no time. So I guess I'm thinking in 'game mode' now anyway." As you go forth with your new content knowledge, game design skills, playful habits of thinking and doing, and newfound gaming stance, I hope you have a "wonderful time of adventuring" (Loh 2007, p. 344).

> *The illiterate of the 21st century will not be those who cannot read and write, but those who cannot learn, unlearn, and relearn.*
>
> – Alvin Toffler

Appendix

Suggested Mentoring Quest Rubric

Criteria	"Wow! I mean, I think this might work." (3)	"Hmm, this might be acceptable." (2)	"I need more convincing." (1)	"Go back to the drawing board." (0)
Tailored to teacher	Teacher pushed just beyond level of tech use with appropriate scaffolding	Adjusted to teacher's level of tech use	Teacher's level of tech use identified	No mention of teacher characteristics
Tailored to content area	Interdisciplinary connections explored	Discussion capitalizes on synergy created when games and content area integrated	Discussion of how games fit or do not fit with content area	No mention of content area
Tailored to students	Discuss adaptations for potential future students including ELLs and special ed students	Range of students in particular class taken into account	Twenty-first-century learners' needs taken into account	No mention of students
Tailored to resources	Ways to capitalize on affordances and counter-constraints discussed	Affordances discussed	Constraints discussed	No mention of resources
Revision cycle	Discussion gets teacher to think of ideas about how to use playtesting to revise game on his/her own	Discussion of how feedback will be used to revise game	Discussion of how feedback will be collected	No mention of revision cycle
Techie (1 extra point)				
Post a comment on an article or blog post about game-based teaching (provide link)				
Tech Savvy (2 extra points)				
Post a description of how you used game-based teaching on a blog, listserv, or other online space that is either public or frequented by teachers (provide link)				
Tech Guru (3 extra points)				
Use of screencasting tools to share examples of your curricular game with others				

Suggested Reading: Non-Fiction

Bogost, I. (2007). *Persuasive games: The expressive power of videogames*. Cambridge, MA: MIT Press.

DeKoven, B. (2013). *Well-played game*. Cambridge, MA: MIT Press.

Fried, R. (2005). *Game of school: Why we all play it, how it hurts kids what it takes to change it*. Hoboken, NJ: Jossey-Bass.

Jenkins, H. (2009). *Confronting the challenges of a participatory culture: Media education for the 21st century*. Cambridge, MA: MIT Press.
McGonigal, J. (2011b). *Reality is broken: Why games make us better and how they can change the world*. London: Penguin Books.
Shaffer, D. W. (2005). *How computer games help children learn*. New York: Palgrave MacMillan.
Turkle, S. (1984). *The second self: Computers and the human spirit*. New York: Simon and Schuster.

References

Barab, S., Pettyjohn, P., Gresalfi, M., & Solomou, M. (2012). Game-based curricula, personal engagement, and the *Modern Prometheus* design project. In C. Steinkuehler, K. Squire, & S. Barab (Eds.), *Games, learning, and society: Learning and meaning in the digital age* (pp. 306–326). New York: Cambridge University Press.
Bransford, J., Brown, A., & Cocking, R. (2000). *How people learn: Brain, mind, experience, and school*. Washington, DC: National Academies Press.
Chatham, R. E. (2011). After the revolution. In S. Tobias & J. D. Fletcher (Eds.), *Computer games and instruction* (pp. 73–99). Charlotte, NC: Information Age Publishers.
Choontanom, T., & Nardi, B. (2012). Theorycrafting: The art and science of using numbers to interpret the world. In C. Steinkuehler, K. Squire, & S. Barab (Eds.), *Games, learning, and society: Learning and meaning in the digital age* (pp. 185–209). New York: Cambridge University Press.
Clark, D., & Martinez-Garza, M. (2012). Prediction and explanation as design mechanics in conceptually integrated digital games to help players articulate the tacit understandings they build through game play. In C. Steinkuehler, K. Squire, & S. Barab (Eds.), *Games, learning, and society: Learning and meaning in the digital age* (pp. 279–305). New York: Cambridge University Press.
De Freitas, S., & Maharg, P. (2011). *Digital games and learning*. London: Continuum.
Doidge, N. (2007). *The brain that changes itself: Stories of personal triumph from the frontiers of brain science*. New York: Penguin Books.
Fullerton, T., Swain, C., & Hoffman, S. (2004). *Game design workshop: Designing, prototyping, and playtesting games*. San Francisco, CA: CMP Books.
Gee, J. P. (2007). *Good videogames + good learning: Collected essays on videogames, learning, and literacy*. New York: Peter Lang.
Gee, J. P. (2008). Video games, learning, and 'content'. In C. T. Miller (Ed.), *Games: Purpose and potential in education* (pp. 43–53). New York: Springer.
Gee, J. P. (2012). Foreword. In C. Steinkuehler, K. Squire, & S. Barab (Eds.), *Games, learning, and society: Learning and meaning in the digital age* (pp. xvii–xx). New York: Cambridge University Press.
Klopfer, E. (2008). *Augmented learning: Research and design of mobile educational games*. Cambridge, MA: MIT Press.
Loh, C. S. (2007). Designing online games assessment as 'information trails'. In D. Gibson, C. Aldrich, & M. Prensky (Eds.), *Games and simulations in online learning: Research and development frameworks* (pp. 323–348). Hershey, PA: Information Science Publishing.
LoPiccolo, G., Squire, K., & Chu, S. (2012). Interview with Harmonix. In C. Steinkuehler, K. Squire, & S. Barab (Eds.), *Games, learning, and society: Learning and meaning in the digital age* (pp. 108–120). New York: Cambridge University Press.
McGonigal, J. (2011). *Reality is broken: Why games make us better and how they can change the world*. London: Penguin Books.
McGonigal, J. (2008). Why I love bees. In K. Salen (Ed.), *The ecology of games: Connecting youth, games, and learning* (pp. 199–227). Cambridge, MA: MIT Press.

Poundstone, W. (2006). Game theory. In K. Salen & E. Zimmerman (Eds.), *The game designer reader: A rules of play anthology* (pp. 382–408). Cambridge, MA: MIT Press.

Salen, K., & Zimmerman, E. (2004). *Rules of play: Game design fundamentals*. Cambridge, MA: MIT Press.

Schell, J. (2008). *The art of game design: A book of lenses*. Burlington, MA: Morgan Kaufmann.

Shaffer, D. W. (2012). Models of situated action: Computer games and the problem of transfer. In C. Steinkuehler, K. Squire, & S. Barab (Eds.), *Games, learning, and society: Learning and meaning in the digital age* (pp. 403–431). New York: Cambridge University Press.

Squire, K. (2008). Open-ended video games. In K. Salen (Ed.), *The ecology of games: Connecting youth, games, and learning* (pp. 167–198). Cambridge, MA: MIT Press.

Squire, K. (2011). *Video games and learning: Teaching and participatory culture in the digital age*. New York: Teachers College Press.

Squire, K. (2012). Designed cultures. In C. Steinkuehler, K. Squire, & S. Barab (Eds.), *Games, learning, and society: Learning and meaning in the digital age* (pp. 3–31). New York: Cambridge University Press.

Stavenga de Jong, J. A., Wierstra, R. F. A., & Hermanussen, J. (2006). An exploration of the relationship between academic and experiential learning approaches in vocational education. *British Journal of Educational Psychology, 76*(1), 155–169.

Tobias, S., Fletcher, J. D., Dai, D., & Wind, A. (2011). Review of research on computer games. In S. Tobias & J. D. Fletcher (Eds.), *Computer games and instruction* (pp. 127–221). Charlotte, NC: Information Age Publishers.

Fiction

Card, O. S. (1985). *Ender's game*. New York: Tor Books. In the novel *Ender's Game*, the main character is led to believe that he is playing a video game as practice for real warfare when, in fact, he is actually orchestrating his side's spaceships. Because he believes he is playing a game (although it is debatable whether or not he is completely duped) as practice and not the real thing, he is willing to take a huge risk, one that pays off in the end.

Appendix
A More In-depth Look at Systems Thinking

It's endlessly engrossing to take in the world as a series of events, and constantly surprising, because that way of seeing the world has almost no predictive or explanatory value.

–Donella Meadows, author of *Thinking in Systems*

Emergent properties: Emergent properties are traits that develop in a system over time (e.g., team spirit, kids getting antsy on a long trip, etc.) (examples from Sweeney 2001, p. 25). This can lead to unintended consequences, i.e., fixes that fail. Temporary fixes can ameliorate the problem in the short-term but have long-term consequences that can end up exacerbating the problem because the emergent properties have a negative effect. For example, caffeine stimulates you, but too much caffeine keeps you up at night. As a result, you do not get enough sleep, so then you end up even more tired (example from Sweeney 2001, p. 30). There are numerous other examples of fixes that fail: pesticides that kill off insects that were eating/controlling another insect species that is even more destructive or that also kill off the predators of the targeted insect allowing insect to flourish; the daycare center that started charging for late picker-uppers but charged too low so then people felt like it was okay to pick up late because they were paying for daycare workers' time and the number of late picker-uppers increased; Georgetown (in Washington, DC) did not want a subway stop because they thought it would bring more traffic, and because there is no subway stop, they now have more traffic and so forth.

Limits to success: In some cases, you can achieve only so much success until you reach a plateau, i.e., a "limit to success." For example, when you post on a social media site like Facebook, people respond; you get a rush of dopamine so you post more to increase that rush, and more people respond, but there is only so much time and energy people can devote to Facebook posting, so eventually that reinforcing feedback loop tapers off.

Drift to low performance: On the other hand, a reinforcing feedback loop can lead to a "drift to low performance." A frog will jump out of hot water but will stay in cold water that is slowly heated up. Initially, there is little discrepancy between the perceived state and the desired state. As the perceived state declines or in the frog's case slowly heats up, so does the desired state. As such, less corrective action is taken: "If this loop is allowed to run unchecked, it can lead to a continuous degradation in the

J.J. Kellinger, *A Guide to Designing Curricular Games*,
Advances in Game-Based Learning, DOI 10.1007/978-3-319-42393-7

system's performance" (Meadows 2008, p. 122). George Bush, Jr. (2000) captured how this occurs in education in his phrase "the soft bigotry of low expectations."

Tragedy of the commons: Sometimes "tragedy of the commons" occurs where everyone decides to do the same thing, overcrowding the situation (e.g., rush hour traffic). In other words, everyone rushes to use a resource that erodes when overused. The rate at which people use that stock is too fast to cause feedback. This long delay in feedback leads to the need for regulation. Parking meters regulate parking in densely populated areas because otherwise, people will park indefinitely and there will be little to no flow due to a lack of open parking spaces (example from Meadows 2008). In the case of rush hour traffic, we see this with high-occupancy vehicle (HOV) lanes to encourage carpooling. However, as Meadows (2008) points out, "If company managers, city governments, the human population do not choose and enforce their own limits to keep growth within the capacity of the supporting environment, then the environment will choose and enforce limits" (p. 103).

Overcompensation: On the other hand, if there is not enough of a time delay, overcompensation can occur, which can lead to large oscillations. For example, when my shower is too cold, I make it too hot, then too cold, and so forth (from Sweeney 2001, p. 35). Instead, I need to wait longer to lengthen the delay to see if my fix worked.[1] This is a common problem in education that Patrick Welsh (2013) points out in his *Washington Post* article, "Four decades of failed school reform" as each reform is introduced, and, when it does not magically solve the problem immediately, it is jettisoned for yet another school reform. How long or short a delay has major implications for the behaviors of a system because "stocks generally change slowly, even when flows into or out of them change suddenly. Therefore stocks act as delays or buffers or shock absorbers in systems… The time lags imposed by stocks allow room to maneuver, to experiment, and to revise policies that aren't working [but] don't expect things to happen faster than they can happen…don't give up too soon" (Meadows 2008, p. 23).[2] The stock is changing as corrective feedback is being taken into account so you have to anticipate the rate of change during the time delay of restocking: "The information delivered by a feedback loop—even nonphysical feedback—can only affect future behavior; it can't deliver a signal fast enough to correct behavior that drove the current feedback" (Meadows 2008, p. 39). Therefore, "A delay in a feedback process is critical relative to rates of change in the stocks that the feedback loop is trying to control" (Meadows 2008, p. 152). Some people think setting the thermostat slightly higher than the desired temperature will cause the room temperature to change faster; however, what it does do is take into account that when that desired temperature is achieved, there is still outflow that needs to be accounted for. The phrase "spinning my wheels" captures this sense of feedback loops that go nowhere.

---

[1] I can also shorten the amount of response time by taking a shower on the first floor rather than on the third floor so that I am closer to the water heater.

[2] According to Meadows (2008), "The time it takes for an exponentially growing stock to double in size, the 'doubling time,' equals approximately 70 divided by the growth rate (expressed as a percentage)" (p. 33).

Taking the long view: Kevin Jennings, a noted gay activist, explains that if you can understand how people advocating for and against gay-straight alliances as having the same motivations—that of ensuring student safety—that gives you common ground to move the conversation forward. He depicts this by drawing two icebergs and showing the overlap as that of concern for student safety. Taking the long view allows people to see "long-term behavior" which "provides clues to the underlying system structure. And structure is the key to understanding not just *what* is happening, but *why*" (Meadows 2008, p. 89). What Kevin Jennings knew is that even when surface features differ, in his case oppose each other, the underlying structure (system that leads to behaviors) can be the same:

> A production system with factories and shipments and economic flows doesn't look much like a population system with babies being born and people aging and having more babies and dying. But from a systems point of view these systems, so dissimilar in many ways, have one important thing in common: their feedback-loop structures. Both have a stock governed by a reinforcing growth loop and a balancing death loop. Both also have an aging process. Steel mills and lathes and turbines get older and die just as people do... systems with similar feedback structures produce similar dynamic behaviors, even if the outward appearance of these systems is completely dissimilar. (Meadows 2008, pp. 50–51)

The similarities in the above example derive from the axiom that "no physical system can grow forever in a finite environment" (Meadows 2008, p. 59). Because of this, "The higher and faster you grow, the farther and faster you fall, when you're building up a capital stock dependent on a nonrenewable resource" (Meadows 2008, p. 63). The example she uses to demonstrate this is our reliance on the nonrenewable resource of oil, and she reminds readers that renewable resources can become nonrenewable "if they are extracted faster than they regenerate, they may eventually be driven below a critical threshold and become, for all practical purposes, nonrenewable" (Meadows 2008, p. 71). It is important to take stock of your stock as well as the inflows and outflows of that stock. As Frederick Pohl stated, "A good science fiction story should be able to *predict* not the automobile but the *traffic jam*."

Paradigm shift: A paradigm is a belief system. Sometimes belief systems contradict each other. For example, Native Americans viewed land as communal, and European invaders did not. Often in a culture, the highest structures indicate the strongest paradigms in that culture. For example, steeples on churches used to be the highest structures in town, signifying the prominence of the religious beliefs. Now, it tends to be skyscrapers as we revere materialism and wealth. According to Meadows (2008), in order to change someone's paradigm:

> You keep pointing at the anomalies and failures in the old paradigm. You keep speaking and acting, loudly and with assurance, from the new one. You insert people with the new paradigm in places of public visibility and power. You don't waste time with reactionaries; rather, you work with active change agents and with the vast middle ground of people who are open-minded. (p. 164)

I have seen this in my lifetime with regard to gay rights. When I first moved to New England, I volunteered for a gay rights group on one of the coldest days of the year passing out Valentines with statements about same-sex marriage. I remember thinking that there was no chance of marriage equality, but I did it anyway. I do not know if those Valentines caused anyone to shift their paradigm, but certainly, the more gay people who came out to family members, friends, and coworkers, the more the messages of "homosexuality as deviancy" were challenged. This cognitive dissonance has changed so many people's minds that when I first came out, gay people would often donate to causes anonymously so they would not be found out. Now, there have been cases of people donating to antigay causes anonymously to avoid being labeled as bigots. This is because "Information is power." Meadows (2008) provides an example of a law that forced companies to release data about their emissions but no fines or penalties. When newspapers started listing the biggest offenders, "within two years chemical emissions nationwide … had decreased by 40 percent" (p. 173).

Making conclusions: Meadows (2008) advises, though, that "before you disturb the system in any way, watch how it behaves" (p. 170) in order to see what varies together, what varies inversely, and what varies independently. She says to "start[] with the history of several variables plotted together [over time] begins to suggest not only what elements are in the system, but how they might be interconnected" (Meadows 2008, p. 171) and suggests asking questions like: "How did we get here? What other behavior modes are possible? If we don't change direction, where are we going to end up? … What's working well here?" (Meadows 2008, p. 171). She says, "The trick, as with all the behavioral possibilities of complex systems, is to recognize what structures contain which latent behaviors, and what conditions release those behaviors—and, where possible, to arrange the structures and conditions to reduce the probability of destructive behaviors and to encourage the possibility of beneficial ones" (Meadows 2008, p. 72). In other words, observe how a system behaves in order to discover the leverage points within that system. Small changes made to those leverage points can lead to very big changes.

We see only what we can talk about.

–Fred Kofman, author of *Conscious Business*

References

Meadows, D. (2008) *Thinking in systems: A primer*. White River Junction, VT: Chelsea Green Publishing.

Sweeney, L. B. (2001). *When a butterfly sneezes: A guide for helping kids explore interconnections in our world through favorite stories*. Waltham, MA: Pegasus Communications.

Welsh, P. (2013, September 27). Four decades of failed school reform. *Washington Post*. Retrieved from http://www.washingtonpost.com/opinions/four-decades-of-failed-school-reform/2013/09/27/dc9f2f34-2561-11e3-b75d-5b7f66349852_story.html

References

Adcock, A., Watson, G., Morrison, G., & Belfore, L. (2010). Effective knowledge development in game-based learning environments: Considering research in cognitive processes and simulation design. In R. Van Eck (Ed.), *Gaming and cognition: Theories and practice from the learning sciences* (pp. 152–168). Hershey, PA: Information Science Reference.

Akilli, G. (2007). Games and simulations: A new approach in education? In D. Gibson, C. Aldrich, & M. Prensky (Eds.), *Games and simulations in online learning: Research and development frameworks* (pp. 1–20). Hershey, PA: Information Science Publishing.

Aldrich, C. (2009a). *Complete guide to simulations and serious games: How the most valuable content will be created in the age beyond Gutenberg to Google*. Hoboken, NJ: Pfeiffer.

Aldrich, C. (2009b). *Learning online with games, simulations, and virtual worlds: Strategies for online instruction*. Hoboken, NJ: Jossey-Bass.

Amtzis, A. (2014, February 4). Personal communication.

Anderson, B. (2010). MMORPGs in support of learning: current trends and future uses. In R. Van Eck (Ed.), *Gaming and cognition: Theories and practice from the learning sciences* (pp. 55–80). Hershey, PA: Information Science Reference.

Annetta, L. A. (2008). Video games in education: Why they should be used and how they are being used. *Theory Into Practice, 47*(3), 229–239.

Annetta, L. A., Minogue, J., Holms, S. Y., & Cheng, M. (2009). Investigating the impact of video games on high school students' engagement and learning about genetics. *Computers and Education, 53*(1), 74–85.

Annetta, L. A., Murray, M. R., Laird, S. G., Bohr, S. C., & Park, J. C. (2006). Serious games: Incorporating video games in the classroom. *Educause, 29*(3), 16–22.

Anthes, E. (2009, October 12). How video games are good for the brain. *Boston Globe*, p. G6.

Baker, E., & Delacruz, G. (2008). Framework for the assessment of learning games. In H. O'Neil & R. Perez (Eds.), *Computer games and team and individual learning* (pp. 21–37). Amsterdam, The Netherlands: Elsevier.

Bandura, A. (1997). *Self-efficacy: The exercise of control*. New York: W.H. Freeman.

Barab, S. (2012). Introduction to Section III. In C. Steinkuehler, K. Squire, & S. Barab (Eds.), *Games, learning, and society: Learning and meaning in the digital age* (pp. 271–278). New York: Cambridge University Press.

Barab, S., Pettyjohn, P., Gresalfi, M., & Solomou, M. (2012). Game-based curricula, personal engagement, and the Modern Prometheus design project. In C. Steinkuehler, K. Squire, & S. Barab (Eds.), *Games, learning, and society: Learning and meaning in the digital age* (pp. 306–326). New York: Cambridge University Press.

J.J. Kellinger, *A Guide to Designing Curricular Games*,
Advances in Game-Based Learning, DOI 10.1007/978-3-319-42393-7

Barker, J. (2013). How I turned my classroom into a "living video game"—And saw achievement soar. *eSchoolNews*. Retrieved from http://www.eschoolnews.com/2013/03/12/how-i-turned-my-classroom-into-a-living-video-game-and-saw-achievement-soar/

Barlet, M., & Spohn, S. (2012). *Includification: A practical guide to game accessibility*. Charles Town, WV: Ablegamers Foundation.

Barrett, K., & Johnson, W. (2010). Developing serious games for learning language-in-culture. In R. Van Eck (Ed.), *Gaming and cognition: Theories and practice from the learning sciences* (pp. 281–311). Hershey, PA: Information Science Reference.

Barseghian, T. (2013). Creating classrooms we need: 8 ways into inquiry learning. *MindShift/KQED*. Retrieved from http://blogs.kqed.org/mindshift/2013/03/creating-classrooms-we-need-8-ways-into-inquiry-learning/

Bartle, R. (1996/2006). Hearts, clubs, diamonds, spades: Players who suite MUDs. In K. Salen & E. Zimmerman (Eds.), *The game designer reader: A rules of play anthology* (pp. 754–787). Cambridge, MA: MIT Press.

Barton, K., & McKellar, P. (2011). From master to games-master: Managing disequilibrium and scaffolding in simulation-based learning. In S. de Freitas & P. Maharg (Eds.), *Digital games and learning* (pp. 226–251). London: Continuum.

Beck, J. C., & Wade, M. (2004). *Got game: How the gamer generation is reshaping business forever*. Cambridge, MA: Harvard Business Press.

Becker, K. (2008). Video game pedagogy; Good games = good pedagogy. In C. T. Miller (Ed.), *Games: Purpose and potential in education* (pp. 73–125). New York: Springer.

Becker, K. (2010). Distinctions between games and learning: A review of current literature on games in education. In R. Van Eck (Ed.), *Gaming and cognition: Theories and practice from the learning sciences* (pp. 22–54). Hershey, PA: Information Science Reference.

Bedwell, W., Pavlas, D., Heyne, K., Lazzara, E., & Salas, E. (2012). Towards a taxonomy linking game attributes to learning: An empirical study. *Simulation and Gaming, 43*(6), 729–760.

Birdwell, K. (1999/2006). The Cabal: Valve's design process for creating half-life. In K. Salen & E. Zimmerman (Eds.), *The game designer reader: A rules of play anthology* (pp. 212–225). Cambridge, MA: MIT Press.

Blair, K. P., Schwartz, D. L., Biswas, G., & Leelawong, K. (2007). Pedagogical agents for learning by teaching: Teachable agents. *Educational Technology, 47*(1), 56–61.

Blanchard, J. (2007, December 29). Anti-bullying program aims to teach students empathy. *Seattle Post- Intelligencer.*

Bloom, B. S. (1980). *All our children learning*. New York: McGraw-Hill.

Bogost, I. (2007). *Persuasive games: The expressive power of videogames*. Cambridge, MA: MIT Press.

Bogost, I. (2008). The rhetoric of video games. In K. Salen (Ed.), *The ecology of games: Connecting youth, games, and learning* (pp. 117–139). Cambridge, MA: MIT Press.

Botturi, L., & Loh, S. (2008). Once upon a game: Rediscovering the roots of game in education. In C. T. Miller (Ed.), *Games: Purpose and potential in education* (pp. 1–22). New York: Springer.

Bransford, J. D., Brown, A., & Cocking, R. (2000). *How people learn*. Washington, DC: National Academy Press.

Brisk, M., Horan, D., & MacDonald, E. (2008). A scaffolded approach to learning to write. In L. Stoops Verplaetse & N. Migliacci (Eds.), *Inclusive pedagogy for English language Learner: A handbook of research-informed practices* (pp. 15–32). New York: Lawrence Erlbaum Associates.

Bronfenbrenner, U. (1979). *The ecology of human development: Experiments by nature and design*. Cambridge, MA: Harvard University Press.

Brown, J. S. (2000, March/April). Growing up digital: How the web changes work, education, and the ways people learn. *Change*, pp. 10–20.

Brown, H. (2008). *Videogames and education*. Armonk, NY: M.E. Sharpe.

Bruner, J. S. (1961). The act of discovery. *Harvard Educational Review, 31*(1), 21–32.

Caillois, R. (1959/2006). The classification of games from man, play, and games. In K. Salen & E. Zimmerman (Eds.), *The game designer reader: A rules of play anthology* (pp. 129–155). Cambridge, MA: MIT Press.

Card, O. S. (1985). *Ender's game*. New York: Tor Books.

Castronova, E. (2002/2006). Virtual worlds: A first-hand account of market and society on the Cyberian Frontier. In K. Salen & E. Zimmerman (Eds.), *The game designer reader: A rules of play anthology* (pp. 814–863). Cambridge, MA: MIT Press.

Cazden, C. (1981). Performance before competence: Assistance to child discourse in the zone of proximal development. *Quarterly Newsletter of the Laboratory of Comparative Human Cognition, 3*, 5–8.

Charsky, D. (2010). Making a connection: Game genres, game characteristics, and teaching structures. In R. Van Eck (Ed.), *Gaming and cognition: Theories and practice from the learning sciences* (pp. 189–212). Hershey, PA: Information Science Reference.

Chasing the dream. (2005, August 4). *The Economist*. Retrieved November 1, 2016, from http://videogames.procon.org/view.source.php?sourceID=009370

Chatham, R. E. (2011). After the revolution. In S. Tobias & J. D. Fletcher (Eds.), *Computer games and instruction* (pp. 73–99). Charlotte, NC: Information Age Publishers.

Choontanom, T., & Nardi, B. (2012). Theorycrafting: The art and science of using numbers to interpret the world. In C. Steinkuehler, K. Squire, & S. Barab (Eds.), *Games, learning, and society: Learning and meaning in the digital age* (pp. 185–209). New York: Cambridge University Press.

Church, D. (1999/2006). Formal abstract design tools. In K. Salen & E. Zimmerman (Eds.), *The game designer reader: A rules of play anthology* (pp. 366–380). Cambridge, MA: MIT Press.

Clark, D., & Martinez-Garza, M. (2012). Prediction and explanation as design mechanics in conceptually integrated digital games to help players articulate the tacit understandings they build through game play. In C. Steinkuehler, K. Squire, & S. Barab (Eds.), *Games, learning, and society: Learning and meaning in the digital age* (pp. 279–305). New York: Cambridge University Press.

Clark, D., Tanner-Smith, E., & Killingsworth, S. (2013). *Digital games for learning: A systematic review and meta-analysis*. Menlo Park, CA: SRI International. Retrieved from http://www.sri.com/sites/default/files/brochures/digital-games-for-learning-brief.pdf

Coleridge, S. T. (1817). *Biographia Literaria*. London: Rest Fenner.

Costikyan, G. (1994/2006). I have no words and I must design. In K. Salen & E. Zimmerman (Eds.), *The game designer reader: A rules of play anthology* (pp. 192–211). Cambridge, MA: MIT Press.

Coulter, B., Klopfer, E., Sheldon, J., & Perry, J. (2012). Discovering familiar places: Learning through mobile place-based games. In C. Steinkuehler, K. Squire, & S. Barab (Eds.), *Games, learning, and society: Learning and meaning in the digital age* (pp. 327–354). New York: Cambridge University Press.

Craster, K. (1871). Centipede's dilemma. *Pinafore Poems*. Ann Arbor, MI: G. Wahr.

Crawford, C. (1982/2006). Eastern Front (1941). In K. Salen & E. Zimmerman (Eds.), *The game designer reader: A rules of play anthology* (pp. 714–724). Cambridge, MA: MIT Press.

Crockett, L., Jukes, I., & Churches, A. (2011). *Literacy is not enough: 21st century fluencies for the digital age*. Thousand Oaks, CA: Sage.

Czikszentmihalyi, M. (1990). *Flow: The psychology of optimal experience*. New York: Harper & Row.

Darling-Hammond, L. (2010). *The flat world and education: How America's commitment to equity will determine our future*. New York: Teachers College Press.

Davidson, D., & Lemarchand, R. (2012). Uncharted 2: Among Thieves—How to become a hero. In C. Steinkuehler, K. Squire, & S. Barab (Eds.), *Games, learning, and society: Learning and meaning in the digital age* (pp. 75–107). New York: Cambridge University Press.

Davis, B., Sumara, D., & Luce-Kapler, R. (2000). *Engaging minds: Learning and teaching in a complex world*. Hillsdale, NJ: Lawrence Erlbaum Associates.

De Castell, S., & Jenson, J. (2003). Serious play. *Journal of Curriculum Studies, 35*(6), 649–665.

De Freitas, S., & Maharg, P. (2011). *Digital games and learning*. London: Continuum.

DeKoven, B. (2013). *Well-played game*. Cambridge, MA: MIT Press.

Dempsey, J. V. (2010). Elemental learning and the pyramid of fidelity. In R. Van Eck (Ed.), *Gaming and cognition: Theories and practice from the learning sciences* (pp. 82–107). Hershey, PA: Information Science Reference.

Devaney, L. (2014, July 7). 5 gaming dynamics that truly engage students. *eSchoolNews*. Retrieved November 6, 2015, from http://www.eschoolnews.com/2014/07/07/gaming-engaging-students-365/

Dewey, J. (1938). *Experience and education*. New York: Collier Books.

Dexter, S. (2007). Educational theory into practice software (ETIPS). In D. Gibson, C. Aldrich, & M. Prensky (Eds.), *Games and simulations in online learning: Research and development frameworks* (pp. 223–235). Hershey, PA: Information Science Publishing.

Dickey, M. (2011). Murder on Grimm Isle. In S. de Freitas & P. Maharg (Eds.), *Digital games and learning* (pp. 129–151). London: Continuum.

Doidge, N. (2007). *The brain that changes itself: Stories of personal triumph from the frontiers of brain science*. New York: Penguin.

Driscoll, M. (2005). *Psychology of learning for instruction*. Boston: Allyn and Bacon.

Dunwell, I., de Frietas, S., & Jarvis, S. (2011). Four-dimensional considerations in serious games. In S. de Freitas & P. Maharg (Eds.), *Digital games and learning* (pp. 42–62). London: Continuum.

Dweck, C. (2007). *Mindset: The new psychology of success*. New York: Ballantine Books.

Edvinsson, B. (Ed.). (2008). Game-based learning: Teacher and student perspectives. In M. Pivec & M. Moretti (Eds.), *Game-based learning: Discover the pleasure of learning* (pp. 46–56). Lengerich, Germany: Pabst Science Publishers.

Edwards, R. (2004). System does matter. *The Forge: The Internet Home for Independent Role-Playing Games*. Retrieved January 7, 2016, from http://www.indie-rpgs.com/_articles/system_does_matter.html

Eisenkraft, A. (2003). Expanding the 5E model: A proposed 7E model emphasizes "transfer of learning" and the importance of eliciting prior understanding. *The Science Teacher, 70*, 56–59.

Erstad, O. (2008). Trajectories of remixing: Digital literacies, media production, and schooling. In C. Lankshear & M. Knobel (Eds.), *Digital literacies: Concepts, policies, and practices* (pp. 177–202). New York: Peter Lang.

Farmer, F. R., & Morningstar, C. (1990/2006). The lessons of Lucasfilm's habitat. In K. Salen & E. Zimmerman (Eds.), *The game designer reader: A rules of play anthology* (pp. 728–753). Cambridge, MA: MIT Press.

Festinger, L. (1957). *A theory of cognitive dissonance*. Stanford, CA: Stanford University Press.

Fine, G. (1983/2006). Frames and games. From shared fantasy: Role-playing games as social worlds. In K. Salen & E. Zimmerman (Eds.), *The game designer reader: A rules of play anthology* (pp. 578–601). Cambridge, MA: MIT Press.

Francis, R. (2002). *Never be sick again: Health is a choice, learn how to choose it*. Deerfield Beach, FL: Health Communications.

Friedman, T. (2007). *The world is flat: A brief history of the twenty-first century*. New York: Picador.

Fullerton, T., Swain, C., & Hoffman, S. (2004). *Game design workshop: Designing, prototyping, and playtesting games*. San Francisco, CA: CMP Books.

Games, A., & Squire, K. (2011). Searching for the fun in learning. In S. Tobias & J. D. Fletcher (Eds.), *Computer games and instruction* (pp. 17–46). Charlotte, NC: Information Age.

Gardner, H. (1983). *Frames of mind: The theory of multiple intelligences*. New York: Basic Books.

Gee, J. P. (2003). *What videogames have to teach us about learning and literacy*. New York: Palgrave Macmillan.

Gee, J. P. (2005). Learning by design: Good video games as learning machines. *E-Learning., 2*(1), 5–16.

Gee, J. P. (2007). *Good videogames + good learning: Collected essays on videogames, learning, and literacy*. New York: Peter Lang.

Gee, J. P. (Ed.). (2008a). Learning and games. In K. Salen (Ed.), *The ecology of games: Connecting youth, games, and learning* (pp. 21–40). Cambridge, MA: MIT Press.

Gee, J. P. (2008b). Video games, learning, and 'content'. In C. T. Miller (Ed.), *Games: Purpose and potential in education* (pp. 43–53). New York: Springer.

Gee, J. P. (2011a). Foreword. In K. Squire (Ed.), *Video games and learning: Teaching and participatory culture in the digital age* (pp. 9–10). New York: Teachers College Press.

Gee, J. P. (2011b). Reflections on empirical evidence on games and learning. In S. Tobias & J. D. Fletcher (Eds.), *Computer games and instruction* (pp. 223–232). Charlotte, NC: Information Age.

Gee, J. P. (2012). Foreword. In C. Steinkuehler, K. Squire, & S. Barab (Eds.), *Games, learning, and society: Learning and meaning in the digital age* (pp. xvii–xx). New York: Cambridge University Press.

Gee, J. P., & Hayes, E. (2012). Nurturing affinity spaces and game-based learning. In C. Steinkuehler, K. Squire, & S. Barab (Eds.), *Games, learning, and society: Learning and meaning in the digital age* (pp. 129–153). New York: Cambridge University Press.

Gibson, D. (2007). simSchool and the conceptual assessment framework. In D. Gibson, C. Aldrich, & M. Prensky (Eds.), *Games and simulations in online learning: Research and development frameworks* (pp. 308–322). Hershey, PA: Information Science.

Girod, G., Girod, M., & Denton, J. (2007). Lessons learned modeling "connecting teaching and learning". In D. Gibson, C. Aldrich, & M. Prensky (Eds.), *Games and simulations in online learning: Research and development frameworks* (pp. 206–222). Hershey, PA: Information Science.

Gladwell, M. (2008). *Outliers: The story of success*. Boston: Little, Brown, and Company.

Grabe, M., & Grabe, C. (2007). *Integrating technology for meaningful learning*. New York: Houghton Mifflin.

Gredler, M. (1994). *Designing and evaluating games and simulations: A process approach*. Houston, TX: Gulf.

Green, E. (2014). *Building a better teacher: How teaching works (and how to teach it to everyone)*. New York: W.W. Norton.

Green, M. E., & McNeese, M. N. (2011). Using digital games and virtual environments to enhance learning. In M. S. Khine (Ed.), *Learning to play: Exploring the future of education with video games* (pp. 79–105). New York: Peter Lang.

Greenberg, J. (2013, November 23). Kids like to learn algebra, if it comes in the right app. *Wired*. Retrieved August 7, 2015, from http://www.wired.com/2013/11/zoran-popovic/?mbid=synd_gfdn_bgfb

Greenfield, P. (2010). Video games revisited. In R. Van Eck (Ed.), *Gaming and cognition: Theories and practice from the learning sciences* (pp. 1–21). Hershey, PA: Information Science Reference.

Harel, I., & Papert, S. (1990). Software design as a learning environment. *Interactive Learning Environments, 1*(1), 1–32.

Hill, L., Brandeau, G., Truelove, E., & Lineback, K. (2014). *Collective genius: The art and practice of leading innovation*. Cambridge, MA: Harvard Business Review Press.

Hirumi, A. & Hall, R. (2011). Presenting content information and facilitating instruction: Design techniques for advancing game flow. In M. S. Khine (Ed.), *Learning to play: Exploring the future of education with video games*. (pp. 55–78). New York: Peter Lang.

Hirumi, A., & Stapleton, C. (2008). Applying pedagogy during game development to enhance game-based learning. In C. T. Miller (Ed.), *Games: Purpose and potential in education* (pp. 127–162). New York: Springer.

Hodgson, J. (2013). Developing and extending gaming pedagogy: Designing a course as game. In R. Colby, M. S. S. Johnson, & R. Shultz Colby (Eds.), *Rhetoric/composition/play through video games* (pp. 45–62). New York: Palgrave.

Holt, J. (1964). *How children fail*. Lanham, MD: Pitman.

Holt, T. (2013, April 19). The ultimate education reform: Messy learning and problem solving. *Powerful Learning Practice*. Retrieved from http://plpnetwork.com/2013/04/19/ultimate-education-reform-messy-learning-problem-solving/

Horn, M. (2013, May 16). What we can learn from a dinner controversy in the desert. *Forbes*. Retrieved from http://www.forbes.com/sites/michaelhorn/2013/05/16/what-we-can-learn-from-a-dinner-controversy-in-the-desert/

Huang, W., & Tettegah, S. (2010). Cognitive load and empathy in serious games: A conceptual framework. In R. Van Eck (Ed.), *Gaming and cognition: Theories and practice from the learning sciences* (pp. 137–150). Hershey, PA: Information Science Reference.

Huizinga, J. (1955/2006). Nature and significance of play as a cultural phenomenon from Homo Ludens: A study of the play element in culture. In K. Salen & E. Zimmerman (Eds.), *The game designer reader: A rules of play anthology* (pp. 96–120). Cambridge, MA: MIT Press.

Jackson, J. (2007). *Unmasking identities: An exploration of the lives of gay and lesbian teachers.* Lanham, MD: Lexington Books.

Jackson, J. (2009). Game-based teaching: What educators can learn from videogames. *Teaching Education, 20*(3), 291–304.

Jackson, J. (2010). Technology and teacher education: What might 21st century teacher education programs look like? In I. Saleh (Ed.), *Teaching teachers: Approaches in improving quality of education.* Hauppauge, NY: Nova Science.

Jackson, J. (2011). Game changer: How principles of videogames can transform teaching. In M. S. Khine (Ed.), *Learning to play: Exploring the future of education with video games* (pp. 107–128). New York: Peter Lang.

Jenkins, H. (2004/2006). Game design as narrative architecture from Jenkins, H. In K. Salen & E. Zimmerman (Eds.), *The game designer reader: A rules of play anthology* (pp. 670–689). Cambridge, MA: MIT Press.

Jenkins, H. (2009). *Confronting the challenges of a participatory culture: Media education for the 21st century.* Cambridge, MA: MIT Press.

Jenkins, H. (2011). Foreword. In S. de Freitas & P. Maharg (Eds.), *Digital games and learning* (pp. xxiii–xxvi). London: Continuum.

Jin, P., & Low, R. (2011). Implications of game use for explicit instruction. In S. Tobias & J. D. Fletcher (Eds.), *Computer games and instruction* (pp. 395–416). Charlotte, NC: Information Age.

Johnson, S. (2005). *Everything bad is good for you: How today's popular culture is actually making us smarter.* New York: Riverhead Books.

Johnson, S. (2012). Theme is not meaning: Who decides what a game is about? In C. Steinkuehler, K. Squire, & S. Barab (Eds.), *Games, learning, and society: Learning and meaning in the digital age* (pp. 32–39). New York: Cambridge University Press.

Johnston, P. (2004). *Choice words: How our language affects children's learning.* Portland, ME: Stenhouse.

Joseph, B. (2008). Why Johnny can't fly. In K. Salen (Ed.), *The ecology of games: Connecting youth, games, and learning* (pp. 253–266). Cambridge, MA: MIT Press.

Juul, J. (2010). *A casual revolution: Reinventing videogames and their players.* Cambridge, MA: MIT Press.

Kafai, Y. (1995). *Minds in play: Computer game design as a context for children's learning Hillsdale.* Mahwah, NJ: Lawrence Erlbaum Associates.

Kafai, Y., & Pepppler, K. (2012). Developing gaming fluencies with Scratch: Realizing game design as an artistic process. In C. Steinkuehler, K. Squire, & S. Barab (Eds.), *Games, learning, and society: Learning and meaning in the digital age* (pp. 355–380). New York: Cambridge University Press.

Kaling, M. (2011). *Is everyone hanging out without me? (and other concerns).* New York: Crown.

Kapp, K. (2012). *The gamification of learning and instruction: Game-based methods and strategies for training and education.* San Francisco, CA: Pfeiffer.

Karp, H. (2004). *Happiest toddler on the block.* New York: Bantam Books.

Kellinger, J. (2012). The Flipside: Concerns about "new literacies" paths educators might take. *Educational Forum, 76*(4), 524–536.

Kimball, M., & Smith, N. (2013, October 28). The Myth of I'm bad at math. *The Atlantic.* Retrieved from http://www.theatlantic.com/education/archive/2013/10/the-myth-of-im-bad-at-math/280914/

Kirkley, J. R., Duffy, T., Kirkley, S., & Kremer, D. (2011). Implications of constructivism for the design and use of serious games. In S. Tobias & J. D. Fletcher (Eds.), *Computer games and instruction* (pp. 371–394). Charlotte, NC: Information Age.

Klingner, J. K., Vaughn, S., Dimino, J., Schumm, J. S., & Bryant, D. (2001). *From clunk to click: Collaborative strategic reading.* Longmont, CO: Sopris West.

Klopfer, E. (2008). *Augmented learning: Research and design of mobile educational games.* Cambridge, MA: MIT Press.

Klopfer, E., Osterweil, S., & Salen, K. (2009). *Moving learning games forward: Obstacles opportunities, and openness.* Cambridge, MA: The Education Arcade at MIT.

Kolb, D. (1984). *Experiential learning: Experience as the source of learning and development*. Upper Saddle River, NJ: Prentice Hall.

Korbey, H. (2013, March 22). Teachers, students, digital games: What's the right mix? *Mind/Shift*. San Francisco: KQED. Retrieved from http://blogs.kqed.org/mindshift/2013/03/teachers-students-digital-games-whats-the-right-mix/

Koster, R. (2000/2006). Declaring the rights of players. In K. Salen & E. Zimmerman (Eds.), *The game designer reader: A rules of play anthology* (pp. 788–813). Cambridge, MA: MIT Press.

Kuchera, B. (2011, February 14). How a song from the 2005 *Civilization IV* won a 2011 Grammy. *Ars Technica*. Retrieved from http://arstechnica.com/gaming/2011/02/how-a-song-from-the-2005-civilization-iv-won-a-2011-grammy/

Kutner, L., & Olson, C. K. (2008). *Grand theft childhood: The surprising truth about violent video games*. New York: Simon and Schuster.

Laurel, B. (2001). *Utopian entrepreneur*. Cambridge: MIT Press.

Lave, J., & Wenger, E. (1991). *Situated learning: Legitimate peripheral participation*. Cambridge, MA: Cambridge University Press.

LeBlanc, M. (2004/2006). Tools for creating dramatic game dynamics. In K. Salen & E. Zimmerman (Eds.), *The game designer reader: A rules of play anthology* (pp. 438–459). Cambridge, MA: MIT Press

Lee, C. (2001). Is October brown Chinese? A cultural modeling activity system for underachieving students. *American Education Research Journal, 38*(1), 97–141.

Leemkuil, H., & de Jong, T. (2011). Instructional support in games. In S. Tobias & J. D. Fletcher (Eds.), *Computer games and instruction* (pp. 353–369). Charlotte, NC: Information Age.

Lenhart, A., Kahne, J., Middaugh, E., Magill, A. R., Evans, C., & Vitak, J. (2008). *Teens, video-games, and civics*. Washington, DC: Pew Internet and American Life Project. Retrieved from www.pewinternet.org/pdfs/PIP_Teens_Games_and_Civics_Report_FINAL.pdf

Levitt, S., & Dubner, S. (2009). *Freakonomics: A rogue economist explores the hidden side of everything*. New York: HarperCollins.

Loh, C. S. (2007). Designing online games assessment as 'information trails'. In D. Gibson, C. Aldrich, & M. Prensky (Eds.), *Games and simulations in online learning: Research and development frameworks* (pp. 323–348). Hershey, PA: Information Science.

LoPiccolo, G., Squire, K., & Chu, S. (2012). Interview with Harmonix. In C. Steinkuehler, K. Squire, & S. Barab (Eds.), *Games, learning, and society: Learning and meaning in the digital age* (pp. 108–120). New York: Cambridge University Press.

MacCullum-Stewart, E. (2011). Stealth learning in online games. In S. de Freitas & P. Maharg (Eds.), *Digital games and learning* (pp. 107–128). London: Continuum.

Macklin, C., & Sharp, J. (2012). "Freakin' hard": Game design and issue literacy. In C. Steinkuehler, K. Squire, & S. Barab (Eds.), *Games, learning, and society: Learning and meaning in the digital age* (pp. 381–402). New York: Cambridge University Press.

Macleod, H. (Ed.). 2008. Games in learning. In M. Pivec & M. Moretti (Eds.), *Game-based learning: Discover the pleasure of learning* (pp. 17–23). Lengerich, Germany: Pabst Science Publishers.

Magerko, B., Heeter, C., & Medler, B. (2010). Different strokes for different folks: Tapping into the hidden potential of serious games. In R. Van Eck (Ed.), *Gaming and cognition: Theories and practice from the learning sciences* (pp. 255–279). Hershey, PA: Information Science Reference.

Malone, T., & Lepper, M. (1987). Making learning fun: A taxonomy of intrinsic motivation. In R. Snow & M. Farr (Eds.), *Aptitude, learning, and instruction* (Conative and affective process analyses, Vol. 3). Hillsdale, NJ: Lawrence Erlbaum.

Marzano, R. (2010). Using games to enhance student achievement. *Educational Leadership, 67*(5), 71–72.

Massachusetts Business Alliance for Education. (2008). *Educating a 21st century workforce: A call for action for high school reform*. Retrieved from http://www.mbae.org/uploads/06102008230519EducatingA21stCenturyWorkforce.pdf

Mateas, M., & Stern, A. (2005/2006). Interaction and narrative from *Expressive AI*. In K. Salen & E. Zimmerman (Eds.), *The game designer reader: A rules of play anthology* (pp. 642–669). Cambridge, MA: MIT Press.
Mayer, R. (2011). Multimedia learning and games. In S. Tobias & J. D. Fletcher (Eds.), *Computer games and instruction* (pp. 281–303). Charlotte, NC: Information Age.
Mayo, M. (2009). Video games: A route to large scale STEM education? *Science, 323*, 79–82.
McGonigal, J. (2008). Why *I Love Bees*. In K. Salen (Ed.), *The ecology of games: Connecting youth, games, and learning* (pp. 199–227). Cambridge, MA: MIT Press.
McGonigal, J. (2011). *Reality is broken: Why games make us better and how they can change the world*. London: Penguin.
McIntyre, A. (1997). *Making meaning of whiteness: Exploring the racial identity of white teachers*. Albany: State University of New York Press.
Meadows, D. (2008). *Thinking in systems: A primer*. White River Junction, VT: Chelsea Green.
Mecoli, S. (2013, March). Game playing=optimized learning? *Technology in the classroom*. Newsletter for Quincy High School, p. 4.
Morris, C. (2013, May 29). *The one Monopoly rule you shouldn't ignore*. Retrieved from http://games.yahoo.com/blogs/plugged-in/one-monopoly-rule-shouldn-t-ignore-190749670.html
Munro, A. (2008). Software support of instruction in game contexts. In H. O'Neil & R. Perez (Eds.), *Computer games and team and individual learning* (pp. 55–74). Amsterdam, The Netherlands: Elsevier.
Murray, J. (1997). *Hamlet on the holodeck: The future of narrative in cyberspace*. Cambridge, MA: MIT Press.
Nemetz, D. (2014, June 24). Whoopi Goldberg explains why she wanted to be on Star Trek. *Yahoo TV*. Retrieved from https://tv.yahoo.com/blogs/tv-news/exclusive-video-whoopi-goldberg-star-trek-213710247.html
Norman, D. (2002). *The design of everyday things*. New York: Basic Books.
Numeroff, L. (1985). *If you give a mouse a cookie*. New York: HarperCollins.
Okita, S. Y., & Schwartz, D. L. (2013). Learning by teaching human pupils and teachable agents: The importance of recursive feedback. *Journal of the Learning Sciences, 22*(3), 375–412.
Olson, C. B. (2007). *Reading/writing connection*. Upper Saddle River, NJ: Pearson.
Osterweil, S., & Klopfer, E. (2011). Are games all child's play? In S. de Freitas & P. Maharg (Eds.), *Digital games and learning* (pp. 152–171). London: Continuum.
Papert, S. (1980). *Mindstorms: Children, computers, and powerful ideas*. New York: Basic Books.
Paul, A. M. (2012, March 17). Your brain on fiction. *New York Times*, p. SR6.
Pelletier, C., & Oliver, M. (2006). Learning to play in digital games. *Learning, Media, and Technology, 31*(4), 329–342.
Pink, D. (2011). *Drive: The surprising truth about what motivates us*. New York: Penguin.
Pittman, C. (June 16, 2013). Indian River lagoon mystery ailment kills manatees, dolphins, pelicans. *Tampa Bay Times*. Retrieved from http://www.tampabay.com/news/environment/die-off-in-indian-river-lagoon-killing-dolphins-manatees/2127017
Plotnikoff, D. (2013). Before reading or watching videos, students should experiment first. *KQED/Mindshift*. Retrieved from http://blogs.kqed.org/mindshift/2013/07/before-reading-or-watching-videos-students-should-first-experiment/
Pooley, E. (1999, May 10). Portrait of a deadly bond. *Time*, 26–32.
Poundstone, W. (2006). Game theory. In K. Salen & E. Zimmerman (Eds.), *The game designer reader: A rules of play anthology* (pp. 382–408). Cambridge, MA: MIT Press.
Powers, R., & Kirkpatrick, K. (2013). Playing with conflict: Teaching conflict resolution through simulations and games. *Simulations and Gaming, 44*(1), 51–71.
Prabhu, M. (2009). Senate bill supports 21st-century skills. *eSchoolNews*. Retrieved November 6, 2015, from http://www.eschoolnews.com/news/top-news/index.cfm?i=58949
Prensky, M. (2001a). *Digital game-based Learning*. New York: McGraw Hill.
Prensky, M. (2001b). Digital natives, digital immigrants. *On the Horizon, 9*(5).
Prensky, M. (2002). The motivation of game play, or the REAL 21st century learning revolution. *On the Horizon, 10*(1), 5–11.

Prensky, M. (2011). Comments on research comparing games to other instructional methods. In S. Tobias & J. D. Fletcher (Eds.), *Computer games and instruction* (pp. 251–280). Charlotte, NC: Information Age.

Putnam, R. T., & Borko, H. (2000). What do new views of knowledge and thinking have to say about research on teacher learning? *Educational Researcher, 29*(1), 4–15.

Rabin, S. (2009). *Introduction to game development* (2nd ed.). Herndon, VA: Cengage Learning.

Rabone, D. (2013). How 'game mechanics" can revitalize education. *eSchoolNews*. Retrieved from http://www.eschoolnews.com/2013/02/12/how-game-mechanics-can-revitalize-education/3/

Raines, C. (2002). Managing millennials. *Generations at Work*. Retrieved November 6, 205, from http://www.generationsatwork.com/articles/millenials.htm

Ravitch, D. (2013). *Reign of error: The hoax of the privatization movement and the danger to America's public schools*. New York: Knopf Doubleday Publishing Group.

Reese, D. (2010). Introducing Flowometer: A CyGaMEs assessment suite tool. In R. Van Eck (Ed.), *Gaming and cognition: Theories and practice from the learning sciences* (pp. 227–254). Hershey, PA: Information Science Reference.

Resnick, L., & Hall, M. (2005). *Principles of learning for effort-based education*. Pittsburgh: University of Pittsburgh, Institute for Learning, Learning Research & Development Center.

Richter, J., & Livingstone, D. (2011). Multi-user games and learning. In S. Tobias & J. D. Fletcher (Eds.), *Computer games and instruction* (pp. 101–124). Charlotte, NC: Information Age.

Rieber, L. P. (1996). Seriously considering play: Designing interactive learning environments based on the blending of microworlds, simulations, and games. *Educational Technology Research & Development, 44*(2), 43–58.

Rieber, L., Barbour, M., Thomas, G., & Rauscher, D. (2008). Learning by designing homemade powerpoint games. In C. T. Miller (Ed.), *Games: Purpose and potential in education* (pp. 23–43). New York: Springer.

Robinett, W. (1984/2006). Adventure as a video game: Adventure for the Atari 2600 from Inventing the Adventure Game. In K. Salen & E. Zimmerman (Eds.), *The game designer reader: A rules of play anthology* (pp. 690–713). Cambridge, MA: MIT Press.

Rowe, M. (1986). Wait time: Slowing down may be speeding up. *Journal of Teacher Education, 37*(43), 43–50. Retrieved from http://www.sagepub.com/eis2study/articles/Budd%20Rowe.pdf

Rushkoff, D. (2011). *Program or be programmed: Ten commands for a digital age*. Berkeley, CA: Soft Skull Press.

Salen, K. (Ed.) (2008). Toward an ecology of gaming. In K. Salen (Ed.) *The ecology of games: Connecting youth, games, and learning* (pp. 1-17). Cambridge, MA: MIT Press.

Salen, K., Torres, R., Wolozin, L., Rufo-Tepper, R., & Shapiro, A. (2011). *Quest to learn: Developing the school for digital kids*. Cambridge, MA: MIT Press.

Salen, K., & Zimmerman, E. (2004). *Rules of play: Game design fundamentals*. Cambridge, MA: MIT Press.

Sandford, R., Ulicsak, M., Facer, K., & Rudd, T. (2006). Teaching with games: Using commercial off-the-shelf computer games in formal education. *Futurelab*. Retrieved November 6, 2015, from https://www.nfer.ac.uk/publications/FUTL49/FUTL49.pdf

Schaffhauser, D. (2013). Can gaming improve teaching and learning? *T.H.E Journal, 40*(8), 26–33.

Schell, J. (2008). *The art of game design: A book of lenses*. Burlington, MA: Morgan Kaufmann.

Schneider, B., Wallace, J., Blikstein, P., & Pea, R. (2013). Preparing for future learning with a tangible user interface: The case of neuroscience. *IEEE's Transactions on Learning Technologies, 6*(2), 117–129.

Schrier, K. (2007). Reliving history with 'reliving the revolution': Designing augmented reality games to teach the critical thinking of history. In D. Gibson, C. Aldrich, & M. Prensky (Eds.), *Games and simulations in online learning: Research and development frameworks* (pp. 250–269). Hershey, PA: Information Science.

Schrum, L., & Levin, B. (2009). *Leading 21st century schools: Harnessing technology for engagement and achievement*. Thousand Oaks, CA: Corwin Press.

Seitles, M. (1996). The perpetuation of residential racial segregation in America: Historical discrimination, modern forms of exclusion, and inclusionary remedies. *Journal of Land Use and Environmental Law*. Retrieved from http://archive.law.fsu.edu/journals/landuse/Vol141/seit.htm?referer=www.clickfind.com.au

Selfe, C., & Hawisher, G. (2007). *Gaming lives in the twenty-first century: Literate connections*. Gordonsville, VA: Palgrave Macmillan.

Shaffer, D. W. (2006). *How computer games help children learn*. New York: Palgrave MacMillan.

Shaffer, D. W. (2012). Models of situated action: Computer games and the problem of transfer. In C. Steinkuehler, K. Squire, & S. Barab (Eds.), *Games, learning, and society: Learning and meaning in the digital age* (pp. 403–431). New York: Cambridge University Press.

Shapiro, J. (2013, July 9). Are kids who make their own video games better prepared for the digital future? *Forbes*. Retrieved from http://www.forbes.com/sites/jordanshapiro/2013/07/09/are-kids-who-make-their-own-video-games-better-prepared-for-the-digital-future/

Sheldon, L. (2011). *The Multi-player classroom: Designing coursework as a game*. Herndon, VA: Cengage Learning.

Shulman, L. S. (1986). Those who understand: Knowledge growth in teaching. *Educational Researcher, 15*(2), 4–31.

Shulock, N. (2010). Beyond the rhetoric: Improving college readiness through coherent state policy. The National Center for Public Policy and Higher Education. Retrieved from http://www.highereducation.org/reports/college_readiness/CollegeReadiness.pdf

Shute, V. (2011). Stealth assessment in computer-based games to support learning. In S. Tobias & J. D. Fletcher (Eds.), *Computer games and instruction* (pp. 503–524). Charlotte, NC: Information Age.

Simmons, A. (2001). *The story factor: Inspiration, influence, and persuasion through the art of storytelling*. New York: Basic Books.

Skinner, B. F. (1953). *Science and human behavior*. New York: The Free Press.

Squire, K. (2008). Video-game literacy: A literacy of expertise. In J. Coiro, D. Leu, C. Lankshear, & M. Knobel (Eds.), *Handbook of research on new literacies* (pp. 635–670). New York: Taylor & Francis.

Squire, K. (2011). *Video games and learning: Teaching and participatory culture in the digital age*. New York, NY: Teachers College Press.

Squire, K. (2012). Designed cultures. In C. Steinkuehler, K. Squire, & S. Barab (Eds.), *Games, learning, and society: Learning and meaning in the digital age* (pp. 3–31). New York: Cambridge University Press.

Staalduinen, J. P., & de Freitas, S. (2011). A game-based learning framework: Linking game design and learning outcomes. In M. S. Khine (Ed.), *Learning to play: Exploring the future of education with video games* (pp. 29–54). New York: Peter Lang.

Stansbury, M. (2008). Students want more use of gaming technology. *eSchool News, 11*(4). Retrieved from www.eschoolnews.com/news/top-news/index.cfm?i=53443

Stavenga de Jong, J. A., Wierstra, R. F. A., & Hermanussen, J. (2006). An exploration of the relationship between academic and experiential learning approaches in vocational education. *British Journal of Educational Psychology, 76*(1), 155–169.

Steinkuehler, C., & Oh, Y. (2012). Apprenticeship in massively multiplayer online games. In C. Steinkuehler, K. Squire, & S. Barab (Eds.), *Games, learning, and society: Learning and meaning in the digital age* (pp. 154–184). New York: Cambridge University Press.

Stevens, R., Satwicz, T., & McCarthy, L. (2008). In-game, in-room, in-world: Reconnecting video game play to the rest of the kids' lives. In K. Salen (Ed.), *The ecology of games: Connecting youth, games, and learning* (pp. 41–66). Cambridge, MA: MIT Press.

Stillwell, R., & Sable, J. (2013). *Public school graduates and dropouts from the common core of data: School year 2009–10*. U.S. Dept. of Education. Retrieved from http://nces.ed.gov/pubs2013/2013309rev.pdf

Strauss, V. (2014, January 18). Everything you need to know about common core—Ravitch. The Answer Sheet Blog, *Washington Post*. Retrieved from http://www.washingtonpost.com/blogs/answer-sheet/wp/2014/01/18/everything-you-need-to-know-about-common-core-ravitch/

Suits, B. (1978/2006). Construction of a definition from the grasshopper games, life, and Utopia. In K. Salen & E. Zimmerman (Eds.), *The game designer reader: A rules of play anthology* (pp. 172–191). Cambridge, MA: MIT Press.

Sutter, J. (2012). The school where learning is a game. *Gaming reality*. Atlanta, GA: CNN. Retrieved from http://www.cnn.com/interactive/2012/08/tech/gaming.series/teachers.html

Sutton-Smith, B. (1997/2006). Play and ambiguity from the ambiguity of play. In K. Salen & E. Zimmerman (Eds.), *The game designer reader: A rules of play anthology* (pp. 296–313). Cambridge, MA: MIT Press.

Swan, R. (2010). Feedforward as an essential active principle of engagement in computer games. In R. Van Eck (Ed.), *Gaming and cognition: Theories and practice from the learning sciences* (pp. 108–136). Hershey, PA: Information Science Reference.

Sweeney, L. B. (2001). *When a butterfly sneezes: A guide for helping kids explore interconnections in our world through favorite stories*. Waltham, MA: Pegasus Communications.

Szalavitz, M. (2012, October 2). Why the teen brain is drawn to risk. *Time Magazine*. Retrieved from http://healthland.time.com/2012/10/02/why-the-teen-brain-is-drawn-to-risk/

Tennyson, R., & Jorczak, R. (2008). A conceptual framework for the empirical study of instructional games. In H. O'Neil & R. Perez (Eds.), *Computer games and team and individual learning* (pp. 3–20). Amsterdam, The Netherlands: Elsevier.

Tobias, S., & Fletcher, J. D. (2011). Introduction. In S. Tobias & J. D. Fletcher (Eds.), *Computer games and instruction* (pp. 3–16). Charlotte, NC: Information Age.

Tobias, S., Fletcher, J. D., Dai, D., & Wind, A. (2011). Review of research on computer games. In S. Tobias & J. D. Fletcher (Eds.), *Computer games and instruction* (pp. 127–221). Charlotte, NC: Information Age.

Travis, R., & Young, M. (2011). Operation KTHMA-Reign of the Demiurge: Game worlds, greek history, and situated learning. In Myint Swe Khine (Ed.), *Learning to play: Exploring the future of education with video games* (pp. 153–166). New York: Peter Lang.

Turkle, S. (1984). *The second self: Computers and the human spirit*. New York: Simon and Schuster.

Van Eck, R. (2007). Building artificially intelligent learning games. In D. Gibson, C. Aldrich, & M. Prensky (Eds.), *Games and simulations in online learning: Research and development frameworks* (pp. 271–307). Hershey, PA: Information Science.

Varlas, L. (2011). Can social media and school policies be friends. *ASCD, 17*(4). Retrieved from http://www.ascd.org/publications/newsletters/policy-priorities/vol17/num04/Can-Social-Media-and-School-Policies-be-%C2%A3Friends%C2%A3%C2%A2.aspx

Vygotsky, L. (1978). *Mind in society*. Cambridge, MA: Harvard University Press.

Wagner, T. (2008). Rigor redefined: Even our "best" schools are failing to prepare students for 21st-century careers and citizenship. *Educational Leadership, 66*(2), 20–25. Retrieved from http://www.ascd.org/publications/educational-leadership/oct08/vol66/num02/Rigor-Redefined.aspx

Wahlstrom, K. (2014). Examining the impact of later high school start times on the health and academic performance of high school students: A multi-site study, Center for Applied Research and Educational Improvement. Retrieved from http://conservancy.umn.edu/bitstream/11299/162769/1/Impact%20of%20Later%20Start%20Time%20Final%20Report.pdf

Wangsness, L., & Estes, A. (2007, June 15). Personal stories changed minds. *Boston Globe*. Retrieved from http://www.boston.com/news/local/massachusetts/articles/2007/06/15/personal_stories_changed_minds/?page=full

Welsh, P. (2013, September 27). Four decades of failed school reform. *Washington Post*. Retrieved from http://www.washingtonpost.com/opinions/four-decades-of-failed-school--reform/2013/09/27/dc9f2f34-2561-11e3-b75d-5b7f66349852_story.html

Wenger, E. (1998). *Communities of practice. Learning, meaning, and identity*. Cambridge, UK: Cambridge University Press.

White, F. (1987). *The overview effect: Space exploration and human evolution*. Reston, VA: AIAA.

Wiggins, G., & McTighe, J. (2005). *Understanding by design*. Alexandria, VA: ASCD.

Index

J.J. Kellinger, *A Guide to Designing Curricular Games*,
Advances in Game-Based Learning, DOI 10.1007/978-3-319-42393-7

D

The manufacturer's authorised representative in the EU is Springer Nature Customer Service Centre GmbH, Europaplatz 3, 69115 Heidelberg, Germany. If you have any concerns regarding our products, please contact ProductSafety@springernature.com

Printed and bound by CPI Group (UK) Ltd, Croydon, CR0 4YY
30/09/2026
02225238-0008